I, Baby Boomer

I, Baby Boomer

David Fletcher

Matador
Unit E2 Airfield Business Park,
Harrison Road, Market Harborough,
Leicestershire. LE16 7UL
Tel: 0116 2792299
Email: books@troubador.co.uk
Web: www.troubador.co.uk/matador
Twitter: @matadorbooks

ISBN 978 1803131 825

British Library Cataloguing in Publication Data.
A catalogue record for this book is available from the British Library.

Printed and bound in the UK by TJ Books Ltd, Padstow, Cornwall
Typeset in 11pt Adobe Garamond Pro by Troubador Publishing Ltd, Leicester, UK

Matador is an imprint of Troubador Publishing Ltd

MIX
Paper from responsible sources
FSC® C013056
FSC
www.fsc.org

For Sue

Contents

Appendices

People are like washing machines. They are produced with in-built obsolescence. So, if one is a Baby Boomer who wants to write his memoirs, one had better get on with it before one's motor packs in and one is carted off to the nearest scrapyard. And that is precisely what I've done, with the results of my efforts set out on the following pages. I therefore now invite you to join me in the recalling of my life as a typical or possibly atypical Baby Boomer, and I do hope you enjoy the ride.

Blob to Rob

I was churned out of the human factory at some unknown (to me) hour on Tuesday 26 October 1948. That is to say, on that day I was delivered to Bill and Pat Fletcher as their one and only son, just four years after the delivery of Tricia, their one and only daughter. Unfortunately, however, there had been a cock-up in Dispatch; the forklift truck driver had ignored the 'this way up' sign on my crate. Accordingly, I was delivered the *wrong* way up. Yes, I was a breech baby. And before the days of compulsory health and safety I was one of those allowed to remain in this breech position right up until shipment, and therefore I emerged into the world brazenly bum first.

Actually, I have to confess that no forklift truck driver played any part in my delivery, and the real reason for my perverse form of entry into the outside world was probably my innate reluctance to embark on an extended period of intense humiliation. After all, like all new-born babies, I was, and would remain for a number of months, nothing more than a pink, doubly incontinent 'blob', smelling of milk or something even worse, and dividing my time between crying, sleeping, gurgling and looking either bemused or alarmed. This clearly wasn't a prospect to encourage me to make a start in life, and I would probably have been far happier remaining in that cosy womb for quite some time, only making my debut on the world's stage when I could have at least dressed myself and found my own way to the bathroom.

Of course, it doesn't work like that, and one has to be very thankful that during this truly embarrassing period of one's life, one is surrounded by loved ones who don't much care how one looks or how one smells. Furthermore, and of far greater importance, one has not yet been equipped with the facility to form memories. One is like a new Lenovo computer with no software inside and not even any Intel inside. I, in common, I suspect, with every other 'blob', have no recollection of those terrible early days, and even when the microprocessors were finally installed and the software-loading process got underway, the memory function was at best spasmodic and at worst completely ineffectual. So much so, that my first fleeting memories – of sitting on a bale of hay, of playing with coloured beakers and of thumping wooden pegs into holes with a wooden mallet – were just that: fleeting glimpses of 'something' in a vast expanse of nothing. Indeed, I have no worthwhile memory of anything until I was officially a toddler and was being walked through a municipal park by my mother and her noticeably older sister, the not insubstantial and the not-that-easily-amused Auntie May. Then I did have a memory, and it was a memory of my being unintentionally amusing.

It concerned the trees in the park, and my observing that their trunks were green on one side. My not being aware at this stage of my life that the green was moss and that moss has a preference for shady locations in order to avoid drying out (and so tends to grow on the northern side of tree trunks in the northern hemisphere), I posed an obvious question to my carers. This was, of course: 'Why are the tree trunks green on one side?' The answer I received – from Auntie May – was not at all accurate, and could have been the result of ignorance or indeed of impatience, because it was a simple: 'Because they are old.' This caused me to ask a second question, which was: 'Well, why aren't you green on one side as well?'

In retrospect, I can well understand why my mother recounted this incident so frequently, and thereby didn't allow my memory of it to sink into the pit of forgetfulness with so many others. Admittedly, it wasn't the sort of anecdote that would bring the house down at the Comedy Store, but it did represent exactly the sort of behaviour that would probably reassure any parent that his or her little darling was well on its way to becoming an almost fully functioning little person; a rapidly ripening human who would one day start to make some sort of sense, and some sort of sense of its surroundings. And furthermore, with such questions and such potential wit rattling around in its almost empty brain, it would no doubt soon be time to begin the process of filling up that brain with a huge amount of essential *education*. Including, quite possibly, the proclivities of various mosses.

Well, when toddler-dom finally drew to a close at the age of four, official education was indeed set to commence, and it would have done so had I not been seized at that time by the dreaded Child Catcher. Or, to give him his not entirely euphemistic name: 'The Catholic Church'.

Now, this is probably the point at which I should explain that I was originally churned out in Rugby, a small town in Warwickshire that can lay claim to being not only the birthplace of the best field game in the world, but also that of the Great War poet, Rupert Brooke, the jet engine, holography *and* selfies! (It was a guy in 1923, and he used a Box Brownie with a self-correcting black lens.) Not a bad record really, and one then added to when (mildly) Catholic Pat and (even more mildly) C of E Bill got around to organising my conception. Needless to say, because of that no-more-than-tenuous Catholic stake in the conception process, the Child Catcher insisted that I, just like my sister before me, was brought up in the true Church, and that, to guarantee my unquestioning acceptance of this Church, I was delivered into the clutches of a Catholic madrassa. Accordingly, I was enrolled at Rugby's single Vatican outpost near the centre of town, and could now look forward to what would be less an education but more an indoctrination.

But hey! Is that a bird or a plane or even Superman arriving to save the day? No, it's my inability to eat school dinners. Not because I had an etymological problem with lunches being referred to as dinners, but because I could simply not stomach the food on offer. This was such a problem that my (saintly) family doctor insisted I return home at lunchtime to be fed by my solicitous mother – with food I could actually eat. This meant that I was wrested from the clutches of the Child Catcher, and moved from his institution near the centre of town to another nearer my home in suburban Rugby. And this institution was an essentially secular primary school, under the notional care of the C of E, which understood that being blinkered might sometimes be good for horses, but that it was never a suitable outcome to aim for in any form of education. I was free of the Vatican's web, free to start my real education, free to learn – and free to enjoy myself. Hooray!

And I did enjoy myself – for the whole period of my primary education at the Paddox Primary School in the suburb of Hillmorton. Inevitably, however, I am unable to recall much detail of this early stage of my learning. Just like me, my memory function was still in its infancy, and all it retains now is a succession of fuzzy images from that time, images of things such as:

- Very high windows that were opened with a window pole
- Hessian mattresses used in 'Physical Education'
- Ceramic ink pots
- Beans grown in a jam jar with wet blotting paper
- Parquet flooring
- Plasticine
- Toy racing cars in the playground
- Marbles in the playground
- And girls in blue gym knickers

Interestingly, these girls, whether in their knickers or more modestly attired, were not associated with sex for at least the earlier years of my primary education. Babies, after all, came from the gas showroom in town. They were all the work of Mr Therm, and when one wanted a baby, one saved up and then visited the showroom and made one's purchase. Everyone knew that.

Yes, this was the first of many of my serious misunderstandings or misreading of messages, and it endured for some time, ably assisted by the prevalent approach to sex education both at home and at school, which was 'none whatsoever'. Instead, all that was known for certain – by 'us boys' – was that girls were somehow different, and that's why they wore skirts and knickers and why they couldn't use our lavatories. Then rumours spread that they didn't have willies, not even really small ones. It was then quite some time before these rumours were in any way substantiated – by the sex education squad in the form of one or two of the older and more knowledgeable boys. And, apparently, not only did girls not have willies, but they had other things that we boys didn't have, and that ultimately would implicate them heavily in the process of producing babies. It wasn't Mr Therm after all, and all you could buy in the gas showroom were gas appliances. They had never stocked babies of any sort whatsoever.

Well, this was all mildly interesting and it did avoid what could have been some rather embarrassing exchanges in the future. However, it didn't have a particularly significant impact on life in or out of school. As far as I was aware, there weren't even many exploratory sorties to confirm the supposed differences between 'us' and 'them'. And this was because boys and girls rarely mixed, especially outside school, where one shared one's time with one's chosen 'mates'. In my case, this was with a dozen or so boys in my class who were able to relish an early life growing up in a suburban environment that was unguarded and unsupervised, but infinitely safer than any that exists today. After all, there were very few cars on the roads, there were no knives, no drug gangs, no roaming paedophiles and, of course, no internet threats. Instead, there were just safe cul-de-sacs and close-by fields to play in, close-by spinneys to explore, and enough adjacent real countryside to provide all manner of adventures and excitement. Indeed, the only dangers I and my young friends were exposed to were those that we ourselves created. And in my case, they involved a bolt, an axe and an air pistol.

The bolt was a replacement for the paratrooper who had been an integral part of my toy parachute but who had been literally lost in action. The bolt was a good substitute for the soldier but, as the method of launching the parachute was to swing the parachute-fabric part around one's head and then release it at speed, the bolt did also constitute a clear and present danger – particularly when it made contact at speed with the front teeth of one of my friends who had been standing just ten yards from the launch point. (In an attempt to empathise with his loss, I soon removed my own front teeth by diving over the handlebars of my bike.)

The axe was one wielded by a friend in order to cut up some wood and, in this instance, it was I who was on the receiving end of its use. Specifically, I was on the receiving end of its head as it was raised to make its next chop – and I received the rear of the head through my right eyebrow. There was lots of blood and, shortly thereafter, my first experience of A&E and stitches.

The air pistol was a weapon we were using to play 'tig'. After all, why go to all the effort of running after all your friends when you can 'tig' them by simply shooting them? I remember that I was shot in the leg and that one of my friends was shot on one of his ears – even though I was aiming at his stomach. I believe his 'hit' was more painful than mine.

However, the point is: we all survived, and we certainly learnt a great deal about risk and about pain and what was and wasn't sensible. We also, through these sometimes foolish but always parent-free pursuits, built up a store of self-confidence and self-reliance that would not only last us a lifetime but that would also enhance this lifetime in so many ways. In fact, to this day, I am so thankful that my early (and later) childhood was not spent wrapped around in cotton wool and that I wasn't cuddled and cushioned by protective parents who saw only threats in the world and not the empowering potential of their offspring's exposure to the raw and sometimes hazardous features of 'life'.

Anyway, I now need to make an important point. It is simple: my parents were in no way absent parents. In fact, quite the contrary. In common with most other parents at that time, they might have allowed their children to discover stuff for themselves, but at the same time they shared their lives with their children. For me – and my sister – that meant that as well as our being taken to pay homage to the North Sea at Skegness, Scarborough and Great Yarmouth, we were also taken into their social circle. Whether this was a visit to a pub garden or the attendance at a greater-family gathering or a smoky evening of card games with friends (and with lots of pennies and halfpennies), we were always included. And we were included in the conversation. One might almost say that it was a time when intergenerational discourse was the norm and most young children would grow up to be young people who could talk not only to other young people but to quite a few older people as well. Just like they can't now.

Yes, quite a few things have changed out of all recognition since the '50s, and it would be remiss of me not to mention a number of things that might be commonplace now but back then were either rare or essentially unheard of. There are so many, but how about: central heating, colour television, interesting food, luxuries (of any sort), political correctness, gender confusion, bulbous bare midriffs, tattoos, anxiety, boredom, being in any way ashamed of our history, being in no way ashamed of displaying one's embarrassing emotions to the whole world – and piped music in pubs and in any other public space one can imagine?

Then, back in that school environment, there were some other features that are commonplace today but that were absent all those years ago. For example, there were no designer clothes, no diagnosed 'conditions', no physical threats to teachers, no smartphones and no other than white kids...

It's enough to send the hairs bristling on the back of a million liberals' necks. But it's a fact. There were only white people at my primary school – because there were only white people available. This was Rugby just a few years after World War II, and Rugby then was a town that was probably entirely white. Black people back then were either in Africa or in the Caribbean (or maybe in London), and Asian people were still in Asia. Indeed, if anybody had asked me at that time what diversity was, I would probably have guessed that he was the third guy in the Welsh front row along with Dai Evans and Dai Jones. (I was, you must remember, a son of the town where that ultimate field game had been invented.) Anyway, this white-only aspect of my formative years should be borne in mind, simply because, despite all those PC considerations, it inevitably shaped my outlook on life – and, I imagine, the outlook of droves of other Baby Boomers as they made their way into the twenty-first century. Put another way, England was once not like it is now, and this should never be forgotten.

Nor should we forget the scourge of school-age bullying. Even if, back in that Paddox Primary School, it was essentially non-existent. Instead, kids just got on with each other, and if they didn't, there was always the opportunity for a really good insult or a harmless, half-hearted scrap, where honour would be satisfied four or five seconds after the first hint of real physical contact. School was a truly benign place. Nevertheless, despite this lack of general bullying, I do have to admit that there were bullies. In fact, there were two of them – for the whole school. One was called Robert Holliday and the other was called Nigel Makepeace (honestly). However, this pair, both of whom were in my year, were more the recognised bullies than actual bullies, and their status was recognised and reinforced more by their manner than by their actions. In other words, they were both seen as 'hard', and nobody would ever choose to cross them or ever engage with them physically. That just wouldn't happen. After all, they were both pretty tough, and what would be the point of upsetting the accepted arrangement of their being the official school bullies, especially when nobody else seemed interested in taking on their role?

I should now add that towards the end of my primary school days, the bully, Rob, did decide to underline his bully status by having a go at me. It was to be nothing really violent, but just a bit of 'I'm superior to you, and I can get the better of you whenever I choose'. Well, he couldn't. I wasn't particularly strong, but by now I was equipped with just enough self-confidence and self-reliance – and I was tall enough – to frustrate his intentions. Essentially, as he approached me in combat, I pushed his head between my legs, grasped his thighs from behind and lifted him off the floor. He was therefore now in an awkward, upside-down position, from which to pursue his bullying aims he would have needed far more strength than he possessed. He was also in front of a sizeable audience of my fellow pupils, and, consequently, very embarrassed. Needless to say, he soon 'sued for peace'. Indeed, thereafter that peace endured indefinitely, and he never tried to impose himself on me ever again. Neither did Nigel. Of course, my reputation in the school surged, and had I been into sex at that stage of my life, I could probably have chosen my next conquest with ease – and certainly have advanced my understanding of the nature and disposition of those fabled female-specific features with no problem whatsoever.

Well, that is probably all that needs to be said about the first period of my life on this Earth, other than one last observation. This is that Rob was inevitably a Baby Boomer as well, and I sincerely hope that he learnt to see the superiority of this status over that of a bully as soon as he left the Paddox. And that, of course, would be just eleven or so years after he'd been a pink and smelly blob himself…

Growing up at a Grammar

I don't know whether the term had been invented in 1960, but that's when I first encountered 'social mobility'. This I did by entering the gates of Lawrence Sheriff Grammar School for boys, along with most of my mates from primary school and seventy or so other boys drawn from just about every rung of Rugby's social ladder. My own rung was quite a way down (Dad was a [brilliant] baker and confectioner). But it didn't matter. The only thing that mattered was that we had all passed our eleven-plus. We were all there on merit and, unlike the pupils at our highly celebrated neighbour, Rugby School, we had not been installed there as a result of the wealth of our parents.

It's difficult to remember whether I knew at that time how fortunate I was to have been admitted into such a wonderful place of learning, but I certainly had no idea that I would be enjoying the fruits of a system that would soon come under some serious attack. In a misguided attempt to improve the fate of all those who had not passed their eleven-plus, a campaign would soon be launched to level the education landscape by ensuring that no high points of excellence were allowed to remain. All grammar schools would be portrayed as elitist citadels to be besieged and finally flattened, and in this way the world would become a better place, and no pupil, no matter how dismally dim, would miss out on that new, possibly-not-quite-so-demanding form of education that would then be devised. And this would be proclaimed as 'progress'.

Anyway, it was still 1960, and my immediate concerns at my new school were nothing to do with meddling with the education system, but all to do with 'How will I manage?' and 'Will I be up to it?' After all, of the three streams that were run at this school and were a recognition of comparative ability/intellect, I had been placed in the middle one: the 'A' stream. I had avoided the to-be-avoided-at-all-cost 'B' stream, but had not made it to the 'want-to-be-there' alpha stream. I need not have worried. Before the end of the first term, I had won my promotion to the alpha stream (without any sort of play-off) and henceforth I would not only stay in this stream but quite often be very near its top. Well, I've always found honesty more appealing than false modesty and, in the interests of honesty, I should now admit that in my eleven-plus English paper, I had discovered in the dying minutes of the exam that I had not answered about 25% of the questions because, even though I had finished it early, I had not turned over the last page where those remaining 25% of the questions lay. It's probably why I started off in the 'A' stream – and why, in no way, can I deny that the sin I most frequently commit is the sin of omission. Just ask my (second) wife.

However, to return to my time at Lawrence Sheriff, I can report that in no time at all I was definitely 'growing up', and definitely relishing my grammar school education. It was very much modelled on a public-school education – with four 'houses' (mine was 'Tait'), Saturday-morning classes, a strong focus on sports (every Tuesday and Thursday afternoon), obligatory Latin lessons, powerful prefects, a strict dress code – but, as far as I was aware, little if anything in the way of buggery or assorted deviant practices. In fact, I was aware of no 'unpleasantness' of any sort either inside or outside school. If there were priests fiddling with little boys, or people in positions of power abusing those below them, they didn't seem to be doing it in Rugby. It just wasn't that sort of place. Heck, paedophilia, sexual assault and sexual harassment would all have been regarded as being akin to dangerous tackles, intentional collapsing of the scrum and arguing with the ref – or possibly even worse. There again, maybe I was just very unobservant or very fortunate. My world remained sweet and unsullied – except for the continued attentions of the Catholic Church.

Yes, I had avoided the Child Catcher during my primary school days, but he hadn't gone away and he hadn't forgotten me. Even though the habit of accompanying my mother and sister to Sunday mass was already becoming less than habitual (helped to no small degree by a growing family-wide disillusionment with Catholicism), my Catholic identity was still with me and now more evident than ever. This was because the thirty or so pupils at Lawrence Sheriff who were 'left-handers' were granted the right to hold their own assembly (in the form of reading magazines and papers in the school library), but also required to receive Catholic-specific religious instruction – once a fortnight at the local Catholic secondary school.

It was great. I was already of the opinion that Catholicism was pretty dreadful and that the whole idea of any religion surviving in a modern scientific and enlightened age was little short of mad. But if I wanted my views reinforced in spades, I could have wished for nothing more than these mandatory sessions with our appointed pedagogue. He was Irish and red (both his hair and his face), and the theme of his lessons was 'bollocks and then more bollocks'. That, incidentally, was not how he himself would have described this theme. But, there again, he was about as mad as the subject matter he was presenting, and he never succeeded in convincing me that what he was spouting didn't belong inside one huge hirsute theological scrotum.

None of it made any sense. It was all fairytale stuff coated in faux gravitas, and about as convincing as a pantomime dame – albeit nowhere near as entertaining. In fact, the more the red man tried to sell us his Catholicism, the more it came over not just as arrant nonsense but as what I'd suspected it was for quite some time: a well-established racket. After all, the idea of imposing the 'stain' of Original Sin on every new-born baby, and then pushing the idea of the Church being the only organisation with access to the right stain-remover is straight out of any mafia handbook you care to mention. Extortion presented as a religion, with the prospect that, through a whole host of other scams, you'll remain a victim for the rest of your life. Oh, and as well as being screwed, you won't be allowed to have any fun either. Fun, remember, is the work of the Devil – or it would be if he actually existed. Which he doesn't. Along with heaven, hell, purgatory, limbo, papal infallibility, miracles, unicorns, phlogiston, magic underpants, flying goats and government competence.

Needless to say, these non-indoctrination sessions didn't last very long. Even red man didn't believe he could work miracles, and eventually I was allowed to ignore my Catholic heritage entirely. I could stay within the bounds of Lawrence Sheriff and get on with learning something useful – like Latin.

Very early on in my grammar school days, I was showing a bent (if one is still allowed to use that word) for maths, physics and chemistry – but not for biology, as I had no wish to cut up locusts. However, Latin really appealed to me as well, and even now I can recite the beginnings of both Virgil's *Aeneid* and Caesar's *Gallic War (Book 1)*, our two set books for Latin 'O' Level. I can also recall the pleasure that was had when, probably in Caesar's work, the story reached a passage involving the Romans' sheaths for their swords. Because as every Latin scholar will know, the Latin for 'sheath' or 'scabbard' is a word that now has a very different meaning in English – which is 'vagina'. And as everyone who has ever been to a boys' school will know, young boys can derive unparalleled entertainment from hearing their teacher having to pronounce this word as he reads it aloud (in Latin) at the front of the class. I recall that he rather hurried through the passage and mumbled his vagina very badly. And I also recall that after the lesson there was general agreement that he had probably seen the real thing, possibly more times than he'd seen a scabbard. And he may even have touched one...

However, moving on, school wasn't just about learning stuff in a classroom; it was also about learning what one's body could do when called upon to play sports. Yes, there were those Tuesday and Thursday afternoons when, no matter what the weather, I and the entire complement of pupils were required to turn out on the extensive school playing fields and give of our best. In winter, this meant our playing rugby (of course), and in summer, cricket (or softball for the... softies).

Well, rugby was fine – up to a point – but it became very obvious very soon that, because I was turning into a sentient variety of a beanpole, I was not the ideal shape for a game that requires its participants to have either mass or a special breed of muscular manoeuvrability. Consequently, I spent no more than a term making a dreadful back-row flanker before I was spotted as a suitable candidate for the school's cross-country brigade. I was destined to spend two afternoons a week straining my lungs, punishing my legs, soaking my feet (part of the school course was up a stream) – and all while being rained on or frozen or both. It was so awful and I always so wanted to finish it as soon as I could that I excelled at it, and before long

I became a recognised star of the school team. Result! I could now spend not just Tuesday and Thursday afternoons maltreating my body but every Saturday afternoon as well, when I and the rest of the team were required to turn out to compete with teams from other schools. In retrospect, I should probably have stuck with rugby, although, had I done that, I would not have come third in the Warwickshire schools' cross-country championship (out of a field of about a million), and nor would I have learnt as much about endurance, stamina, fortitude, pig-headedness, suffering and blisters.

It was a similar story with cricket – in that I didn't play it, but instead spent my summers as an athlete. Well, more accurately, I 'did athletics', and spent many a happy summer afternoon testing the efficacy of a jock strap in the long-jump pit and over the high-jump bar (it was in the days before the Fosbury Flop) – and running around an oval track and sometimes throwing a javelin, albeit never at the same time. The javelin throwing, I really enjoyed. I wasn't very good at it, but there is clearly something atavistic about throwing a spear, and I couldn't get enough of lobbing a slender shaft of aluminium as far as I could – and sometimes getting it to stick in the ground! This was much more enjoyable than trying to hurl a discus, a skill I never really mastered. After all, throwing an overweight frisbee called for the same sort of coordination skills required for cricket, and I most certainly did not possess these. In fact, I had very few coordination skills, as was only too apparent when I was obliged to tangle with the school's giant trampoline. Maybe it was something to do with my being born bum first…

Well, that's probably enough about school for the moment, other than to record that Lawrence Sheriff had no bullies at all (really), but it did have one fat kid (called 'Slim'), one slightly portly teacher (called 'Porky') and, later on in my time there, one black kid. I can't remember where he was from, but he was as posh as the black guy in *Rising Damp*, and I don't imagine he ever ended up as a rapper. Just like I was never going to end up as any sort of musician…

I did have music lessons – for both the piano accordion (!) and the guitar – but there were far too many keys and buttons on my accordion and six too many strings on my guitar. I was declared officially musically inept – just before I was judged to be pretty well useless at being a Boy Scout. I couldn't tie knots. I couldn't cook over a fire. I couldn't whistle and smile at the same time. And I couldn't contemplate going on another serious camping expedition after the first such expedition – to Borth. That little outing was hideous. It rained continuously. It was cold. Most of the food we cooked ended up in the 'wet pit'. Some of the more fragile scouts had to be shipped back home. And the only small ray of sunshine breaking its way through the dismal Welsh gloom was the clandestine securing of tobacco in any one of Borth's amusement arcades. Back then, if you could get a ball bearing to disappear through the right slot, after sending it around a circular path in a glass-fronted machine, you won a cigarette! And then you smoked it. Even if you were still wearing your woggle...

Of course, Wales didn't rank as the most exotic location that I visited during my grammar school days. There was also Austria – with my parents and on a coach – and then Jersey and Guernsey, still with my parents, but now in a flying machine. On each of the two or three occasions we visited those Channel Islands, it was on a Viscount – a small, noisy, propeller-driven aircraft that flew from a very small Birmingham Airport and on which one would be treated to a barley-sugar sweet before take-off. Possibly gin and tonics hadn't been invented then or, more likely, they couldn't get a trolley on the plane. Viscounts were, after all, very small.

I don't remember a great deal about any of these holidays, other than in Austria I made my first acquaintance with lederhosen, duvets, salamis and horse-flies, and in the Channel Islands I took an increasing interest in both chicken in the basket and female swimwear. Indeed, I was taking an increasing interest in what was in that female swimwear, but it was still very much 'look but don't touch'. It wasn't that I was a particularly late starter, but this was still the '60s, a time well before the introduction of the terms 'sexting', 'intimacy', 'heavy petting' and 'underage sex'. We had to make do with just staring, imagining, occasionally chatting – and waiting. No doubt somebody would tell us when we could do something more.

Yes, naivety was in common circulation back then, and it was still very much in evidence when it came time to take my first set of 'O' Levels at the end of my fourth year. This was the alpha stream norm: collect one's first batch of qualifications a year earlier than the 'A' and 'B' stream pupils, enter the lower sixth a year earlier and collect a second batch of ('O' Level) qualifications before entering the upper sixth, when it would then be the time to focus on 'A' Levels in earnest. Modesty almost stops me from reporting that eleven (very good) 'O' Levels were acquired in this way – but not quite. And no amount of modesty will stop me reporting that on entering the sixth form, even though I wasn't equipped with a girlfriend, I was equipped with a new barathea blazer. Yes, I had been made a prefect (prematurely)! Not, I imagine, because I really merited it – because I didn't – but probably because I was now six foot two, and that made me a foot or two higher than all the little sprots who needed to be kept in order. If I'd have been John Bercow, I wouldn't have been considered. Unlike his wife...

Anyway, I really had grown up now in more ways than one, and I began to take an interest in other than Lawrence Sheriff (and Rugby High School for girls). First there was an intensifying interest in cars. It was, after all, a fabulous time for British motorcars, and there was even that incomparable E-Type in my world. There was also a whole slew of new, incomparable music to enjoy. It was as though the Beatles and a whole string of other British groups had set out to provide me with the best soundtrack to my life that they could possibly devise. And they seemed to be having more and more success as the months rolled by. Even now I can remember sitting in the prefects' room – supervising the detention of some miscreant who'd be busy completing his 500-word essay on the subject of the inside of a ping-pong ball – listening to the prefects' radio playing Chris Farlowe's 'Out of Time', and wondering whether popular music had simply hit a sweet spot or whether there was much more to come. Fortunately, as we all now know, the sweet spot would last for years. What a great time it was to be young.

It was an even greater time for me when I passed my 'A' Levels, and now, with a year to spare, I could devote myself to some extra studying and a lot of playing bridge with my fellow prefects. It was possibly one of the most enjoyable periods of my life and definitely the most idle. So much so that after two terms, with a place in the University of Birmingham's chemistry department in the bag, I left school and took up a spell of paying work. For three months I became a sort of (paid) intern at what were then AEI's central research laboratories in Rugby (later to be subsumed into Arnold Weinstock's GEC conglomerate).

I'd like to say that my time there was interesting and that it was a good preparation for my forthcoming time reading chemistry at university. But it wasn't. It was quite often very dull, and on odd occasions it was just a hoot. The dullness was largely the product of my being assigned to work with two analytical chemists (dull rating 9), and then being set to work on a ceramic and platinum contraption to measure trace quantities of oxygen in metals (dull rating 100). The hooting was all to do with the way the analytical chemists spent their time, which was only rarely anything to do with analysing something. One spent most of his days plasticising fish keepnets for his fishing friends. The other devoted most of his time to silver-plating his own and his friends' cutlery. And both of them relished the misuse of the liquid air that was piped through the building in the same way that water was. (They would fill a metal wastepaper bin with the stuff, wait for the nitrogen to boil off, and then throw a lighted cigarette into what would then be just liquid oxygen. The effect was quite dramatic.)

I maybe should have taken more notice of what this all said about a future career in chemistry. And I do recall that I did take notice of what a future career in chemistry might do to my health. That was when I observed the silver-plater of the pair, 'pickling' some cutlery in a bath of weak hydrochloric acid – not just with his hands actually in the acid, but with plumes of hydrogen chloride gas emerging from his nostrils as this gas made it back out from his lungs. Oh, and I discovered when I was working there that, for those ICI chemists who actually made it to retirement, the average retirement life span was not much more than a year. Shit! I may have chosen a dangerous career.

It was probably safer on the building site – the pre-health-and-safety building site I laboured on to get some more cash together before I went to university and before I went on my first unaccompanied-by-parents holiday. This 'foreign expedition' was instead accompanied by one of my friends from school – and it wasn't exotically foreign. It was just a hitchhiking/camping expedition to the South of France. Well, that was the intention. And it certainly wasn't planned that our one and only lift would be terminated when my friend informed me rather insistently that the (male) driver of the 2CV van who had picked us up in the very north of France was feeling his upper thigh. (So that was it. Nothing naughty was happening in Rugby because all the perpetrators of naughtiness were busy in France.) Anyway, having ditched the idea of hitching, we made it to Paris by train, only to head north again when we were prevented from sleeping on one of the platforms at the Gard du Nord station by a pair of *gendarmes*, and when we'd formed the firm opinion that our reaching the south coast of France was as likely as either of us reaching the end of *War and Peace*. We settled instead on Le Touquet, the rather stylish resort that had once been even more stylish. And there we divided our time between lazing in its far-from-stylish campsite and being picked up and abandoned by a very attractive French woman. I can't remember much about this particular incident, but I do remember that we were left with both our thighs and our virginity intact. If only it had been the '90s and not the '60s. Although, there again, the '60s had seen me being given the best education I could ever imagine, and before the '60s were out, I was now set to be given a whole lot more – at the University of Birmingham! I could hardly wait…

Party Time

I arrived at university driving my dad's Ford Cortina and wearing my brushed-denim hipster jeans. Yes, I had learnt to drive and how to dress – sort of.

I had with me my sister (to drive the family car home), a good selection of my worldly possessions, and a big bundle of excitement tied up with a long length of trepidation. I was, after all, taking the biggest step in my life so far, and it was a step into a very daunting unknown. Not only was I entering an entirely new environment without the cushion of my longstanding circle of friends, but it was an environment stuffed with what I believed were exceptionally bright people.

Remember, this was 1967, a time long before the days of 'uni on demand', where half of all school pupils now get shipped off to their institution of choice in order to accumulate a mountainous and often pointless burden of debt. Instead, there were just 7% of school-leavers making it to university, and frankly one had to be very bright to get into this privileged 'pick of the crop'. That meant I had to be very bright myself, but not necessarily extremely bright (and I say that, having long ago learnt to live with conceit in the interests of accuracy). I might have 'looked good' academically at school, but now I might be revealed to be just a rather 'plain' contender in a field of real beauties. I might prove to be a very ordinary university student or even a bit of a dummy, and that was somewhat scary. Of course, only time would tell, and before then there was the serious business of settling into a wonderful university – and of meeting some of its wonderful girls...

I had been installed in a university hall of residence, with the imaginative name of 'High Hall' – probably because it was a high-rise construction sitting on the highest point of a landscaped halls-of-residence park. There were five halls of residence in total on this 'Vale' site, three of which were full of students of the female variety, and one of which, just brimming with these distracting ladies, was actually connected to High Hall via a shared lounge and bar! This was Ridge Hall, and it came equipped with one particular lady who would feature very heavily in my university days, and in a great number of days thereafter. But more of her later. Now it was time for High Hall's rather alluring canteen manager and her not quite as alluring but still quite attractive canteen friend.

I had a roommate – Keith – and Keith was a barrow-bow type guy from London with a big intellect, a very big smile and an even bigger ego, the sort of ego that allowed him to chat up a canteen manager who he had just met, and a canteen manager who would have looked more at home in a house of ill repute than in any canteen. And she'd have been nowhere near the dishes. She wore a beige canteen tabard, but above the tabard was the face of a temptress, and under the tabard was almost certainly the pulsating body of an impatient siren. It moved under that tabard and it constantly looked restless, as though it was just waiting to burst out in all its remarkable nakedness to overwhelm the emotions and the restraint of any passing hapless male. And certainly a young brash male such as Keith, who had the temerity to approach it to within just inches and at the risk of turning blind.

He, of course, did manage to keep his eyesight, and his eye on his purpose – which was to invite the seductress to accompany him to the freshers' disco and to ask her to bring along her attractive canteen friend to make up a foursome with his decidedly diffident roommate. And it worked. Nothing, of course, to do with the fact that we had tickets to this extravaganza and Femme Fatale and her sidekick did not. Which is why Keith and I set out so confidently with our new female companions on the appointed night and, much to the surprise of many other fresh-faced freshers, turned up to the disco with two delightful dishes on our arms.

It was just a shame that after they immediately retired to powder their noses, they couldn't ever find us again, and had to make do with a succession of other dancing and snogging partners until they disappeared a few hours later with a couple of obvious gigolos. This was at about the same time that Keith and I were wondering whether we would finally get on the dancefloor ourselves or whether it might be better to give the dancing – and the snogging – a miss, and go back to High Hall to check out one of the table-tennis tables in its basement.

In retrospect, it could have been a better night, but it was still early days, and even the diffident member of the twosome would start to have some measurable success with girls, to say nothing of the odd (quite often surprise) conquest. Not that these encounters always involved what might be called actual sex. More often it was one or more forms of advanced fumbling, where intimacy might entail the use of hands and lips but not necessarily those other parts of the body that were designed for the purpose of intimacy *per se*. And, after all, it wasn't as though university was just about girls. There were also parties – with girls. And drinking – with girls. And very late nights – with girls. And even clandestine night-time visits to the neighbouring Edgbaston Golf Course – with girls. And of all these demands on my time, it was probably parties – with girls – that was the most... demanding. There were lots of them, some organised, some more or less spontaneous, some in someone's room, some in someone's flat, some verging on the raunchy, some verging on the entirely inebriated – but none of them furnished with drugs.

Drugs were about – somewhere – and there was definitely a supply of LSD in the university – somewhere. But I never encountered – or sought – anything more stimulating than very cheap wine and French cigarettes. My 'trips' were only ever fuelled by one-litre bottles of Rocamar or Hirondelle or sometimes by some upmarket Mateus Rosé, and always accompanied by repeated drafts of either some Gauloises or some slightly superior Gitanes. Parties back then always seemed to smell like the inside of a Marseilles brothel, thoroughly steeped in stale wine – and, occasionally, as though their recent patrons had included a band of joss-stick-burning Buddhists. Real drugs would have just screwed things up, and they would also have got in the way of relishing all those girls – and what they were all wearing. Which, as I remember with great clarity, was generally a combination of a tight sweater or a tight blouse – and a miniskirt. And to encapsulate what this form of attire meant, I can only say that by the end of my first term

I had become very well acquainted with both the size and shape of a huge range of upper chest parts and the size and length of a huge range of thighs. And, on numerous occasions, I had also been obliged to avert my eyes from the sight of some blatantly exposed underwear. Albeit not always with complete success...

Young ladies today would be amazed, even those displaying their midriffs and a great deal more on a Friday night. Because, those tight tops and miniscule skirts weren't worn just for parties. They were worn throughout the day – at lectures and in the lab – and, as far as I was aware, without any great degree of resentment. Following a fashion, showing off your legs – if not more – and maybe flirting a bit, still hadn't been hounded out by feminism, and most if not all of the women I knew then seemed positively to enjoy it. There may not have been a real equality of the sexes back then, but there was a distinct equality of pleasure. Girls were only too pleased to put on a show; boys were only too pleased to relish the show. And if that sounds like the sexist view of a dinosaur male, then I can only point out that I am a dinosaur, but that it is definitely not a sexist view, just an honest account of how women and men behaved in those days and how they enjoyed themselves in those days. And all without any great threat of unwanted advances, inappropriate behaviour, out-and-out harassment or actual molestation. What has changed is a little difficult to pin down, although I suspect the remedy for every form of sexual abuse and grossly improper behaviour that we witness nowadays does not lie in the reintroduction of miniskirts and the consequent display of intimate apparel. If only it did...

Anyway, I seemed to have neglected to mention that the primary purpose of my attending university was to learn. And before getting on to the purely academic aspect of learning – about chemistry and all its wonders – it is probably worth my listing a number of other things that I learnt in my first year at university. I learnt:

- How to budget
- How to write up somebody else's lecture notes
- How to use a Grundig tape recorder
- How to be not entirely honest with women when one was getting out of one's emotional depth (sorry)

- How to use a High Hall canteen tray as a sledge on the slope down to the Vale site's lake
- How to make a coffee last for an hour in the Students' Union
- How to exist on instant mashed potatoes on toast when required
- How to use the urinals in the Students' Union loos without banging one's head on a bizarrely placed air duct
- But not how to deal entirely proficiently with the fasteners on bras – or with Saturday-morning practicals

Yes, my main subject at university – as you will recall – was chemistry. However, as there were also three subsidiary subjects – physics, maths and German (!) (supposedly to enable us to read scientific papers in that language) – there was rather a lot of pressure on our timetable. So much, in fact, that we had to endure five solid mornings of lectures, and not just five solid afternoons of practical work, but a sixth practical on Saturday morning as well. It was Lawrence Sheriff all over again, only with my weekend starting with burettes and flasks rather than with textbooks and pens. This was a little dispiriting, not least because many of the best of those party-type gatherings previously referred to were held on a Friday evening, and woe betide you if a few hours later you were incapable of pouring some sort of liquid from one glass container into another, or worse still, incapable of sucking on a pipette with the required degree of suck. It was all very unfair, with some courses, such as Classics and English Literature, requiring students to attend for just two or three brief tutorials per week and never on a Saturday. Heck, even the hard-working gorillas in Mech Eng were granted a completely undisturbed weekend.

Nevertheless, I learnt to cope, and I also learnt what the three branches of chemistry were all about. That is to say, organic chemistry, inorganic chemistry and physical chemistry. Well, what they were not about were, respectively, 'live chemistry', 'dead chemistry' and 'chemistry in the gym' – although there is a hint of truth in the 'live chemistry' bit. This is because organic chemistry deals with the chemistry of carbon, which has a lot to do with the chemistry of life. And it needs its own separate branch of this science because, if I've remembered correctly, there are more compounds of carbon than there are of all the other elements in the periodic table taken together – and which form the substance of 'inorganic chemistry'. Then there is physical chemistry, which deals with stuff like entropy and enthalpy, and which is designed to give most normal people a headache. Indeed, looking back at my university notes – which, of course, I still have – it is this branch of chemistry that is still the most impenetrable. (Not that I can understand a great deal of any of my university notes, which now serve only to remind me of how much I have forgotten and how much my intellect must have shrunk...)

Anyway, notwithstanding the potentially detrimental aspects of physical chemistry, I did really enjoy being immersed in the seemingly infinite world of chemistry in all its forms. I particularly enjoyed organic chemistry – for its order, its logic, its predictability and its pure magic – and I really began to enjoy practical chemistry, even though I struggled to achieve the results required. After a whole week of quite often demanding work, that naphthalene-based derivative I'd synthesised and which was supposed to be a residue of 'sparkling white crystals' would more likely look like a very mean helping of crumbled burnt bacon. The only consolation was that this was far from a unique outcome. Most of the other one hundred souls in their first year of chemistry had just as much trouble as I did in ever ending up with 'sparkling white crystals' and, like me, would probably go on to be entirely useless in a kitchen.

I was pretty poor at practical physics as well, but that was because I adopted the common approach taken by all my fellow (male) experimenters in our designated physics lab – which was to use one hand at all time to shield our gonads. There were radioactive substances in that lab, and most of us assumed (rightly or wrongly) that one day we might want to have children. And one could never be too careful. There again, I would always have chosen the physics lab over the language lab. Here was not the danger of being sterilised but the danger of being traumatised – by not understanding a word of what was going on. I had collected a German 'O' Level at school, and this had persuaded the university authorities to put me on an advanced German course in pursuit of the passing of my mandatory German subsidiary. It was '*lächerlich*' – or, as we say in English, 'ridiculous'. I couldn't understand a word, and spent most of my time in the language lab's cubicles either thinking about forthcoming parties or about some... well, some very forthcoming girls.

There were a number of them, and even though very forthcoming, none of them turned into a serious contender for anything approaching a lasting relationship. That said, some were quite fun. There was a student from Aston University who was studying pharmacy but not the art of restraint in her dealings with men. There was a student nurse from the nearby nursing school who didn't know the meaning of restraint. And there was an international entrant – from Swansea University – who knew a lot about restraint other than when broaching the subject of marriage! And then there was Daphne. Daphne played the double bass in the Midlands Youth Orchestra – and fast and loose with me when we went to see a university production of *Waiting for Godot.* She gave a whole new meaning to the term 'intimate theatre', and in due course she gave me glandular fever. Strangely enough, I probably enjoyed my subsequent two-week stay in the university's medical centre more than I enjoyed *Waiting for Godot* – by quite a long way. In fact, I've since heard say that this play is one of the most 'stripped-down' plays ever written. Just like that emperor when he took off his clothes.

Incidentally, that encounter with glandular fever led to my missing a good part of my second term, which was not good news, in that party time had already robbed me of quite a chunk of studying time and would do so again when I'd returned for my third term. And then there were those other demands on my time, demands such as a very long weekend in London...

This was shared with Keith and another guy from High Hall called Ian, and Ian's girlfriend, Christine. Ian had a car – a clapped-out Ford Popular – and this was our means of transport down to London (along a still rather empty M1). We got there – despite a hint of smoke in the interior of the car combined with a smell of roasting plastic – and when we were there, we were treated to two highlights. One was an all-night card game with Keith's father, who lost so much money that he might thereafter have lost his wife. (She looked murderous when she appeared in the morning to find her husband still in a card game – and broke.) And the other highlight was a visit to Windsor Great Park, where serendipity had laid on for our entertainment a polo game, attended by what appeared to be every senior member of the royal family (the Queen, her consort and her two elder children). And such was the security in those days that, between chukkas, all four of us visitors from Birmingham could wander on to the polo field to stamp down the divots no more than a few yards from where the Duke of Edinburgh was doing just the same. He and I didn't speak, but there again, I'm not sure he recognised me...

Anyway, much later that afternoon, we set out on our return journey, and got a very long way up the motorway before that smell of burning plastic returned in earnest – this time followed shortly thereafter by a cloud of black smoke that soon filled the interior of Ian's car. We had to stop on the hard shoulder and call the AA (from, of course, a motorway telephone). And when their friendly representative arrived, he confirmed that all the electrics associated with the car's exterior lights had been incinerated and that, as it was now getting dark, all he could do was escort us off the motorway to a suitable lay-by where we could wait for the morning light to appear and then hopefully limp back to Birmingham before any more of the car's wiring spontaneously combusted. This he did, and he left us in a lay-by, near an AA box on a road that led into Northampton.

Well, to make ourselves comfortable – and to enable us to play cards – we extracted the seats from the Ford Pop and set them below a lamppost that the AA man had assured us would remain illuminated throughout the night. As it was a slightly chilly night, we then put on our pyjamas (over our clothes), and, as we were peckish, we sorted out the store of strawberries that Christine had purchased back in Windsor. And then we got on with playing bridge. Nobody was around, so there was nobody to take any notice of us – until there was. It was a guy who had pulled into the far end of the lay-by and who, after just glancing in our direction, had made off into the night – on foot. We then just carried on playing until we had a closer encounter with another night visitor. This was a policeman who had turned up in his police car to ask us whether we had seen where the first visitor had gone. We, of course, told him where he had gone, and he took off in his police car in the indicated direction – having made no comment whatsoever about the practice of playing bridge in one's pyjamas in the middle of the night in Northamptonshire – with strawberries.

Ten minutes later he returned – with an apprehended car thief in his car. He thanked us for our assistance, and then informed us that he had been observing this character back in Northampton because what he'd been doing 'didn't look quite normal'. Clearly, had the car thief gone about his business in pyjamas with a deck of cards in one hand and a strawberry in the other, he would have avoided the attention of any of Northampton's constabulary. (Or given that he had chosen to carry a strawberry, might he have been arrested and charged with 'handling stolon property'?)

Well, I have recounted this story, because it woke me up to the fact that life is often absurd and should never be taken too seriously, even when it involves the police. And to wrap up the story, all I need to say is that we did get back to Birmingham in the morning and in due course, after she had parted company with Ian, I did have a fleeting encounter with Christine when she was not wearing any pyjamas. But that is a completely different story, as is the tale of my search for a millennial who might actually be aware that strawberry plants possess 'runners' otherwise known as 'stolons'. After all, it's not the sort of information that often trends on Twitter.

However, to return to my first year in academia, I have to report that as much as I enjoyed my chemistry, I did enjoy long weekends in London – and in Swansea and in bed – and socialising, drinking, meeting lots of girls and going to lots of parties a helluva lot more. Which meant that at the end of my first year (and after missing a chunk of that year thanks to darling Daphne) my academic performance was well below par. And it was official. I was informed that unless I pulled up my academic socks, I was heading for an Ordinary degree, the sort of miserable outcome of a university education that has now been banned on the basis that it might infringe a student's human right – of being able to walk away with an Honours degree just as long as he or she is still able to walk.

So, it was time to raise my game – just as soon as I'd raised my bank balance with another summer-long spell in the building trade.

Although I couldn't imagine that in my second year of university there wouldn't be room for a few more of those lovely parties…

Still Party Time

I had, it may be recalled, served my building apprenticeship back in 1967. So, when, in the summer of 1968, I rejoined the same small firm of builders in Rugby to ply my trade, I was more than well prepared for any number of building-type tasks. I had learnt how to use a spade, how to clean a spade, how to use a brush, how to clean paint splashes off bathroom suites, how to shovel gravel, how to use a brush, how to climb a ladder, how to use a kanga, how to use a brush, how to make very milky tea, how to unload a brick lorry, just two bricks at a time (before the days of palleted bricks), how to use a brush, how to wheel a heavy wheelbarrow, how to use a brush, how to use a hose, how to use a brush… and how to use a brush.

Well, in 1968, some of these skills were soon put to the test, and I was happy to discover that I had forgotten little since my last spell in the construction industry. My use of a brush, in particular, was as sharp and precise as ever. However, it wasn't long before two further skills would be needed: one concerning excavations and one concerning, amongst other things, exclamations.

The excavations in question were a dozen or so large holes that had already been dug in the middle of a field, somewhere in the extensive grounds of Rugby Radio Station, and intended to be used for the anchor points for a couple of new radio masts. I and a naturally work-shy colleague had been given the job of finishing off and generally tidying up these holes, for which task we had been provided with two spades and a rather dinky dumper truck, a vehicle that would prove to be our salvation. Because not only could we put it to good use to carry away excavated soil – when we'd eventually worked out how to put it into reverse – but we could also 'use' it as a much-needed distraction from the tedium of shovelling soil – in between not shovelling soil. Yes, I have to confess that if one has been abandoned in the middle of nowhere in order to perform a job that is neither urgent nor absolutely essential (the holes could have served perfectly well for anchor points in their original marginally untidy condition), it is very difficult to remain diligent in the performance of one's duties. Especially when these duties involve lifting spadeful after spadeful of soil until the foreman, who abandoned one at eight in the morning, returns in his Land Rover to pick one up in the late afternoon. That is too much to ask of anybody, especially when it would involve doing far more work than one's work-shy partner. I have to say that I was not proud of my contribution to the maintenance of Rugby Radio Station's longwave communication facilities, but I did, at least, learn to drive a dumper truck – and my enforced period of tedium and skiving may have added to my eagerness to do something a little more interesting and even a little more demanding when my excavation responsibilities had concluded. This was just as well. Because very soon thereafter I was on a roof and charged with the task of saving people's lives…

I had accompanied two of the building firm's brickies to the centre of Rugby, and then, up a ladder, to the roof of an old building overlooking the town's High Street, its main (and busy) shopping drag. Here there was a large chimney stack that required repointing. And, in accordance with standard working practices of the '60s, we soon set about this task in let's say something of an improvised 'freestyle' manner. One of the brickies sat on the ridge of the roof on one side of the stack, his colleague on the ridge on the other side of the stack. Yours truly then returned to ground level to prepare the modest amount of mortar they would need for the job, in order that the repointing work could be completed in a trice. Oh, and to avoid any inconvenience to the shoppers on the High Street, no warning signs or protective measures had been put in place down below. After all, it was just a bit of repointing somewhere up above.

Anyway, it was as I had reclimbed to the top of the ladder and was just about to crawl towards the brickies with my first small consignment of mortar that I noticed that they were still in their chosen positions on the ridge of the roof, but that they were not surveying the chimney stack to establish where the mortar was required, but instead they were both embracing the stack – very tightly – to prevent it from rolling off the roof and onto those not-inconvenienced shoppers on the street down below. A few individual bricks had already made that journey, which is probably why the two ridge-situated brickies were… well, bricking it. There was terror in their eyes, and it took one of them quite some time to advise me that I needed to get down onto that street and warn the passers-by of the danger hovering above them, before then setting off at speed in the firm's van to get some help. There were, of course, no mobile phones in those days that might have expedited the necessary rescue mission.

So, it was onto the street to make some loud exclamations, which ultimately got through to the bemused occupants of Rugby High Street, and caused a couple of their number to appoint themselves as amateur marshals to keep the innocent of Rugby out of the danger zone below the stack. When this had been done, I attended to the equally vital duty of finding and then bringing back the cavalry as soon as I possibly could. And ultimately, I succeeded in my task, and disaster was avoided – by the brickies and the cavalry joining forces to dismantle, brick by brick, the whole damn chimney stack, with not more than another twenty bricks falling into the street as they did this. Job done, and without all that silly health and safety stuff. And, as there was no longer a chimney stack there, we even saved on the amount of mortar we used. Quite a result. And quite an addition to my growing list of building skills. Indeed, it was almost a pity that the summer eventually came to an end, and it was time to return to my university. Although, there again, I would now have a new single room!

I had gone up in the world in more ways than one, as, in addition to securing some much-welcomed privacy, I was now ensconced on High Hall's twenty-first floor rather than on its sixth, and I now had an unparalleled view over leafy Edgbaston. Incidentally, Keith, my first-year roommate, didn't. He had disappeared entirely, and whether this was due to shortcomings in his work or to rather too many full-length comings and goings with that delectable canteen manager, I never established. I could only hope that he went on to enjoy a really satisfying life in every way possible.

It has to be said that Keith had been drifting out of my life even in the first year of university. He had moved away from my circle of friends in High Hall and he never got close to my other circle of friends in the chemistry department – because he hadn't been studying chemistry. I therefore didn't miss him a great deal. And, in any event, I would in due course realise that many friendships formed throughout my life would not be of the everlasting variety (even if they had involved sharing a room). Looking back, I have enjoyed the company – and the real friendship – of many men and women, and when those friendships were active, I could not have imagined that they wouldn't just go on and on. But, at the same time, who would have imagined that one's 'sloppy joe' sweater would finally lose one's affections – or one's shapeless corduroy jacket and one's coordinated brown suede tie would completely lose their appeal? Well, they did (thank goodness), and moving on from old friendships to new ones is not that different from moving on from dreadful '60s fashions to... well, to whatever comes next. If one retained all the clothes one ever owned, one would end up with a wardrobe overflowing with stuff that one would never wear. If one retained all the friends one had ever had, one would end up with a *life* overflowing with all sorts of people, many of whom would ultimately prove to be as about attractive as a classic deep-green Bri-Nylon shirt. Everybody changes, and one needs to adjust one's wardrobe of friends all the time, keeping some and discarding others – if they haven't already done the discarding themselves. Keith was just an early example of this process in action, a process that would continue right up to the present...

However, it is still 1968 in this story, and I should now return to what was my second year of academic life by reporting that, although I had ended my first year at university on the watch list, I was soon able to raise my game, largely because I had told myself that I would be at university only once and I had better make the most of it. Furthermore, I had also discovered that I could still party while at the same time putting in the required amount of work. I was back on track, and back into learning an improbable amount of chemistry.

Some of it was really hard. Not just most aspects of physical chemistry, but stuff like quantum mechanics and something called solid-state chemistry. The quantum mechanics was just impossible, and very early on in the coursework I knew I would have a problem with it when I was called upon to get my head around the concept of a one-dimensional box, inside of which the potential was infinity and outside of which the potential was zero. Just the sort of thing one would never encounter on a modern university course in event management. And, as regards the solid-state chemistry, my only recollection is that our lecturer in this subject was the only human on the planet to study it and that, as a by-product of his work, he had discovered that there were only twenty-seven basic designs for wallpaper. Which, having deducted exactly twenty-seven, is, I suspect, precisely the number of people who ended up following him in his pioneering footsteps.

Anyway, on the subject of numbers, it is worth pointing out that the student population of the University of Birmingham towards the end of the '60s was about 6,000. That is to say, just one fifth of its current humungous complement of 30,000. This meant that it had a very 'manageable' feel about it, and one felt as though one was a member of a large but reassuringly close-knit family. It was probably why 'student mental issues' were somewhere between being as rare as a three-cup bra and essentially unheard of. Or maybe that was also something to do with the fact that, although sometimes naïve, most if not all of those admitted to university in the '60s were not still children dependent on their parents for guidance, advice and comfort. I, for example, usually made one phone call home to my mum and dad each term, and the first time they visited me at university was on my graduation day. And that sort of distant, not to say remote, relationship was not that unusual then. It was such a different world – with no mobile phones, no rampant immaturity and no umbilical cords that could stretch for more than 300 miles. In fact, if one wanted to seek out the only real manifestation of student immaturity back then, one would have to take a look into the world of university politics…

Yes, some university students had not quite shaken off the remnants of their kindergarten existence, and felt the need to immerse themselves in university/union politics in order to recreate their infantile pasts. And if that wasn't the reason, then I've yet to learn what the real reason was. It was certainly nothing to do with 'us', as in any of us normal folk who saw a university only as an institution devoted to our education and our general development – and not as some sort of adolescents' playpen in which we could indulge our childish and quite often churlish behaviour. Essentially, university politics was a joke, and those who participated in it were regarded as jokers and were to be avoided at all costs. And, as regards university politics at the national level – as represented by the workings and machinations of the National Union of Students – well, even back then they were seen at best as ridiculous and at worst an assault on our combined intelligence. It was a hotbed of hotheads – and chumps – students who would see black as white and white as a nice shade of avocado. They'd all clearly been fixed up with a common-sense bypass, probably as a precursor to their entering 'real-world' politics when they finally graduated. Indeed, one only has to look at the number of dippy left-wing activists who have emerged from the NUS to see the veracity of this statement. And one only has to look at a recent president of the National Union of Students, one Ms Zamzam Ibrahim, to see that the NUS has maintained its asinine credentials to this present day. Anybody who has listened to this woman – and who has tried to understand a little of what she has said – will realise that she has never had a rational thought in her head, and was only in post to satisfy the NUS's desire to be hyper-radical, if necessary, by choosing as its president somebody who was the antithesis of a white Christian English male. Even if she did suffer from having two usable legs.

Of course, there are two serious points arising from my mild castigation of university politics and they are these. In the first place, those who engage in politics of any sort while they are still at university are just the sort of people to be kept away from politics for the rest of their lives. In the second place, those who do not do this – and who will then probably go on to ignore politics and fail to inform themselves about the political issues of the day for quite some time – should only be allowed near politics when they've turned thirty, and only allowed to vote when they've turned thirty. Constructing a democracy on a foundation of ignorance is not very clever, and that's why it so often just doesn't work. Better to construct it on understanding and genuine engagement. That way it might just work. And I do know what I am talking about here. *I* very definitely was not politically aware until I had turned thirty, and I should have not been given a vote at thirty, let alone eighteen. Although now, of course, now that I know everything, I believe I should be given multiple votes. Obviously...

Anyway, moving on from political immaturity, it occurs to me that I might be giving the impression that all was just so improbably ruddy good in the appropriately named 'good old days' that I am simply mis-recollecting the past. That my early childhood and schooldays were nowhere near as idyllic as I've described, and that my time at university wasn't a near perfect combination of challenge, camaraderie, common sense, hedonistic practices, stimulating relationships, sexual awakening and pure fun – even though it was. Well, if so, I can do nothing about it, other than maybe reinforce just how marvellous it was back then by talking a little about money, spending and debt.

To start with, I have to mention the size of the student body half a century ago compared to that of the present. And whilst my university's population has grown fivefold in that period, with the proliferation in the number of universities in this same period on top of their ballooning into giants, I imagine the total student population has increased by more than seven times. That's why students now have to pay fees and then set out on a working life loaded down with debt. No longer is it feasible to expect free tuition and local authority maintenance fees – which I and my contemporaries were fortunate enough to enjoy.

However, even with no tuition fees to pay and a maintenance grant in one's pocket, back in the late '60s one would still not be able to support oneself through three years of university study. One would either have to receive parental support (which was the privilege of the few) or one would have to furnish oneself with some additional resources by pushing a broom around a building site or by making a negligible contribution to the excavation of holes at Rugby Radio Station. It sounds almost implausible, but the 'credit world' was somewhere over the horizon back in the late '60s, and one simply did not borrow to live. Hell, even democracies hadn't adopted this practice to any great extent back then, and it wouldn't even have occurred to any student to do this – if for no other reason than there were no institutions from which one could easily borrow.

However, to make this work-and-save system succeed, one also needed to look at one's spend. Even with a summer's worth of pay packets in one's pocket, one was still essentially skint all the time, and one had to be super careful not to run out of money before the next summer. I have already mentioned that I learnt to budget at university, and that this was simply an unavoidable necessity, especially if I wanted to be able to buy cheap wine and (back then) cheap fags to take along to all those parties. So, for example, I learnt that I could live on a minimum of food, and that this food could consist largely of baked beans, spaghetti hoops, sausages, canned soups, bread, jam, toast (sometimes with those instant mashed potatoes) and, for the occasional treat, boiled-egg curry in the university refectory (this being the only meal they served there with the magic ingredient of 'taste').

The nearest I got to fast food fifty years ago was chicken-and-mushroom pie and chips. But that was a rarity. Not only did it involve big money, but it also involved a long trip. There were no takeaway food outlets of any sort near the halls of residence, and none on the university campus. One would have to make a special expedition to Selly Oak, and even there it was merely a choice between a couple of chippies. Put another way, there were simply not the temptations to spend that there are today. No Nando's, no McDonald's, no Kentucky Fried Chicken and certainly no Deliveroo or Just Eat. There weren't even any packaged sandwiches for sale. They hadn't been invented. Neither had white chocolate mochas, iced-coconut lattes, 'wraps' of any description, those calorific bombs called muffins – or, indeed, any of those super-expensive food and drink offerings, the consumption of which has now become almost a human right. Nobody, these days, could be asked to exist on a combination of Heinz baked beans, Heinz tomato soup, Wonderloaf sliced bread, Wondermash mashed potatoes and Marmite – all washed down with a mug of Co-op coffee. Furthermore, nobody these days could contemplate an existence that didn't lead to a whole raft of financial demands that simply didn't exist back in the Ice Age. So, that's the financial demands of greedy mobile service providers, the outrageous financial demands of a rank of designer label outfits, the preposterous demands made by a bunch of tattoo artists and, for female students, the additional demands made by eyebrow-threading exponents, fingernail bars and even intimate-waxing salons. I can't imagine how hard it must be for these young folk now, and maybe it even contributes to those 'student mental health' issues I've referred to before. These, I am sure, are not due just to immaturity and insecurity – or, indeed, to an inability to deal with close personal relations. Talking of which, it must be time to introduce that particular lady in Ridge

Hall, referred to previously, who sometime around the middle of this otherwise free-wheeling second year, introduced herself into my life…

Her name was Kathy and she was a law student. I think I first saw her in the Ridge Hall/High Hall common bar, but I have no real recollection of that event or, at a later date, whether I approached her or she approached me, but I suspect it was – in some way – the latter. Kathy, after all, was a 'bauble', a glittering ornament set apart from all her Ridge Hall companions by her looks and her dress. Her face was incredible. Even though she was (another) Catholic she must have had some Jewish ancestry, and in the right light she could have been mistaken for a rather appealing version of Barbra Streisand. As regards the rest of her body, one might say that she wasn't very tall, but she was just tall enough and she was 'very well formed'. Indeed, taking everything together she made up a fairly attractive package. But what really made her outstanding – and earned her that 'bauble' designation – was the way she presented herself. Quite simply, she didn't dress like a conventional woman student – which in the late '60s was normally a fusion of a miniskirt-length skirt (of course) with, above it, either some sort of (tight-fitting) 'passive casual' or some sort of (maybe less tight-fitting) 'active hippie'. It was a style that never, even when these desirable young gals dressed up for a party, could be accused of being 'smart'. But that is exactly how Kathy did dress. More like a young professional than a grungy student. And even though her outfits conformed to the mandatory 'don't for God's sake bend over' skirt regime, she always conspired to look not just elegant but also 'glossy' – helped to no small degree by her impeccable makeup and her thick, well-groomed shiny hair. So… she just wasn't my sort of girl. In fact, she was just about the antithesis of my sort of girl. Not willowy, not the owner of long tresses of auburn hair, not in any way Pre-Raphaelite – and not studying the right subject at university. Hell, she was a law student, and everyone knew that law students were just a bunch of tedious stuck-up tossers (an opinion, I might say, that I still hold to this day). So how likely would it be that I would approach her, even if I was not entirely sober? A bauble like that I would have noticed, but I would never have wanted to hang it on my tree.

Well, however it might have started, I had somehow managed to embark on my first serious relationship with a woman and there was precious little sign that it would end any time soon. Indeed, it seemed to get more serious by the week and, within no time at all, Kathy and I were receiving joint invitations to parties. That should have rung some very loud alarm bells but, if it did, the bells were muffled by a childlike fascination with my new plaything and by Kathy's disarming and quite often charming behaviour. She made me feel as though I had a real 'catch', even though it was probably me who had been caught.

She also made sure I was kept on a fairly short lead. I was free during the day when I was in the chemistry department and she was in the law faculty (and without even a dumb phone let alone a smart one to maintain any contact), but for most evenings and weekends I was under observation. Of course, I didn't really see it like that then, and the same sort of disparaging observation could well have been made about my own behaviour. Indeed, I was more than keen at that time to extend my range of social experiences, which meant that as well as turning up to parties together or hanging around High Hall's bar together, I often accompanied Kathy to the Rendezvous café.

This was situated, a long walk away from High Hall, at the end of Broad Street in Birmingham, when Broad Street was just an ordinary rather shabby sort of street and not the city's somewhat unconvincing answer to Hamburg's Reeperbahn, which it is now. In the late '60s it hosted no restaurants and no nightclubs or pubs, but just two coffee bars: the moderately respectable Rendezvous and, just across the road, the much less respectable Tow Rope. Needless to say, the Tow Rope was avoided, and whenever they could afford it, Kathy and Dave would be found ensconced in the Rendezvous, listening to 'Ain't Nothing Like the Real Thing' by Marvin Gaye and Tammi Terrell, and husbanding their hot, frothy-topped chocolates, quite often into the early hours – and quite often with an improbable number of butch-looking women ambulance drivers sitting at the other tables. (They never seemed to go to the Tow Rope.)

Inevitably, I cannot quite recall when this serious relationship moved up to the acute category, but I suspect the first visit to Kathy's home in Manchester was well before the end of my second year. Here I met her mother and her obnoxious younger brother – and her auntie and uncle who lived in the same large house – but not her father, who had many years before left the matrimonial home (under undisclosed circumstances) and had since died. It was a feature of Kathy's life that had clearly shaped her nature and certainly developed her determination – whether in respect of securing a career as a lawyer or the husband of her choice.

Yes, I was in it up to my armpits, and when my second year came to an end, and Kathy returned to Manchester for the summer, I was already wondering whether I would ever be able to drag myself out of the quicksand of total commitment. Or whether, perversely, a bauble would drag me down even further…

Tricia

Having rejected the idea of either a summer sailing around the Seychelles or a summer of debauchery in the South of France, I settled on a summer in Birmingham – driving an Austin J4 pickup. Yes, my parents would be seeing even less of me, because, as well as having discounted these two improbable fantasies, I had also eschewed the opportunity to hone my building skills back in Rugby, and instead I had taken up a summer-length job at a motor-parts setup in Brum.

Unfortunately, this meant my living in a truly grotty flat in Bournville, which lacked any hint of the Seychelles or the South of France, but it did mean that I would earn some serious money and that I could indulge my interest in vehicles in general and driving in particular. My role would be as a delivery driver for the company, taking all sorts of parts and components from its main depot in Selly Oak to a string of workshops and garages where these products were required. And to do this I would be given my very own Austin J4, a vehicle which combined primitive design with a whole sackful of soon-to-be-superseded technology. Whether it was rubbish drum brakes all around, unsophisticated suspension, a really noisy engine (housed between the two seats in the J4's basic cab) or a clunky, awkward-to-use gearbox, the J4 had it all. And as a consequence, it was an absolute joy to drive!

Despite it having a little problem in holding the road, especially around bends, it was surprisingly quick, and it was all too easy to finish the delivery round early (up into the northern suburbs of Birmingham and beyond) and thereby have time to take the J4 for a spin around the centre of Birmingham, or maybe even for some speed trials around the centre of Birmingham. There were, after all, no speed cameras in 1969 and, at the age of twenty, not much in the way of responsibility or caution in my make-up. It was all just fun, even when the engine of my chariot caught fire at a petrol station next to the petrol pumps. It was only smoking before I took off the engine cover, but it then burst into flames and I had to politely ask the wide-eyed attendant in his kiosk for use of his extinguisher. (And after I had put out the flames, I started up the engine and then drove the J4 back to base – an indisputable testament to the quality of British *uncomplicated* engineering which we have lost for all time.)

Anyway, it was a remarkably enjoyable summer – and an educational one as well. Before I worked at that depot, I had no idea of the amount of thievery that could be conducted in the workplace. Some of the full-time drivers were loading onto the back of their J4s all the body parts one would ever need to rebuild the front of a Mini. And either nobody noticed or the managers were in on the scam as well. And no, I didn't snitch. Reckless driving was one thing; informing on an affable workmate was quite another. Particularly 'Big Jane' whose husband had apparently expired during their love-making, the recounting of which only added to what I saw as the educational theme of that summer.

Then the summer was over, and it was time to head back to university – and to take up residence at Number 106, Oxford Road.

Third-year students weren't really welcome in halls of residence and, in any event, most students, after two years in a hall of residence, wanted only to get out of their *table d'hôte* existence and try something a little more *à la carte.* I did, and so did Ian (of Ford Popular fame). And Ian, a geology student, had two geology friends who also wanted out, and one of whom had found that *à la carte* option in the form of a generously sized flat in what had once been a rather posh road in Moseley. That is to say, Oxford Road. In fact, by now, it may well have reverted to 'posh', as the vast majority of houses along the length of this road are substantial bay-fronted piles that must these days command an enormous price. Number 106 was no exception. It was 'only' a semi, but this was a semi with three floors, and our second-floor apartment comprised a large kitchen, a bathroom, two sizeable bedrooms and a lounge that was easily big enough to house a harem – if only we'd equipped ourselves with any concubines. We hadn't, of course. We just had ourselves – in the shape of Ian, Clive, Tom and yours truly – and a desire to make our final year at university the best year of all.

The first step to fulfilling this ambition was to sort out the domestic arrangements in our new home. And I'm pretty sure that we had succeeded in this quest well before the end of the third term. Yes, it was all a bit *ad hoc*, with no rotas, but just a willingness on the part of us all to do a bit of cooking and a bit of washing and cleaning as the need arose. It certainly wasn't a *Young Ones* scenario, and I do have distinct memories of cooking rice (and discovering to my amazement how much it expands in water), grilling our offcuts of bacon (supplied by a friendly butcher), pouring something strong down the loo, and ironing my shirts – on the lounge carpet (we didn't have an ironing board). And I suppose we must have done something with our bed linen as well...

Anyway, nobody caught anything and we weren't reported to any authorities – which meant that we could get on and enjoy our student apartment life, the high point of which, each week, was *Top of the Pops*. Somehow, we'd obtained a telly. And having avoided watching this contraption for two years, we now just avoided watching the news and most other programmes, but we did make a point of gathering to watch Pan's People and all those young things who would bop around self-consciously in miniskirts, but not necessarily in time to the music. One of us who shall remain nameless, but who was not Ian, Clive or me, was quite fixated on this programme – or on the length of the skirts on show. I can't quite remember which. He was also my roommate, and the only one of us to own a working vehicle (Ian's Ford Popular having a long time ago been put down in order to bring to an end its suffering). This was a minivan, and it was often used to ferry all four of us to the university campus a few miles away. This was an exercise that always entailed a painful crush in the back of the van – where two of us would have to install ourselves – and quite often, before take-off, the 'cooking' of the distributor cap in the oven to take the chances of the engine starting to somewhere above zero. Minis were notorious for suffering from damp. Just as notorious as students were in their seeking of distractions from their studies...

After all, one could not live on a diet of *Top of the Pops* alone. One had to organise a whole variety of amusements and diversions, and that's what we did. We sometimes (but not very often) visited the swimming baths in Northfield. We home-brewed some disgusting but powerful home-brewed beer (powerful enough to blow the corks off the flagons it was stored in). We had a fireworks-night bonfire in the back garden – when we realised that there was a back garden. We listened to a lot of music – in what was still a golden age for popular music. We often socialised with a group of (female) student dentists who lived just down the road, and some of us socialised with certain of these students on a one-to-one basis. But not me. I, of course, was still 'firmly fastened' to Kathy.

It is less than gallant of me to report this, but I did 'dump' her. I knew early on in that third year that if I didn't, I would end up marrying her, as in she would end up marrying me. However, the dumping didn't work. One dark and stormy night she turned up on the doorstep of 106 in a state of collapse – followed shortly thereafter by the collapse of my resolve, and I took her back. I must have been brainless, particularly as I knew that she would wheedle her way back into my affections and end up making me feel guilty that I had ever tried to spurn her in the first place. And she did. In retrospect, I think that I subsequently forged an ever-closer relationship with her – a woman who I still believed had quite openly 'reeled me in' – in the same way that a hostage develops positive feelings towards his or her captor. I had succumbed to a close relative of Stockholm Syndrome, and there was now no way that I would ever seek to escape my captor.

Nevertheless, Kathy would be instrumental in sorting out my life in terms of my lifelong career. She was, after all, destined to become a lawyer. Not a solicitor but a barrister. She would therefore become a 'professional'; somebody who would successfully side-step the distastefulness of the 'rat race', and who instead would proceed through life at arm's length from the nasty realities of any sort of commerce, industry or even science. That made me think, especially because, whilst I was still enjoying chemistry as an academic subject, I could not see how it could provide me with a satisfying career. In the first place, to get a decent job in the discipline, I would need to embark on a second degree, either an MSc or a PhD, and I had no desire to do that. Nor did I want to end up making my way along an ever-narrowing path, where eventually I would be a community of just one, informing people that there were just twenty-seven basic designs for wallpaper. Instead, I might like to become a professional myself, somebody who would sit in a wood-panelled room, advising widows on their pensions and the advantages of trusts. Yes, I could become a chartered accountant! And more. I could earn a lot of money. Mike, one of my chemistry friends, had a brother who was a chartered accountant, and although he was only thirty, he was already earning £3,000 a year! Heck. As a chemist, I might make that much money by the time I was twice his age. If I survived to that age...

However, I was still regarding the accountant path as merely a possibility, and I hadn't by any means discounted a career as a research chemist. Indeed, I had already made some tentative enquiries into the possibility of working as a chemist in the field of ceramics. (Although God knows why.) But that was before a certain chemistry practical on a Friday afternoon, where I received some very convincing advice that chemistry was not the discipline I was destined to follow, and that I should get out of it as soon as I'd earned my degree.

It was an organic chemistry practical, as usual in one of the chemistry department's vast labs, with scores of students attempting to synthesise some complicated compound without inhaling too many noxious fumes or scalding themselves with the contents of an oil bath or otherwise coming to grief. I have no idea what I was attempting to do on that particular day, but I recall vividly what the guy who worked next to me on the bench was trying to do. It was coming up to five o'clock and, before he left the lab, he was trying to clear a blockage in a large glass vessel, a big globe of a vessel with a (blocked) glass tap at its base. To do this he had filled the globe with a mixture of concentrated nitric acid and acetone, having first checked with one of the university's postgrad supervisors that this was an appropriate thing to do. Unfortunately, the postgrad had not remembered that commercial acetone contains a measurable amount of propyl alcohol, and propyl alcohol and concentrated nitric acid get on just about as well as an ultra-orthodox Jew and a member of Hamas. Albeit their coming together would lead to a bad reaction, whereas the acid and alcohol coming together would inevitably lead to a very good – and very vigorous – reaction.

So vigorous that a great deal of energy would be generated and a glass globe full of these components would quickly start to heat up in its owner's hands.

That's what it did, and that was why my panicked neighbour set the globe on the bench and ran away at speed, neglecting, in his haste, to warn me that he had just left a bomb no more than a metre from where I was standing. When it blew up, I was showered with the contents of the vessel and, as these contents were a mix of hot concentrated nitric acid and hot acetone, laced with a few traces of hot propyl alcohol, it wasn't the sort of shower that would ever be refreshing. No, it was a shower that burnt, and it first burnt my face and, having burnt its way through my fawn polo-neck jumper, it then burnt my chest and my right arm. This was a little disconcerting. And then events became even more disconcerting when I ran my face under a water tap at the end of the bench and doused myself with hot water rather than the more efficacious cold variety.

On the way to the hospital, the culpable supervisor asked me whether this was my first accident. I remember telling him that it was, but also that I intended it to be my last. I had been wearing safety specs, something I rarely did. Had I not been, I would now be looking forward to a life with a glass eye and not just a life as a disfigured ex-chemist. No way was I going to put myself in the path of chemical danger ever again. Even if it meant becoming the most boring accountant on the planet.

However, there was still the aftermath of my accident to deal with first, and this meant my second stay in the university's health centre (after that first stay for glandular fever) and a surprising easing of my burns within just days. By the end of the week following the explosion, they were only just visible, and I had improved so much that I was allowed to accompany Kathy to Manchester for a weekend visit to her mother. It was during the second night there that the itching started, the itching that accompanies the formation of 'skin nitrate', a layer of yellow glutinous guck that could quite easily pass as a film of translucent oozing puss. When I returned to Birmingham on the train on Monday morning, I had the entire carriage to myself, and before me the prospect of either another stay in the health centre or a call to audition for the next Hammer Horror.

Well, Hammer Film Productions missed out, and I was soon in a hospital bed again, and I stayed there until the skin nitrate had dissolved and I could go out into the world without the likelihood of causing pregnant women to suffer spontaneous births. I could also expect to hear from the university authorities what compensation I might receive for the harm I had suffered. After all, they were undeniably liable for this harm, as it had been one of their own representatives, the postgrad supervisor, who had given the go-ahead for the construction of the home-made bomb. And indeed, they did not deny this liability. Why would they? Hell, what university wouldn't be prepared to cough up £5?

That is the amount of compensation I received. And it was principally a generous award to cover the cost of a replacement polo-neck jumper. My injuries, it appeared, warranted no compensation whatsoever. And the remarkable aspect of this munificent payout was that I accepted it without challenge and without much in the way of resentment. Had the same misfortune befallen me thirty or forty years later, I would have been hounded by a whole pack of compensation lawyers and they'd have been exploring not just the cost of a replacement jumper, but the mountains of cash that would be needed to recognise the physical pain I'd endured, the anguish I'd had to endure as a result of the defacement of my supple young skin, the intense indignity I'd had to deal with on public transport, the possible deep mental wound I'd incurred as a result of the trauma, and possibly even the infringement of my human right to live a safe and peaceful life within the confines of a university lab. I would have been awarded an absolute packet.

However, that is what happens now. Back then, most people's reaction to an accident was that it was an accident. It wasn't 'Who can I sue?' That may have been wrong. But when the NHS now pays out more than £2 billion a year in compensation (which it can't afford), when councils pay out hundreds of millions to people who can't manage to negotiate a wonky pavement, and when even prisoners in jail have worked out how to turn the compensation culture into an income stream, one wonders whether it might be better if all claims were capped at £5. At least that way an army of ambulance chasers, claims brokers and compensation lawyers would have to clear off and find themselves a proper job. And hooray for that.

Anyway, that dramatic advice received in the form of a shower of hot chemicals hadn't removed the need to complete my degree, no matter what

I ended up doing thereafter, and I was keen to get a good degree, which, in 1970, meant securing an upper second – or a '2.1'. First-class degrees were only ever awarded to genuine geniuses or very clever students who had failed to engage in university life and who had spent the whole time with their nose in a book and their mind on just work. They would have no social life, no experience of hangovers, no embarrassing episodes with members of the opposite sex, no possibly rewarding episodes with the opposite sex, and no ability to distinguish Jethro Tull from the Moody Blues. Well, as I wasn't a genuine genius and as I was still very much enjoying every aspect of university life, there was no way I was on course for a first, and my objective was to leave the University of Birmingham with 'just' a prized 2.1.

This probably sounds odd, when nowadays a 2.1 is quite often seen as something of a failure. Only a first can be regarded as a real success. But that is to ignore some arithmetic. As has already been pointed out, I was one of just 7% of school leavers who went on to university in my generation and, of those fortunate enough to be in this group, a mere 7% were awarded firsts. That means that just one in 200 school leavers managed to secure this ultimate prize. (And slightly less if one studied chemistry at Birmingham where there were normally only five people awarded firsts each year out of a year class of one hundred.) Well, as 50% of school leavers now turn up at university, and between 25% and 30% of these masterminds are being gifted a first, that means, even if we go with that lower 25%, one in *eight* school leavers is now apparently capable of securing a first. So… either we were a load of real dummies back in 1970 and our modern counterparts have somehow achieved a twenty-five-fold improvement over our performance or, just possibly, degrees have been grossly devalued over the last fifty years to the point where they are just ordinary in every sense of the word. Not that I am bitter, more just a bit… disappointed.

Happily, I was entirely ignorant of this impending devaluation back in 1970 and, as my finals approached, in common with all my colleagues and my three flatmates, I got my head down and devoted myself to ever more work and ever more revision. A lot of this – and especially the revision – was done in 106 Oxford Road. Here I would stay with Tom, while Ian and Clive applied themselves to revision on campus – and both of us would get our heads down for the whole of the day, stopping only to set up the occasional booby trap for our returning friends. We even used the 'bucket full of water on the top of a door' trick, and I am able to report that it does actually work...

Well, this last period of my university life was something of a trial, but in its own way it was still enjoyable. There was a real purpose to all the study, and I was sharing my efforts and my concerns with a group of close friends. In poetic terms, I was still cantering through the pastures of a charmed and privileged life – right up until the day I was brought to an abrupt and unexpected halt. And it wasn't a hurdle or some other barrier that had done this. It was an event; something that was more shocking than anything I'd ever encountered before. It was my sister, Tricia. She had died.

At the age of just twenty-four, and in the company of her devastated husband, she had suffered a massive brain hemorrhage and had died within hours. Worse still – if that were possible – was the fact that she was pregnant and her unborn baby died too. It was simply horrible, and so horrible that it was almost impossible to accept. But I had to, just as my parents had to accept that their daughter – who, unlike their absent son, had stayed in Rugby and played a part in their lives – would no longer be turning up on their doorstep. Ever again.

I could have tried to support my parents through this awful time by just 'being there'. But I knew and they knew that this would achieve nothing, and I would be better employed – and better distracted – by returning to my interrupted studies and having a go at taking my final exams. And that's what I did, despite the university authorities offering me an aegrotat pass. That is to say, that they were prepared to award me an examination pass without my taking any exams on the basis that I was not fit to do so. This option didn't attract me at all. Despite everything, I still wanted that 2.1, and I certainly wanted all the distraction I could get. And an intense spell of further revision would be ideal.

It worked. So that a few weeks later I was receiving my 2.1 degree – from the university's vice-chancellor, Anthony Eden – and celebrating the event in my mortar board and gown and in the company of my mum and dad. But without Tricia. She wasn't there. And that hurt. It hurt both my parents more than I can describe. And it hurt me more than I could ever have imagined. It also removed any vestiges of my belief in any supernatural power. It wasn't just Catholicism that was wrong. So too were all belief systems that had some all-seeing, all-wonderful, benign god at their centre. If there was any god then he was the sort that would pull the wings off flies – and snuff out the life of an innocent young woman and her unborn child on a whim. As far as this shiny new graduate was concerned, he could just go and comprehensively stuff it…

Double Entry

My post-university life started in another Austin J4 and in a state of pseudo-wedlock with the lovely Kathy.

As regards the latter, what this meant was that Kathy had moved into the Oxford Road flat after my male flatmates had left, and had already become my designated wife-to-be. I might even have been engaged to her, but, along with many other aspects of my relationship with this legal lady, that particular memory has been auto-expunged. As regards the former, that reacquaintance with an Austin J4 meant that I was back in the parts-delivery business for a second time, and I stayed in this business even when my true love departed to spend her summer with her Mancunian brethren – and gave me the opportunity to take on a second job to fill in my evening hours.

Yes, I was clearly eager to scrape together as much money as I could before I embarked on a period of impecuniosity inherent in starting a career as a chartered accountant (for that was what I had chosen to do). And what better way to fill up the coffers than by spending my days delivering parts and components around north Birmingham and my evenings delivering liquid refreshment to the patrons of one of the most disreputable pubs in the whole of Birmingham, an underground dive at the back of New Street station that must have formed the template for a whole host of shabby shebeens. It was pretty unpleasant – and it was pretty large. With a huge horseshoe-shaped bar at its centre, it generally had a staff of at least a dozen barmen and barmaids, and it was overseen by two Micks. Not micks in a racially derogatory sense, but two Irish guys who were both called...

Mick. As I would soon discover, their overseeing duties did not prevent them exploiting their positions of authority in much the same way that most of the bar staff were exploiting their own positions in a cash-rich environment.

When I first started at this dreadful drinking den, my major concerns were how not to cock up what was expected of me and how to deal with beer-impregnated trousers. But as I got to grips with these challenges, I couldn't help noticing one very peculiar thing, and this was how a majority of the bar staff seemed indifferent to the arrival of Thursday night – which was pay night. I then realised why. They were fiddling far more money behind the bar than they were being paid to be there. It was phenomenal – and all too easy. One simply had to take a large drinks order, adding up its cost in one's head, and then retire out of sight to the other side of the horseshoe-shaped bar and there enter in a till an amount that was £1 or even £2 below the true cost of the round – and pocket the difference. The practice was so rife and the bar staff so adept that the pub ran at a loss, and the two Micks could do no more than try to catch the malefactors in the act and dismiss them on the spot.

That is all they did. They never pursued a prosecution. Probably because, as I've already indicated, they were up to all sorts of scams themselves. There were little ones like requiring all the bar staff to sell (slightly cheaper) pale ale as lager (in the days when lager was sold only in bottles); making sure that the drip trays were fed back into the barrels of mild in the cellar (!); and, if they did it themselves, measuring out shots of spirits with one of their thumbs in the measure (or serving vodka and blackcurrant with no vodka at all). But their principal method of defrauding the punters was to emulate what all their dishonest bar staff were doing, but with a twist. That is to say that there was a 'house directive' that was supposed to be applied every time a sizeable order was placed at the bar. This involved adding up its cost in one's head (as was normal) and then simply adding a round £1 to its total, or £2 if it was something like a large hen-party order. And if anybody was smart enough to challenge the incorrect total, it was all too simple to confess that it was an easily made mistake when one was trying to do mental arithmetic with pounds, shillings and pence, especially when the shillings and pence totals would always be precisely correct.

It all constituted another indispensable education. Not just the ease with which people could conduct their fiddles or indeed the myriad fiddles that people could devise when presented with tempting cash, but the virtual guarantee that these fiddles would work. Hardly anybody questioned the cost of a round, and nobody noticed that partial or total absence of spirits in a drink – and only one person ever questioned the authenticity of his lager. I remember this because it was I who had served him his pale-ale substitute (probably because the emergency supply of bottled lagers had run out). As I gave him his change, he informed me that this was his second lager, but that his first had not been a lager at all but a pale ale. I apologised for what I claimed must have been an unfortunate mistake, at which point he took his first sip of his second pale ale and announced that 'now, this is a lager, but what I had before certainly was not'. And another satisfied sucker went happily on his way…

Other punters were less prepared to go away happily – ever. And to underline the unwholesome nature of this subterranean saloon, I have to report that every evening two security guards appeared just after closing time – with two German Shepherds. And as often as not, their services were essential. Drink seemed to turn certain punters into man-sized limpets, and no amount of polite entreaties would get them to leave the premises before dawn. In the same way that no amount of polite interaction with one pair of punters would change the fact that one of them was passing a pistol to the other…

It was early one evening, and there was no mistaking what I had seen. As I turned from the till to hand over some change, desperado number one was passing a handgun to desperado number two. And, as it would turn out, they were real desperados.

My initial reaction was to gulp – as discreetly as possible – and my follow-up reaction was to report my observation of this firearm exchange to one of the Micks. He called the police, and within only a very few minutes a plainclothes Sergeant Raincoat and his four plainclothes constables arrived to arrest the gun-toting duo – and one of their companions in the gents – but not another one who got away. This failure to apprehend the whole gang – who were apparently on their way to do a 'blag', having first had a pint and a pee – was just a little bit problematical. Particularly because Sergeant

Raincoat, immediately after the event, had made a point of thanking me for my sharp-eyed observation, which had allowed him to disrupt the commission of a crime, and then gone on to inform me that it was highly likely that I would be called as a witness in the forthcoming trial of the trio of villains (but probably not of a quartet of them).

Shit! Each evening, I finished my stint at this tavern just before midnight to take a night-service bus back to the centre of Moseley, from which I would take a distinctly unaccompanied walk back to 106 Oxford Road. And there was no way that those who'd been apprehended wouldn't know who'd fingered them and no way that they wouldn't relay this vital piece of information to their still-at-large companion. He, no doubt, would have a whole host of villainous buddies who would be only too keen to deal with a blabbermouth barman – and I would be the easiest target imaginable. Even without a bullseye on my back.

Needless to say, my night-time journeys back to Oxford Road were more than a little fraught for the remainder of the summer, and one night I nearly suffered a cardiac arrest with incontinence complications when somebody emerged from the gloom of a churchyard at the beginning of Oxford Road. A one-hundred-yard dash at a qualifying speed for the Olympics ensued, and I promised myself then that in the future even bazookas could be freely passed between punters at my place of employment and I would look the other way. After all, there was no point in provoking fate once again, and following the all-clear on the potential witness front, I just wanted to embark on my chosen career, and put to good use all those lessons I'd learnt about the ingenuity of humans and their ability to subvert any sort of system that others had devised. I'd had the best possible grounding for accountancy, even if a couple of my pairs of trousers were now so beer-soaked and stiff that I could have flogged them off as umbrella stands…

So, at the beginning of September 1970, armed not just with new trousers but with a couple of new suits, I did indeed take up my role as a naïve and underpaid articled clerk. With thirteen other graduates I had joined the Birmingham office of a large national accountancy practice with the rather exotic name of 'Touche Ross', and all fourteen of us were soon grappling with the mysteries of double entry. Now, this isn't, of course, a reference to the sort of thing that might feature in a hard-core porn film, but merely a standard form of bookkeeping where every entry into an account requires an opposite entry into another account. Every debit requires a credit and every credit requires a debit. Simple really – until one is exposed to it for the first time when, even with a 2.1 in chemistry, one can become irritatingly confused. And one can stay irritatingly confused for quite some time. Right up until that day arrives when it all falls into place and debits and credits and where to put them becomes almost second nature and no longer a source of acute embarrassment. In much the same way as it is with sex. Only not so absorbing.

Anyway, as I was setting off along the double-entry path to my chartered destination, my prospective-barrister partner was treading water as a law lecturer at Birmingham Polytechnic (now, of course, Birmingham City University) – and both of us were not enjoying the experience of occupying a so-called furnished flat on the edge of the badlands of Balsall Heath. It was grim, and so grim that it motivated Kathy to find somewhere a little less threadbare and certainly somewhere that was anywhere other than Balsall Heath. And she succeeded in her quest, finding a small but beautifully situated one-room apartment in leafy Harborne, an area of south-west Birmingham that has as much in common with Balsall Heath as I do with Donald Trump. This apartment was really very small indeed, with just one room housing a bed and our living space (a little like those we'd experienced in a hall of residence) together with a bijou kitchen and an equally bijou bathroom. In fact, I think it actually stated in the lease that the swinging of cats was categorically forbidden. Nevertheless, the flat's miniature proportions did mean that we had to acquire the minimum of furniture and we could legitimately not offer overnight accommodation to Kathy's mother or her brother – which was a significant if unspoken (by me) bonus.

So, each weekday, Kathy and I would set off towards the centre of Birmingham, Kathy to the polytechnic and I to a rather pleasant office on the top floor of Chamber of Commerce House. This was a fairly modern building that had been installed in the elegant surroundings of 'professional Edgbaston', a matrix of roads lined with what had once been the smart homes of Birmingham's elite but were now the offices of architects, quantity surveyors, solicitors – and accountants. It was a very pleasant place to undertake a whole host of mundane tasks – which is essentially the full-time job of a new articled clerk, otherwise known as a 'junior'. Yes, I had fallen off that lofty pedestal occupied by freshly minted haughty graduates and was now just a lowly peasant labouring away amongst ledgers and files, and forgetting an awful lot of chemistry very quickly. And frankly, even a knowledge of the periodic table wasn't required when you'd been asked to cast several hundred columns of figures. (It may be difficult to believe, but pocket-sized electronic calculators were not even in sight in 1970, and when they did finally arrive their cost was only a little less than my monthly salary after tax, which to begin with was a whole £60.)

Of course, not every day was spent in the office undertaking mindless tasks. On the contrary. It very soon became the norm to spend one's days out at clients' premises undertaking mindless tasks. Auditing, after all, was the office's principal function, and that meant us lowly peasants, responsible for every sort of lowly chore, had to install ourselves – along with more senior audit staff – in all sorts of accommodation in all sorts of enterprises in all sorts of locations. One week we might be housed in the Dickensian surroundings of a goldsmith in the Jewellery Quarter; another week it might be in a corner of a warehouse of a pallet manufacturer out in Acocks Green. Or one might be very fortunate and end up in the company of a hundred women at a knicker factory in Hinckley (really). And then, of course, there were the 'out of town' assignments...

Touche Ross in those days had only a limited number of offices outside London, and many clients were rather remote from any of these offices. So, in the Birmingham office, whilst it was quite acceptable to drive daily to somewhere like Stafford or... Hinckley, it was necessary to stay away if one was undertaking one's mindless tasks in somewhere like Hull – in, of course, a hotel! This was quite an experience for a former penniless student who had now been indentured as a penniless peasant, and even a two-star hostelry in Bradford or Merthyr Tydfil was a source of enchantment. Not only would somebody make one's bed, but somebody else would provide one with a cooked breakfast every day. And theoretically, at least, one could devote one's evenings to study. One could make progress with one's Foulks Lynch correspondence course and so edge ever closer to that goal of being a fully fledged chartered accountant, free at last from the bonds of servitude and from the need to live on a diet of just mindless tasks.

Of course, that Foulks Lynch stuff never happened, and away-job evenings were normally spent eating, drinking and playing darts, if, that is, they weren't spent doing even more of that auditing stuff. You see, it became apparent very soon in my professional life that being an accountant in practice – at any level – was going to be bloody hard work. There would always be a deadline to meet, a pile of work that had to be cleared without delay, and long hours would be the norm and responsibilities would be loaded onto one's shoulders far sooner than one expected. And to start with, on top of all that, there was then that damn Foulks Lynch correspondence course, which might get neglected on away jobs but that did demand attention at some point – and very often, quite a lot of time. It wasn't like being at university, where missed lectures could be copied up and one could occasionally have a few more hours in bed, but instead it was unavoidable professional education somehow squeezed between the demands of a full-time job. The only real positive was that there was no nitric acid and acetone around...

Anyway, in the interests of restoring some balance, I should admit that these early days of my career were not entirely about constant toil and mind-numbing tasks. There was plenty of fairly interesting stuff to engage in as well, and I did meet an awful lot of people who were either good fun or at least a source of enduring fascination. And furthermore, even as a humble ignorant junior, one did command a certain degree of respect from all those workers out in client-land who did not properly appreciate that one was just a humble ignorant junior. One was seen as 'one of the auditors', one of some superior race that had been put on Earth to monitor the behaviour of mere mortals – and to catch them out if they had committed just a single cardinal sin such as not signing off a dispatch note or not initialising a clock card to authorise maybe two hours of overtime. Such was the power of authority in those days – even unearned authority. And such was the nature of an experience back then that had a great deal of seasoning to spice up the otherwise very bland diet of checking and ticking. Furthermore, there were my fellow graduate peasants, a bunch of young men – and just one young woman – who were generally as bemused as me but, by and large, really good guys who I would get to know very well indeed over a period of months.

We all shared a particular camaraderie because we were the very first wave of graduate recruitment into Touche Ross. Those who had joined the firm before were mostly school-leavers, with only one or two graduates within their numbers. And I should add that this didn't mean that they were any better or any worse than us upstart clever-clogs, but it did mean that we tended to stick together as the new-style new kids on the block. Even if some of us were bordering on the downright peculiar. Like Bruce, whose middle name was Peris and whose 'r's were indistinguishable from his 'n's and who, when drunk on half a pint of bitter, would seek out a piano to play with his elbows – or Paul, who would sometimes appear in the morning with mud on his trousers from doing some very-early-morning gardening and who had an extremely unappealing relationship with his dandruff...

Anyway, my overall recollection of my first year as a budding accountant was one of tedium and hard work blended with discovery, satisfaction and sheer enjoyment. I had jumped off the reassuringly familiar '*SS Chemistry*' and I had found myself sailing along happily in the elegant, full-rigged '*Double Entry*', a beautiful barque heading for the shores of true professionalism and crewed by a load of agreeable sailors, not all of whom had a drink or a dandruff problem. And furthermore, I think I was beginning to take an interest in what was going on in the slightly wider world. By visiting places like Bradford and Merthyr Tydfil – and by reading the occasional newspaper (!) – I was beginning to break out of the bubble of university life that I'd lived in before.

So, for example, I learnt that Britain was negotiating for the membership of something called the EEC. Northern Ireland was limbering up to be the biggest pain in our arse for the next half-century – and counting. Rolls-Royce was indulging in a spot of bankruptcy in preparation for it being nationalised (for a time). Decimalisation was arriving – which admittedly was quite difficult to miss if you were working in a firm of accountants. And *The Sun* was just beginning to decorate its third page with some prominent, not to say formidable, ladies' breasts...

Oh, and one last item to mention about this first year in the nearly real world. It was towards the end of this year that I took my Intermediate Exam (the first of three exams on the way to charter-hood) and I passed it. In fact, out of the 1,800 people who passed at that sitting I came in at number sixty-nine! This was the only exam I had ever sat – or would sit – where my place in the field of successful candidates would be published. It was also the only exam that allowed me to boast that I had achieved a proper *soixante-neuf* – even while I still had my clothes on.

And what's more, I would soon lose my status as a junior…

Ah... Marriage

It is a truth universally acknowledged that a married man in possession of a wife – of any sort – must attempt to remember the date of his wedding anniversary...

Yes, with apologies to Jane Austen, I am conceding that it is incumbent on any married man not to forget the anniversary of the day on which he and his loved one were joined in holy matrimony, which does of course mean that, to start with, he must never forget the date of that actual day. Well, forgive me, but not only can I not remember the date on which I married Kathy, but I cannot even remember the year. It might have been 1971 or it might have been 1972, and I am almost certain that it wasn't 1973. But I'm really not sure...

So, for the sake of this tale, I will take an unknown date in 1971 as the presumed date of our sacred union, and proceed to say just a few well-chosen words about this historic event.

In the first place, the wedding itself took place in a church which, with the help of Mr Google, I have recalled as St Monica's Roman Catholic Church in the parish of Flixton (on the edge of Manchester). St Monica's would struggle to receive plaudits from Prince Charles for its architectural merit, and were he still alive, John Betjeman might indeed have redirected one of those bombs destined for Slough to this modernist mistake in the north of England. That said, there was plenty of room inside it for the modest band of invited wedding guests and there was no ban on the throwing of confetti on the tarmac outside. I know this because I still have five (proof) photographs of the event, and in one of them my new wife and I are being assailed with confetti by a young lady in a short dress and a big hat, whose name has long ago been consigned to the 'inaccessible archive' of my mind.

What I can remember – with the help of those photos – are what Kathy and I wore for this famous day. Kathy had on a rather nice high-collared, white wedding dress, and I was draped in what can only be described as early-1970s super-cool. This comprised a blue and brown pinstriped three-piece suit, worn over a high-collared coffee-coloured shirt (enlivened with a wide brown and yellow tie), and mirrored in a pair of glossy, pale-brown shoes. With what I have to confess was a carefully crafted, almost bouffant style of long hair that completely hid my ears, I could have been taken for a fashionable playboy or maybe a colour-themed character from a Ken Russell film about the excesses of the Italian garment industry. And I must say, the cut of the suit was pretty splendid...

Anyway, I do not need photographs to remind me who the best man was, as I well remember it was Mike of chemistry department fame, who, like me (and his brother), had followed a path into accountancy. Similarly, I have no problem in remembering who was Kathy's matron of honour, because this was one of her old school chums and someone who was actually very famous. This was Paula Wilcox, who had appeared with Richard Beckinsale in Jack Rosenthal's TV sitcom *The Lovers*, and, in due course, would go on to appear in *Man About the House* and, much later on, in *Boomers* (yes, *Boomers*!) and *Upstart Crow*. But back on that day she was just attending to the needs of the bride – and forming the principal source of interest at an otherwise very ordinary set of nuptials. In fact, the post-nuptials reception was pretty ordinary as well, and whilst it was held at a very pleasant country hotel somewhere nearby, it probably cost no more than is now spent on a modern wedding's elaborate invitations and place cards, and certainly less than might be spent on a dose of what I believe now goes by the name of 'official wedding videography'...

As regards some of the actual particulars of the event... well, recollections of these have gone for all time. I don't even remember how I got to Manchester for the wedding (as I suspect that I had not equipped myself with my first car by then) and furthermore I have no idea how I and my new wife got from Manchester to the Lake District for the three or four days of our modest honeymoon. Oh, and as regards the particulars of our honeymoon… well, there will be delight all round that recollections of these have gone for all time as well. Other than a very vague memory of something rather diaphanous being worn at bedtime. But not by me…

So, having dealt with my conversion from bachelorhood to well and truly wedlocked, it is probably time to shed some light on what I was doing for most of the second two years of my articled clerkship – which might just be summed up as 'lots of work'. Having got that Intermediate exam out of the way, there was now 'Part 1' of the professional exams to prepare for – with more of those Foulks Lynch question papers to complete – and there were all those audits to deal with as well. Two, in particular, were very demanding. The first was the audit of one or more of the dozens of companies making up the GEC Group, and the other was the audit of Chrysler UK.

GEC (or the General Electric Company) was then a huge industrial conglomerate involved in electronics, communications and engineering – and, for somebody like me, who was beginning to realise that he relished all aspects of manufacturing, it was also a source of pure fascination and almost envy. When I saw some of the remarkable products of this business, whether they were giant turbines or enormous generators, I was marginally jealous that I hadn't had a hand in their creation. I was having to make do with what was very much a vicarious involvement – generally in offices that were nowhere near the design department or the factory floor. And that was a little sad. After all, what went on in that humungous enterprise was just so impressive, albeit impressive in a very different way from the guy who ran the whole thing, a 'gentleman' by the name of (Lord) Arnold Weinstock. I never met him, of course, because he was far too important and he was generally holed up in his fortress HQ in Stanhope Gate in London. But I was well acquainted with his less than gentlemanly style of management and his terrible reputation. Essentially, he seemed to rule through a combination of fear and focused interference, and he was pretty well ruthless. In fact, the apocryphal story relating to his behaviour, which best sums up the man, concerns his spotting from his top-floor office, a Stanhope Gate employee clearing snow from the steps of his London citadel, and immediately firing off a demand to know how this lowly individual usefully spent his time when he wasn't shovelling snow – with the implicit understanding that unless an adequate response was received, the employee in question would soon be an ex-employee. Needless to say, 'Arnold' wasn't much loved, and even the City criticised him for his caution and what many saw as an oppressive style of management. Nevertheless, GEC thrived under his stewardship, and it had to wait for his successor to make a series of ill-judged acquisitions before it would all go pear-shaped, and GEC would fracture into a series of smaller concerns.

Now, it may be thought that GEC and its formidable managing director have only a tenuous connection with the story of a young trainee accountant making his way to qualification. But GEC really did cement my interest in everything surrounding the process of manufacturing, and Arnold, although he would never know it, did manage to provide me with a template for how I would *not* go about treating anybody 'below' me. As I gradually took on more responsibility and more and more people ended up working 'under' me, I would always endeavour to see things from the steps of Stanhope Gate and not from the executive floor above it. I would also try to remember that very little of anything should be taken that seriously, thanks in no small part to the time I spent on the audit of Chrysler UK…

This was conducted at the beginning of the calendar year in a vast warehouse of an office on the outskirts of Coventry, and it provided an insight into what can be the manic behaviour of a huge enterprise and the equally manic behaviour of a good number of those who work in such an enterprise. It was all so demented, with a whole army of people seemingly not focused on making profits, which is the supposed primary purpose of most businesses, but instead on increasing the market share of their vehicles at the expense of their competitors – at whatever cost. It was never going to be a recipe for long-term success, and indeed the operations of Chrysler UK eventually passed into the hands of Peugeot Citroën – who did appear to want to earn some profits out of making cars. But back in those Chrysler days, it was 'sales and marketing' before anything else, and a reluctance to admit that with so many cars leaving the factory with 'runs', 'drips' or 'sags' in their paintwork, there might be merit in paying some attention to other aspects of the business – such as the quality of its product. Nevertheless, it was fun to be on Chrysler's audit, not least because a special sort of camaraderie would develop within whatever team of 'tickers' had been condemned to spend many long working days in a windowless audit room – and who would therefore barely see any daylight for the whole of January. Oh, and one got mileage as well...

Yes, it wasn't too long before I had my own car (a scary Triumph Herald 13/60), and I was then able to earn mileage by driving it to work in Coventry and sometimes picking up a couple of juniors on the way. For I was now a 'senior', and for the first time ever, I had a degree of real authority. Unfortunately, however, I still didn't have much money. And when Kathy left to pursue her bar-exam training in London (requiring a flat in that metropolis), I had even less money. What was left of her previous earnings from her lecture work was now going to maintain her in London, and what I was earning was just about keeping our heads above water – but only just. I still vividly remember hiding from the milkman once when we simply had no money at all. And I would recommend that everyone should experience this sort of milkman moment in his or her life at least once. I can guarantee that it teaches one the value of money in a way that nothing else can, and it also, of course, encourages the consumption of coffee without milk. I've now been drinking mine black for nearly half a century.

Anyway, to return to life at work for a moment, I should first report that I was successful at my attempt at Part 1 of the professional exams and I was equally successful in acclimatising to life in a professional office. It really wasn't very difficult, probably because the office was far from huge, and with its no more than maybe eighty personnel, it managed to maintain a really friendly, almost family feel to it. Furthermore, it had a clearly defined hierarchy and clearly defined paths of progression. Everybody knew where they were in the hierarchy and where they were going – up to a point.

Now, this 'up to a point' qualification is important, and what it means is that for 'technical staff' (that is, people such as myself), the path started in their first year as a lowly junior and, if they passed their exams, it would almost certainly take them through a two-year stint as a senior right up to the point at which they became qualified accountants. After this they would then either be promoted to a 'supervisor' – or they would scuttle out of the office door just as soon as they could and get themselves a job in 'the real world'. Professional accountancy practices are, after all, as much about feeding the insatiable accounting demands of industry and commerce as they are about providing professional accountancy services (and a living for those who remain within them). However, if one is a supervisor who has chosen to eschew the real world – for at least the time being – and instead stay in 'the profession', one may then find oneself promoted to assistant manager. Alternatively, one may be 'counselled out', a very professional euphemism for being dumped on the grounds that a supervisor grade is as far as one's limited abilities or one's limited application is going to take one.

Now, though, it gets serious. As an assistant manager, one has effectively announced one's intention to proceed to a full manager grade and from there to being admitted into the partnership – to being elevated to the company of those exalted gods of the accountancy profession who are not only omniscient but very much omnipotent as well. I mean, we are talking about some really powerful guys here, guys who own the whole game as well as running the whole game, and that's why it turns out to be very difficult indeed to become one of their number. Some of those assistant managers don't even become managers. Some of those who do make it that far soon learn that they will never get any further, and end up retiring in their sixties as managers, or they jump ship – maybe to a client company – as soon as they're able to do this. Which just leaves a few persistent souls who have reconciled themselves to quite a few years of pretty demanding work in the belief that one day they will get that call from the managing partner in London to join him and his buddies on Mount Olympus. Not all of these are successful by any means, and to make partner in a firm like Touche Ross, one needs a truly magical combination of ability, resolve, stamina, application, intellect – and more than a little bit of good luck. Very few, I have to say, even get their hands on a wand.

So, who were the representatives of this master race in the Birmingham office of this 'Big Eight' accounting firm, and how did I see them from the perspective of a lowly senior? Well, two of them were very old school and just very old. One was the partner in charge of the office and the other was his number two, who was seemingly partner in charge of nothing. He was rarely in the office, and if he was, he was generally tied up with 'Institute' or 'Society' affairs (as in the snappily titled Institute of Chartered Accountants in England and Wales' affairs or the local West Midlands Society of

Chartered Accountants' affairs – both of which organisations were even duller than the dullest aspects of professional accountancy). Needless to say, I saw little of this gentleman and only marginally more of the equally venerable 'PIC'. He, the top man, seemed to spend most of his time on trusts and other equally riveting stuff, and was attended by a small retinue of faithful retainers who were as deferential to their master as they were old and dusty-looking. Their appearance really did suggest that they'd been in the office before the office even existed – and, like their master and his number two, they had little to do with us thrusting articled clerks and even less to do with the other partners.

Yes, there were four other partners, a quartet of younger souls, with whom we minions were allowed to interact. Indeed, we were able to address them by their first names, even PBJ, the most senior of the quartet, who was also the one with the permanent smile. Peter – for that was his name – was a large gentleman with an even larger personality. If he wasn't smiling, he was laughing, and by approaching the world with such a beaming face and with so much irrepressible affability, he was able to generate all sorts of new work for the firm and a great deal of affection from the staff. Indeed, one day I witnessed an outstanding example of his overwhelming charm in action when he was on the phone to his wife. I was in his office, and 'Pet' (his wife) had rung him with the good news that the vet had visited their home and had fixed the donkey – and the bad news that, as the vet was leaving, he had run over the cat and killed it. Cue Peter, and a heartfelt assurance offered to his wife that the cat would probably have felt very little pain and, as it had enjoyed a very long and very happy life, its departure was hardly premature. And all this soothing verbal balm was delivered in such a saintly and 'smiley' voice that it would no doubt have set at ease even the cat's own mother.

Peter wasn't, by any means, regarded as the top technical partner in the office. That honour fell to John, the Scary Spice of the office, who not only didn't take prisoners but was not unknown to shoot his own troops. He was very clever, very clinical in his approach, and very feared. When the position became vacant – on the retirement of both of the oldies – it was a foregone conclusion that he would take over the leadership of the office. And it was no great surprise thereafter when he moved to London and took over the leadership of the whole firm. John was not only clever, clinical and potentially terrifying, he was also single-minded. And he never got on to my Christmas-card list.

Neither, in fact, did the other two young partners, although in due course I would socialise with them both. One was the tax partner, Charles, who had the looks of a featherweight boxer and the aspirations of a country gent. The other, Tony, was the 'deals' partner, who was quite simply the antithesis of the accepted image of a chartered accountant. Strangely enough, like me, he had graduated in chemistry from the University of Birmingham, but he must have taken up accountancy as a dare. That said, he was one of the most capable and imaginative accountants I have ever met. And one of the most alcohol-resilient.

Talking of which, you may recall one of my fellow articled clerks with the middle name 'Peris', who was not resilient to alcohol at all, and who would either fail to play the piano proficiently after just a couple of halves or fail to stay conscious after three. Well, I bring him back into the story because he featured in what for me was a very memorable event that kicked off in North Wales…

Somebody in the office – probably Charles, who was sort of responsible for training – had decided that to reinforce the efficacy of those Foulks Lynch correspondence courses, use could be made of a residential 'crammer' in a gothic-type mansion just outside Conwy – called Caer Rhun Hall. This place, I have recently discovered, is now a desirable hotel, but back then it was just an austere pile with little in the way of comfort and nothing in the way of relief from work. For those of us who were sent there to prepare for either Part 1 or Part 2 of our professional exams, it was four to a room, minimal heating, minimal facilities, prunes with every meal (including breakfast), and a study day that started at 8.30am and only finished at the conclusion of the final session of the day, which was held *after* dinner (with prunes). It was relentless stuff for three solid weeks, Monday to Sunday, with only two brief respites – on the afternoons and evenings of the first and second Saturdays. These were our only chances to escape the stifling atmosphere of Caer Rhun Hall, and all of us grasped these chances without a second's hesitation. On the first Saturday, I joined a group who had decided to visit Chester – where I purchased a wonderful life-like rubber rat. And on the second Saturday, I was one of five who sought out some early-evening sustenance in Anglesey.

Well, at the risk of upsetting the *Visit Wales* guys, back in 1973 the dining options in Anglesey were such that we ended up in Liverpool. Here is where middle-name Peris features, because he was also one of the five and he was easily the most outrageously dressed of us all. I do not have to imagine what he wore because I still have a photo of him in his chosen regalia (standing next to me in a group of us in the grounds of Caer Rhun). This is reproduced in the photo section of this book, and it clearly shows that my 'most outrageously dressed' description could not be more apt. Indeed, with his (not quite long enough) flared trousers, his flared, white plastic coat complete with a huge fake-astrakhan collar, all finished off nicely with a white panama hat sitting precariously on his huge mop of collar-length hair, he still reminds me of a Christmas-tree fairy who has undergone a sex change and, in the process, has lost any dress sense that she or he might have originally possessed.

This appearance was, of course, not a problem in the grounds of Caer Rhun Hall, but it threatened to be a very distinct problem on the streets of downtown Liverpool on a Saturday night. And so it was. Indeed, so much so that we had only one quick drink in very awkward circumstances and then returned to base somewhat earlier than planned.

Nevertheless, notwithstanding this reckless sortie into urban danger, the Caer Rhun experience did its job, and just a few weeks later I was in receipt of a pass notification for my Part 2 exam and, after the normal formalities, I was pronounced a fully fledged, albeit still-wet-behind-the-ears chartered accountant. And I was still, of course, married to Kathy…

Brum, Barmy Driving, the Big Apple and Bermuda

At the outset of 1974, Kathy, having passed her bar finals, was now back in Birmingham, and she would soon be joining a set of chambers in the city to embark on her pupillage, otherwise known as a period of working under the direction of a senior barrister for something between nothing and a pittance. I was already a 'supervisor' – with new responsibilities and maybe a new sense of purpose, and that was to progress up the promotion path and, of course, to get to its very top. So, both of us now had a clearly defined ambition: Kathy to become a successful criminal and matrimonial barrister, and I to become a partner in Touche Ross. And both of us were looking to pursue our respective ambitions in familiar Brum. Never did we contemplate moving to London or anywhere else – although in due course we might have to do just that…

However, for now, Brum was our world and, in many ways, it was a world that was sweet. Even though Kathy seemed to be operating as a charity, she was certainly enjoying the role she had been working towards for several years, and I was equally engaged with my work for the firm. It might be a difficult concept to grasp, but conducting audits – which was what I was doing for most of the time – isn't necessarily a quick route to brain death. On the contrary, it's actually quite demanding, quite intellectually challenging and quite interesting generally, not least because much of it involves dealing with people and not just numbers. And if that sounds like a statement made because I currently have a gun held to my head, it isn't. It's true. Working on the audit of a company's results may not be up there with flying F35 Lightnings or reporting from war zones, but I found it very rewarding, and that's even before taking account of the people with whom I worked.

They were all bright people. In a way it was like still being at university – surrounded by people of a similar intellect and with a similar ability to provide a stimulating environment. And then there were all those bizarrely named 'non-technical' people back in the office, all those secretaries, administrators and receptionists who made the world sweeter than ever. Yes, when discussing office life in the previous chapter, I shamefully focused on just the 'technical staff', all those folk who were either accountants or on their way to becoming accountants, and I neglected to point out that their job would have been impossible to do without the 'support staff' who answered phones, typed up reports and accounts (in a pre-computer world) and generally ensured that the business actually functioned as a business. And they certainly brightened up the place no end.

Virtually all us technical types were male. Virtually all the non-technical types were female, and most of them were young as well as female. And flirting, teasing, 'joshing' and even 'associating' – whether initiated by a *beau* or a *belle* – hadn't yet become capital crimes. I was never aware of anything unpleasant going on and never aware that any of the women in this now long-lost environment felt oppressed or abused – because they weren't. In fact, they were more often initiators of some of this 'cross-gender interaction'. And I can't help feeling that, in the current 'Me Too' world, women have ended up swapping something that was largely benign – and fun – for something that simply engenders suspicion and hostility but allows no bloody fun whatsoever. But what do I know? I'm only a man – and back then a happily married man who only ever indulged in a bit of mild flirting...

That last statement, incidentally, wasn't meant to be facetious. Despite my previous lukewarm comments about my spouse, we were both having a pleasant enough time, and it probably helped that for much of the week she was busy pursuing her career and I was busy pursuing mine. We were travelling through professionalism on parallel tracks that never met, but in an odd way this meant that we now had more in common than ever – and more money. Not a great deal more, but with Kathy eventually earning some fees – and sometimes even being paid these fees – and my salary going up quite rapidly, we weren't needing to hide from the milkman anymore. Nor did we need to rely on a clapped-out Triumph Herald and have to live in a one-room flat. Instead, we could afford a smart second-hand Beetle and a not-so-smart 'starter home' on a new estate in a nowhere-near-smart suburb of Brum called Lye. (But at least it was our property and we weren't looking forward to years of renting or years of living back with our parents…)

Anyway, our world wasn't entirely sweet, and in certain respects it was bitter in the extreme. And the reason for this was the state of our nation back then. Essentially, the country was in a right old pickle, principally due to a devastating miners' strike which had caused the government to introduce a 'three-day week' at the beginning of 1974. And what this meant was that commercial users of electricity were limited to three specified consecutive days' consumption each week, and prohibited from working any longer hours on those days. It wasn't a very jolly time, especially as we auditors were still expected to turn up at a client's premises every day of the working week and, if necessary, conduct our tasks without the benefit of any heating and by the light of candles. We had in a way reverted to the nineteenth century. And I remember sitting at a desk one day – in my overcoat and in the gloom of a candle-lit office – wondering whether I should furnish myself with a proper quill pen and maybe a dose of consumption or rickets to create that genuine Victorian feel.

This nonsense did end, but only through our being lumbered with a supine Labour administration that would oversee a period of rampant inflation and fail to cure that other great national malaise of the time known as IRA terrorism. Yes, future members of the Northern Ireland Assembly were busying themselves back then with murdering as many people as they could by blowing them to bits, and making everybody's life a real fucking misery in the process. There were bombs everywhere, and I was actually in earshot of two of them: one in London and another small one just down the road from our office in Edgbaston – which killed at least one person. Then in November of 1974, these monsters in human form killed twenty-one people who had the temerity to go for a drink in a pub in the middle of Birmingham – and that left a really bitter taste, and a taste that for some remains to this day. I know I cannot put into words the disgust I feel for these people and their miserable ambitions for their miserable little corner of the world, and I doubt many in this country would shed a tear if one day we all woke up to learn that the whole of a particular part of Ireland had been abducted by aliens. Although, of course, there might be a large outpouring of sympathy for the aliens...

Michael would definitely not have shed a tear. This was not Mike, my best man, but Michael, a barrister who had qualified with Kathy and who had remained in contact – to the extent that we both met him occasionally either in Birmingham or more often in London. He was unique: a young man who was highly intelligent, highly inventive, highly active – and highly reckless. His intelligence, his inventiveness and his high activity level I had witnessed when I'd first met him. However, it took a particular weekend in London to discover his reckless disposition.

This became blindingly apparent when he and I were, for some reason, passing Gray's Inn, the Inn of Court at which both Kathy and Michael had studied for the bar. It was a Sunday morning, and one middle-aged barrister who lived in an apartment in a four-storey residential wing of the Inn had put his Sunday roast in the oven – and had then locked himself out of his apartment. Cue much consternation and an immediate offer by Michael to provide his Superman service and so save the roast from incineration and the flat from any subsequent conflagration. Needless to say, Michael had no real Superman powers and not even a Superman costume. All he had was me and an idea that if we got ourselves onto the roof of the building, I could hold a rope and he could climb down this to the barrister's second-floor flat and then enter it through a window.

I have no idea where we found a suitable rope, but I remember vividly being on that roof with a rope and somehow facilitating my reckless friend's descent of the building in much the same way as those SAS guys invited themselves into the Libyan embassy a few years later. Then, having let the very relieved barrister back into his unburnt apartment to enjoy his unburnt Sunday lunch, we set off in one of Michael's several cars – a Mini – to drive out of London along the M4 towards Windsor. Again, time has erased the purpose of this journey, but it certainly has not erased what happened on the journey – which made climbing down a building on a rope look like the least reckless thing one could possibly do.

The start of the journey was uneventful but, as we got nearer to Windsor, we were met with the sight of myriad brake lights ahead and then more and more warning headlamp flashes from the vehicles on the opposite carriageway. There was clearly an accident up ahead, and Michael – who was driving – began to slow down. At the same time, events began to speed up, and the first of these events was the appearance of two saddled but riderless horses galloping towards us. This was no ordinary accident – and probably no accident at all (yet) – but, instead, two animals who were not only in acute danger but also causing mayhem on the motorway. As they got nearer – at gallop speed – cars were swerving all over the place, and it looked as though some sort of accident was now inevitable, and in all likelihood the horses would come off second best.

I probably took this into account when I agreed to Michael's suggestion that we do a U-turn as they passed us in order that we might add two saved equines to our existing count of one saved barrister's flat and one saved barrister's Sunday dinner. And anyway, I, like Michael, had always wondered what it would be like to drive down a motorway the wrong way.

Well, I can now report that it was quite exciting. With both of the Mini's doors open, we attempted to usher our wayward duo towards the hard shoulder with a view to guiding them down the next slip road. This, I have to admit, didn't work very well, and after one of them had kicked in a car windscreen as he passed it, they both avoided the slip road and continued on their way. No further windscreen encounters were made, but I do recall that never before had I seen so many frightened and startled expressions on the faces of motorway drivers, and I had rarely felt more relieved when our tactics did finally pay off and we were able to convince the two horses to take the next exit. They trotted down the slip road, and, at the bottom of the slip road, they then just ambled into a field as if nothing had happened.

Well, neither of us knew anything about horses, other than they were really very nice chaps and, if they had a bridle on, then they would probably not object to being helped to avoid another rendezvous with a busy road. We therefore left our car, strolled towards where they had stopped in the field, successfully took hold of their bridles, and then led them back to where we had parked and where there were now four police cars...

The policeman in charge took our details, but seemed unsure as to what to do. He knew that we had just driven the wrong way down a motorway – which is counter to the directives of the Highway Code – but he also knew that we had saved two horses and maybe even some Sunday drivers who had not prepared themselves for a meeting with Black Beauty and Champion the Wonder Horse. He also had an immediate problem to deal with, which was how to return two large beasts to their rightful owners – or to anywhere – when he clearly couldn't get them into the back of his Rover 2000. It's probably why he was eager to let us go on our way without even a caution. And maybe, we thought as we drove away, not only would we not get any sort of punishment at all, but we might instead get an MBE! After all, this was the Windsor area, and Princess Anne and Captain Mark Phillips were still very much in the romancing stage back then – and they were both horsey people. So, it was just possible... that they had parked up their steeds for a bit of impromptu nooky and, as they had made out, their horses had made off. In which case, the consequent royal gratitude would certainly lead to some suitable reward. And if not an MBE, then at least an invite to the next royal wedding.

But it didn't happen. In fact, nothing happened. We were neither rewarded nor punished for our motorway madness. This outcome, I am convinced, simply encouraged Michael to continue with his reckless ways. No consequences meant no caution and, as I would witness later on in my relationship with this guy, Michael would remain without any noticeable reck for a good many years to come.

I was much more careful. Obviously. I, after all, was an accountant. Nevertheless, I did throw caution to the wind in 1976, when I accepted a dangerous posting overseas: a posting to the urban badlands of the New World.

Well, that may be overdramatising things just a little bit, and what actually happened, shortly after I had been promoted to assistant manager (!), was that I was offered an exchange trip with our firm in America – for two and a half months at the beginning of the calendar year. This was all part of a longstanding arrangement where we provided trained staff to Touche in the States – and in Canada and Australia – to help out in their busy periods, in exchange for some of their staff turning up in Blighty to help out in ours. It was also something of a perk, in that those taking part in this exchange programme were paid their normal salary back home, but they also received 'subsistence' expenses from the receiving firm to allow them to... subsist for the duration of their visit. Oh, and it provided a useful perspective on how the firm operated in a different jurisdiction. In fact, the offer to participate in this exchange programme was all good news – other than the fact that I was originally destined to be sent to one of the firm's (safe) Canadian offices, until a manager from our London office got cold feet at the prospect of being shipped off to those urban badlands, otherwise known as New York. Hence, an offer to swap with him, which I *recklessly* accepted. I would be going there with a full manager from my own office – by the name of Phil – and both of us would have to gird our loins and all our other vulnerable bits for a spell in the Big Bad Apple, a city that back then was apparently riddled with lots of thieves and baddies and simply brimming with guns and knives. So, just like London is now...

Anyway, I was still thrilled to be going there – and thrilled beyond measure at the prospect of getting there on a Jumbo Jet! Remember, for me it had been just Viscounts up to now, and the fact that I would be flying across the Atlantic in an aerial cathedral was simply mind-blowing. Even if New York turned out to be as terrible as threatened, it would still be worth going there just to experience a 747. And in the event, I was not disappointed. Even now, I can remember looking along the length of its enormous cabin as it took to the air, and finding it difficult to believe that anything that size could actually get airborne and then stay airborne. And they even gave you food and drinks as well!

'They', however, didn't give you a very warm welcome to America. In the shape of American Immigration officials, 'they' offered us only a frosty reception, and then the taxi driver who took us from the airport to Manhattan went via somewhere like Wisconsin to clock up the most unfair of fares possible. It was simply extortionate. Neither Phil nor I was impressed, and in due course there would be other experiences in New York that left a lot to be desired. Early on in our stay, we were saved from an assault only by the locked doors of a bus terminus, and then I was hijacked by a 'bag lady' who tried to claim that I had assaulted her, in a brazen attempt to win some on-the-spot compensation (which she didn't get). Then there was being aggressively abused by a restaurant waiter for not leaving the required (grossly excessive) tip, the accusation that Phil and I were homosexual (made by a camera shop owner who had failed to sell Phil a zoom lens that he didn't want), the completely non-aggressive but worrying encounter with a black, bearded transvestite on a deserted railway platform – and most dramatic of all, the sight of the aftermath of a stabbing. It was only early evening and, in a crowded street, a man who had clearly been punctured by a knife was chasing his assailant. And both the assailed and the assailant were being ignored by everyone else. It seemed that the reputation New York had earned back in the '70s was not false after all.

Nevertheless, there was much to enjoy in the ten-week stay, not least the easy pace of work, where hours spent at work seemed infinitely more important than the quality or the efficiency of the work. And then there was the opportunity to see the sights of New York and even opportunities to see parts of Washington and Boston and bits of Pennsylvania. With Phil and with another guy from the Birmingham office who was on an exchange trip in New Jersey, I tried to make the most of my first time in the States and succeeded more than I could ever have imagined, thanks in no small part to the welcome intransigence of the New York office…

Phil and I were each receiving an expense allowance of $42 per day, of which $38 was to cover the cost of our rooms in the hotel on Broadway that had been chosen by the New York office to act as our temporary home. We didn't like this hotel or its situation (think *Midnight Cowboy* street scenes and then add in another layer of sleaze). So, we found a short-lease furnished apartment in a much more salubrious part of Manhattan that worked out at a cost, for each of us, of just $7 per day. We immediately reported this fact to the local partner who was responsible for us, and suggested that he might want to reduce our daily allowance to reflect our significantly reduced accommodation costs – but he wouldn't. $42 per day was the agreed rate and it could not be changed. So, if you do the arithmetic, you will discover that our daily subsistence of $4 ($42 minus $38) had immediately risen to $35 ($42 minus $7) – an almost nine-fold increase that we… well, that we reluctantly had to accept. And bear in mind that back in 1976, one could –

believe it or not – live on $4 a day in New York. So, with so much money to play with, Phil and I ate out every day, built up a pile of unspent money (which for me would be used to finance a new car when I returned to the UK), and we still had enough money to have a ten-day holiday in Bermuda on our way back home. It certainly made up for that frosty reception to the States and for the aggression and violence we'd witnessed in the city. And it even went a long way to making up for those ten weeks of celibacy we'd had to endure…

Talking of which, our stay in Bermuda was not planned to bring our celibacy to an end (perish the thought), but we did think that our respective wives might not be too upset if we sought out some female companionship during our stay there (especially if we didn't tell them). Accordingly, we turned up at a disco one night where we had been assured that there would be piles of US college girls on their spring break, who would simply melt at the first sound of an English accent. Well, maybe word had somehow got back to our wives, because the venue was in darkness, and we were obliged to channel any desires we might still have into a game of ping pong back in the basement of our hotel. It was a little like the freshers' ball all over again.

However, by coming back early, we did have the thrill of sharing the hotel's lift with Hughie Green. So, the evening turned out to be not quite a complete write-off. Even if Hughie didn't look to be in the best of humour. Maybe because, just like us, opportunity for this rather sinister-looking game-show host had, this evening, failed to knock.

(Baby Boomers will understand…)

Abigail's Party

Star Wars arrived in 1977, and one would have to have been a hermetically sealed hermit holed up in a literal hole in the Hebrides not to have known about it.. It was quite an event. Nevertheless, there was something else that arrived that year, no doubt produced without the benefit of a *Star Wars* budget, but with the capacity to make a *Star Wars*-level impact on any number of Baby Boomers. And this was, of course, the unforgettable *Abigail's Party*.

This remarkable play, written by Mike Leigh, was shown on television in November of that year. With Mike Leigh's words – and apparently some improvisation – Alison Steadman and her fellow thespians were able to confront a burgeoning new middle class with its not entirely laudable tastes and aspirations. Not every critic would agree with this statement, and some might see it more as an exercise in disdain for this new middle class – a new middle class that undoubtedly included one recently minted barrister and one tenderfoot chartered accountant. However, it did capture an 'essence of the age', whilst at the same time allowing the vast majority of its audience to comfort themselves in the knowledge that 'they weren't anything like that – thank God'.

Kathy and I, I am confident in saying, had very little in common with the characters in the play, and virtually nothing in common with their tastes, especially those tastes in music and drinks that were relentlessly imposed by the irrepressible 'hostess from hell' on her guests. We recognised them, but they weren't ours. They were alien as well as cringeworthy. Unlike the aspirations on show. Which, I have to admit, were rather more difficult to disown...

Yes, I have already admitted that Kathy was seeking success at the bar, and I had a partnership in my sights. And on top of this, we were both entirely sold on the idea of 'advancement'. We had aspirations that would be reflected in every aspect of our lives up to the end of the decade and beyond. In fact, it could be said that realising these aspirations had now become our full-time occupation. Just like it had for a whole swathe of that new middle class...

For me, the clear path to fulfilling these aspirations was the simple four-letter word 'work', albeit that this 'work' was quite often accompanied by the eight-letter term 'more work'.

Now, even I think that sounds creepy. It no doubt conjures up an image of a distinctly unappealing, calculating drone who seeks to impress his masters by keeping his nose so close to the grindstone that he risks nasal eradication. However, nothing could be further from the truth. In the first place, the accepted work ethic in the firm, accepted by all of us, was 'work and then more work' – and don't complain about it. Especially if one has been elevated to the ranks of the firm's middle management. So, there was simply no alternative. Other, of course, than leaving the firm. But on top of this work ethic imperative, there was something else, something called motivation. And this is where I have to take a short detour into the memorable (for me) run-up to a particular managers' conference.

It was when I was still an assistant manager (before becoming a full manager), and when I was asked to deliver a presentation at a regional managers' conference on the subject of... motivation. Inevitably, my first reaction to this 'request' was the triggering of some premature action in my peristaltic wave. But, when this had passed, my more considered reaction was to conduct some research on the subject of motivation, in order that I might have more than a sentence worth of material for my address. And this was when I learnt not only about what motivating factors are in the workplace, but how they are often confused with 'hygiene factors' in the workplace.

Forgive me for a dose of didacticism here, but what I discovered was that 'hygiene factors' are aspects of the work environment that do not give 'positive satisfaction' or provide any real motivation, but instead lead to dissatisfaction if they are absent. So, for example, usable chairs and glass in the office windows are hygiene factors. Their presence does not motivate people to perform better or to work harder, but their absence probably leads to a degree of dissatisfaction that may well end in mass resignations. No matter how interesting or challenging a job might be, if you have nothing to sit on, and an icy draught is blowing in through a hole where a window should be, you're not going to stay around for very long. And interestingly, money is a hygiene factor as well. More of it won't motivate people to up their game, but too little of it will encourage them to seek a career somewhere else. Which leaves us to explore what are the true motivators; what are the features of any job that encourage people to excel and willingly give their all?

Well, it's obvious, isn't it? It's being provided with interest and challenge in one's work, along with being given increased responsibility, enhanced independence, new opportunities and appropriate recognition, all of which were present in abundance for both managers and assistant managers in 1970s Touche Ross Birmingham. Indeed, 'challenge' was a ubiquitous feature. Whether it was the challenge of understanding a client's business, the challenge of understanding his systems and the anomalies in these systems, or simply the challenge of getting him to pay your eminently reasonable fees, all were there all the time. Just as were meeting his expectations, meeting the onerous requirements of accounting and auditing standards, meeting deadlines (oh so many deadlines), and meeting the copious and varied demands of the partnership. And then, of course, there was drinking...

Yes, in blathering on about the heroic nature of what was involved in fulfilling my aspirations, it would be remiss of me not to mention what was a critical aspect of the 'coping mechanism' adopted by all of us hard-pressed manager types, and this was our routine ingestion of alcohol – as in the daily consumption of beer at lunchtime. It sounds positively scandalous now, but with most of us working in the office – rather than out at a client's premises – there was always a quorum for a visit to a local hostelry at one o'clock. And at this hour the assembled members of the pub expeditionary force would proceed to the chosen watering hole, and there, each of us would down at least two pints of bitter. Quite often, it would be three.

Something with chips would provide a modicum of ballast to stabilise this liquid intake, and both taken together would furnish not just sustenance but also sufficient invigoration for a full afternoon's work, work that would generally not be concluded until the early evening. (Except on Friday, when more pints would be consumed at a favoured hostelry in Edgbaston – starting late afternoon and in the company of an improbable proportion of the entire office.)

It is probably worth dwelling for a moment on what would now be regarded as near criminal behaviour, and I will do this by making three pertinent observations. The first is that whilst some modern office workers would claim that I and my fellow managers could in no way be invigorated by lunchtime drinking, they would be ignoring not only the work imperative I have discussed *ad nauseam* but also the absence of modern-day office distractions. Unlike the current crop of white-collar workers, we were not spending time at work updating our Facebook page, checking our Twitter feeds, and Googling the best LGBT-friendly hotels in Magaluf and Gran Canaria. We were just working. In fact, our productivity was probably embarrassingly colossal compared to that of the smoothie-drinking, wrap-eating social-media junkies of the current era. And alcohol can never kill as many brain cells as a smartphone…

Then there's the second point: drinking encouraged socialising, and socialising built bonds. This was certainly true for my close-knit group of managers, and equally so for the wider group that would gather in that Edgbaston pub each week, and that encompassed secretaries, receptionists, all grades of 'technical staff' and even the anointed ones. Yes, partners would often attend these events, along with their open wallets. Which I still think is a more effective way to build firm loyalty and firm morale than writing a passionate foreword in the (online) staff magazine.

And then there's point three. Nearly everybody drank in the '70s, just as most people smoked back then. And whilst these habits could never be described as commendable, they weren't quite up there with child molestation and flamingo-strangling as some of the most despicable activities one could choose. (And drinking, by the way – quite often to excess – is in our culture. And it's far less dangerous than any form of zealotry, something which is happily still missing from our [native] culture.)

Anyway, back to aspirations, because I haven't yet mentioned what all that alcohol-lubricated hard work – with its attendant promotions and pay rises – delivered in terms of meeting my and my wife's material aspirations. And these were plenty. First the Beetle was replaced with an MG MGB GT (!), which was then joined by a second car in the family, and then replaced with a company car – a not-so-aspirational Chrysler Alpine, the sort of car that car enthusiasts look on with pity. But, there again, at least it was free...

It also looked not in the least out of place sitting in the drive of our new house in a real village! For we had forsaken the delights of Lye and minimalism in bricks, and had moved to the sort of property that would have been considered far too grand for *Abigail's Party*, a detached house situated in what might be considered a top-tier aspirational destination. Because not only were we now 'out in the country' – but we were in genuinely rural Worcestershire, in a settlement called Inkberrow, which was the village that had inspired *The Archers*. Not that it had a population of just 200, as it did when *The Archers* first aired in 1951, but it was still a pretty nice place to live. And a pretty nice place to contemplate what other aspirations Kathy and I might want to realise...

Amongst these were brushing up on our home entertaining, 'eating out' with friends, acquiring more and more essential possessions – and, most important of all, 'taking foreign holidays'. Since getting married, we had made only domestic excursions to places like Cornwall and the Lake District. But now we wanted to spread our wings. Or at least make use of a ferry, and try out that place over the Channel.

I'm talking about France, one of only five countries in the world with just one syllable in their name (the others are Spain, Greece, Chad and Laos), and the only one in the world with the vowel and consonant combination of 'ance', the same 'ance' as one finds in 'elegance', 'nonchalance', 'insouciance' and 'arrogance'. Perhaps it was this list of indisputably French characteristics that attracted both of us to our nearest continental neighbour – rather than Spain or Greece – or maybe it was because we had been asked to join another couple who were going there, and their offer of a joint holiday sounded irresistible...

This was John and Sue. John was a fellow manager at work and my 'best friend', and Sue was his (attractive) wife. They both had a little experience of

France, and they both felt sure that Kathy and I would enjoy a *soupçon* of its rural charms, along with a taste of its unsurpassable cuisine and its infinite assortment of home-produced alcoholic beverages. Especially its excellent and – back then – ridiculously inexpensive wines.

They were right. Because in 1978 we undertook our first French sortie, and devoted ourselves wholeheartedly to the consumption of every delicacy and every drop of fermented or distilled liquor we could manage. Remember, this was a time when I and my three holiday companions had livers that were impervious to the assault of any amount of alcohol – as well as lungs that were indifferent to the ingress of tar and nicotine, and bodies that had not yet learnt how to convert calories into layers of stored fat. Accordingly, we imbibed freely throughout the day, 'smoked for Britain', and packed away any number of multiple-course meals (with only aperitifs, table wines and digestifs to aid us in our task).

It was a revelation. Not just the delights on offer in France – and how stupidly affordable they were – but also how one does not need comfort and luxury to make for a perfect experience. Here, I am referring to our accommodation, a *gîte* by name, a dump by nature. A tumbling-down farm outbuilding in the Dordogne with, instead of a swimming pool, a jacuzzi, a shady terrace, a collection of designer furniture and a stock of scented candles, just a garden hose, four chairs, a table, two beds, a bath, a wash basin, a square ceramic sink with a curtain beneath it, and gaps in the first-floor floorboards that compromised the privacy of the downstairs bathroom quite considerably. It was lovely. And so lovely that the four of us went back there the following year. Chez Cannon (for that was its name) was the perfect introduction to France, even if it might by now have fallen down. Without anybody's help.

A similar fate may well have overtaken the next two *gîtes* we visited – in 1980 and 1981. Yes, we were still the same group of four, and still more than willing to accept the sort of accommodation that in today's world would probably be honoured on Trip Advisor with an exceptional and quite generous *negative* rating. The first of these was situated in the south of the Dordogne (which had yet to be overrun by Brits), and its singular outstanding feature was its view of a shit-shoveller across the road. This was an aerial conveyor device, that conveyed farmyard *merde* from wherever it was produced on the farm to a stockpile of the stuff within smelling distance of our rustic retreat. It barely ever stopped working, probably because it was earning its owner a guaranteed income under some early manifestation of the EEC's Common Agricultural Policy. Furthermore, I am quite sure that it did not feature in the *gîte*'s given particulars on the basis of which we made our original booking – as none of us was especially interested in the excrement-ejection techniques adopted by French farmers. Nor were we that interested in the way that some of them held on to their less than charming antiquated practices. Such as the housing of their goats on the ground floor of their isolated hovels.

This was a feature of 1981's 'cottage': a *gîte* in the Tarn area of France, so isolated itself that its only neighbour – for miles (or indeed for kilometres) – was one such hovel – a tiny stone-built construction that was home to an ancient lady who had stopped changing her clothes at some point in the '60s and whose live-in geriatric son had adopted this same eco-friendly dressing convention. Or maybe the goats had just eaten his and his mum's other clothes – despite these goats having been given comfortable ground-floor lodgings in their keepers' humble abode.

He used to let them out each morning, for a nibble of grass. And quite often she would wander along the track – on a remote stretch of a remote plateau – to assail us with stories of her youth and her life. Not in French, but in a local Occitan dialect, which, in all honesty, was about as impenetrable as a nun's knickers. I think only her son and her goats could understand her.

Nevertheless, any number of unwashed and incomprehensible neighbours – and any amount of *merde* on the move – were small prices to pay for our being able to indulge ourselves in all things French before millions of our fellow countrymen did the same. Especially when the French things in question included *crudités, écrevisses, langoustines, aiguillettes de canard, tarte au pommes, sauce Espagnole*, more *fromages* than you could shake a stick at, *îles flotantes*, blackcurrant sorbet, both yellow and green Izarra, a whole host of Armagnacs and, of course, the incomparable pastis. None of these delights, as far as I can remember, featured in *Abigail's Party*, but maybe that was part of their attraction – a treasure trove of pleasures uncovered before the rest of the world had arrived to spoil them. I and my three fellow vacationers were very lucky, and furthermore, we also knew how lucky we were. Especially when we stopped to think what was going on, not just in crowded places like the Costa del Sol and other European holiday hotspots, but also in the wider world – and back in Britain.

The Iranians were taking hostages. The IRA were not. They still had a preference for blowing people up. China had equipped itself with a billion Chinese (an event that even then filled me with a degree of foreboding – in a time when boding was rarely to the fore). And back on the home patch there were interminable strikes, inflation was rising faster than a porn stud's chopper, 'racial unrest' was putting its boots on, and Margaret Thatcher was warning that many Britons felt they were being swamped by people of a different culture (but, of course, not being listened to). It was all enough to make one want to stay in the most awful *gîte* imaginable, and overdose on *vin rouge* and Izarra Vert while the world fell apart. But unfortunately, that was not possible. There was that genuinely tempting work to re-engage with, and a marriage to re-assess (of which more later).

However, right now, as I have just reminded myself, there is a story to complete, a story concerning my presentation at that regional managers' conference – on 'motivation'. Because, although I say it myself, the presentation was a resounding success, and for the first time in my life I experienced what it was like to make a roomful of people laugh. For that was the way I had approached my topic. *They will all go to sleep*, I thought, *if I keep it serious. But they might just stay wake if I make it marginally funny.*

Indeed, the laughs were so many and so unrestrained that for a few hours after the event – and with the help of some Brew XI and some pastis chasers – I considered chucking in the accountancy stuff and taking up a career as a comedian. It was only when John pointed out that I would never be left wing enough or egotistical enough that I abandoned the idea. And after all, there were those aspirational aspects of *Abigail's Party* to consider. It was no less than my duty to plough on with those debits and credits – and reap the further rewards that they would inevitably provide…

Jersey – Part 1

The natives of Jersey despise the natives of Guernsey, just as much as the natives of Guernsey despise their Jersey counterparts. This deep-seated antipathy for each other stems from their respective ancestors taking different sides in the English Civil War. In simplistic terms, Jersey was largely Royalist while Guernsey supported the Parliamentarians. And now, after nearly 400 years, this historical divergence in allegiances has come to define how each set of islanders sees its immediate neighbour: as the detested nearby enemy to which it is implacably opposed.

I learnt this in early 1982. And I also learnt a few other features of this longstanding feud. How, for example, the Jersey people refer to their Guernsey neighbours as 'donkeys', and how these 'donkeys' refer to their Jersey rivals as '*crapauds*' – as in 'toads'. How, at certain times of the year, the donkeys are said to gather on the east of Guernsey when there is the promise of a red sunrise, in the hope that they might observe what they can then imagine is the island of Jersey (to the south-east) going up in flames. And, more realistically, how Guernsey's animosity towards Jersey had increased in recent years due to the performance of its neighbour's 'finance industry' so much outpacing its own. Envy had now sharpened its resentment into outright hostility.

Anyway, this reference to Jersey's 'offshore financial services' is the cue to my explaining what was going on in early 1982 and why I was learning so much about Jersey's relationship with its immediate neighbour. Quite simply, I had moved there. Without, for the present, my adorable wife.

She was still wrapping up her legal affairs back in Birmingham, with the intention of joining me later in the year. By then, I would have had our new house in Jersey decorated to our taste, and, all being well, I would be well on my way to bringing Touche Ross's brand-new practice on the island into the established Touche fold.

Yes, the firm had acquired an existing independent practice in St Helier, and I had been dispatched from Birmingham to Touche Ross-ify it. And whilst I had been made no promises, it had been made very clear to me that this would be a 'very good move'. It certainly looked that way when I arrived at the practice's newly built offices, situated on St Helier's esplanade, and designed to house about forty people over two floors. Because, unlike the ground floor, which was all open plan, the first floor had, in addition to an open-plan area, three (sea-facing!) offices, only two of which were occupied – by the practice's two existing partners. Furthermore, one of these guys was a Welsh (notional) Protestant, the other was an Irish (notional) Jew – and I was that English (notional) Catholic. I felt like the last piece in a very simple three-piece jigsaw. And, in fact, everybody in the office had already assumed that I would soon be pressed into place. Indeed, as soon as April arrived, which was the month in which new initiates were admitted into the Touche Ross holy of holies. That is to say when that year's handful of uber-fortunate managers were admitted into the partnership.

The call came one morning – from the managing partner in London. At the time, I was sitting at my desk in the open-plan area of the first floor, just outside that empty third office. But within minutes I had been installed in that office, there to receive a parade of congratulations, just before being taken out by Geoffrey (the Welshman) and Paul (the Irishman) for not so much a slap-up lunch but more a hefty thump-up of a meal – all washed down with a couple of bottles of Richebourg Grand Cru Burgundy (for which one now has to take out a sizeable mortgage). Needless to say, I was a very happy bunny. Very happy indeed. I was thirty-three years old. I had achieved my ambition of becoming a Touche Ross partner. I had a rather nice house on a beautiful (low-tax) island. I had an office with, out of the window, a view of Elizabeth Castle sitting in the middle of St Aubin's Bay. I had a new car (a beautiful red Mk 1 Golf GTI). And I had… a lovely wife. Well, at least, one was scheduled to join me later that year. And meanwhile,

I had a new pile of challenges. What would I have to do to discharge my new partner-type responsibilities in a new and largely unknown environment?

This was a good question, because I had already established that whilst Jersey was one of the more civilised places on the planet – in terms of food, conviviality, scenery, general pleasantness and absence of squalor – in respect of accountancy and allied affairs, it was the untamed and very Wild West. All the rules, regulations, laws and standards that I had known for twelve years no longer applied. I know this all sounds a bit techy and has a whiff of boredom about it. But when, in place of reams of UK company law, one finds that Jersey company law runs to just twenty pages, that it was written in the middle of the nineteenth century, and that it is still in impenetrable Norman French, even those allergic to accountancy might appreciate that this could represent just a few minor problems. Like, in what form does one draw up accounts? How does one discharge one's duties as a liquidator when there is no reference whatsoever to a liquidator and his duties in those twenty pages of Norman French (I had immediately acquired three such appointments)? And how does one protect oneself from litigious scoundrels when there are no appropriate laws to use as a shield?

Well, the answer is that one muddles through. And one bears in mind that whatever risks one is running in 'making it up as one goes along', they are as nothing compared to the risks to life being endured by an expeditionary force in the South Atlantic. Because, of course, my admission to partnership coincided with some beastly behaviour by an Argentinian junta that required a dramatic response from our own military – to return the Falklands to their rightful owners.

It was on the telly every evening. Like a captivating, well-written action-packed serial. Only it was real. With real loss of life and real pain and suffering. I remember it made me feel just a little bit guilty that my own life had just taken a turn off Charmed Boulevard into largesse-lined Easy Street. Because, despite that untamed environment, real professional challenges were few, and the pace of work was… well, not what it had been in Birmingham. And if, on any workday, I was still in the office at one minute past five, I would be the only person in the office. Jersey's banks, lawyers, assorted financial institutions – and the island's other accountants – all closed down at five o'clock. And, of course, we did too. It was something

I had to get used to very quickly: being landed in a sinecure. And I am proud to say that I very soon did...

Nevertheless, going back to my words of wisdom on 'motivation', I did begin to think that an absence of real challenges might become a problem. So too might the absence of 'real' clients. Many were offshore paper-type entities, the sort that one could neither touch nor interact with. And only two had stuff like physical premises and physical stock. One of these was RCA Jersey, which imported US television cameras from the States and converted them into cameras that were compliant with the European system, and the other was Bass Charrington (Channel Islands), which imported booze from England and converted this into sozzled *crapauds*.

So, these two client companies were something of a godsend. As, in a way, were the guys who ran them. RCA Jersey was under the control of a very nice American – from New Jersey – who often experienced problems when travelling between his home in the States and this particular Channel Island. As in when he attempted to book a flight back from New Jersey to Jersey (via London), he would generally be told very politely that 'Sir, you are already in Jersey.' Then there were the two managers of Bass Charrington CI, both of whom had superpowers. Even without underpants and capes, they could both apply their unique superpowers, and turn alcohol into spring water, or something with a similar effect on their own metabolism. I thought I had developed a certain resilience to the impact of alcohol by the time I'd arrived in Jersey, but these two chaps were in another league. They were impregnable, and the stronger the booze, the less it seemed to register in their systems. They always remained completely sober, while all those around them who were trying to keep pace with their Armagnac ingestion fell almost literally by the wayside. If they are no longer with us, I suspect their bodies remain as perfectly pickled specimens. They were quite amazing.

That said, they were not exceptional in their affection for bottled beverages. Drinking in Jersey was up there with rifle-shooting (for which it was famous) and making money (for which it hardly had to try). Booze was, of course, cheap, and was seen by many as more of a grocery item than something that had the capacity to render you senseless. I can think of no better example of this than our immediate neighbours, a delightful old pair who believed in adding a touch of tonic to their gin rather than the other way around. As I discovered one night near Christmas 1982, a succession of gin and virtually no tonics, consumed next to their roasting Aga, and immediately after a session with Bass Charrington's superheroes, could prove near fatal – even for a fit young partner who'd been in training with lunchtime drinking for years. Jersey's per-capita consumption of ethanol in all its forms – back in the beginning of the '80s – must have been world-beating. And certainly better than Guernsey's…

However, I am getting ahead of myself. I have omitted to mention the arrival of my wife on the island, and how her installation into the new matrimonial home wasn't… very satisfying. For either of us.

We did both try, and we even had mad Michael there to help us. He and his wife had fortuitously already moved to the island, and the two of them became our joint friends – and something of a distraction. Like when I flew to Dinard airport – in Michael's own plane – to help him 'rescue' one of his cars from its car park. It had been there for months, and for so long that it had now attracted a total of fines that easily exceeded the car's value. He had therefore decided that a covert removal of the recidivist vehicle under the cover of darkness was the best way to resolve the matter. And so my attendance, and in due course, my steering the object of the mission out of the car park – as Michael towed it with another of his cars, and before we had attended to its two flat tyres. Michael had still not learnt how to acquire any reck, and indeed may well have become even more reckless since he had moved to Jersey.

Anyway, Kathy and I were definitely not getting on, even though she had plans to qualify as a Jersey advocate, in order to enable her to continue her legal career on the island. Before then, however, she and I had another appointment with John and Sue and with another no-stars *gîte* in France, this one down in Provence, and equipped with the odd scorpion rather than a mechanised shit-shoveller. It was a pretty good holiday, but the fact that its highlight – for John, Sue and me – was the local farmer's rupture of a water main with his digger says a lot about the sorry state of my relationship with Kathy. Oh, and I should just add that the farmer did this when Kathy was having a shower, and had fully 'sudded up' just before the water stopped, giving her no ability to sluice off the suds. My, how we laughed. Albeit I do remember that Kathy didn't find it quite so amusing. Or indeed, amusing in the least…

I remember feeling quite sad when Sue and John left *ma femme et moi* at a small Normandy airport to fly back to Jersey. It was as though I was being left to confront my fate all on my own, a fate, certain (matrimonial) aspects of which I didn't much like the look of. It was just as well that fate also included all four of us getting together again for that mid-winter festival, otherwise known as Christmas… Which reminds me, that as well as the prospect of John and Sue joining us for this event (something that had been agreed over the fourth bottle of wine on the first evening in that Provencal *gîte*) there were also some Jersey-specific aspects of the run-up to Christmas that would no doubt lift my spirits.

The first of these was the installation at the Esplanade entrance into St Helier of the crumpled remains of a car, which, the previous Christmas, had become the entrance into the underworld for three intoxicated unfortunates. This was an annual tradition: a reminder to all the piss-heads on the island (aka the islanders) that drinking and driving could have consequences that were a little more lethal than they were festive. It was a commendable effort, but I doubt even the installation of a car with dead bodies still in it could have done a great deal to curb the locals' enthusiasm for imbibing to excess. And who wouldn't want to go out in a possibly literal blaze of glory in the season of goodwill to all men?

Well, not the local fuzz. That's for sure. In fact, they wouldn't want to go out full stop. And here I am talking about another Jersey-specific feature of the Yuletide season and its possible attendant wintry weather. Because, when it snowed in the run-up to Christmas, it was announced on the local news that all police cars were being withdrawn from the streets in order to avoid their coming to grief in the impossible conditions – just like they'd been withdrawn the previous year and the few years before that. Even though the technical term for the effects of this major snowstorm was 'a dusting'. I reckon they all just wanted to stay in their stations and get pissed themselves…

Anyway, in no time at all it was Christmas proper, and through a haze of Xmas excess on the booze front, John and Sue hove into view (having nearly been stranded in Guernsey by a weather event rather more common than a snow flurry and known as very thick fog). They had come to celebrate Christmas with Kathy and me – and to provide a shift in our combined tectonic plates, the like of which we had never experienced before.

The first hint that plate tectonics might become a feature of this particular Noel were interactions between Sue and John that mirrored those between myself and Kathy. There was a prickliness there that was only too apparent, and one that pointed to there being a serious underlying problem in their relationship. Which is why I made quite sure that Sue and I had some time together doing the Christmas Day dishes, and why I proposed that on Boxing Day, I should take (just) her out to observe the sea from a suitable random headland. In retrospect, I cannot understand how John and Kathy allowed this to happen. But maybe they had felt those tectonic plate movements as much as Sue and I had, and were resigned to the inevitable: that I would leave Kathy and take Sue as my new partner.

It may have been that Wild West aspect of my work that had caused me to make such a momentous decision. Or maybe that is not a particularly chivalrous way to explain what I'd done, and I would be on safer ground to mention the word 'love'. But whatever was going on, it caused me to act more precipitously than I had ever acted before and with more resolve than I normally got through in a year. Which meant that the day after Sue and John returned to England, I banished my wife back to the mainland, and three days later Sue returned and we began our life together.

That probably deserves a genuine 'Wow!' and just a handful of ancillary observations. The first of which is that Kathy and I were finished and had been for years. It's just that we'd never got around to admitting it. That would have been too much like a further act of *Abigail's Party*. The second is that Sue and John were finished as well – as John's new girlfriend would have attested. The third is that there was no pre-planning to this event, in the same way that there had been no mutual carnal knowledge before the event. Whilst I had always 'been attracted' to Sue (and, one must assume, she to me), this mutual attraction had never led to any sort of actual action as opposed to 'attr'-action. This, despite the fact that Sue was something of a cracker to look at, as well as being far more appealing than Kathy in just about every department that mattered. Anyway, this lack of any sort of exploratory manoeuvres definitely meant that it was to be a leap in the dark in every conceivable way – for both of us. And then there is a fourth observation, concerning reckless Michael and his wife, Mary.

She was in St Helier Hospital, having her big toe operated on (!), and I thought it wise to visit her there when Michael would be in attendance, so that I could confess my heinous act to the two people who were Kathy's closest mates on the island. It was a good move, because their joint immediate response to my confession was 'What the hell took you so long?'

So… in conclusion, I am not passing any judgement on my first wife here. (And, in many ways, she could rightly claim that it was I who was the villain.) But I did learn a big lesson. And this is that no one should not confront what he or she knows to be wrong. Whether that's a moribund marriage, the attempted annexation of some peaceful islands in the South Atlantic – or the use of 'infer' when it should be 'imply', something that really gets on my tits.

And why the BBC does not make this a sackable offence for its presenters, I do not know. No more than I know why this first part of my Jersey chronicle has ended up on such an unconnected pedantic note. Maybe I'm just getting old…

Jersey – Part 2

Well, the tectonic plates settled down remarkably quickly. At least they did for Sue and for me. (And I suspect for John, but not for Kathy…) Not only were we soon enjoying what can only be described as a honeymoon period, in every sense of the word, but we were also enjoying an acceptance of what we had done – from everybody. It wasn't just Michael and Mary who thought we'd done the right thing, but also my two partners, Paul and Geoffrey, my other friends on the island, our mutual friends back in England, and even those in the office who'd only had limited exposure to my now absent wife. It was only a pity that I nearly screwed the whole thing up by having a serious 'quake' only a few weeks after that geological rearrangement, when I frightened myself by carefully considering all the implications of my actions. It's probably enough to say that the resulting wimpish behaviour on my part was soon forgiven by my new dearest beloved, and we were then both able to channel all our energies into relishing the undeniable if sometimes odd delights of an island off the northern coast of France. Starting with its incomparable culinary delights…

Essentially, Jersey in 1983 was overrun with sensational eating establishments, most of which must have operated at a loss. They were just so remarkably cheap. Indeed, it soon became apparent to the new chief housekeeper that it was less expensive to eat out than to prepare meals at home. Which, within no time at all, meant that we began to dine out at least three times a week – whilst saving money in the process. Listing all the restaurants we visited would, of course, be tedious in the extreme, but one in particular is worthy of mention, if only to illustrate the irresistibility of what was on offer. And this place was known as Bistro Frère.

This was a fairly ordinary-looking building on the north-eastern coast of Jersey, with an extraordinary view from its windows – of the Normandy peninsula of France. It also offered extraordinary views inside – of its attractive waitresses. Because they all wore 'string-vest-grade' crocheted dresses, as in there was probably enough material in half a dozen of these dresses to make one respectable dress. And furthermore... three-course Sunday lunches at this place cost just £5 (or £6, if one chose a whole lobster for one's main course), and these suitably lubricated lunches would last all afternoon. Even taking account of the cost of living then – and before factoring in the arousal credentials of all those lovely waitresses – that was still remarkable value. Unfortunately, the place was eventually burnt to the ground. And I strongly suspect that it had been set alight by the wife of a patron who had himself been set alight by what was visible through those flimsy veils of crochet. Only the arsonist, I assure you, wasn't Sue. She just bought a similar dress for herself...

So, moving on, there were many other aspects of Jersey to discover and explore – and to find either engaging or amusing. At the engaging end of the spectrum was the Jersey 'countryside' and how it began to completely fill the new Lilliput world in which Sue and I were living. Jersey is an island measuring just ten miles by six. But its roads are so narrow, so winding and so labyrinthine that it seems much larger than this as one makes one's way across it. So much so that one soon begins to resent having to make a 'long journey'. Indeed, with Paul and Geoffrey living in the north-west of the island, and our living in the south-east, a trip to see them often made us consider an overnight stop...

Then there was the preponderance of Scots people on the island, reputedly the result of so many Scots visiting Jersey for a holiday, and then deciding to stay indefinitely after discovering its liberal licensing hours. And, of course, the local 'Jersey beans', the genuine Jersey articles, who were quite difficult to meet and even more difficult to properly engage with. Which meant that yours truly joined a rifle-shooting club, not only because he quite fancied learning how to shoot a rifle properly, but also because this was a popular Jersey pastime, and it held out the promise of a very good helping of 'beans'. Yes, I would no doubt meet a number of the locals who, otherwise, would remain hidden in that extensive Jersey countryside. Well, I did become acquainted with a few, but I became much more intimately acquainted with my inadequacies with a weapon. Whilst the rest of the shooters were refining their skills to get a place in the next Commonwealth Games, I was still tussling with the need to take on the stillness of a cadaver. Which was no less than essential to stand any chance whatsoever of hitting a target at the end of their super-challenging 1,000-yard range. And, unfortunately, I couldn't get out of the habit of breathing.

I also couldn't get out of the habit of watching the news on Jersey's local TV. Because this would start off with reports on stuff like Michael Foot's latest mumblings or maybe bombings in Beirut, but then it would slide towards that amusing end of the Jersey spectrum by announcing that a green budgerigar had escaped in St Ouen, and that he answered (inevitably) to the name of 'Joey'. If only our present global news was filled with more stories of escaped green budgerigars. And if only it was filled with more stories of converted minesweepers owned by 'colourful characters'…

Here I am referring to a bit of midsummer madness in Jersey, where a client of our London office (but not of the Jersey office) had arranged to make a bit of a local splash – and announce himself to 'Jersey society' – by throwing a party on his luxurious yacht. And this 'yacht' wasn't a regular yacht, but instead, as was noticed when it steamed into St Helier's marina, it was a very large converted minesweeper. (There were rumours that he had two of these vessels, but that the other one was in Dubai being gold-plated.)

This gentleman, whose name will be withheld on the grounds of self-preservation, was an SAE. Not a 'stamped addressed envelope', but a 'successful Asian entrepreneur' (with friends in high places). He had been kicked out of Uganda by Idi Amin, and had arrived in Britain with more children than pennies, but despite this paucity of loot had then gone on to build up a substantial business involved in 'shipping, trading and commerce'. This had led him to avail himself of our services in London. And with his empire already having a few tentacles in Jersey, the likelihood was that he would soon be looking to become a client in St Helier as well. Which is why Paul, Geoffrey and I – and our respective other halves – were included on the guest list for his 'lobster and champagne' bash.

It was the only party I have ever been to on a (very opulently appointed) converted minesweeper, and the only one where lobster and champagne were genuinely in oversupply. He must have robbed Bistro Frère of a year's worth of these goodies. In fact, it was such a splendid evening that Sue and I were almost the last to leave in the early hours of the next day, hopeful even then that our host would in some way share with us some of the images of our enjoying ourselves. There had, after all, been a guy with a professional-looking cine camera taking a film of all the proceedings – and of all those participating in these proceedings.

Well… a couple of years later, back in Britain, I would have a slightly different hope. This was well after our London office had dropped this particular SAE before they (or ourselves) were seriously burnt, but only shortly after his business had collapsed and he'd ended up with the promise of spending some serious time at Her Majesty's pleasure. I'm sure it was all a terrible mistake, and especially his conviction for perjury – all something to do with his supposedly concealing his personal assets. But whatever the truth, he did, in due course, merit a two-episode exposé on *Panorama*, where there was no guarantee that its producers would not spice up their tale with a bit of film taken from one of his hedonistic soirees – but every guarantee that the firm's managing partner would be watching to see just how much mud might be splattered on the firm's good name. So, that different hope was that my drunken features would not appear on prime-time national TV, courtesy of that busy cameraman, or, if they did, that I might look more professional than pickled.

It was OK. There was nothing on screen from that orgy of indulgence. Maybe the cine camera had been for show. Just like that deep-carpeted, wood-panelled, brass-encrusted minesweeper had been for show. Along with the other one in Dubai. Or maybe the film had been confiscated by the Jersey constabulary the morning after the event on the grounds of indecent behaviour. After all, the constabulary would have taken a very dim view of anything quite so indiscreet and so contrary to Jersey's conventions. Which is probably my cue to dwell for a moment on Jersey's police force, and how it operated back in the '80s and how its rather quaint methods were my very welcome salvation.

It may be a little different now, but back then Jersey's police force (that is to say, its uniformed police officers) did not have the power of arrest.

That lay with the 'parish constables': twelve daily-appointed civilians – each chosen on some arcane rotation system to represent Jersey's twelve parishes – who provided leadership (and the power of arrest) to the boys in blue. (Their names would be published daily in the universally read *Jersey Evening Post*, and unsurprisingly I don't recall any of their names being other than those of Jersey beans.)

Anyway, my first and only real contact with this rather eccentric system of policing began one hot afternoon in July, when, after a trip to the beach, I was returning home with my visiting parents – in my still pristine Golf GTI. It wasn't, however, still pristine a split second after I had pulled up to a junction with a major (i.e. slightly less narrow) road. And this was because it had sustained a direct hit from another car which, through having been driven at an excessive speed on a slightly wet road surface, had ended up partly on the wrong side of the major road and partly on the pavement of the wrong side of this road. Indeed, the driver had managed to scrape his vehicle along the granite wall that backed this pavement just before its progress was brought to a sudden halt by the front nearside of my Golf.

Nobody was hurt, but my feelings were when the driver of the projectile that had been fired into my stationary vehicle immediately claimed that it was I who was at fault, in that I had carelessly pulled out in front of him – when I clearly hadn't. Now, in the UK, this would have caused me a considerable problem. Because, as nobody had been hurt, the police would have had very little interest in the collision and, in the absence of any independent witnesses, the subsequent insurance claim would inevitably have resolved itself into a case of his word against mine. And I could well have got stuffed. However, because Jersey parishes are so small, the parish constable – who was in a nearby field on his tractor – heard the collision, and was at the scene of the crime before you could say 'Bergerac'.

What happened then was a delight. The other driver was still protesting his innocence and claiming that it was all my fault. But as soon as the farmer/constable pointed out the tyre tracks on the pavement and the scrape marks on the granite wall that matched a number of scrapes on the side of his vehicle, he had to concede that he was lying through his teeth. He had been netted by the operation of a police system that seemed to have more to do with Toy Town than the real world. But it had worked –

beautifully. And it even saw the arrival of uniformed police, who promptly put themselves under the guidance of the constable, who himself was keen to use their services to help him compile his official report of this major parish incident. After all, he would soon be convening a parish hall inquiry, to which I and the other driver would in due course be receiving a literally irresistible invitation…

This inquisition took place about three weeks later (in the local parish hall), and involved the constable informing me that I was totally innocent and would face no action by the authorities – but informing the other guy that he was not so innocent and that he would be charged with careless driving and would soon have to make an appearance in the island's Royal Court. The constable then adopted an avuncular tone to advise the condemned man that it was the original open-and-shut case, and that he should not waste his money on an advocate, and just plead guilty. He'd only get a fine anyway, and life was far too short. Which all meant that my insurance was kept intact, and furthermore that no monies would be needlessly channelled into the local legal profession. All in all, quite a result for such an apparently risible approach to policing. And maybe a taste of what I might expect from certain other authorities on the island – when, after two months, my seriously bent Golf had been unbent and I wanted to check that it still worked properly, even when driven at speed.

This, of course, was impossible to do on Jersey. Nowhere could I drive it at more than 40mph. However, I really wanted to confirm that all was well before I took it to France (for our first just-the-two-of-us holiday), where on some French motorways I might be driving it just a little more quickly. It really did look as though I had an insurmountable problem. But then somebody told me that the island's equivalent of our Ministry of Transport had a rolling road, on which I would be able to drive my Golf as fast as I liked. I therefore rang this mini transport ministry, only to be told that the rolling road was only available in cases where there was a complaint against a garage and, as I had no complaint, I would not be able to use it. I must have sounded very disappointed on the phone, because the man from the ministry then suggested that I took my Golf to Five Mile Road early on a Sunday morning – where I could 'easily get it up to a ton'!

This road is famous on Jersey. It is on the extreme west of the island, and it runs in more or less a straight line for five miles. Consequently, it was and, no doubt, still is a popular venue for the owners of the island's extensive collection of Ferraris, Maseratis, Astons and similarly powerful beasts. These frustrated racers take their cars there for a bit of illegal speeding and, as I imagine is still widely known if not widely acknowledged, they take their cars there early on Sundays for a bit of very excessive illegal speeding. All elements of Jersey's police force judiciously stay away, and any number of rev counters, for a brief period at least, move out of the idling range and even up to the red. It is a very important safety valve for some of the island's drivers; one not condoned by the authorities, but one just sensibly ignored by them. And one that is very infrequently actually recommended by them. Although that's just what this ministry guy was doing. 'Can't help you, mate. But why don't you go and break the law? That should sort it.'

Imagine that happening in this country. It would be akin to phoning Revenue and Customs about importing shedloads of fags and being told of a small cove in Cornwall where you could land them without any possibility of challenge. 'And make sure you enjoy a few puffs yourself.'

Anyway, the advice was taken. As was the Golf – up to the magic ton – and in due course to France, where it performed perfectly on the French *autoroutes* – for more than just five miles. And while I think about it, it meant that Sue and I had another perfect French holiday, this time in another part of Provence, where there was only one marginally awkward incident in the whole of our two-week stay. This is when we went for a Sunday lunch in a restaurant in Orange, which turned out to be the same restaurant that Sue's John and his new *amour* had chosen for their Sunday lunch! We did acknowledge each other – when we'd overcome our acute surprise – but we didn't share a table. No more than we shared the ultimate fate of their trip to France, which, we later learnt, involved the write-off of John's car in a road traffic accident that was not attended by any injuries or by any French constables. Fate, I decided then, is not only strange but also unpredictable. A bit like Michael's relationship with the tax authorities in Britain.

Now, before I give a prime example of this relationship, I should first explain that, with Kathy now absent from the scene, Michael – and his wife – had extended their friendship with me to encompass Sue, and the four of us would meet almost every week. Sometimes we would even house-sit for them – when they were away from the island and their pets needed a couple of carers. And on one occasion we even assisted them in hosting Michael's number one arch enemy when Michael invited him for a home-cooked evening meal...

Michael had by now established himself as an international tax adviser – and a thorn in the side of what was then the UK's Inland Revenue. And this was because he had not just pushed the envelope on what was legitimate practice, but he had poked so many holes in the envelope that there was now a warrant out for his arrest – one that would be executed the minute he returned to Blighty. And there was one guy in the Revenue's investigation branch who had been charged with bringing him to justice, the very same guy who, as Michael had discovered, was about to visit Jersey with other business to pursue but without any powers. He would be out of his jurisdiction, and should he have met Michael in the street, he would not have been able even to have cautioned him. Which is why, when Michael learnt of this tantalising situation, he invited him for dinner at his house!

It was surreal. Here was the hunter and his quarry, both sitting at the very same table. And, with the help of his mates, the quarry being as hospitable as possible – and the hunter reciprocating this hospitality with grace. He behaved himself perfectly, and although he was undoubtedly a 'Revenue man' through and through, he was also quite a star. Which is probably why, years later, he finally caught his quarry – when his quarry had been foolish enough to set foot in England – and was then able to ensure that Michael was subsequently convicted and sentenced to four years in jail! I believe, even now, that this ex-con still offers his tax services – from somewhere like Switzerland – but not as a barrister anymore (he was disbarred), but instead as someone with the unique selling point of being able to claim that he was prepared to serve jail time for the benefit of his clients. If only his intellect and ingenuity had been put to a rather more productive purpose. Which might, of course, be an observation that could also have been made about me...

Yes, Jersey was fun, and it had a great deal to offer – other than any real challenge. And we're back to that motivation thing again. I was beginning to learn to live without it, but only by adopting more and more a Jersey outlook on life. Which meant more and more a focus on what was happening in its ten miles by six, and barely any focus whatsoever on what was happening elsewhere. Heck, it wasn't until years later that I learnt that 1983 saw the first ever McDonald's chicken nugget being foisted on an unsuspecting public. I was clearly insulating myself not only in physical terms, but also in mental terms and in terms of my curiosity. Which is why when, in early 1984, I was 'asked' by the managing partner to return to Birmingham, where my services were apparently sorely needed, I had mixed feelings. One part of me saw the obvious attractions of an extended idyll on a slightly peculiar but very attractive island retreat. Another part of me could not fail to see the less well-defined attractions of a 'proper' professional life in a part of the world I knew well, and a part of the world where I could regularly drive at more than 40mph.

In any event, the decision was not really mine, and I just needed to focus on the attractions of real challenge and real driving – and push to the back of my mind short working hours, visits to the beach, visits to Dinard and St Malo, preposterously cheap booze, lost budgerigars, Toy Town policing, Jersey/French cuisine, lobsters – and, of course, crochet when worn to reveal.

Although naturally, always at the front of my mind would be the superiority of *crapauds* over donkeys...

Spindlewood, New Responsibilities, Religions and God

Well, returning in 1984 to what was by now Arthur-Scargill-Land was a bit of a shock. Not only did I observe that striking miners were causing mayhem throughout our benighted nation, but I was quickly reminded that (back then) gastronomic delights in Birmingham were in the same situation as mobile phones – as in 'not due to arrive for some time'. And if anybody came across a lobster, it would make the front page of the *Birmingham Evening Mail*. Nevertheless, there was plenty to distract me from the less than idyllic conditions to which I'd returned. And this plenty included my new workload, which probably warranted the title 'excessive', and my need for somewhere to live with Sue, which definitely warranted the term 'pressing'.

The firm had arranged for us to be billetted in an apartment in Edgbaston, but with a new puppy in our family (called Freddie) and a distinct distaste for city life, we were desperate to find a proper new home, and this new place to live in would have to be somewhere 'in the country'. So, while I reconciled myself to my new workload, Sue was charged with finding us a suitable rural refuge. And her search was focused on the inviting countryside of Worcestershire, that little slice of England where both of us had lived before we'd ended up in Jersey.

Sue found lots of promising properties – which only broke the promises they'd made in their particulars when they were confronted in person. Only then would it become apparent that they had minor drawbacks, such as close-by caravan sites, close-by major roundabouts, gangrenous-looking thatched roofs, impractically high ceilings, impractically low ceilings, mined drives, extensive bomb damage or tattooed squatters in the loft. Or any combination of these various unappealing features. So, it was with great excitement that we finally turned up to one property that Sue had selected on the basis that it could not possibly be any worse than its depiction in its particulars – and that it came with four acres of land…

This was Spindlewood, one of the small number of dwellings that made up the unspectacular and rather linear hamlet of the less-than-poetically named Stock Green. And as soon as we had made our way up its drive (still peppered with concrete blocks to deter its then owner's many creditors) we knew that we had found our ideal home. And who could have foretold that this ideal home would have features that included no central heating, numerous decaying windows, several rough concrete floors, kitchen units embedded with glass fragments and internal doors decorated with painted insults (the owner and his wife had recently divorced after an all-out uncivil war), a wilderness 'garden', a falling-down lean-to, a decrepit, asbestos-roofed garage, various outbuildings housing a collection of lathes, and, lying around everywhere, enough other stuff to keep a couple of hoarders happy for a lifetime? Oh, and in four acres of unkempt land in need of all sorts of attention, were three railway wagons that had once provided shelter for chickens, and an old 'sit up and beg' Rover that was now barely able to sit up and beg at all. It all added up to a 'tip' – a wonderfully enticing, couldn't-wait-to-get-our-hands-on-it tip. And within weeks it was ours! We had found a place that had real promise, and that stood a very good chance of becoming our home for life. Which is exactly what it did.

Well, home improvements rarely constitute suitable material for inclusion in any sort of literary work. And whilst 'literary' might be stretching a point for this particular tome, home improvements of any sort will certainly not be included in this one. Other than to say that over the years we managed to create our own little island in the middle of Worcestershire, with a comfortable (extended) house at its centre, eventually surrounded by newly planted trees, a completely 'unimproved' wild-flower meadow and a substantial pond – and all nestling within the shelter of a ninety-acre wooded hill. And despite transforming that tip into such a wonderful place to live, we decided not to rename it Smug Towers, but instead to keep its original name of Spindlewood – along, we believe, with quite a lot of its original character. No longer do frogs make their way into our lounge under the bottom of a very badly fitting outer door, but there is still some wildlife in the loft and we are very proud to be home to one of the country's national collections of house spiders whilst, at the same time, offering a refuge for scores of hibernating ladybirds. And then, outside, there are the foxes, the muntjac deer, the roe deer, the herons, the woodpeckers, the sparrowhawks, the bats, the butterflies and, very gratifyingly, a great many other delightful critters.

Of course, transforming anything – other than base metal into gold – generally costs, and these costs have to be paid for. Which is why Sue took on a part-time secretarial post, and I kept gnawing away at that sizeable workload.

My life as a partner in the Birmingham office of Touche Ross was very different from that I'd experienced in Jersey, and not only in terms of much more work to attend to, but also in terms of being loaded with more responsibilities. At the partner level, we were simply short-staffed. So, everybody had to take on whatever they could, whether they were comfortable with it or not. And I was certainly not comfortable with being made 'partner responsible for IT'. Despite producing my Luddite Society membership card and claiming that I was allergic to software, I was obliged to pretend that I had any interest in this fast-developing new technology and some sort of understanding of it. And in reality, I had neither. Which didn't, incidentally, make me unique in the office. Quill pens had gone, but for my fellow partners and even for most of the managers, there was nothing quite like a sharpened pencil and a pad of high-quality, narrow-lined paper. Neither of which ever broke down or caused you to tear your hair out.

On a more positive note, I should mention that I was soon given a rather more appealing responsibility, and this was to become the firm's 'car man'. This was a national responsibility, and it meant, amongst other things, that I would now have to lead the firm's development of business within the country's automotive sector (meaning the nation's car manufacturers, its component manufacturers, its motor retailers and its providers of motor finance) and I would have to polish up my knowledge of all things to do with four-wheel vehicles. This, I was very happy to do. Unlike computers, I had always been interested in cars, and I even had an inkling of how they worked. It was still early days, but over the coming years, more and more of my time would be absorbed in running the firm's 'automotive sector' and more and more, this would provide some relief from the purely technical demands of my job. It would also lead me to performing my first high-speed 720-degree spin on a race track. But that is to get ahead of myself. We are still in 1984 here, and I should now make it clear that, despite taking on new responsibilities and the various demands of a new home, I was already coming out of that insular outlook on life that had overtaken me in Jersey. I was beginning to apply my mind to all manner of stuff, and to shape my opinions on various aspects of the world around me. And there is no better way to illustrate this widening of my mental horizons than to set out a brief résumé of the thoughts I had now arrived at on the subject of 'religions'.

You may recall that very early on in my life I was relieved and indeed delighted that I was able to avoid the clutches of the Catholic Church. However, I now understood more clearly than ever that it wasn't just Catholicism that could ruin people's lives, but that all organised religions should come with a serious health warning. After all, how can any institution that commits child abuse through its forced indoctrination of innocent unformed minds not be regarded as bloody dangerous? Especially when we know that, with the help of a band of captured souls, it then goes on to cultivate misogyny, ignorance, exploitation, divisiveness, aggression (aimed at followers of other religions or no religions at all), and even a good helping of fundamentalist lunacy. And these rotten fruits of religious husbandry are for real. They are not just a fanciful crop that I've dreamt up myself. One only has to take a closer look at any one of them to see that this is true. And why don't we do that with 'misogyny', one of the oldest and, some might say, the most important rotten fruit of them all? Indeed, in conjunction with an attempt to make sense of what could not be understood, it was probably one of the main reasons that religions came about in the first place.

You see, in my opinion, (most) men are on a constant quest to increase their sense of significance and status. (Blame that damn testosterone.) But at the same time, they are all too conscious that they are vulnerable to women – and their wily sexual ways. And they don't like it. Consequently, most cultures have had within them a noticeable antagonism towards women. They have viewed them as impure and intrinsically sinful creatures who have been placed among men to lead them astray. And guess what. The major Abrahamic religions – all run by men, of course – have gone out of their way to reinforce this belief. For them, sensual desires were (and still are) regarded as base and sinful. And whereas men are associated with the 'purity of the mind', their second-class neighbours – all those terrible women – are associated with 'corruption', as in the corruption of their temporal form.

If you doubt this deep-seated prejudice within our principal religions, I can only suggest that you consider references in the Bible to Eve popping out of Adam 'to serve him and obey him'; instructions such as 'thy desire shall be to thy husband, and he shall rule over thee'; and observations made by the famous second-century Christian author, Tertullian, including 'a woman is the gateway to the Devil' and that she is also 'a temple built over a sewer'. Needless to say, Christianity does not have a monopoly on these sorts of sentiments, with Judaism making references to 'women are evil, my children… they use wiles and try to ensnare (men) by their charms' – and Islam making references to… Well, let's not bother with any specific references, but just say that a combination of mullahs who are simply misogynistic by nature and any number of the basic tenets of sharia law have not in any way led to an age of enlightenment for that religion's female adherents.

Well, sorry to drop such a heavy load on you, without much in the way of a warning, but I'm afraid I'm far from finished yet. Because even if you want to discount the inbuilt misogyny in religions, I would like to suggest that it is almost impossible to dismiss the connection between religions and the phenomenon of 'moral licensing'.

Now, I confess I had no knowledge of the term 'moral licensing' back in 1984, but I *was* aware of its manifestation in the behaviour of 'pious people'. Because it seemed to me that the 'holier than thou' were often not very nice people. The more they turned up at church (or at their temple or their mosque), the more judgmental they became and the harsher they became in their tendency to want to punish. They were often simply not as nice as their agnostic and atheist cousins. Well, there have now been some scientists who have proved that my observations were correct. Because they have studied the pious and the not-so-pious, and have discovered that the religious pious types come to believe that they have done something good simply by being religious, and that this gives them the licence to do something bad (like being judgmental or being unwilling to share with others). Which they then, quite often, proceed to do. They are, all of them, the scientists decided, suffering from the affliction of 'moral licensing' – without even knowing they are afflicted.

This is pretty heavy stuff. Because what this research is actually saying is that religion is by no means vital for an individual's moral development, but indeed quite the contrary. It is the secularisation of childhood, and not its capture by a world religion, that can lead to an increase in human kindness. Which means that religions are not just ridiculous, obsolescent, a cover for questionable cultural practices, counterproductive in the way we care for the Earth, and the cause of most of the deadly conflicts in the world, but they are also a genuinely negative force in our development as kind and considerate human beings. Just think of some of our current problems with 'religious types' or the treatment of humans in those countries where 'religious types' are in power, and you may find you can agree with this conclusion. Or at least question the overpowering righteousness of religions that is still constantly thrust down our throats.

Anyway, I'm not prepared to let religions off the hook just yet, because there is one further failing of them all that I have still to mention, and this is the fact that they all rest on the existence of responsive divine beings – in the plural or the singular. And to prevent this chapter turning into a PhD thesis, let me just stick with the Abrahamic religions and their choice of a singular divine being, otherwise known as God. And let me examine the behaviour of this all-powerful, all-seeing, supernatural deity, a guy who apparently created us in his own image.

Right, well, we weren't first on his 'to do' list, were we? Or, if we were, he took a really extraordinary route to bring us into existence. I mean, to start with, 13.7 billion years ago, he set in motion the creation of the universe.

And this turned out to be very, very, very big. After all, it now contains maybe 100,000,000,000,000,000,000,000 stars, which means it may well contain 50,000,000,000,000,000,000 habitable Earthlike planets. And that is definitely very, very, very big indeed. Anyway, those Earthlike planets took more than a little time to come into existence. Which meant that God had to wait more than 9 billion years for our own Earthlike planet – known as Earth – to condense into what would become our home world, but a home world that we would not occupy ourselves for a further 4.5 billion years (when *Homo sapiens* turned up just 150,000 years ago). However, with his chosen ones eventually established on their rather small rock in an unfashionable stretch of his almost infinite universe, he could reveal himself to them. Or at least he could when he finally got round to it – just 2,000 years ago. Oh, and in that special peaceful haven of good sense on this planet, otherwise known as the Middle East.

Now, taking account of that potted history of our coming into being, I believe it is very difficult to dismiss the view that not only did God demonstrate a breathtaking degree of extravagance in creating 'his children', but he also lacked any sense of urgency whatsoever. All those unused stars and planets and all those 13.7 billion years gone to waste. One would be forgiven for thinking that he was more the universe's chief bureaucrat rather than its God, a bloke who gave no thought to creating a universe within budget and even less thought to securing the required deliverable within a reasonable timescale. Either that, or he did not know what he was doing. Indeed, looking at the quality of that deliverable, any sane God would have gone for a recall, and started work on humanity Mk II. He would also, after 13.7 billion years, have waited just 2,000 more years to have done his revelation bit. That way, he would have avoided the need for a clutch of holy books that would soon be out of date (and were certainly in no way future-proofed), and he could have set up his own website and even his own Twitter account. That little delay would have been what is commonly known as a no-brainer.

I know this is all highly irreverent, but it's what this particular Baby Boomer believes. And just to ram home my point one last time, let me just invite you to consider one quite important aspect of one of those holy books, namely 'the temptation of Eve'. Well, I think it might just be possible to give some credence to this Garden of Eden incident if the tempter had been portrayed as a rather suave monkey with the voice of Richard Burton. But a snake! How many women do you know (or men for that matter) who would stay around to listen to a talking serpent anywhere near long enough to take in any of what he was saying? I think the answer to that question is probably 'none'. And almost worse than the absurdity of this story, is the harm done to the reputation of all snakes by this disastrous piece of miscasting. It is no less than a reprehensible exercise in emphasising their unwarranted reputation as something bad. I mean, if you dream up a fairy story, you should at least try to ensure that it won't do any damage.

In the same way that if you tell your own story, you should give your readers a chance to digest an unexpected diatribe, and remind them that in 1984 you weren't on a soapbox calling for the abolition of organised religions, but instead sitting at a desk, working, or standing on a ladder, painting. And when time allowed, formulating more views on life in the twentieth century, some of which will no doubt have to be exposed in the following chapters. For the benefit of all those of you who might just manage to get past this one…

To help you do that, I'll quickly mention our 1984 holiday. Which, as might be expected, was another Sue-and-me expedition to France. This time to its Alpes-de-Haute-Provence region, where we stayed for two weeks in a rather unappealing chalet. There is little to recount of this trip, other than the fact that I learnt two important lessons.

The first is that if one is visiting a mountainous area, one should be careful where one stays. It is a mistake to choose a chalet or other habitation that sits at the bottom of a steeply sided valley, where the sun emerges mid-morning and sets mid-afternoon. This is not conducive to comfort if the chalet or other habitation, whilst at the bottom of a valley, is still very *haute*. Even in mid-September, one will never be very warm. (One might also want to take account of the dismal quality of what is definitely not *haute* cuisine. The food on offer in alpine eateries can be either uninteresting or greasy.)

The second concerns the wiring in French hotels (which may have improved since 1984). I have in mind here a small French hostelry we used as an overnight stop on the way down to the *Alpes*, where I attempted to plug in a hairdryer – without the benefit of a plug. What I learnt was that even if one pokes the bare wires into what were undoubtedly the right holes in the socket, one can still cause a small explosion, and plunge the whole hotel into darkness. Such was the fragile nature of French wiring in those days. As I had to explain to Madame, 'The whole thing just went "puff"'.

And unfortunately, there was no God around to say, 'Let there be light…'

The Antipodes – and Antipathy (to Human Rights)

Now, I could just say that for the years 1985 to 1990, I was simply working hard and getting five years older. But no self-respecting Baby Boomer would be satisfied with such a spartan account of well over 40,000 hours of his life. So, let me expand just a little on this second half of the '80s, and first of all by talking about where Sue and I chose to travel to in this period – and whom we chose to travel with – and what these choices said about our changing views and our changing circumstances at the time.

Well, 1985 is easy. We went for a lazy, do-sod-all holiday in Corfu. And what this said about us then was that, after more than a year of knocking our new house into shape – on top of our both working – we were completely knackered. We couldn't even contemplate a drive through France. It was a good choice. Because it was good fun. Even the fact that the first car I hired there was more knackered than we were, and when I reported to the hire company that we had been obliged to push it on a number of occasions to get it to start, they advised us always to park it at the top of a hill! They did, however, eventually replace it with a vehicle that responded to the ignition.

1986 saw us back in France, near a delightful place in the deep south of the country called Olargues. What this said about us was that we'd still not had nearly enough of this country, or maybe we just weren't being very imaginative. There are, after all, getting on for nearly 200 other countries in the world.

Well, nothing had changed by 1987, and we had chosen yet another *gîte* in France, this one down in what would prove to be the delightful region of Gascony. However, we would not be visiting this *gîte* on our own. We would be going there with our mums! And what this choice might have said about us I am not quite sure. But there was a very good reason for this choice, a very good reason indeed.

You see, my dad had died earlier that year and, as we knew that our Gascony *gîte* could accommodate six people, we thought it would be wrong to leave my mum on her own when we could easily take her with us. And then *I* had the bright idea to provide her with a companion in the shape of Sue's mum who, for some time, had been estranged from her husband.

Whether we were being naïve or reckless in organising this intergenerational group vacation is hard to say. But it worked, even though it meant a blasted roof rack on my latest (two-door) Golf GTI and, on the way down and back, my doing a number of heavy-luggage lifting jobs on each of our overnight stops. Indeed, it worked so well, that the four of us would holiday together over the coming ten years. And Sue and I didn't even apply for an MBE.

What we all did on this first shared French holiday is by no means particularly interesting (it was just a lot of eating and drinking). But we did establish that a single man can withstand the company of three women for at least two weeks, even if one of these women has never fully accepted that the man (her son) is no longer just a child, and another of the women carries the burden of being that most dreaded of creatures: the (unofficial) mother-in-law. Although whether exposure to such a trio of females could be endured for any longer than two weeks is definitely open to question. The man would, in all likelihood, soon be in need of a far less crowded holiday.

Then came 1988, and we went to Australia. This might suggest that we had finally become a little more interested in the world beyond France, but in fact we embarked on this long-distance trip in response to an invitation from Tom (as you may remember, one of my university flatmates) to join him and his wife on their visit to Ian (another of those former flatmates, who now lived in Perth [Australia]). We didn't take much convincing, and if nothing else it would give us our first taste of long-haul flights – which turned out to be beef and alfalfa, served up in delicate sandwiches and in some quantity. It is strange what one remembers, isn't it? But those beef and alfalfa snacks are seared into my memory, along with the fact that the Qantas jumbo on which we were flying was hardly a quarter full. Maybe word had got around (but not to us) that Australia was currently not just full of flies but also teeming with mosquitoes...

I don't wish to be rude about this Antipodean giant, but both insects did make a lasting impression on me – as did, in due course, the Western Australia Police Force.

It all started within hours of our landing in Perth. We made the mistake of spending a long, lubricated evening out on Ian's inviting verandah. Which proved to be just as inviting to a host of unseen, military-grade mosquitoes as it was to some old university chums and their respective other halves. I discovered this the next morning when I awoke with numerous mozzie bites on and around my ankles that soon started to suppurate and to become so painful that I had to spend my first full day in the Southern Hemisphere in bed. I should just point out that Sue was unaffected, as were our hosts and our fellow visitors. This was because, as I already knew from a visit to the Camargue in France, I am regarded by all the world's mosquitoes as the tastiest thing on two legs. And I now know that wherever I go on the planet, word will go out on the mosquito grapevine that the Tasty One has arrived, and all mosquitoes within flying distance should make their zizzing way to meet me as soon as possible. That said, I do not believe that I have ever since had as bad a reaction to mosquito bites as I did in Perth. Maybe it was the beef and alfalfa still in my system (?).

Anyway, as it was December 1988, Ian had booked us to join Father Christmas (really) on a steam train that would be taking a party of day-trippers to a small town to the north-east of Perth called Gin Gin (really). The plan was to get there and then, along with all the other day-trippers, visit a shaded park in the middle of Gin Gin and there have a barbie. It wasn't long before we were approaching the promised municipal glade of eucalyptus, and we were intrigued to see that above every brick-built municipal barbecue was a cloud of smoke. All of them seemed to be already in use. I can't then remember who then said it. It was probably Ian. But what he or she said was that what we were seeing were not clouds of smoke but clouds of flies. 'Because, didn't you know? Gin Gin is the fly capital of Australia.'

Yes, it was the second insect to make a lasting impression on me in Australia. And whilst we visitors had already been bothered by them as we simply ambled around the streets of Perth, we had never before seen them in such huge and disturbing numbers. I will not go into detail, but let me just say that most of the sales being made by a local food kiosk were not of food items but instead of insect repellant, and when one was handed one's barbie-cooked food, one had to walk around as one ate it, to avoid it disappearing under a... blanket of flies. Oh, and there was no demand made by any of us visitors to pay Gin Gin a second visit.

Instead, on the penultimate day of our stay in Perth, we drove south to visit a winery near Margaret River. And this is where the Western Australia Police Force took over from flying insects in the concerted irritate-the-foreigners campaign.

The day did not start particularly well. We stopped in a 'town' to buy some postcards – a town that looked like the lot for a low-budget western. It was little more than a single street with just one-storey shops on either side and a distinct absence of either people or domestic dwellings. There were just a very few cars parked on this street, so that's where we parked our own car as well. After all, there were no 'no parking' signs anywhere. So, I, as the driver, was more than a little miffed when, having returned to the car, I found it had a parking ticket on its windscreen. Because I had apparently parked my vehicle facing the wrong way!

Never mind. We would soon be at that winery, doing some agreeable wine-tasting and then having some lunch. Which is precisely what we did before then setting off back north to return to Perth. Our road was straight out of *Mad Max*: a strip of tarmac through an empty landscape, devoid of bends and much in the way of traffic. Indeed, when another vehicle approached us from the other direction, we regarded it as quite an event – and then, when it emitted the sound of a police siren as it passed us, just before it did a rapid U-turn behind us, as quite a significant event. It appeared that it was a plainclothes police car, and one whose onboard radar had been able to detect, as it approached me, that I was speeding...

I did everything right. I stopped. I got out of the car. I was polite to the police officer, and I didn't even debate with him that I had barely been speeding at all (because I hadn't been). And why should I? When I told him I was a visitor to his country, he was bound just to tick me off, before asking me whether I and my friends had enjoyed our stay in his beautiful country. But he didn't do this. Instead, he issued me with a speeding fine, and then commanded me to report to a Perth police station in the morning and there present one of his fellow stormtroopers with my driving licence. I can't remember now whether I was more shocked than infuriated or the other way around. But I do know that before I was back in that car, I had decided that I would do a runner...

The next day, we were due to leave for Sydney, and the day after that for Fiji, before then embarking on our long-haul home. And I was confident that a failure to respond to a (largely unwarranted) speeding charge – even if this failure was exacerbated by an unpaid (completely unwarranted) parking ticket – would not cause the Australian authorities to launch an international manhunt. I was right. They didn't. Although the Western Australia Police Force did turn up at Ian's house in an attempt to find me and, for all I know, I am still a wanted man in that western chunk of Australia. (I did have to visit Adelaide on business a few years later, and I was a little concerned at the time that the handcuffs might appear as I presented myself to Immigration. But there was nothing. It seems that this particular fugitive from justice merely has to remember not to revisit Perth.)

And just before leaving this tale, I think it's worth pointing out that, although by 1988 I was nominally a staid and respectable professional, in reality I was still a bit of a subversive, and certainly subversive enough in my behaviour to deny what I saw as heavy-handed policing, and to do this without any qualms whatsoever. Maybe this was connected with the fact that, although a partner in one of the biggest professional services firms on the planet, I still thought that one day 'I would be found out'. People would realise that they had a fraud in their midst – someone who often could barely take himself seriously. So how on earth were *they* taking me seriously?

Well, nobody did ever attempt to expose me, and that is why by 1989, with partner earnings still flowing into my pockets, I was able to trade in my last Golf GTI for a Jaguar XJ6. And in my defence against an accusation of extravagance, I can only say that Sue was very agreeable to another

French holiday with the mums as long as I swapped the two-door Golf for something with four doors. And the XJ6 definitely had four doors. (And, incidentally, if this defence doesn't work, may I simply offer it in mitigation before the passing of sentence. Thank you.)

So, despite that taste of far-off places, the sweet taste of France still won out, and in September of 1989 we made yet another excursion into France, this time to the same *gîte* in Gascony that we'd visited in 1987, and with both mums travelling in style in the back of the Jaguar mobile. It was another enjoyable, if uneventful, holiday (as would be the *next* visit to France with the mums in 1990), but it did furnish all four of us with a genuine *You've Been Framed* moment on our journey back to the north coast of France. And it all happened at one of those convenient Campanile hotels…

We were having our breakfast in the hotel's modest restaurant, taking in the view of the hotel's crowded car park through the restaurant's windows. Here we could see that there were cars parked tightly together around three sides of the parking area – with my Jaguar sitting almost in the middle of the line of cars directly opposite the restaurant. There wasn't much in this scene to capture our attention – until, just as we were finishing our *petit déjeuners*, 'monsieur' arrived. And 'monsieur' was a genuine caricature of an old French peasant: an old man with a crumpled beret, blue dungarees, a face with dark sagging jowls and a moustache-adorned mouth that was currently housing a half-smoked cigarette.

Even though it was still early morning, he didn't look entirely sober. This is probably why he captured our attention quite so comprehensively, and why we all looked on in concern when he approached a small car at the end of the right-hand rank of vehicles and then got in it. Then something strange happened. The car reversed out, but only by a couple of inches before it lurched forward to its original place, and then it repeated this fidgeting movement four or five times. Eventually it tired of this game, and it successfully abandoned its spot, turning as it came so that eventually it was pointing forward – towards the back of my Jaguar. Then it stopped, with monsieur presumably lining it up for an exit from the car park. Only it didn't then move. It just started to judder…

This is when I spotted that between its near-side front wing and its near-side front wheel, there was one of those concrete bollards that are generally found at the perimeters of car parks and not normally within the wheel arches of cars. The idiot had somehow managed to park so badly that when he'd been leaving his parking spot, he had collected this chunk of concrete, and even though it had very much impaired his reversing, he had just not noticed. Just as he was now not noticing that, because the front wheels of his car were still turned to one side, this same chunk of concrete was impairing the forward motion of his vehicle to the point that it was not able to move forward at all. Instead, it just sat there juddering, with its driver revving its engine and no doubt puffing on his fag in befuddled consternation.

With keen eyes and without the burden of alcohol in his system, the hotel's chef did notice the bollard – and where it was – and he therefore rushed out into the car park to rescue both the hotel's concrete property and the hotel's 'hazard to shipping'. Because, apart from anything else, the hapless driver was now preventing the (safe) use of the car park by the hotel's guests. The chef first succeeded in persuading the driver to get out of his car, and he then seemed to have succeeded in showing the driver the nature of his problem. So that when the chef crouched down and tugged on the bollard, the driver allowed him to do this. He just stood there and watched. And when the bollard fell free from the wheel arch he then just stood there and watched his car move forward – towards the back of my pristine new Jag!

It was clearly an automatic car, which its brainless and sozzled driver had left in 'drive' – just as he'd left its engine running. And it was now on a collision course with my pride and joy.

But no. Those front wheels were still turned, and there was just enough lock to take the driverless car around to the right in an arc, so just missing the back of my car, and instead ploughing into the side of the car in the right-hand row of cars, next to which it had originally been parked. Just as the owners of this unfortunate car were emerging from their room. They looked distraught. Monsieur just looked indifferent, and merely underlined his lack of concern for the result of his actions with an archetypal French shrug. His shoulders went up and his moustache moved a little. And that was it. Except for my rushing out to the car park to move the Jaguar to an overflow car park around the corner. I was not convinced that there would not be a possibly disturbing finale to monsieur's performance. And I didn't want it to involve an XJ6. Not even as a member of the audience.

Anyway, to return to the theme of what our choices were saying about the views and circumstances that Sue and I shared, it is indisputable that buying that luxury motor meant that our circumstances were very healthy by 1989. Just as our shared views were by this time 'more developed' than they were a few years before. And in part this was a result of our interpreting the significance of certain world events. Because there were some unmissable world events in the second half of the '80s that we believed had some unmissable ramifications.

For example, in 1987 there was the outbreak of BSE (Bovine Spongiform Encephalopathy), the cause of which cemented our belief that humans had a diminishing respect for other animals. Then there was the Chernobyl disaster, which confirmed our view that what was then the USSR was a world leader in shoddiness and incompetence. Just as the Lockerbie bombing and the fuss over the *Satanic Verses* made us more certain than ever that there was a far bigger villain than the IRA waiting in the wings to make our lives as miserable as possible and possibly to threaten our very existence. And then there was the massacre in Tiananmen Square, which sent us all a signal that China was lining up to become the world's biggest evil empire, where increasingly its malign and damaging conduct would be focused not so much on its own citizens but more on the citizens of every other country on the planet. Of course, we cannot forget the Berlin Wall coming down either, as, whilst this was clearly a 'good thing', we did see it as an indicator that the age of secure borders was coming to an end and that the free, but not necessarily wanted, movement of people would soon replace it. And by golly it certainly did that.

There is one last event that I should mention – a national event not a world event, but one with huge implications for everybody in Britain. Although maybe this wasn't as clear in 1989 as it should have been. Because what I am talking about here is the rebranding in that year of the National Council for Civil Liberties as 'Liberty'. Someone had thought it a good idea to excise the all-important reference to 'civil' in the organisation's title.

I don't think that this made me cross at the time, but I've lost count of how many times the consequences of this rebranding has made me cross ever since, these consequences being the promotion and protection of *human* rights at the expense of *civil* rights.

You see, I do not believe in human rights. They are a chimera, something cultivated over the past thirty years to provide not only a rich living for a host of lawyers but also an existential threat to our long-established *civil* rights. Quite simply, just like lions, hamsters, pelicans and earthworms, we are born into a world without any *inherent* rights. Instead, the society into which we are delivered confers on us some *civil* rights, rights that are anchored in reality and rights that can be enforced. Universal *human* rights, on the contrary, are merely unrealistic aspirations that can do no more than raise unrealistic expectations in the minds of millions, and then go on to cause untold damage – other than to all those droves of human rights lawyers.

If you consider this view very mean-minded, I would ask you to consider the huge difference between human rights, which, because they are inherent, require no responsibilities on the part of those who claim them, and civil rights, which exist only if the members of the civil society that has granted them sustain that society and police the maintenance of those rights. Both of which tasks constitute enormous responsibilities.

Essentially, human rights encourage people to think selfishly about their entitlements; civil rights promote an understanding of the responsibilities that all rights entail. And this isn't just some philosophical musing. More and more, it means trouble for all those of us who would never dream of claiming any sort of human rights, and an opportunity for a whole bunch of other people to really take the piss. I'm talking here about how the operation of human rights – with the help of an army of lawyers – serves to further the sovereignty of the individual over the sovereignty of the state (i.e. us), and often in the most perverse manner imaginable. In short, the ascendency of human rights at the expense of civil rights has handed a weapon to the likes of the charming Ms Chakrabarti that can be aimed at common sense and decency whenever they like. Which is every day of the bloody year. And they even get us to pay for their ammunition…

Well, that wasn't too polemic, was it? And probably because over the years I have learnt to put all sorts of stuff into perspective. Even stuff that really gets up my nose. No doubt because I have enjoyed the calming influence of a soulmate who, in 1990, was still 'just' my partner and not my wife. Although, as will be seen in the next chapter, this situation was just about to change. Sue and I would finally be in a position to confer some special rights and special responsibilities on each other. By mutual consent and without the assistance of a single, state-funded, over-rewarded, human rights lawyer.

And very much without the blessing of that one lawyer to whom I'd been hitched twenty years before…

Marriage (Again)

Now, before moving on, I think it is only right that I address a 'structural' feature of this book that may have become very apparent in the previous chapter. This is the fact that it can move effortlessly from such things as innocent tales of inebriated French peasants to subjects such as the threats posed by the armed cohorts of human rights lawyers. This might be unsettling for some and possibly not what they were expecting. However, in the first place, I believe an autobiography should deal with what was going on in the subject's head as well as what was going on in his or her world. And in the second place, this is the autobiography of a Baby Boomer, one of a crop of post-war babies who were set to break all sorts of conventions as they grew up. It can be no surprise then, that my approach to setting out my life on the pages of this book is following a slightly erratic and maybe unconventional route. And it will continue to do so until its end. You have been warned. Which is more than I was when I hooked up with wife number one. Who will now feature once again in the opening of this new, possibly all-over-the-place chapter...

I really don't want to be mean here, and, whatever faults my first wife had, it was I who terminated our relationship in such a precipitate and ruthless manner. That said... despite my paying her maintenance for some time, and despite my eventually coming to a financial settlement that left her with everything and me with just my clothes, my car, my record collection, and my depiction of the Rape of the Sabine Women rendered in matchsticks, she would not give me a divorce. She was, after all, a matrimonial barrister – and someone who wanted to frustrate my marriage to her successor.

Nevertheless, under the rules of the game that pertained at the time, a man (or a woman) could win his (or her) freedom after seven years (of separation), on the basis that each party to the marriage might well have forgotten the name of his or her other half after such a long passage of time. And whilst I don't think I will ever forget Kathy's name, I finally got my incontestable Decree Absolute in 1990 (or 1991?), which meant that I could now proceed to marry Sue. Even though Kathy still had one further cartridge in her magazine…

I should remind you here that I was baptised a Catholic, and so too was Kathy. However, we were, both of us, as far estranged from the Catholic Church as it was possible to be. After holding our marriage in that Catholic edifice in Manchester (on the grounds of convenience and 'convention') I don't think we ever set foot in another outpost of Rome during the whole of our married life. We were both practising atheists/agnostics/couldn't-care-less-about-religion *bon viveurs*, and we had long ago mislaid both our creepy rosaries and our belief in that guy with the beard.

I have made this point at this stage of my tale because it might help you understand my surprise when, shortly after that Decree Absolute, I received a letter from the secretary to the Bishop of Manchester asking me whether I would like to provide 'evidence' to an ecclesiastical court, which was being convened to decide whether I had the 'right thoughts' in my head when I had married Kathy just twenty years previously! It appeared that Kathy had petitioned the bishop to annul our marriage, not on the grounds of non-consummation (because quite a lot of consuming had gone on) but on the grounds that I had entered into the marriage without the requisite 'right thoughts' in my noggin, whatever they were. So, just to be clear, a bunch of grown men were going to sit down in a room somewhere in Manchester, and somehow establish what had been going on in my head twenty years earlier.

I had, for some time, found it hilarious that grown men could sit around in a room in Rome, and talk seriously about supposed miracles and the need to make someone a saint. But that undertaking seemed positively rational compared to what these chumps in Manchester were planning to do – and without my help. I didn't just decline the invitation; I scorned it, pointing out to the secretary in my response that most of the rest of the world had moved on from medieval times. And if he wasn't quite sure, he should just make a note that heretics were no longer burnt at the stake and that the Sun was at the centre of the Solar System. And had been for some time.

Well, whatever decision those plonkers came to, it was not relayed to me. And I certainly never experienced a sensation of being nullified. Furthermore, I can honestly say that I have as much interest in discovering the outcome of their deliberations as I have in discovering the taste of earwigs. Albeit earwigs do have a connection with the real world…

Anyway, notwithstanding the discharge of that last, very silly cartridge, I was now free to have another go at this marrying stuff. Only in this instance I would not be entering into wedlock with one eye closed and the other dazzled by a mix of presumptions and social conventions. Instead, I would be marching towards my new chosen fate with both eyes wide open – and through the doors of the Stourbridge Register Office, a public facility just off the third floor of Stourbridge's town-centre multi-storey car park. It must be one of the most convenient places to get married anywhere in Britain. At least for those who wish to drive to their wedding…

It was an amusing ceremony, attended by just six people: Sue, me, our two mums, the registrar and her assistant. Or, as far as I knew, her live-in lover. After all, registrars must be able to operate on their own. Especially when they're unlikely to be facing any crowd trouble. Or even a photographer…

I do remember that some titters were heard in the crowd of four when, after the deed had been done, the registrar asked us whether we would now like to take some photos. It was wrong of us really, but we knew that this was just the business side of our nuptials, and that the wedding celebrations proper wouldn't kick off until we'd transported ourselves to one of our favourite riverside restaurants in Worcester, where our assembled guests would be waiting to greet us. And where they would then join us for a fabulous lunch, before all decamping to Spindlewood for a catered afternoon and evening of more food and booze.

The whole thing went exactly to plan. That is to say, not only did the day go precisely as we'd hoped it would, but also, by deciding to depart on our honeymoon the day after the day after, we were able to recover from the excesses of those celebrations and be entirely sober when, on that day after the day after, we stepped onto an aeroplane bound for Malaysia. We were even in a reasonable state when we landed in Kuala Lumpur. Which was just as well, because I had ahead of me – immediately – a drive across the mountainous spine of the Malaysian Peninsula to its faraway east coast (in fact, a coast some 300 miles away, and not along a motorway, but along the winding roads of the Campbell Highlands).

We had decided on this wheeled rather than winged conclusion to our journey, because the only available connecting flight to this east coast would be taking off a whole ten hours after our arrival in Kuala Lumpur. And I'd reckoned that even on those mountain roads, I could be at our destination well before the connecting flight had even been fuelled. It would land hours after we had checked into our 'honeymoon hotel', the still extant seaside resort of Tanjong Jara. And that's exactly what happened. We beat the aeroplane really easily. Even if a certain passenger slept for most of the way, and even if the drive triggered a two-day migraine...

I will not mention this again, but my life, until quite recently, has been plagued with migraines, and they tended to arrive when they knew they would cause me maximum consternation. Like at weekends or at the commencement of a honeymoon. And, on this occasion, I was in no condition to do anything for a full forty-eight hours. I couldn't even face another Chicken Maryland (the incongruous choice of meal that we'd both made on our very first evening in the exotic East). Fortunately, day three saw me returning to the world of the living, and I could now start to relish all the various delights on offer in our outpost of decadence on the otherwise chaste coast of Eastern Malaysia...

Tanjong Jara is near a place called Kuala Terengganu. And Kuala Terengganu, back in 1991, was at the centre of what was probably the most Islamic slice of peninsular Malaysia at that time, and a very different place from the west of the peninsula. In fact, this had been one of Tanjong Jara's attractions. It was in what was definitely not a touristy area, and therefore it held out the prospect of a bit of adventure and a bit of the unknown. It also (although we had no idea it would) held out the prospect of intimate encounters with flying mammals. Without the need even to get out of bed...

The accommodation at Tanjong Jara was – in 1991 – made up of a number of huge traditional wooden buildings, each of which contained four very expansive, very handsome rooms. Two were at ground level and two were on the first floor. It was one of these latter rooms that we had chosen, not only because it would provide us with an elevated view of the sea but also because we could see from the resort's (pre-internet) brochure that it had a huge vaulted ceiling which emphasised its exotic credentials and set it apart from any of the more conventional ground-floor chambers. It was lovely. But certain bats thought so too.

This became apparent on our first night in the room when we began to hear noises in the dark apex of the vaulted ceiling, and even more apparent when we found bat poo on our polished wooden floor the next morning. However, I was still in migraine-land, and they didn't seem too interested in us. Nor did they on the second night. But on the third, it was a very different matter. I came face to face with one on my pillow, and I have to say its face was quite demonic-looking. He or she (I was not collected enough to bring my bat-sexing skills into play) may very well have thought my face was demonic as well. But whatever he or she thought, he or she didn't have a towel, and I did. With this I made a skilful capture of the non-paying guest, and directed it out of our room. That just left a couple of his/her mates flying around out of reach.

When we turned up at reception at about 1.30 in the morning to report the overcrowding in our room – and our desire to move to a ground-floor room – the male receptionist didn't even question our request. Instead, he just reached behind him, took a key (to a ground-floor room) off a hook, and handed it to us. He then, in a very laconic manner, told us where our new room was, and bid us a bored goodnight. He clearly did this most nights. Because the resort knew very well that those of its guests who had chosen a first-floor room would, at some point, ask to be moved downstairs. Unless they were dedicated chiropterologists – but not batologists, because they're the people who undertake the study of brambles. Although I suppose there might be a few brambles enthusiasts who are also turned on by bats. (As I am – normally – but not when they're trying to share my bed.)

Anyway, settled in our new room, we got on with enjoying our new formal relationship together. Which lacked only one thing: a bottle of spirits from which we could pour ourselves a modest nightcap...

We could buy spirits at the resort's bar, but it was impractical to take a worthwhile amount of any booze back to our room to be consumed in bed, which was something we really wanted to do on our honeymoon. And why not? So… we decided that we would hire a car and drive into the metropolis of Kuala Terengganu, and there buy a couple of bottles of brandy from one of its many off-licences. This seemed like a good idea when we hired the car, but not such a good one when we arrived in Kuala Terengganu and started to walk around its centre. This is when we began to appreciate the impact of Islam on the local retail trade – as in finding alcohol for sale was going to be as likely as finding images of Muhammad for sale. (And, as it turned out, much less likely than finding, next to a Family Planning Association clinic, a restaurant called 'Soon Fatt' – honestly.)

We had almost given up, and had reconciled ourselves to returning to our Malaysian-made Proton car, when Sue noticed a small Chinese supermarket and reminded me that in general the Chinese were more in favour of alcohol than they were in the faith of the Prophet. So, wouldn't it be worth having a nose around? And bingo! There, at the back of the supermarket, was a very small kiosk, hiding behind a heavy metal grill – in which there were bottles of booze. Not many of them, but certainly enough for our requirements, and we therefore presented ourselves at the kiosk and waited to be served. Eventually a Chinese man arrived, fully equipped with a disapproving scowl, and, with the use of a key, he let himself into the supermarket's evil inner sanctum. He was clearly struggling to decide whether the prospect of making a probably high-value sale trumped the prospect of trouble from the authorities as a result of providing a couple of odd-looking foreigners with firewater. After all, this was such a strongly Muslim area that the tolerance of any trade in alcohol was probably even more fragile than the local tolerance of fun. Anyway, the prospect of that high-value sale won out, and after paying over a wad of cash – and signing a register to admit to our despicable purchase – we were soon out of the supermarket with our two bottles of Napoleon brandy. And, all being well, we would be out of the country before the register was examined, and a team of religious police were dispatched to inform us of the error of our ways and the need to respect local norms. (Only kidding. But I do now wonder whether that kiosk is still there. After all, Malaysia has hardly become more secular in the last thirty years.)

We did, incidentally, use the availability of a car to explore the local countryside, which seemed to consist of banana plantations and road verges being strimmed to near death by men with their noisy machines. It wasn't exactly 'the lost world', and it had little in the way of charm. No more than did the sight of some of the local weekend visitors to Tanjong Jara, who obviously avoided any encounter with alcohol, but 'happily' bathed in the sea still fully kitted out in their modest attires. I remember thinking at the time that it must be like going for a dip in a washing machine full of sheets, only a little less invigorating.

Singapore wasn't very invigorating either. It was more unbelievably enervating. This is where we were ending our honeymoon, on what had once been a swampy island that was now a hive of commerce and unsurpassed Asian 'activity'. It was interesting, but it soon got slipped into that file named 'never really want to go there again'. Even if it got rid of its disgusting Chinese food market. And who the hell would want to live anywhere where one's sweat pores are only ever closed when one finds the sanctuary of an air-conditioned building? Good luck to the Singaporeans, but frankly I'd always choose a weekend in Swindon to a weekend in 'Opened-Sweat-Pore'.

OK, time for a lurch. Because we were now back in England, and it was soon time for Freddie Mercury to depart this mortal coil. This I found not devastating news but very sad news. Much of my musical tastes were still firmly anchored in the '60s and '70s, but Freddie and his fellow band members in Queen had been a beacon of musical excellence well into the '80s, and now the brightest element of that flame had been snuffed out. Just because he had sought to taste every forbidden fruit in the garden, which, in my mind, should never have come with a death penalty attached. He was one of my heroes and, as with the untimely death of John Lennon, I felt as though just a little bit of me had been chewed away. And it wouldn't be the last time that the passing of people I knew – from their music, their acting or their comedy – had given me the sense that integral to life was its diminishing through the loss of certain of its 'fixtures', and particularly those fixtures that had so enriched it when they were alive. Just like the USSR hadn't…

Yes, that was running out of road as well, a close-neighbourhood empire, built on bullying and repression, which was now breaking up as most of its subjugated states were coming to realise that having something called Russia ruling over them was about as attractive as having a flesh-eating disease as their sponsor. Russia then was as Russia is now: third-rate and about as fit to run an empire as were the elders of Kuala Terengganu. Albeit the elders of Terengganu wouldn't have been pissed on vodka all the time. Or as keen to turn a whole country into the biggest kleptocracy on the planet.

But I am drifting off the point. Which is that, in 1991, I was not only a married man again, but I was also beginning to understand life and the passing of life. It was therefore incumbent on me to make bloody sure that I made the most of my own life, and that, with Sue, I looked for no other purpose in my life than to enjoy it whilst, at the same time, trying not to do harm to others. Whether these others were other people or all those other life forms on the planet. And if that sounds risibly virtuous, then jolly bad luck. Because I think, back in 1991, I was already well on my way to seeing that 'other animals' had just as much legitimacy on this planet as we did. They might not have been our equals in all sorts of ways, but they were just as deserving of space, consideration, respect – and life.

However, not wishing to attract the attention of the saint-makers in Rome, I suspect it is now time to move on, and to end this chapter with an acknowledgment that marriage can work (at least it has done for Sue and me) – and a report that although we have since been back to Malaysia (just once to its province of Borneo) no Muslim zealots turned up to admonish us for our choice of beverages in Kuala Terengganu. Or, indeed, for any aspect of our behaviour on our honeymoon...

Fermat's Last Theorem

Well, the honeymoon was over. It was now time to reapply my nose to the grindstone and get on with some work. By 1992, I now had more of this than ever, which is probably why it filled so much of my waking life. Indeed, it was so much of my life for so much of the time that it deserves just a little mention in this chronicle. But not too much, because I am keen not to lose my entire audience…

So, I was a partner in a firm that had originally been one of the 'Big Eight' accounting/professional services firms in the world, but that was now on its way to being one of what would be reduced to the 'Big Four' (us, PwC, EY and KPMG). And this reduction process would be achieved through a series of mergers and acquisitions – and one total collapse (of which more much later). Needless to say, our survival and ultimate success meant that we were always on the winning side, in that all our mergers were in fact acquisitions – and we were never acquired by anybody else. Although we would change our name from Touche Ross to Deloitte and Touche and then to just Deloitte, the firm that exists today with that name is still the firm I joined in 1970 and which tolerated me as a partner for over twenty years. Not that this march to success occupied much of my thoughts in 1992. They were still largely lost in the day-to-day work of the Birmingham office, and what this meant in terms of always-demanding technical work, a never-ending succession of problems arising from failed attempts at delegation, and that already-mentioned constant challenge of meeting deadlines. I rarely felt that I wasn't earning my earnings.

Of course, it wasn't professional hard labour all the time, and often there'd be some welcome light relief in the form of such things as preparing proposals for new work, attending to the demands of my developing role as the firm's car man, and turning up for all sorts of meetings, most of which were just as unproductive as they're reputed to be. And... on top of this light relief, there was some genuine respite, first in the form of a variety of residential courses, and secondly, in the form of the much-anticipated 'annual partners' conference'...

This was, as is apparent from its name, an annual event. But what is not apparent from its name is that it was also an opportunity to test the resilience of the human body to excessive amounts of alcohol, and to establish, over three long days, just how close one could get to alcoholic poisoning without actually triggering some *bona fide* toxicity. Many partners made use of this opportunity, having, most of them, for many years, honed their drinking skills at national and regional *managers'* conferences. Which isn't to suggest that the firm was one large collection of soaks, but just to acknowledge that in the twentieth century, many norms in Britain were not the norms we have in the twenty-first century – even if we would all be better off if they were (livers excepted). Anyway, these annual bashes were great fun, and their highlight was an after-dinner 'review', staged by a number of the younger partners on the final evening of the get-together, and designed to ridicule the senior management within the partnership – absolutely mercilessly. It was a real 'roasting' of those at the top of the firm, and, despite its cruel and sometimes uncompromising nature, I suspect that all those top guys probably enjoyed it even more than those applying the heat. But not so our visitors...

Let me step back here – to a speech I heard from the European president of Microsoft probably sometime in the late '80s. Because this French man was recounting his experience of the different national traits he'd encountered within his European bailiwick, and which he believed fell into one of just three regional types. There were, according to him, the Anglo types (us), the Latins (principally, for the sake of his argument, the French) and the Teutonic types (the Germans). He claimed that it was very easy to tell these three types apart – at meetings. The Anglo brigade, he maintained, would regard meetings as a means of discussing various issues and possibly coming to some decisions. The Latins would regard them as an opportunity for discussion – without ever coming to a single decision. And the Teutonic types would see them as a gathering where all those attending would be informed of the decisions already made. And he was right. From some painful personal experience, I can certainly vouch for the French desire to avoid a decision at all costs – even outside of a meeting.

Anyway, the point of this tale is to underline my own belief that national traits do exist, however much this might offend universalists, and however much they might claim that this recognition of the blindingly obvious is tantamount to racism. Which it isn't. It's just the result of people being observant – and being honest. And this brings us back to those savage end-of-conference reviews, and our visitors: partners invited from our overseas firms to witness their British brethren indulging themselves with beverages and with fun. And, in particular, partners from the American and Japanese firms. Because these guys, when they witnessed the disrespect being showered on our own top management, would, essentially, be appalled. It just wasn't what would happen in their own countries, where their national characteristics precluded the ability and even the desire to take the piss out of those 'who were to be respected'. Indeed, their reaction to the behaviour on show was almost as much fun as the review itself, and it certainly left me in no doubt that the peoples of this world, even those who share the same language as ourselves, are not necessarily exactly like ourselves. And some of them, with very different national traits, are like visitors not from the USA or Japan, but from another planet, possibly in another far-off, not very attractive universe...

However, in order to dodge the attention of our liberal arbiters of what constitutes allowable thinking, why don't I quickly move on to the subject of holidays, because between 1992 and 1994, as well as taking our mums back to France – and to Lanzarote and to Cyprus – we made an unaccompanied visit to Mauritius. This was notable for two reasons. The first was that it indicated that Sue and I were experiencing a stirring of interest in the world beyond Europe. (Which still lay semi-dormant, even after visits to Australia and Malaysia.) And the second was that I was becoming reconciled to being bitten by mosquitoes. Having made a meal of me in Australia (and, earlier on, in the Camargue) they had, of course, dined on me again in Malaysia, and there was no way that they wouldn't be sorting out the cutlery in anticipation of my arrival in Mauritius. Which is exactly what they did – but to no avail. I was prepared to suffer in order to taste our chosen delights. And, in any event, it was only ever likely to be mosquitoes. There could never again be a Gin-Gin-sized multitude of flies…

And talking of bloodsucking and irritating pests, it's probably time to say a few words about MPs – and their contribution to our wellbeing. After all, by the early '90s I had formulated some fairly strong opinions on these esteemed 'representatives of the people', just as I had on the well-oiled machine of which they were part, otherwise known as British democracy. And maybe, in setting out these views, I should start with the machine rather than any of its components. I should start by making clear just how much admiration I had already developed for British democracy. If possible, without the use of an electron microscope…

Democracy, we are told, is 'a form of government where supreme power is vested in the people and exercised directly by them or by their agents elected under a free election system'. Which is rather odd, because under our British representative democracy, I have yet to meet a British voter who thinks that he or she is anything but powerless, or that those agents who do have the power have any intention of using it for the common good. Instead, they are focused on using it for their own advancement, which generally means using it for the benefit of those organisations that can provide this advancement, otherwise known as the major political parties.

Now, this might point to a couple of problems. Because, to start with, voters are rarely party members. (Only 1% of the UK electorate are members of a political party, which means that the combined membership of all the principal political parties in the UK is less than that of the RSPB – and much less than that band of sceptics who subscribe to the belief that Wee Jimmy Krankie had a hand in the procreation of Nicola Sturgeon.) Then there is the way that under our 'first past the post' system, the political parties end up with stakes in the legislature – our Parliament – that bear little relationship if any to the wishes of the electorate as expressed in the popular vote. If it did, it would mean that by the time we had reached the 2015 general election it wouldn't have taken 3.9 million people to elect one

UKIP MP, while at the same time an SNP MP could make it through the doors of the House with the help of just 26,000 misguided voters. Even if he or she was one of those sceptics who was absolutely convinced of Ms Sturgeon's Krankie-assisted provenance…

Yes, this party-infected, first-past-the-post system almost guarantees that our representative democracy will not do what democracy has printed on its tin. It will certainly not empower any voters in this country – unless they are also MPs – and it will rarely result in those in government ever doing what us plebs would like them to do. (For example, a whopping 84% of the public support the choice for assisted dying for terminally ill adults, and yet our current crop of faint-hearted representatives choose to sit on their hands, and subject countless people to real pain and suffering. So as not to risk their own political careers…)

I could go on at length about all the other aspects of democracy as practised in this country that I don't much care for, such as the bribing of the electorate with promises of spending money that doesn't exist, the absence of an English-only legislature, the unfortunate presence of a sclerotic revising chamber full of self-important fools – and the inclusion in this chamber of 'Lords Spiritual' – but I don't want to test your patience, and I really want to get back to those greasy cogs of the democratic machine, otherwise known as MPs. Which is what I will now do.

You see, these people are portrayed as our representatives; the people we have selected to act on our behalf in the greatest institution of the state – when they are nothing of the sort. We haven't selected them. That job's been done (on our behalf!) by some form of constituency candidate selection panel, a small number of *party* activists, who will undoubtedly have chosen the guy who they think will promote the aims of the party (or its local clique) as opposed to the guy who might make a better job of representing his/her constituents in Parliament. This really matters, because in almost 80% of all constituencies, the voting outcome is a foregone conclusion. In some of these constituencies, the Conservative selection panel could put forward a performing stoat and it would win, and in others the Labour selection process could provide the voters with a rubber dildo as their candidate and it would have a walkover – and it would possibly do a better job than some of the two-legged dildos who are chosen instead.

So, just to be clear, most constituents in this country do not choose their agents. Those poorly supported political parties do, with the help of their candidate-selection panels. Indeed, I have rarely if ever found anybody who has voted with enthusiasm for his or her take-it-or-leave-it candidate, and the real reason that a particular candidate's box on the ballot paper is being ticked is that it might mean that the other candidates don't get in. Democracy, in reality, boils down to selecting the least-worst option; keeping the party that you detest out of power, by voting for a representative of the party you can just about tolerate. And furthermore, who could really assemble any enthusiasm for those products of the party selection procedures, that motley bunch of wannabes and losers who believe their time on Earth would be best spent grooming their egos whilst at the same time interfering in the lives of other people? And finally, we are back to where we started – with my reference to those pesky pests known as Members of Parliament…

Let's be honest. They might themselves claim that they are all upstanding folk who want no more than to bring about social and political change and a better life for their fellow citizens. But we all know that they are largely a bunch of arrogant and generally incompetent tosspots whose main interest, other than accumulating more power and supposed status, is to impose a mix of misguided and half-baked ideas on a host of other people who would rather be left to muddle through their own lives as they want. Indeed, when one takes account of the lurid stories that have swirled around our three established parties for years, one might be forgiven for concluding that the majority of those seeking office and those in office are either bullies, tinpot despots, preening prima donnas, common-or-garden thugs, unprincipled chancers or scheming psychopaths. And, as is apparent all too often, many of them are not very bright…

It would be insensitive and grossly uncharitable of me to single out any examples of these intellectually challenged heroes of the nation. So, I shall single out only three. One is the guy who, to everybody's amazement, finally ended up as Deputy Prime Minister: our old friend John Prescott. And how could anybody with an IQ and a BMI within touching distance ever have got that far up the greasy pole? Then there is the charming Diane Abbott, a woman who has demonstrated that not only is she as sharp as a hammer, but also that she has a penchant for stuff like hypocrisy and insincerity, but isn't too interested in stuff like humility and integrity – and certainly not an understanding of basic arithmetic. And let's not forget David Lammy, a man who holds out hope for every aspiring plank of wood. Or at least every plank of wood that has too much to say...

Well, that was very cruel of me, wasn't it? But to lessen the offence to these chosen three, I would like to emphasise that they are not unique in their outstanding limitations, but merely good examples of what I am trying to convey: that, with a few notable exceptions, our lives are in the hands of a bunch of inadequates, given bogus legitimacy by a bogus version of true democracy. And unfortunately, there is little we can do about it, other than comfort ourselves by reminding ourselves of two important facts. The first is that the country is run by the Civil Service, not politicians. (Which is seriously comforting, isn't it?) And the second is that we are getting no more than we deserve. After all, there is one further drawback to every democracy in the world that I have yet failed to mention, and this is that it involves voters. Because, without wishing to be insensitive and grossly uncharitable again, many of these chaps could give David Lammy a run for his money, and many more know as much about the democratic process as they do about gravitational singularities and Schrödinger's wave equation, and they may well think that the House of Commons is a new sheltered housing project in Brent...

So, there you have it. Thirty years ago, I had already become disillusioned with both democracy as practised in this country and the majority of its practitioners. And I haven't become in any way illusioned ever since. Although I have, of course, become much more agreeable in my nature, and so much so that I am already regretting my comments on those three hard-working public figures. But not quite enough to withdraw those comments. Instead, I shall jump clear of this draining political topic, hoping to land safely on the upholstered theme of 'cars', as in the growing demands of what was now the 'automotive sector group'.

Good. I made it. And let me begin by explaining that by the early '90s, being the firm's car man was no longer a solo occupation, but one that entailed my leading a small gang of car-interested partners and managers in the firm, who together made up that 'automotive sector group' referred to above. Based in a number of offices throughout the country, they all had various automotive-related skills and interests to bring to the party, and together we endeavoured to raise the firm's profile in the automotive industry with the intention of generating work from its constituent businesses. With, I might say, a modest degree of success. However, we did ultimately decide that, as an automotive group, there was one thing we lacked. And this was a car...

In 1994 I set about dealing with this oversight. And I did this by begging money from a string of regional partners – and the managing partner – to fund the procurement of our very own racing car. By pulling together all this spending power, I was therefore able to give the go-ahead to the construction of a purpose-built TVR Cerbera coupé, which would be capable of travelling at 185mph and which would meet the entry requirements for an event I'd followed since my early childhood: the Le Mans 24-Hours endurance race!

This car would be put together by a specialist car builder in Coventry. Although not quite in the way I had expected. I realised this when I visited the builder's premises for the first time, and after I had burnt through exactly one half of my excessive budget. Because, there, on the concrete floor of these premises, was a matrix on aluminium struts and nothing else! They were not converting an existing Cerbera into a racing Cerbera; they were building one from scratch. One that, at the halfway point, didn't even have wheels, let alone the semblance of some sort of body and maybe an engine.

I was a little shocked. But I should not have been. They knew what they were doing. And only weeks later – and without busting the budget – they were able to wheel out the completed racer at Castle Combe Race Circuit in Wiltshire. And our race director/driver (a six-foot-five semi-professional speed freak from Birmingham) was able to take it on its first run as a racing machine. This went well – until, when it was being brought down the home straight at top speed, our coupé became an open-top (as its cab blew clean off), just before it was driven back into the pits, where it lost its off-side front wing in a slow-speed argument with an Armco barrier. I was comprehensively shocked for a second time. Which is probably why I made my first 720-degree spin in a car when, later that day, I was let loose with a TVR Griffith to experience what it is like to race around a proper race track at speed. Something I've never done since. Neither the racing nor the spinning...

Anyway, again I shouldn't have been shocked. When racing cars come apart, they are just put back together again. And it wasn't long before our Cerbera was racing in something with the snappy title of the BRDC GT Championship, which wasn't quite Le Mans (that idea was soon filed under 'impractical and unaffordable'), but was nevertheless populated by Le Mans-type cars. Every race within this championship was quite a spectacle – and quite a good excuse to conduct a bit of 'client entertaining' at various race circuits. I had found another very attractive, long-running respite from all that unrelenting work.

Now, some of you might recall that in the same year that our Cerbera was losing its head before losing part of its front to an Armco barrier, BMW was acquiring the Rover Group. This was very big news at the time, and so big that the BBC, in their Birmingham Pebble Mill studios, decided to put out a live evening radio programme – on the very day of the announcement of the takeover – where a panel of 'experts' would field questions from the public on the implications of this troubled business falling into German hands. What might the 'Boche' have in store for our brave English Tommies?

Well, I was, of course, pretending to be just the sort of expert they might need, and the subterfuge worked so bloody well that I received a telephone call in the morning to join the panel that evening, and there was no way I could refuse the invitation. All I could do was tremble at the thought of having to answer any question on a transaction I knew little about, concerning two car manufacturers about which I knew even less.

I was still trembling when I arrived at the studios and met the programme's host, but was just composed enough to ask her who else was on the panel. When she replied, 'There is no one else; you are the panel', I think my trembling increased so much that it could have been picked up by the British Geological Survey's nearest seismic monitoring station – and have triggered an earthquake warning. Nevertheless, I immediately switched into stoic mode, and was thereby able to get all the way through a live, hour-long question session without anybody realising that my authoritative tone was concealing a mix of trepidation and more or less complete ignorance of the issue in hand. Indeed, Sue taped my performance – which I still have – and I would challenge anybody to claim with certainty that I was simply bullshitting like a pro. Hell, on the basis of that performance, I could have become an MP.

Of course, I didn't become an MP. Neither did I make my mark, not as politician, but as a mathematician. After all, the year before, as I'm sure you'll all remember, some other bloke solved Fermat's Last Theorem, and thereby deprived me of the opportunity to do the same, something I'd always dreamed I would do – in my dreams. Yes, whenever I was awake, I had to accept that there was as much chance of my solving that theorem as there was of my avoiding mosquito bites. Or the consequences of living under a system of government populated by professional bullshitters and worse. With recourse to no gunpowder whatsoever, but only the possibility of occasionally disappearing overseas – to somewhere exotic, like somewhere in Africa, for example…

Africa – At Last!

Well, not quite yet. Because it has just occurred to me that I have so far neglected entirely 'life in Stock Green'. I may have therefore given the impression that my waking hours were spent exclusively at work, or on holiday or within the confines of our Stock Green retreat of Spindlewood. But this was certainly not the case. Stock Green – together with its sister village, Bradley Green (making up the parish of Stock and Bradley) – dispensed a full and engaging social life to all those who sought it. There may have been a paucity of raves and rockfests (or indeed parish-sponsored orgies), but there were enough pig roasts, travelling suppers, village hall quizzes, village hall dances and other functions to keep most villagers very happy indeed. And that included newcomer villagers like ourselves as well as the two settlements' more established residents. In fact, Sue and I, along with other newcomers, were made to feel very welcome by all 'the locals'. Even by the supposedly curmudgeonly farmers, one of whom, together with his wife, would probably have organised a welcoming drink for a bunch of invading North Koreans. What Stock and Bradley might have lacked in 'chocolate-box picturesque' (we're talking here about two linear collections of motley houses), it certainly made up for in hospitality. And, right up to this present time, without it embracing the joys of socialism.

Anyway, with that omission of a reference to village life now rectified, it is time to justify the above chapter heading, and to talk a little about how Sue and I similarly rectified our not having stepped foot on the continent of Africa despite our having been on Earth for nearly half a century. (If you don't count Mauritius, that is. Or, if you're a real pedant, and you do want to count Mauritius, then make that 'mainland Africa'. OK? Satisfied now? May I please go on now?)

I think I got a 'yes' there. So, I will go on, and I'll do this by describing how one day I suggested to Sue that we go on a safari holiday to Tanzania. Possibly because there was a lapse in our conversation, or I had forgotten something important. I now cannot remember. However, the point is that Sue agreed to my suggestion, and in due course we were sitting in a Boeing 747 that was just coming in to land at Julius Nyerere International Airport, the international airport of Dar es Salaam and (back then) Tanzania's repudiation of the world's growing obsession with cleanliness. It looked as though it hadn't seen a mop or a duster since it was built. That said, it was a pinnacle of good housekeeping compared to the next-door domestic airport, to where Sue and I had soon been ferried. Because this place wasn't just dirty, it was gruesome; a sort of sty on steroids, but without the charm of any pigs to redeem its squalor. And I'm barely exaggerating at all.

Now, before I continue to apply my metal-capped boots to this aeronautical edifice I should just say that I am fully aware that it is discourteous in the extreme to be so disparaging about any facility to be found in a poor country. Well-off people should always be careful what they say about any aspects of a down-at-heel nation. Especially when, with their own free will, they have chosen to visit this nation – and not with the intention of recolonising it. However… this domestic airport terminal really was indescribably awful, and something of a shock for two naïve, antiseptically clean travellers from sanitised Britain. And in my defence against the charge of being gratuitously derogatory, I will mention the loos, which would have scandalised *The Young Ones*, and the two or three settees in the 'departure lounge', which had clearly arrived as part of a 'Couch Aid' project, and just as clearly had been sourced from a drug den in the Gorbals, where they had quite likely already done forty or more years of sterling work. Sitting on them, I still believe, might have proved fatal.

Fortunately, Sue and I did not have to endure this place for very long. Unlike the scores of locals who appeared to be using it as a day shelter, and who seemed to have no interest whatsoever in its connection with powered flights. Not one of them left the facility to get on a plane, and some of them looked quite surprised when we did. When we walked out onto a broken-concrete apron to meet our pilot and his fun-size flying machine – a coffin-shaped vehicle with wheels and wings that would (possibly) take us to our safari destination. If it got airborne and if it managed to stay airborne for long enough.

I am attempting here to convey our thoughts when we first saw this diminutive craft. Because never before had we flown in anything quite so petite, or quite so old. (It was clearly a post-war aeroplane, but it was far from clear which war it was post.) Subsequently, we would discover that Africa is brimming with these ancient diminutive workhorses and, in no time at all, we would willingly board any of them, knowing full well that we would be in for a thrill but not a scare. But then, when we were walking towards that scruffy little crate, we both felt that we had possibly made a big mistake, and it might even be the last mistake we'd ever be able to make. Nevertheless, we did get on board and we certainly took comfort from the fact that the pilot looked very relaxed – and so young that he had a lot more of a remaining life to lose than we did. And furthermore, his willingness to join us on board had to be some sort of statement of his confidence in his antique machine. Or possibly a reflection of his insanity or his acceptance of fate…

Well, at least the engine started. First time. (Albeit it sounded like a 1956 Mountfield mower in need of a service.) And soon the pilot was taxiing his craft out onto the runway, and doing all those things that pilots do – other than closing the door. This was still open as he began to line up for take-off, and he only got around to closing it as the plane started to pick up speed for its ascent into the ether. And then we were there. We had lost contact with the ground, and we were soon well above the ground, overcoming gravity and our own unjustified doubt in the aeroplane's abilities. It really could fly very well, especially if it avoided those big looming clouds, which, with the help of the observant pilot, it did every time. And after maybe only fifty minutes of this stimulating experience, our thankfully competent pilot turned around to inform us that he would soon be landing – just as soon as he'd checked that the grass airstrip he was about to use was free of antelope and giraffe. (He didn't want a repeat of the previous accident here, which had proved fatal – and not just for the poor beast that had been struck.)

He had our almost undivided attention for this piece of information. The remainder of it was directed to attempting to identify the whereabouts of our safari camp – which was currently nowhere to be seen. Maybe he was in entirely the wrong place...

No, he wasn't. After a bumpy but entirely collision-with-wildlife-free landing, we were soon out of our transport and being met by the camp's pint-sized camp manager, the first of a whole brigade of competent and resourceful South African/Australian/British camp managers who would meet us at the end of a long journey – spread out all across the whole of the continent of Africa. And, just like many of her counterparts would do, she was soon ushering us into her Toyota Land Cruiser in order to drive us a short distance to our riverside camp – and a welcoming drink.

We were in wild Africa! And we were soon in our accommodation: a grown-up Scouts sort of tent, with a loo and shower at its rear and a modest deck at its front – complete with a couple of canvas chairs. It was one of half a dozen or more of these tents stretched out in a line on the banks of the Rufiji River, and it did not put me in mind of Borth. Instead, it made me realise that we were somewhere very different from Stock Green, or from anywhere else in Britain. The African bush just has this very different feel to rolling farmlands, country lanes, orchards – and Esso service stations. And of course, it is fairly well furnished with insects...

We were making our way along a path that linked the spaced-out row of tents to the camp's centre, which consisted of a big open-sided dining tent and a few service tents. It was now nearly 7.00pm on this first day in authentic Africa, and we were only able to negotiate this path by following a chain of very dim oil lamps suspended from posts. They provided almost zero illumination, but they did their jobs as markers pretty well. Even when I began to get bitten around my legs, I could still see where we needed to go.

Yes, I was wearing a long-sleeved shirt, regular jeans, and I had covered myself in insect repellant, but those mozzies were still inflicting some serious damage to my legs. But how? And why, when we'd arrived at our destination – a riverside blaze surrounded by more canvas chairs – did the painful bites subside almost immediately? Why weren't they beginning their trip into itching hell, after making just a short stop at itching purgatory?

I would discover the answer to these questions on the second evening. Because on this occasion, as we embarked on that same path to the dining area, we were met by one of the camp guards – carrying a gun. This was because the previous night an elephant had sat on one of the provisions tents, and he (and it was a he), might still be around. Together with the local hippos, this definitely warranted the need for an armed escort (even if his arms probably consisted of a gun but no bullets). Anyway, he also had a torch, which made our progress along the dimly lit path that much easier, and enabled him to stop us as we reached one particular stretch of this path. Because here, as he showed us with his torch, was an enormous column of some sort of chunky-size ants that completely carpeted the path – and through which I had clearly unwittingly strolled the previous evening. It hadn't been mosquitoes at all. It had been scores of ants – ants that had run up my trouser legs to bite the invading Gulliver and persuade him to leave post-haste. Which would, of course, explain why the bites were so immediately painful and why the pain then receded so quickly. Although it never did explain why I had been bitten but Sue hadn't. Was it that I was irresistible not just to mozzies but to all biting insects, and that all these same *Insecta* found my wife no more attractive than I found unruly children? (Albeit, in extremis, I have, of course, sometimes been tempted to bite them…)

Well, I'm making it sound as though our safari was something of a trial. But it wasn't. It was quite the reverse. Our Rufiji River camp was situated in the Selous Game Reserve, one of the largest uninhabited areas anywhere in Africa and, back in the '90s, visited by only a handful of people housed in a handful of non-permanent tented camps. Serendipity had played a hand in our first visit to Africa, and had deposited us in one of the most pristine and most rewarding wild places on the entire continent. And not only was it full of animals and birds, but it was one of the few places where one could walk through the bush (with a man with a rifle) rather than being driven through the bush. This was greatly enjoyable – and far less fear-inducing than taking to the river in a small tin boat.

It wasn't the water that was the problem – or the small size of the boat or even the presence of numerous crocodiles. It was the hippos.

Hippopotamuses are wonderful creatures, and in a way absolutely adorable. However, they do have two very disturbing habits. One is to trample you to death if you inadvertently get between them and their favourite river. And the other is to upend your small tin boat if it just happens to be where they've chosen to surface in that river – and they might then go on to chomp you. This wasn't just a 'scare the tourists' yarn. They really do upend boats. So, when in one of these boats, one sees a hippo's head poking out of the water some way ahead, and then one sees it disappear (which is always what happens) one becomes conscious that there is every possibility that a leather-bound mini-submarine might return to the surface in that one patch of the river currently being occupied by one's overgrown bathtub, and that one might then get a closer look at the submarine's substantial noshers than one would otherwise choose. And being bitten by a hippo is not like being bitten by either a mosquito or an ant. One is very unlikely to feel any discomfort thereafter – or anything.

Needless to say, no capsizing events of any sort were experienced on any of our river outings. And we were still without toothmarks about our body when, on our last afternoon in the bush, we were delivered back to the airstrip to be collected for our trip back to Dar es Salaam – on our way to Zanzibar…

The pilot was late arriving with his winged wonder, and he was therefore late back at Dar es Salaam airport. So late that when he'd taxied to a stop, somebody appeared out of nowhere and shouted out the question, 'Is this the pair for Zanzibar?' It was our next pilot, a guy who flew another modestly sized aircraft – which was waiting for us on the apron to whisk us away to our island destination. Directly. No tiresome arrival procedures, but just a transfer of our bags and ourselves into his awaiting craft. And, within minutes, another take-off and another journey through the sky in the company of a rackety mower engine. I can't really remember how long this journey took, but I do remember that when we arrived in Zanzibar, we were 'today's entertainment'.

We had landed on what might have been an airstrip or a football field. It was now getting dark and it was difficult to tell. However, when we were escorted into a tiny customs shed/club house, it was very easy to tell that we were not simply going to be waved through. A couple of officials insisted we open our cases, in order that they could search through their contents – and display to their extended families what exactly we were bringing into their fiefdom. There certainly were a lot of people in the audience. (Or should I say a lot of men and boys?) And bear in mind also that this was another domestic flight. Tanzania, as its name suggests, includes the island of Zanzibar. And yet here we were being given a thorough customs going-over without having crossed an international border. I distinctly remember feeling less than completely amused. And I certainly wasn't convulsed with laughter when I and my other half were kept awake half the night...

We were staying not in a regular hotel, but instead in a 'traditional characterful hostelry' in Zanzibar Town, right next to the sea and close to the town centre. It was indeed so traditional and so characterful, that one expected to encounter a suitably garbed Rudolph Valentino lurking in its inner courtyard or, more aptly, Bob Hope and Bing Crosby, both putting in their final scenes for *Road to Zanzibar.* What one did not expect, however, was a riotous assembly outside one's ground-floor room that was both inconducive to sleep and extremely disconcerting. Hell, the locals here weren't into booze, which meant that there wasn't a bunch of drunks outside, but a bunch of seemingly very upset people. Whether they were upset with us, we could not tell. Our room was so traditional that its only window was about ten feet off the floor. So, we could only speculate that it was either nothing to do with us – and just something harmless, like the beginnings of a national insurrection – or just maybe one of those onlookers in the customs hall had spotted the Swiss army knife in my case, and had misinterpreted the cross on its side...

They finally moved off – maybe to burn down a government building – and thankfully, there was no sign of them at all in the morning. This meant we were free to go about our exploration of the island – which involved a sweat-inducing trip to a nutmeg farm, a sweat-inducing visit to a former royal palace, a sweat-inducing walk around Zanzibar's famous Stone Town and an X-rated, sweat-inducing stroll around Zanzibar's principal meat market. And I should perhaps just mention that Zanzibar was hotter and even more humid than hot and humid Singapore. Which was, of course, the reason for all that perspiration.

It was refreshing to finally reach an air-conditioned atmosphere – back in Dar es Salaam. We had flown there in another diddy plane (having already become big fans of this sort of personalised flying) and we were spending a night in one of Dar es Salaam's 'international' hotels. There is little to say about this fleeting visit to Tanzania's capital, other than that the city failed to impress me – without it having to make much of an effort to do so – even though the hotel's restaurant did serve up a very passable meal of prawns in Pernod sauce. Oh, and getting out of the place proved quite problematical. This was because Air Tanzania simply cancelled our flight to Nairobi, and we had to wait for over ten hours in Dar es Salaam's fastidious-free air terminal for the next flight to Kenya's capital. That meant we missed an onward flight to Mombasa, and had to make an unscheduled overnight stop in one of Nairobi's hotels before moving on to Kenya's coast.

We did finally get to our intended destination: the very smart and very agreeable Indian Ocean Beach Club. But to avoid this biography turning into a detailed, interminable travelogue (entirely), I will just note that it is the only place we have ever stayed where one of the security guards who patrolled the perimeter of the resort did this armed with a bow and arrow. One can only hope that the resort's situation, far to the south of Kenya's border with Somalia, means that his successors have not had to swap their bows and arrows for AK47s and bazookas.

Well, what did this first trip to Africa do to shape my thoughts for the future? The answer is 'quite a lot'. In the first place, it had made me – and Sue – eager to explore more of the world. France was no longer going to be enough. Furthermore, travelling itself could be fascinating, even if it meant festering settees and having to fly around solid-looking clouds. And surely that meant there were lots of other fascinating experiences waiting for us out there if we were prepared to make travelling an integral part of our future expeditions. And then there was Africa and Africa's wildlife...

In retrospect, I'm not sure how our Tanzania experience didn't cause us to want to go back to Africa almost immediately. Despite the rude things I've written about this country, 'wild' Tanzania was fabulous, and so were its animals and birds. Indeed, its wildlife was certainly instrumental in triggering, for both of us, what would become a life-long interest in all sorts of fauna, and particularly birds. We would never become twitchers, but we would definitely join the ranks of happy and harmless birdwatchers. Just as long as searching for that last bird of the day didn't delay one's first gin and tonic (or allow time for the next).

As regards Africa *per se*, maybe both of us wanted time to digest the experience, and spend some of this time exploring other far-off places in the world before returning to what would become our favourite continent on the planet. And this is what we did. It would be another five years before we returned to Africa's clutches, and then become captured by it for life. And meanwhile, we would just have to make do with bits of the Indian Ocean, and bits of the Caribbean and South America. Yes, life would be really tough. Or '*ngumu*' as they might say in Swahili. Or maybe they might say '*rahisi sana na bila ubishi haiba*', which means 'very easy and indisputedly charmed'. I'll let you be the judge.

Wellies and Welfare

In the previous chapter I omitted to report one important feature of that expedition to Tanzania and Kenya. This was that it had to be deferred at the last minute, and this was because my mum had unexpectedly died only days before we were due to fly off. She had been sharing afternoon tea with a neighbour, and had just informed this neighbour that she felt a little funny. Then she was gone – before she even knew she was going. A massive aneurism had snuffed out her life instantaneously – and painlessly.

Now, I tell this tale not as a sombre reminder of how all of us will one day meet our end but, on the contrary, to celebrate the fact that some of us may still be able to take a dive into oblivion without any of that increasingly common drawn-out suffering stuff. We might just find that, even in the absence of some much-needed changes in the law, we can still secure an end to a life well led 'promptly' and before getting entangled in some horrible chronic ailment that causes either the loss of one's physical faculties or the loss of one's marbles. And I don't think I am being entirely insensitive if I say that many of my fellow Baby Boomers, who are themselves now responsible for fragile and/or distressed parents, will understand exactly what I mean. Living should be about living the best life possible, not the longest life possible. And if it can be ended 'cleanly' (and not desperately prematurely!), then this is the best possible outcome, both for the cleanly-departed and the cleanly-departed's relatives. Even though these relatives will probably experience both shock and sadness in the immediate aftermath, before they then begin to accept the fact that everybody concerned has just experienced a dose of very good fortune. And my golly, I do hope this is the way I go – albeit not quite just yet. And certainly not before I've finished this book. Which will now continue with a couple of brief references to my 'car responsibilities' within what was now Deloitte and Touche.

These responsibilities were consuming more and more of my time – especially in the area of surveys and publications. If I wasn't organising a study on the financing of company cars or on 'personal contract purchase schemes', I was producing glossy reports on these studies – or I was even talking about them on the telly. Not that often, but I did make two authoritative appearances on Sky's Business News – once when I was sober and once when I was under the influence of alcohol. In the latter case, I had been participating in the (very wet) lunchtime initiation of a new partner, and directly afterwards had made the mistake of agreeing to an interview on some critical car issue of the day – without realising that the interviewer and his cameraman were already on the premises and eager to get going asap. I had thought I was being invited to do an interview at a studio the following day or the following week, but I had thought wrong, and I could not now back out.

Well, objective assessors have opined that my performance was marginally better in that wine-augmented interview than in the one where I'd not touched a drop. And, having seen recordings of both, I tend to agree. It seems indisputable that as long as one can avoid any slurring, a certain hint of 'merry nonchalance' is bound to add to one's authoritative persona, and it might even distract viewers from the substance of one's discourse. Which might not be a bad thing. Unlike taking one's first scuba dive, which can be a very bad thing indeed...

Now, unless you're already missing some of your recollection marbles, you should have no problem at all in recollecting that I only recently alluded to having to endure tough times in the Indian Ocean, and in 1996, this meant having to endure a holiday in the Seychelles (which, in fact, was so tough that Sue and I didn't return there until the following year). And what, I hear you say, was so tough about the Seychelles? Well, mozzies to start with and, on the unbearably beautiful Bird Island (to the north of the main Seychelles group of islands), a gecko landing on my face as I slept in one of Bird Island's less than hermetically sealed cabins. Which was 'quite a bloody fright'. However, these were minor burdens to bear compared to my first encounter with self-contained underwater breathing apparatus – and the PADI personnel who 'taught' me how to use this apparatus and who accompanied me on my first (and only) dive.

I knew it was all going wrong when I turned up to the resort's swimming pool to grapple with the scuba gear in a safe environment, and was asked to sign a document that I couldn't read because I had turned up without my specs. (Which, not unreasonably, I had decided, would not fit well under a scuba face mask.) Anyway, the PADI people passed me as fit to be let loose in the deep blue sea. And if you're wondering what PADI stands for it is the Professional Association of Diving Instructors, although maybe it should be the 'Perfunctory Assessment of Diving Incompetence'. Because, if they'd done a proper assessment of my level of diving incompetence, they wouldn't have let me near the beach, let alone into the deep blue sea.

I and a small gang of other beginners were taken beyond a reef – to where the water was seriously deep – and all of us soon found ourselves fifteen or more metres under the sea. And one of us found that he had incredible earache – as in excruciatingly painful ears. It was awful, and even worse than knowing that one had the weight of a fifteen-metre column of water pressing down on one's body, and – because of an inability to recall any of the prescribed hand signals – no possibility of saying, 'I've really had quite enough, thanks very much. May I now return to the bar – immediately?'

This underwater purgatory did come to an end, but only after my suffering the indignity of having to haul myself back into our little boat – with half a hundredweight of scuba gear on my back. Which meant I spent about as much time extracting myself from the Indian Ocean as I had spent extracting myself from my first marriage. (Or so it seemed at the time.) And thereafter, I had severe earache for four days, which only decided to abandon me when it accompanied me in an unpressurised cabin of a small aeroplane on our way to another of the Seychelles islands. Needless to say, I have ever since made do with a snorkel, and if I'm ever threatened with a close-fitting wetsuit and a cumbersome metal backpack, I claim hydrophobia, and begin to foam at the mouth just to prove it. Alternatively, I simply avoid all oceans and seas and, with Sue, take myself off to tropical jungles and similar environments, where the only water in evidence is that which is leaking out of one's skin. Which is a suitable introduction to our first 'group holiday' – which, still in 1996, was taken in Venezuela…

We had clearly decided to be a bit more adventurous – in a part of the world we knew very little about, other than it might be as well to be adventurous there not entirely on our own. 'Safety in numbers' considerations made us choose to taste this enticing unknown with a few others, and, most importantly, with someone who could act as a leader for us and those others – and as our protector if the need arose. We therefore opted for a group birding holiday, run by a firm called Naturetrek – a firm with which we would become very well acquainted over the coming years. And I should just say that the birding aspect of this holiday wasn't an imposition, as by now we had cemented our interest in our avian cousins, and Venezuela promised a veritable smorgasbord of feathered fliers. And it also promised a few hazards…

This became apparent when the joining instructions arrived. Not only were we advised to bring a sockful of flowers of sulphur to be dabbed around our ankles in order to avoid the attention of burrowing chiggers (!), but we were also advised to bring with us our wellington boots. It seemed that not only would we be walking through chigger-infested grass, but we would also be walking through standing water, where any number of undesirables might be living who could be kept at bay only by a barrier of moulded rubber. We, of course, took this advice seriously. Although the sockful of sulphur was a lot easier to pack than the two pairs of wellies. (And when we had arrived in Venezuela, its sweat-inducing climate guaranteed that those wellies would remain in our cases. Once they were on, we would never have got them off.)

Anyway, our group of just seven adventurers, having arrived in Caracas, had first to negotiate not grasslands or swamplands but the city's hyper-manic roads – in our 'tour bus', an ancient American minibus with a sort of suede interior, which managed no more than 0.1% of its intended itinerary before it broke down. Its engine was still working but, just two miles into its journey, its ancient air-conditioning system began to fill the vehicle's interior with clouds of white and probably fairly toxic gas. We were obliged to debark it pretty damn quickly – and then wait for a replacement bus while we contemplated what we had got ourselves into: a more than marginally dysfunctional country where things just about worked or didn't work at all. (Although we had no idea then that this was something of a golden age in Venezuela, and that in only two years' time, a certain Mr Chavez would take over as head honcho and set his country on its path to total ruin.)

Well, the next thing to break down was me. We were making our way west from Caracas, and had spent a couple of interesting nights in a couple of interesting hostelries, before embarking on our first proper jungle expedition and our first *al fresco* lunch at some half-derelict research station. I do remember that there was salad with this lunch, but I don't remember being concerned by this fact. However, I should have been. Because that salad had been hosting within its greenery a small platoon of very small critters that, when ingested, lost no time at all in mounting an attack on my guts. You will have no desire to hear any of the sordid details of the sordid outcome of this assault, but I will just say that I was in dire straits for a number of days, and I have never since suffered anything quite so intestinally disruptive and so absolutely debilitating. It was so bad, Sue and I even considered returning home prematurely. Fortunately, we didn't. And, after I recovered, I was able to join the rest of the group in lapping up what was a fabulous, never-to-be-forgotten wildlife trip, one that would take in not just jungles, but also a stretch of the high Andes and, best of all, a taste of Venezuela's incomparable Llanos – its treeless grassy plains that (once) hosted an abundance of birdlife, at its best in an enormous ranch by the name of Hato Piñero.

This is where we stayed – a mostly untouched idyllic haven, owned and run by an elderly saint, whose considerable wealth had been used to maintain its idyllic credentials, and all that birdlife. It was such a refuge for wildlife of all sorts that it was internationally famous and a 'must go' destination for any birders or naturalists visiting the country. Which is why it is so sad to report that when Chavez took the helm of his country, he lost very little time in expropriating the place and then ruining it. It mattered little that Hato Piñero had been in the saint's family for about as long as Venezuela had existed. Because socialism has no time for fairness and decency and, if it is socialist thugs who are in power, it is they who prevail.

I hate to think what happened to the kindly owner – who was even kind enough to lay on two small planes to take us 'Naturetrekkers' back to

Caracas when our bus transport failed to turn up. He was so old back then that it's beyond doubt that he is no longer with us. But for him to have seen his life's work torn apart – and his family's heritage thrown aside – must have been devastating. And, of course, Hato Piñero remains expropriated even now. Mr Maduro, Chavez's idiot successor, still manages to hold his country in his tyrannical gangster-socialist grip, and, inevitably, he is much more concerned with preserving his and his cronies' wellbeing than that of any bird who might need an untouched environment out on the Llanos. Shit, birds have got even less say in modern-day Venezuela than most Venezuelans have. So, they count for absolutely nothing…

OK. There are three themes developing here, aren't there? One is my growing interest in wildlife back in the '90s – shared with Sue. Another is my growing realisation back then that the behaviour of humans towards wildlife leaves a lot to be desired, again shared with Sue. And the last is my burgeoning distaste for socialism, which, as much as it might be laudable in theory (possibly), is a bloody disaster in practice. Sue, not surprisingly, shares my views on this as well.

So, if I might be allowed to ignore themes one and two for the moment (which will not be ignored indefinitely), I would now like to explain how it wasn't just socialism as a concept that was earning my displeasure back in the '90s but also its real-world manifestation in Britain – in the shape of the welfare state. And I might just say that the formulation of my ideas on this subject didn't even need the booster rockets that Venezuelan socialism would make available at the end of the '90s and beyond. I already thought – and still do – that the operation of any welfare state inevitably leads to a country's undoing. And it's certainly been leading to this country's undoing for several decades – a statement I would now like to expand on…

Where I'd like to start is where I and all Baby Boomers started: just after the Second World War. Because that's when the welfare state was introduced – not necessarily to eliminate 'want, disease, ignorance, squalor and idleness (!)', as was its advertised purpose, but more to pacify an expectant populace who were unwilling to just pick up from where they'd been before the war – in terms of social conditions. Indeed, if they weren't granted what they wanted, there was a fairly strong likelihood that they might have become marginally belligerent. Which means that the introduction of the welfare state was more an exercise in containing the threat of class conflict – and thereby keeping the capitalist system afloat – than it was an admirable step forward in the development of our society. It was also very much 'of its time' and, in reality, no more than a pragmatic response to the demands of that time.

And, to begin with, it worked! Even a jaundiced Baby Boomer like myself has to admit that. And it worked for a number of reasons. The first was that it was rolled out across an ethnically homogeneous nation, containing a workforce with a strong cultural work ethic. This meant that it was very much seen as a safety net and not as a nicely plumped cushion. It was primarily designed to look after the country's citizens when they needed to be looked after, and then return them as soon as possible to a situation where they could look after themselves – something that was at the core of a society that had for centuries espoused the principle of self-responsibility. And furthermore, that ethnic homogeneity meant that those in work didn't resent those being helped. They might be on hard times, but they were part of the 'tribe'. And, of course, it also worked because it hadn't yet propagated all the many problems that would soon become its hallmarks, whether these problems were in the form of the chronic abuses it was about to endure or the cankerous attitudes it would slowly engender.

If you're a Baby Boomer yourself, you'll already be listing these unavoidable negative impacts of our welfare state. So, you might want to check your list against mine, which is:

1. The creation of a dependency culture and an unjustified sense of entitlement
2. The theft from many people of the pride that comes with having a job
3. The infantilisation of people by undermining their sense of self-responsibility
4. (Very often) the encouragement of people to have more children than they can afford
5. The enormous financial burden placed on those called upon to fund the welfare system (which is now colossal)
6. The facility given to tens of thousands of people to commit welfare fraud

This isn't a comprehensive list, but one designed to underline why, back in 1996, I was already so disillusioned with a misguided state support system that was clearly doing so much damage to our society – and to our economy. Albeit it had a lot more mileage in it yet. Because just consider how much further damage it has managed to wreak in the last two and a half decades.

As regards the economic damage, one cannot deny that our economy (in common with those in the rest of Europe) has become less competitive because the high tax rates needed to fund welfare payments have stifled economic growth. Cossetted Europe, which accounts for just 16% of global domestic product, accounts for a full 50% of all welfare spending on the planet, which is one of the major reasons why we and other European countries have been taken to the cleaners by China, India and a whole raft of other nations where self-reliance is still the order of the day. But that's not the end of the story. As well as our welfare system enfeebling our economic performance, it has also acted as a magnet for all those people who are prepared to come to our shores to do the jobs we no longer want to do – all those jobs we do not have to do because that original safety net has now become a comfortable cushion. Indeed, our 'welfare for all' attitude has unfortunately coincided with a period of rapid population growth around the world, and particularly in a number of failing African and Islamic countries. And it is little wonder then, that if you are in the ranks of one of these 'excess' populations, you will be more than eager to reach the golden shores of welfare heaven – whether through a legitimate route or otherwise.

One doesn't have to be a Baby Boomer to see the end result: a crowded island becoming ever more crowded with people who will look to the state for support. And many of these people will not share the group loyalty that was so important for the initial success of the welfare state, and they may not have the sort of cultural background that is necessary to sustain a welfare system of any sort. In short, the high levels of 'national trust' that were prevalent when Baby Boomers were popping into the world is diminishing by the day and may soon have disappeared entirely. When that happens, it will become all too apparent that the welfare state has done rather more than 'just' screw up our economy. It will also have screwed up our whole country.

Mind… I think when we've already arrived at the point where an undeniable 'mission creep' of the welfare state has made virtually all of us clients of the state, where the majority of the population believe that it is the state's responsibility to provide for them in their old age (irrespective of how they have managed their finances up to that point) and where overpaid footballers can convince a similar majority that parents should be relieved of the duty of feeding their own children, maybe we're screwed up already but just haven't realised it yet. And maybe we won't until we've sunk to the depths of Venezuela…

Now, I did point out a little earlier on that this book would be covering what was going on in my head as well as what was going on in my world, and that's why you've just had to make your way through a far from humorous mugging of the welfare state. And what was going on in my head isn't just part of *my* story, but I suspect, if they sat down and put pen to paper, it might be part of many a Baby Boomer's story as well. Of course, not all would be quite so compassionate or quite so empathetic as I have been, but growing up in a self-reliant society and seeing it shrivel into one of increasing dependency on others will, I'm sure, mean that many of my contemporaries will share my views. Just as long as they've been rational enough to have dumped any affection for socialism quite some time ago. Obviously.

And one final point. I've recently discovered that if one is in receipt of certain welfare benefits, one might be eligible for a free phone and broadband package. Possibly a very good practical idea, or just possibly… well, where does it end? Probably at something called the buffers.

Anyway, I'm sure there are other, far more favourable views on the operation and efficacy of the welfare state that are just as valid as my own. It's just that all of them are, unfortunately, indisputedly wrong…

Dragons, Crabs and Robbers

OK, time to lighten up a bit. No doubt about it. And what better way to do this than to return to my 'automotive man' responsibilities within the firm, which by the second half of the '90s had expanded even further, and so much so that I now had a dedicated assistant to help me. This was a young woman who had once worked in our Glasgow office, and who therefore came with an intimate knowledge of the workings of the firm – and a noticeable Scottish accent (but fortunately, no likeness whatsoever to Nicola Sturgeon).

She ended up accompanying me on a couple of trips to the States, two of half a dozen of such visits, designed (supposedly) to publicise the existence of our UK automotive group within the US firm and to generate some work. Whether they succeeded in these objectives is still being debated by various historians, but that they were difficult and demanding tasks is beyond question. They certainly – if not probably or even possibly – were. Or there again, maybe they weren't...

Anyway, the first (an unaccompanied trip) was to San Diego, which, I have to say, I agonised over for quite some time before I finally decided to go. Because, you see, 'agonised' is an anagram of San Diego, and I want you to feel that you're learning at least something from this book that you might actually remember after you've finished it – if you do ever finish it. This anagramic fact is certainly about the only thing I remember from my trip there. And then there was Detroit – twice – which, as far as I am aware, does not provide a worthwhile anagram – or much in the way of scenic splendour. My recollection of the place is that it was falling to bits, as well as it being very cold and bereft of any thatched or half-timbered buildings. None of which surprised me in the least.

Then there was Orlando, not quite the automotive/commercial capital of the USA, but a place that has some extremely large hotels that can host mega conferences, including a few hosted by the US firm to which I was invited – in my role as the car man. Strangely enough, the content of those conferences is now something of a blank in my mind, but I do remember there being an awful lot of food on offer, and I do remember having to evacuate one of those giant hotels in the middle of the night as a result of a (false) fire alarm. This I will never forget, because, as I emerged into the corridor outside my room – in response to the demand to evacuate – so too did dozens of very small people in dressing gowns and pyjamas. They were all Japanese. And the reason I had not set eyes on them before was because they had all been spending their entire days at one or other of Orlando's many theme parks. They'd clearly wanted to make the best use possible of every minute of their holiday in Florida.

Of course, I and my assistant had better things to do, and we barely managed more than half a dozen rides a day. And even then, we had to turn up early at the Universal Studios park – to make quite sure we could bag a couple of rides on its 'Dueling Dragons'. This was a pair of 'intertwined inverted roller coasters', where two 'trains' were dispatched simultaneously along two unique courses to create a number of (high-speed) near-miss encounters for their two sets of riders. It was scarier than a meal of sushi, but of course infinitely more enjoyable. Although not for everyone…

Apparently, somebody on one of the dragons lost an eye when he was struck by a 'loose object' from the other dragon. This inevitably led to an inquiry and then a decision to require all punters to deposit all their 'loose objects' in lockers before they were allowed to participate in a ride. This rather stringent rule didn't go down too well, and the ride became much less popular, and was eventually dismantled. Well, I think they missed a trick. They should have gone above and beyond the minimum requirements of health and safety and have demanded that not just loose objects were placed in lockers but that all the riders' possessions were placed in lockers. And I mean all. That way, Universal could have delivered Orlando's first nude ride, and they would have had a hit on their hands. Hell, even the interminable queuing would have been fun. You know, sometimes I think I followed the wrong profession…

Maybe I should have become a theme-park director or, failing that, a TV news editor. That way I might have been able to stop the rot.

Yes, I think it was really beginning to set in during the last decade of the last century, and it certainly got a boost from the unfortunate demise of Princess Diana in that Paris underpass. That let loose such a surge of unwarranted but completely indulgent 'public emotion' that what, up until then, had been a trickle became a flood. And what I am talking about is the unhealthy corruption of news coverage in the United Kingdom. We Baby Boomers, you see, grew up in an age when 'the news' was broadcast dispassionately, and it consisted predominantly of facts. This was quite a good way of going about things, because by facts being provided – in an entirely dispassionate manner – we could form our own views as to what that news meant for us, for our country and for the world.

Fast forward to the present age, and I challenge you to watch any newscast, and not count more 'emotional personal experiences' than actual facts. This has got far, far worse recently. Probably because of the impact of social media, where everybody sees the world through the blinkered lens of his or her own experience. But I still believe that this degradation in news broadcasting has its roots in the '90s, roots that received a healthy dose of Baby Bio when Diana was transformed from a princess into a saint.

One can argue that this doesn't matter. But it does. In the first place, presenting those emotional personal experiences as real news is clearly designed to persuade us to empathise with the person in question and not to form our own considered opinions – which we might do if we were given just facts. And in the second place, that blinkered lens of personal experience is also a very distorting lens. And I can think of no better example of just how distorting it can be than to recount a reported discussion between a white customer of a black physiotherapist in London, a guy who had become an activist in the cause of getting more diversity into the ranks of the nation's physiotherapists. He was appalled, he told his client, that only 3% of this country's physios were black. However, he probably found it difficult to remain appalled when this same client informed him that the percentage of black people in the whole population was… 3%. Living and working in an area of London where there were a lot of black people had led him to believe that this same situation pertained throughout the whole of the country. Had he stopped to equip himself with some facts rather than looking through his hopeless pair of distorting 'Emotional' brand goggles, he might not have made quite such a fool of himself. Although he's hardly unique in how he was going about obtaining and processing information, just as the BBC is hardly unique in fertilising this sort of misguided behaviour with its personal-experience-over-facts news coverage. All news channels do it; it's just that the BBC is by far the worst. But enough of all that. Because now it's time to move on from minor rant to major holidays – or where Sue and I went to get our breath back after that trip to Venezuela…

Well, essentially and maybe not surprisingly, it was a beach somewhere hot, and where we could really get our breath back – not just from Venezuela but also from that unavoidable pastime called 'work'. In the years running up to the end of the millennium, I was probably working harder than ever (despite the odd ride on Dueling Dragons) and I doubt I could have contemplated any sort of vacation where I would have to do much more than walk between the surf and a lounger – and occasionally have something to eat and to drink. I think I've already mentioned that one of these lazy holidays involved a return to the Seychelles, but before that we made our first visit to St Lucia. We stayed at a small beach resort that was renowned for its food (by the name of East Winds), and I remember not only that its food deserved its fame but also that the resort housed the noisiest cicada in the world. Unfortunately, he lived in a bush just outside our chalet, and was responsible for our making a trip into Castries, the capital of St Lucia, just to buy a pair of earplugs. They didn't work, but it was still nice to have made a small contribution to the island's retail sector and to have become the owner of artefacts that are really quite rare in Britain. In fact, I am not aware of any of my friends who have ended up owning a pair of St Lucia moulded ear bungs. Neither am I aware of any who have suffered a psychotic episode in Zanzibar…

Yes, despite that riot outside our bedroom on our previous visit to that island, we had returned to Zanzibar, in order to spend a couple of weeks doing nothing at a beach resort on the east of the island called Mapenzi.

It was ideal for our purposes: simple but comfortable – and so steaming hot that one was tempted to do two thirds of three eighths of sod all. Any energy one had needed to be husbanded in order to mount the 10,000 steps between the beach and the dining area. And if it wasn't 10,000, then it could seem like 10,000. Especially after one had experienced a disturbed night as a result of taking Lariam.

Unsurprisingly, Sue and I were sharing this Mapenzi resort with a few hundred squadrons of malaria-carrying mosquitoes. We were therefore taking anti-malaria medication, not our preferred benign 'Malarone' but, for a reason I cannot recall, its bad-ass brother, otherwise known as Lariam. And this guy was a bad-ass because it was known to have psychotic side effects – side effects that have resulted in it being banned in many jurisdictions. Nevertheless, after several days at the resort, no such side effects had emerged, and we were soon both too relaxed to even recall that there were any side effects. We were instead more focused on the beauty of the resort and the idyllic charm of our beachside chalet, a small white-painted construction just yards from the sea, and surrounded during the day by dozens of quite adorable ghost crabs – tiny little critters that spent their days crawling around and providing a constant source of fascination. They were lovely.

Then, one night – in the middle of that night – I was woken up by a crab in our bed. But it wasn't a small ghost crab; it was an enormous, sinister-looking spider crab – white like the ghost crabs but about a hundred times bigger. Needless to say, I was soon out of that bed, and informing Sue – in a rather high-pitched voice – that her sleeping companion was no longer me but instead an oversized crustacean that had no business being even in our room. And it was still there when I was providing her with this information, and it only vanished when Sue was able to convince me that it did not exist in reality but instead just in my mind. I had suffered a genuine psychotic event. And I didn't much like it.

In retrospect, it could have been a lot worse. I could have been taking Lariam on our trip to Australia, the one where we'd ended up at 'fly central', that little settlement outside Perth where flies outnumbered its citizens by about 1,000 to one. And who would have wanted to wake up to a foot-long bluebottle in his bed – with a disturbingly low buzz? Not me, that's for sure.

I'd want that about as much as I'd want a return trip to the Maldives...

This was the last of our twentieth-century lazy holidays, a stay on a Maldivian island called Reethi Raa, which was little more than a strip of sand awaiting its turn to be submerged by rising sea levels. It was very pleasant in a way (because it hadn't yet been upgraded into a luxury resort), but it was barren in so many senses of the word. It had no decent cuisine; it had no female staff (in accordance with the prevailing Muslim practices); it had virtually no birds; it had no calm (the wind blew viciously all the time); and it had no love for alcohol. This was served only rather resentfully in the restaurant at an exorbitant price. Among its few plus points – other than sun, sea, sand and some exotic fish – was that it was also deficient in Russian and Chinese visitors. And I say that not as an overtly racist observation, but with the knowledge that the increasingly opulent resorts which are now found on the Maldives' tiny islands have become a magnet for rich Russians and rich Chinese, the presence of whom I am told is not conducive to a relaxing stay. If you can't hear them, it's only because they are in the sea somewhere, disturbing the sea cucumbers, harming the coral or otherwise disrespecting the fragile and sensitive environment. And I believe my defence against the accusation of libel there will be the one of 'truth'. In any event, I am more likely to go back to Detroit than to the Maldives. Apart from anything else, there are more birds in Detroit.

OK. Time to get back to work. Because, as I've tried to emphasise, there was a lot more of that going on than there was of lying on beaches. And some of it, I'm afraid to say, was becoming rather less than satisfying. Indeed, two aspects of it in particular were becoming something of a pain. The first was the blossoming of 'tick box' methodology. Instead of being required to use their brains, our young, front-line troops were more and more being required to tick a box to indicate that they had done a certain task. This was supposed to introduce efficiencies into the firm's operations and also provide substantive evidence of work having been done, should the unfortunate happen and we were taken to court. Well, in some instances, I believe a tick in a box indicated little more than an ability to tick a box, and there were certainly too many instances of the box-tickers not being able to answer what should have been simple questions if they'd done the called-for work – properly. In my mind this was undermining the whole concept of what it meant to be a 'professional': somebody who was supposed to bring his or her intellect into play to solve a problem, first by understanding the nature of the problem and then by devising the required solution. It had to involve more than being able to make a mark with a pen – or latterly, making a mark on a screen by pressing a key. And that leads on to the second aspect of work that was causing me grief: how that pen or those keys were being used when there were letters involved and not just ticks.

Yes, we were employing graduates – with 'good' degrees – who knew little about grammar, even less about spelling, nothing about punctuation, and for whom 'structure and composition' could well have been a new-wave comedy duo and not the essential components of a well-written, well-presented report (for which some poor client was having to pay). In essence, I was becoming a proofreader, corrector of prose and a report rewriter rolled into one, and I didn't much like it. No more than I liked an education system that, whilst constantly improving (or so we were told), was churning out a product that was far inferior in terms of its basic abilities than… well, yer standard Baby Boomer. And it wasn't just the writing and composition that had gone downhill. Numeracy (whilst never very important in accountancy) had slipped significantly as well, as had the understanding that work involved turning up for work as agreed and then working when you were at work, rather than checking your mobile phone all the time.

Ah well, if I'm beginning to sound too much like a curmudgeonly Baby Boomer, maybe I should talk about one other aspect of the firm's work, one which wasn't giving me a problem, but one about which I now had a very different opinion. And this was its business of dreaming up (legitimate) tax avoidance schemes to assist generally well-off people pay rather less tax. For years I had regarded this as a somewhat distasteful practice, as well as it being a misuse of good intellect on the part of those who devised such schemes. Why didn't everybody just pay their 'fair share' and get on with their lives? And then those scheming intellects could be channelled into some much more worthwhile endeavours. Well, now, I had changed my mind. Now, I was all in favour of any legitimate scheme going. In fact, I was in favour of doing away with tax entirely. And I will now explain why.

I will start by introducing the term '*corvée*', which was the earliest and most widespread form of taxation, levied on people who were too poor to pay other forms of tax. And what it was, of course, was just forced unpaid labour. Whoever was wielding power at the time would require you to work (for nothing) for a few days, weeks or months – to maybe build a pyramid or a castle or maybe just to gather in their crops. It was an exercise in one group of people – the ruling elite and their hangers-on – imposing their demands on another group of people against their will. And now, whilst we may have consigned *corvée* to the dustbin of history, we have replaced it with something far more onerous, and we call it variously income tax, capital gains tax, stamp duty, VAT, customs duty, council tax and so on and so on. And the money rather than the labour we are now required to provide – to the elite and their hangers-on – can easily amount to 40% of all our income, and it may well represent a far more onerous burden than dragging a few stones up a pyramid.

Now, the really important point I want to make is that *corvée* and our modern forms of taxation are really precisely the same thing. They are both forms of robbery. After all, if a bunch of heavies demanded 30 or 40% of your income every month and threatened you with dire consequences if you didn't comply with their 'request', you'd know very well what was going on. You'd know that you were being robbed. But that is exactly what is going on under Britain's tax system. Only the heavies can't be touched because they just happen to make the law as well. That, however, doesn't remove the fact that these 'establishment' heavies are seizing our property without our consent. Which is unquestionably theft. And just to be as clear as I can here: tax is theft because it is a government/administration/clique/gang transgressing the property rights of an individual – because it can, because it wants to and because the individual can do nothing about it (other than maybe ask a firm of accountants to help him with a bit of valid tax avoidance).

Now, I know there will be some who regard this view as somewhat radical. To those I will point out that the principal beneficiaries of all these taxes appear to be the robbers themselves: that vast host of people who often have (well-protected) jobs for life and armour-plated pensions – or even chauffeur-driven cars of the sort not available to mere tax-paying plebs. And as regards those funds that are left over – for social security, health, infrastructure and whatever – well, this is the principal reason I developed this deep-seated antipathy to tax in the first place. After all, if one wants to spend money in the most inefficient, careless, wasteful and misdirected way possible, it is common knowledge that one puts it into the hands of 'the authorities': those modern-day robber-barons who go about their business under the flag of 'the Democratic Government and the Civil Service'. Much better if all those taxpayers were allowed to keep their property, and sort out what are currently monopolised services for themselves, while, through the sort of charitable giving that was once common in this country, those others in need or who had fallen on hard times could be cared for as required. And so many people would finally be released for productive employment (having all of them lost their Establishment jobs), the amounts available for this charitable giving would no doubt just soar.

Anyway, while you work out just how much my radical views would assist the cause of self-responsibility in this country – and whether my tongue might be nestling firmly in my cheek – I want to end this chapter with something far more important than robbery, and that is the demise of a dog.

Freddie, the best cocker spaniel in the world, who had spent his whole life with us, died in 1998, and his place was now occupied by Max, the next 'best cocker spaniel in the world' who had joined us in 1994. They had shared their doggie lives together for four years, but now Max would have to make do with just Sue and me, and we would have to get by without Freddie. I hope Freddie might not mind my using this tale of his going to state quite categorically that losing a pet, and especially a dog, is no less painful than losing a close relative or a close friend. And if the dog in question is as magic as Freddie was, it can be even more painful. It is the sort of personal emotional experience that can easily reduce one to tears – but one that should always remain personal and not be broadcast on a national news bulletin.

Sorry, Freddie, but I thought I should just get that one in as well. And, by the way, featuring in my autobiography does not amount to a national broadcast. Far from it…

Two Brazilians and Three Books

As one approached it, one was confronted with a floating deck populated by a significant number of irritating sweat bees. Then the first evidence of the lodge proper was a thatched shack and a couple of challenging-looking hammocks. And our actual accommodation, when this came into view, was entirely in keeping with the rest of this isolated establishment. It was a small, unadorned thatched hut, one of just four such huts in the lodge. And we were here in this lodge only because Sue and I had read an article in a Neotropical Bird Club magazine...

Our interest in birds had now become almost serious, and somebody on that Venezuela trip had mentioned this particular magazine, as it was designed to be read by those who were interested in the birds of South and Central America. Sue had a number of its editions, including one in which there was an article about a magical birding destination in Brazil – where the food provided to visiting birders was out of this world. Now, this reference to the quality of the cuisine wasn't just unusual; it was unique. Dedicated birders are interested in only one thing: birds. They are certainly not foodies, and most of them would probably not notice whether they were being fed a beautifully cooked duck confit or a budgerigar's spray of millet. And the fact that a comment on the excellence of some food had found its way into the pages of this earnest birding magazine was quite remarkable – and quite enough to lead us to decide that we ourselves should visit the aforementioned magical birding destination. In autumn 1999.

Well, it just so happened that within walking distance of my Birmingham office was an American Express travel bureau. You know, a physical, pre-online thing, where it was possible to walk through a door, sit down across a desk from a human, and ask him to arrange and then book an expedition to the middle of Brazil – with some R&R at its conclusion in Rio de Janeiro. And even though I'd never in my life had an American Express card, there was no charge whatsoever for this service. Presumably, they earned their income through commissions. And, in this case, they certainly did earn their income. The itinerary took weeks to sort out and went through about eight iterations. And still that guy behind the desk smiled every time I walked through his door. Maybe, I had provided him with a real professional challenge. After all, our getting to that spot in the middle of Brazil would involve a flight to Rio, an onward flight to Sao Paulo, an overnight in Sao Paulo, five flights (in the same plane) into Brazil's interior, an overnight in a place called Alta Floresta in the Mato Grosso, a trip in a 4x4, and then a ride in a tin boat up a river called the Rio Cristalino. In any event, he did a splendid job, even arranging a Bank of England loan for the cost of our business-class flights to and back from Rio. Well, no, but they were the most expensive business-class tickets I've ever acquired. And they had to be acquired. I'd been hooked on business-class flying ever since I'd made those earlier visits to the States (when the firm was paying). And for long hauls I was now an irredeemable junky. There was no way I could manage in economy. Neither, it appeared, could Sue. Which I suppose, in retrospect, was only to be expected.

Anyway, we made it to Rio. Then we made it to Sao Paulo. And after a chain of flights in a modest Embraer that had an outside window in its loo, we made it to Alta Floresta. Then, after an overnight stay, it was just that 4x4 and a small tin boat, navigated to our final destination by our guide for the next ten days: a really delightful guy by the name of Francisco. He spoke no English. Nor did Naira, the provider of that promised good food. And, as no other guests were in residence or were expected for quite some time, these two Brazilians would be our only company for those forthcoming ten days. In what appeared to be something of a dump.

It wasn't just the outward appearance of the Cristalino Lodge that looked a little basic. Everything looked a little basic. Our hut had a wire 'n' wire-coat-hanger wardrobe arrangement, a chair, a couple of candles and a couple of very simple beds (and a tiny, distinctly non-*Grand Designs* bathroom). And that was it. The thatched shack (the dining room/bar) was similarly sparsely furnished, and the whole place was dependent on an ancient diesel engine that ran for just four hours a day. (Visits to the bathroom frequently required a candle.) Oh, and then there were the wild pigs that snuffled around our hut every night, the eruption of termites *in* our hut on one very special night – and the ever-present danger of ticks (of which there were far more than we had encountered in Venezuela).

So, all in all, those ten days spent in that tiny, beyond-rustic lodge in the middle of nowhere turned out to be some of the best days that Sue and I have ever spent on this planet. And to justify that statement, I should probably start with the food, which wasn't just excellent, but literally superb. Naira, who had no real kitchen, but just a cooking area under a shelter, was a culinary genius up there with Raymond Blanc and Paul Bocuse. Her dishes were exquisite – and generous. And each evening, the main meal of the day would be preceded by a bowl of her home-made (of course) salted manioc chips, which were completely irresistible, and then, after the meal, one would be required to tackle one of her preserved sweets – such as cashew fruits in syrup! Just imagine melt-in-the-mouth, syrup-infused, pear-shaped, cashew-tasting bombs of delight, and you'll probably understand how these were just as irresistible as the manioc chips – and why, when we finally returned to Britain, there was a full one stone more of me than there had been when I'd set out from Britain. Naira's food may have been the best I have ever tasted, and it was only right that it should have found its way into the pages of that bird magazine. Indeed, when compared to what's on offer in some of the more pretentious eating places I've encountered, the term 'knocked into a cocked hat' soon has to feature.

However, neither Sue nor I had lost sight of the official reason for our expedition to Cristalino Lodge, which was to soak up the ambience of its surrounding rainforest and to observe some of its wildlife – other than its pigs, termites and ticks. We were not to be disappointed. The forest was primary, which meant that it was as airy as it was fascinating, and it had within it some truly magnificent trees. There was a beautiful (naturally) buttressed fig tree with surface roots spreading out from its trunk that were longer than most trees in Britain are tall. There were a number of Brazil trees, which are so massive, one cannot understand how they just don't sink into the ground. And there were a number of 'walking palms', all equipped with their set of stilt roots, but none of which we ever caught walking. And, of course, in and around these trees were all manner of birds...

As just a sample, may I offer the incredible-looking 'umbrella bird', whose head-crest puts one in mind of the Fonz on speed, or a pair of hyacinth macaws who are the biggest, bluest parrots in the world, or a gang of dark-winged trumpeters who, as they tiptoe through the forest, put one in mind of a troupe of miniature ballerinas. And maybe I should also mention a clutch of nightjars, all resting on a patch of high ground next to a wild pineapple (which is the size my thumb) and not moving even when one almost stands on top of them. Such is their faith in their disguise. And I suppose they know that by being on high ground, they will never be bothered by giant river otters...

Yes, the Cristalino Lodge is on the banks of the Cristalino River, and this river doesn't only attract animals like tapirs and anacondas, but it's also the perfect environment for giant river otters. Or Tarkas on steroids with a mouthful of huge pointed noshers. They were around almost every day, snaking through the water with ease, and making life pretty miserable for anything that lived in that water – as I did for just one of the river's residents, when, with Sue and Francisco, I went fishing for piranha.

My only previous fishing experience was in France, when Sue's first husband, John, had tried to teach me to fly fish. That didn't work out too well, because the only thing I caught was my cheek. However, it would be impossible to injure myself in quite the same way on this occasion, because the fishing involved no more than sitting in Francisco's tin boat, holding a rod supporting a line, at the end of which was a hook baited with a small chunk of meat. Strangely enough, although Francisco was employing exactly the same technique as I was, he caught half a dozen of these little chaps, whereas I managed only one. And I certainly didn't manage to separate him from the hook. I wasn't only squeamish, but I was also very attached to my fingers, and wanted all of them to remain attached to me and not to lose one to a piranha's bite. These guys really do have a terrifying mouthful of teeth. Albeit, one is able to put this out of one's mind when, together with a load of ginger, they have been converted by Naira into a delicious river-fish soup. (Although I still preferred her salted manioc chips…)

Every day at Cristalino brought new pleasures – whether these were observing fireflies, observing (very carefully) the rather more alarming fire ants, or 'just' tasting yet another fabulous dish from Naira's 'jungle kitchen'. And being in the company of two exceptionally nice people who had even fewer words of English between them than we did Portuguese was no problem at all. Indeed, it proved an object lesson in how one can communicate without a common language, even though we had to rule out a debate on the wisdom of investing in floating-rate corporate bonds, and soon had to give up on an exchange of views about the influence of Proust's sexuality on both his wardrobe and his writing. It was going to be something of a wrench to leave this place – and to leave those two brilliant-in-their-own-way Brazilians. I still feel exceptionally lucky that we met them – in such a fabulous situation – and even more so now because I suspect they have been 'obliterated' along with the old lodge. That has now gone, and in its place is the new Cristalino Lodge: a glossy establishment that has various classes of rooms, various classes of 'bungalow', a reading room (!) and even a perishin' conference hall. It all looks very lovely, and, as you will discover, Sue and I have stayed in similarly opulent eco resorts elsewhere. But it's just that in the case of Cristalino, we had been fortunate enough to have tasted the real thing, before it was wiped away and replaced with… well, with something that would be unlikely to have a place for two special Brazilians. I wonder what they're both doing now.

I wonder also whether I should spend too much time describing how our return journey to urban Brazil was interrupted by the weather, meaning we had to spend ten hours at Cuiabá airport to the south of Alta Floresta, waiting for a 3.20 am (!) flight to Sao Paulo – which turned out to be a packed 737 – or whether I should just move on to our arrival at a hotel in Rio, situated just a few yards from Copacabana Beach. Maybe I should choose the latter, and simply mention that one of the first jobs to do in this hotel was to remove a couple of ticks that had concealed themselves in some very awkward places… (This, incidentally, can be best done by applying to the affixed-to-skin ticks a brandy-bottle cork, recently charged with more brandy by holding the bottle upside down. This works. Maybe because ticks are teetotallers. And it is, of course, the only reason we take care always to travel with a bottle of brandy to hand.)

Anyway, we had three days to spend in Rio and a task to complete that was infinitely preferable to tick removal. It was to meet up with one of Sue's childhood friends who now lived in this city, and who had some sort of job with Rolls-Royce. Not the car company but the aero-engine setup. And he did indeed have a job with this firm. It was to head up all its activities in the whole of South America! He was the head honcho, the top guy. And, as became apparent soon after meeting him and his wife, his job came with a very nice BMW and a very nice chauffeur to drive his very nice BMW. And because he would have no immediate need for either his car or his chauffeur, he put both at our disposal for the full three days.

It was a bit of a shock. We had just spent ten days in a beautiful wilderness with only two other people and with not even a bicycle let alone a car anywhere near. But now we were being driven around a teeming metropolis in a shiny black Beemer – avoiding any number of imminent collisions with other cars. Because Carlos (for that was the chauffeur's name) drove everywhere very quickly and often through impossibly small gaps in the traffic. Fortunately, he had retro-fitted the Beemer with a device that could shrink its width to just three feet, and thereby he could avoid all those imminent collisions with ease. Ever since, I've always meant to get a similar device myself.

Anyway, after a visit to that giant super-elegant scarecrow that overlooks Rio de Janeiro from the top of Corcovado – otherwise known as Christ the Redeemer – it was time for Sue and me to fly home from Rio and for me to start thinking about how to lose that extra stone. And I would also have to start thinking about what to do with the rest of my life…

I had now spent just over half a century of my allotted span. And not knowing the full length of that allotment, I was beginning to think that I should make damn sure that what was left of my life was utilised in the best way possible, which meant in a way that best reflected my interests, my ambitions, my desires and my dreams (none of which conflicted with Sue's).

I have already made passing references to population growth and to this population's less than admirable treatment of wildlife. Well, I was now aware that the world's population had grown by almost two and a half times since I was born, and I had witnessed first-hand what this frightening growth rate was doing to the world: how it was not only decimating its wildlife or simply swallowing up its wilderness, but how it was also despoiling the world. In so many places where mankind had made its mark it had also made a mess. The world was not covered in pretty Cotswold villages; it was covered in shacks, hovels, slums – and waste and filth. This was the nature of the suburbs of Rio, the great concrete expanses of Sao Paulo, much of Dar es Salaam, and even many of the settlements in Zanzibar and Mauritius. And things were not going to get any better. There would be no relief for the world from the burgeoning masses of people yet to be added to its burden, and certainly no relief for all the world's hard-pressed fauna and flora. These were already on a path to devastation or, in the worst cases, extinction.

So... Sue and I, probably shortly after our return from Brazil, made a decision. And this was a simple decision: it was to see as much of the world's natural treasures as we could before they had been ravaged by the onslaught of man. We would travel to as many wild places as possible, with probably a focus on rainforests and other tropical environments and, although it wasn't clear at the time, with an increasing focus on Africa. France might see us at some point, and there might even be the odd appointment with a beach somewhere. But our priority would be wilderness destinations in all their many forms – while there were still some wilderness destinations remaining.

This isn't, incidentally, a retrospective interpretation of our worldview at that time. And I can be certain of this because I had already embarked on one other activity that would be a focus of my remaining time on Earth, and this was the writing of books! And not just any old books, but books that dealt with what we were doing to the planet and how we weren't winning many awards for our performance. Oh, and these books were supposed to be funny (to sweeten their serious message).

I can't now remember quite when I wrote my original three masterworks, the three books that delivered their castigation of our behaviour through documenting the adventures of an ex-accountant in the far distant future. But I do remember that some of this writing was begun on some of those last beach holidays and that some of the books' contents reflected my experiences of both Tanzania and Brazil.

As I'm sure you are now all thirsting for just a little more information on this seminal trilogy (all involving that ex-accountant, one Renton Tenting), I can tell you that the first book had, and still has, the title of *Dumpiter*. It is an absolutely cracking story, with, as its focus, a planet (called Dumpiter) which is the most abused, polluted and generally screwed-up planet in the universe. It is the universe's appallingly managed breaker's yard, and it was meant to represent all the despoilment I had already witnessed on my travels. But unlike that despoilment, there might just be a chance that Dumpiter's condition will be addressed. Although you'll have to read the book yourself to find out whether it is.

Then comes *Ticklers*, which is more an oblique assault on our behaviour in that it deals with mankind's greed. It was also an exercise in catharsis that enabled me to deal with some of the 'less than equitable' stuff that was going on in Deloitte at the time. But if pressed on that aspect, I shall deny it with the threat of legal action if necessary. Or I might just invite those doing the pressing to read the final work in the trilogy, which is *Lollipop*.

This story concerns an enormous spaceship that caters for both the normal and the aberrant sexual demands of its fare-paying passengers, but that is, in fact, no more than a warning that we should not export our destructive habits to other worlds. Just because we've wreaked so much damage on our own planet, we shouldn't think that it is a good idea to replicate our global mutilation on other worlds. Particularly by our colonising them and then indulging in our favourite pastime of breeding out of control and overwhelming the indigenous inhabitants – whether these inhabitants are anything like ourselves or more like any of the more benign creatures that are desperately trying to cling onto an existence on our own increasingly fucked-up world.

I should point out that all three of these works of genius were written in the period just before the end of the millennium and just after it, but they did not appear as published works until sometime later. But that is to broach the subject of the world of publishing – and especially the world of literary agents. And, as I haven't preceded this chapter with an X rating, I think it would be sensible to leave all that stuff for later on in this tome.

Instead, I will mention just one last aspect of our excursion to Brazil. Which is that I suspect that it was while we were completely cut off from the rest of the world in the Cristalino Lodge, that the all-important national referendum took place in Britain. You know, the one where we were asked whether we wanted to move from what was essentially a reasonably healthy monoculture society to an exciting multicultural one. And, you know, as much as I have attempted to discover the detailed results of what was obviously a 'yes' vote (was it a landslide or a marginal win?) I have been unable to find anything. Nor have I been able to find out why we were prepared to take such a reckless step into the unknown. How, for goodness' sake, did any of the Baby Boomers vote 'yes'? And heck, they're often the only people who bother to vote.

Ah well, one day I might find out a little more. And in the meantime, I will comfort myself with the knowledge that whatever we do to dismantle what I and my fellow Baby Boomers knew as our own country, this will pale into insignificance when set against what everybody around the world is doing to bring this planet to its knees. We are, after all, 'all doomed'. And we were already doomed, of course, before we entered the new millennium. Which, even back in 1999, I suspected would never earn the title of 'the golden millennium'.

And, on that optimistic note, I will finish this chapter – and maybe once again Google '1999 referendum in Britain'. There must be something about it somewhere…

Cadillac, Rover and Land Rover

Well, the new millennium arrived – without any noticeable millennium bugs – and, to begin with, it didn't look too bad. All the tall buildings in New York were still standing. Trump was still just a sideshow – in the 'objectionable hustler' tent. The finance industry hadn't yet perfected its 'let's put the world into meltdown' routine. And taking long-haul flights hadn't yet become a capital offence...

Now, just a word about this last item – before I move on to my taking one of the many such flights Sue and I would take over the coming few years. And it's really a heartfelt defence of what, within the context of the undeniable impact of air travel on global warming, will be seen as our increasingly irresponsible actions.

I could start by stating the bleedin' obvious. Which is that it's all a bit too late now, and that however few aeroplanes take to the sky, it's not going to make a blind bit of difference to the forthcoming roasting of the world. But that's too easy. Instead, I would like to point out that many wild places in this world – and their constituent wildlife – are entirely dependent on revenues earned from overseas visitors, most of whom would not be prepared to swim and walk thousands of miles to reach them. When recently surveyed, 99.99% of these potential visitors said they would only go to that reserve in Botswana or Guyana if they could climb aboard a jet in order to get there. (The other 0.01% comprised a mix of journalists and celebrities who were not sufficiently acquainted with world geography [or much of anything else] to make a reasoned response.) Anyway, the point is that the immediate survival of countless animals and birds – and insects and trees, etc etc – depends on somebody coming to observe them. If that doesn't continue to some degree, then they will all be long gone, well before our planet resembles a giant baked potato.

Then there is the matter of 'credit'. And I can think of no simpler way of explaining this than to ask you whether two people who make a few trips on aeroplanes will end up doing more damage to the Earth than somebody like Ursula von der Leyen, the current president of the European Union, who has burdened this planet with seven children. After all, at least some of these kids will no doubt go on to use jet aeroplanes themselves and may well have seven children of their own – who, in turn, will want to fly and have numerous offspring – or, just possibly, have far fewer children, because they will see that primarily it is the number of people on this planet that is set to destroy it, and that the habits of these people are almost incidental. Which means that Sue and I – who never signed up to be procreators – might just have more credit to use (on air flights) than all those intemperate shaggers who believe it is quite in order to leave a mark of their time on Earth in the form of more kids than there are in a reception class of goats.

Incidentally, neither Sue nor I are looking for an award for our not inaugurating more new lives. We certainly didn't take this path for altruistic reasons. But we both get a bit pissed off when we hear – as we did recently – somebody like the co-leader of the UK's Green Party, assuring people that they should have as many little sprogs as they like, just as long as they don't ever step foot on an aircraft. Which is so the wrong way round, so illustrative of misunderstanding the nature of the problem and so simply naïve, that I can only think that the 'Green' in Green Party refers to the expression 'green behind the ears'. It certainly can't refer to preserving green places around the world by enabling paying punters to visit them. But there again, one always has to bear in mind that sagacity is a distinct rarity in virtually all our politicians…

Anyway, now I've got all that off my chest, I can tell you about our first long-haul trip of the new millennium, which, had it been a few years earlier, would have been to British Honduras but, because we were so dilatory, was to Belize. (British Honduras had a name makeover in 1973, prior to it gaining full independence from Britain in 1981.) Our itinerary had been put together by Reef and Rainforest Tours, a point I mention because this firm would go on to arrange a number of our future expeditions. Our first overnight was (unavoidably) in Belize City, the capital of Belize, and an example of a certain lack of imagination concerning the naming of capitals prevalent throughout the whole of Central America. (Just think Panama City, Guatemala City and Mexico City, and you'll understand what I mean.)

The only event worth mentioning during our stay in Belize City took place when Sue and I – and her mum – had together just seated ourselves at a table of one of the city's nicer restaurants. This table was on an exposed verandah, which offered no defence whatsoever against the Queen Kong of mosquitoes who, before I had even taken my napkin from its ring, landed on the very centre of my forehead and there proceeded to insert her lance-length proboscis into my skin. It was a warning – as if I needed it – that Belize was a tropical destination, teeming with mosquitoes, all of which were probably aware of my arrival.

There were certainly a few more of them at our first jungle destination, a place in the country's interior, reached by a small plane and bearing the name Chan Chich Lodge. It is still there, and it still looks much as it did in 2000. I wonder therefore whether it still has the same miserable lodge manager and the same miserable lodge food. It also, of course, had, and presumably still has, much to recommend it, including oropendolas, bat falcons, ocellated turkeys, tarantulas and three-inch-long cockroaches that look like fallen leaves – but maybe it no longer has a white 1970s Cadillac to take its guests to their next destination.

Actually, I don't think it was the lodge's Cadillac, but instead it was the property of its driver, who usually hired it out for weddings but, when business was a bit thin, wasn't put off by the prospect of driving it along unmade jungle roads – and even roads that took him through the realms of the Mennonites!

Now, I have to take a couple of steps back here, and first of all add to that earlier statement that many of the wild places in this world are sustained by paying visitors. And this addition is to note that many of those wild places are still there to sustain at all because they are owned and protected by wealthy individuals. It is something that Sue and I had already observed in Venezuela and Brazil, and would go on to observe in places as far apart as Madagascar, Namibia and Panama. Furthermore, we had just experienced this 'survival of the finest' approach in Belize, in that Chan Chich sits in a huge stretch of pristine forest, owned by one of the country's richest men (who, I think, owned the country's biggest brewery). Indeed, having left Chan Chich, we remained in this pristine patch of the world for quite some time, and right up until our Cadillac entered the neighbouring Mennonite territory, which is my cue to go much further back in this book and pile even more opprobrium onto… religions. And certainly onto those religions that actively seek to desecrate the world.

Yes, I'm talking about Mennonites: a bunch of characters superficially like the Amish in their dress and habits, but more like barbarians with bulldozers when it comes to their treatment of the natural world. Unfortunately for that part of the natural world within the borders of Belize, a number of them had arrived in this country some time ago, and had proceeded to 'farm with no regard for environmental laws', and to 'use farming practices that lead to widespread deforestation'.

However, those statements simply cannot convey just how destructive these buggers have been in their desire to feed their oversized families – with no regard whatsoever for what their God supposedly put on this world for us all. I, also, will find it very difficult to convey just how destructive they have been, but I'll give it a try. And I'll do this by asking you to imagine sitting in the back of a white Cadillac being driven through the deep greenery of a tropical forest when, without any warning, it comes to a turn in the track where the forest stops abruptly and in its place is a vast landscape of ravaged vegetation, acre upon brown acre of chopped-down and ripped-up trees, with not a single tree left standing anywhere. This wasn't just shocking; it was gut-wrenchingly awful. And it definitely didn't do too much to lessen my antipathy towards religions. Furthermore, it was also a very important event in the development of my view of all mankind in its treatment of the natural world. What had been some serious reservations were now stiffening into rock-hard convictions. In fact, almost as rock-hard as the space between the ears of all those fuck-awful Mennonites. I just hope that if I'm wrong and there is a God, he makes it known to them in the afterlife that he much preferred the world he created to the miserable one they did with the help of chainsaws and bulldozers. And Joseph and Mary didn't have ten kids either…

Fortunately, the devastation eventually ran out, and our Cadillac was able to complete our journey through more greenery before depositing us at another jungle lodge, this one next to a lagoon and near some famous Mayan ruins, and bearing the name Lamanai Outpost Lodge. Well, the highlights of this place in no particular order were a real Mayan guide – who took us to those Mayan ruins – some night-time birding, an early-morning canoe ride across the lagoon, a snakeskin sloughed overnight in our cabin, an absence of Mennonites, and a nearby airstrip from which we could fly to the south of Belize, to make our way to one of its offshore cayes.

This final destination had no highlights, but just a series of drawbacks, which, in no particular order, were the amount of open water between it and the mainland (which had to be negotiated in a worryingly small open boat), the accommodation in the form of a room in an old wooden-built former convent, a copious number of sandflies, truly dreadful food, and defective door furniture. This last item merits a brief explanation, because the defective door furniture in question was on a door that connected our room to the one adjoining. It appeared to be up to the job of supporting Sue's wet swimsuit when she hung it there on the second night of our stay. But, as became apparent in the very early morning, it was not. The swimsuit's weight had caused the door furniture to 'subside' and thereby to let that door swing open into the adjoining room.

I noticed this as I woke, and I immediately thought the door would be better closed, even if it meant reaching into that other room – while I was still stark naked. So, I did. And I was thereby immediately presented with the opportunity to nod a morning greeting to the couple who were still in bed in that room but not asleep. Instead, they were staring at me in disbelief.

Well, that was it. We would be leaving the far-from-paradise island as soon as we could, even if it meant an unscheduled overnight in an 'international' Belize City hotel – and, in due course, another unexpected event involving the occupants of a next-door room (to which there was another connecting, not very sound-proof door). This probably involved some nudity as well. Because – to cut a long story short – it involved a lady in that room whose vocal emanations put me in mind of a bird we had heard earlier on the trip, which rejoices in the wonderful name of a screaming piha. Although, I have to say, she was a great deal louder than any piha, and she'd probably consumed rather more piña coladas than any piha ever had before she'd got herself into that screaming situation. She could probably have been heard in Guatemala. And, if orgasmic screaming had been an Olympic event, Belize would no doubt have been assured of its first ever gold…

Anyway, approximately forty-eight hours later, having got back to Britain, I was driving down the M40 to embark on a further forty-eight hours – in which I would be allowed to sleep for no more than two hours. On that first Sunday back, I had received – mid-afternoon – a telephone call from one of my Deloitte partners to tell me that he, another couple of partners and myself, had until just Tuesday morning to put together a deal to buy the Rover Group from BMW. And I had better get my skates on and get down to London. This I did later that afternoon, and the magic of my Belize adventure was immediately replaced by the demands of trying to do the impossible in an impossibly short timescale.

However, by having those two hours of sleep that night – and none the next – the impossible was achieved, and for just £10, the 'Phoenix Four' became the owners of an iconic manufacturer of British cars. I don't remember too much of what went on in that manic marathon, but I do remember driving back up the M40 around lunchtime on that deal-securing Tuesday, with the windows of my car fully open and lots of vigorous thigh-slapping to help me keep awake.

I felt very proud of our combined achievements. And when, in due course, I'd prepared some completion accounts that led to BMW having to throw in an additional engine factory and a few other odds and sods to make up for a deficiency of net assets I'd identified, I felt even prouder. Needless to say, that was a high point in pride terms, and in due course my involvement in the Rover group would first become something of a trial and ultimately one of the reasons I would seek early retirement. But that's a story yet to be told, and meanwhile I can't leave the year 2000 without mentioning that it was a year rounded off with Sue and I making what would prove to be the first of many expeditions to Namibia and Botswana.

OK. Let's kick off with a spot of instruction on the first of that pair of countries, Namibia, and in particular let's see what of its features might make it a very attractive destination. Well, to start with, it is the second least densely populated nation on the planet (after Mongolia – and if you don't count Greenland, which isn't yet a proper nation). Even now, it has a population of just 2.6 million people in a country that is well over three times the size of Britain. Next: it is very warm there, not to say hot, but also so dry that mosquitoes just can't cope. You'll only ever find them in the extreme north of the country where it abuts Angola. Furthermore, the locals speak English, and they drive on the right side of the road – that is to say, the left. Then, not to be forgotten is the fact that it is noted for its wildlife and, in particular, for its birdlife. And in addition to its many private reserves, it hosts a national park (the Etosha National Park) which, at 22,270 square kilometres, is slightly bigger than Israel.

The positives just keep coming, and they, of course, include quite a few positive negatives (apart from the lack of mozzies). For example, there is barely any traffic on Namibia's roads, and these roads lack any (fixed) speed traps. There are certainly no smart motorways. There are no congestion zones and no low-emission zones. There are none of *those* caravan sites. There are no fashionable hotspots. There is no Channel 4 News, no London elite, no Emily Maitlis, and no Kay Burley. And there are no Kardashians, no fundamentalists, no Chechens, and no Mennonites!

So, it can be no great surprise that this is the country that Sue and I chose as our reintroduction to Africa, and that because it is next door to Namibia, we tacked on a visit to Botswana as well. It was probably one of the best decisions we had ever made, and this became only too evident when we had begun to taste what the first of these two remarkable countries really had to offer.

We were going to see it with a guy called Uanee, and with his helper and general dog's body, another guy called Jan. Uanee and Jan were both employees of the Sandyacre Safari company, but they were very different in appearance terms, Uanee being a six-foot-six black guy, and Jan being the same colour but much smaller and not much more than about half of Uanee's body weight. Oh, and all four of us would be travelling around in an extended-wheelbase Land Rover, with a trailer towed behind.

Our itinerary would be the 'standard itinerary for beginners', and it therefore kicked off with a visit to Sossusvlei in the Namib desert to see the stunning sand dunes, followed by a stop in the distinctly German-flavoured town of Swakopmund. (Namibia was, after all, formerly a German colony, and the Germans had very much left their mark.) After Swakopmund, it was a spot of camping on the banks of the (dry) Huab River, before making our way to the magic Etosha Park, and from there it was a drive back south to the private reserve of Okonjima. This would be our last stop prior to our returning to our starting point of Windhoek, in readiness for our flight to Botswana.

A report on all we did and all we saw would be tedious in the extreme. Suffice to say that we had decided even before we had got back to Windhoek that we would be returning to this country, although on that second visit we would try not to embarrass ourselves by again mistaking the herd of donkeys that had made a middle-of-the-night pass of our tent on the Huab for a herd of elephants. As Uanee had explained the next morning, had they been elephants, he would not have been out of his own tent trying to shoo them away. That was about as likely as our arriving at any of our destinations, and Uanee not 'meeting up' with one of the many girlfriends he had stashed all around the country. He was a very popular boy.

He was, nevertheless, quite cautious (in certain other respects). And he warned us to be on our guard in Botswana, where the local guides were quite reckless, and quite oblivious of the dangers to which they were exposing their clients. However, he need not have worried. Our guides in Botswana – in its wonderful Okavango Delta – always had our welfare in mind, even if they did sometimes get us very close to animals with large teeth and exclusively carnivore habits. But we hardly noticed, such was the paradisiacal quality of this unique watery environment. It was another place that we knew we would visit again, and I am afraid there will be a few more references to it in the forthcoming chapters. But for now, I will limit myself to comments on just two of its features. The first is that it is furnished with some of the most beautiful (small) safari camps anywhere in the world (of which Little Vumbura, our accommodation for this trip, is just one). And the second is that it is not furnished with mosquitoes! What looks like an insect-infested swamp from the window of the four-seater aircraft that takes you into the delta is in fact a huge tract of crystal-clear water studded with islands – and that water is running water. Nowhere is it stagnant, and that means nowhere does it provide a nursery for mosquitoes.

Shit! Two wildlife-filled countries without one particular species of wildlife. How could we not return to them both? Especially when, on top of all I've already explained, Namibia has some of the most scenic landscapes in the world, Botswana has some of the best safari nosh in the world – and there is a guy in Windhoek who is a fount of knowledge on both countries. This is Martin Webb-Bowen, the owner of what was then the small Sandyacre Safari company – soon to become the much larger Ultimate Safaris company. Just as Martin was to become our friend and the organiser of a whole string of our visits to that part of the world.

All in all, taking account of our African trip, that earlier sortie to Belize – and that Rover stuff – it had been an interesting and enjoyable start to the new millennium. And this first year with a '2' at its beginning was also something of a catalyst. It certainly increased the rate at which we wanted to explore the world – before the Mennonites and much of the rest of mankind had reduced it to a wasteland. And it probably increased the rate at which I would become disillusioned with being an accountant, especially one with a part-responsibility for Rover.

However, that is something to deal with in due course, and I should probably end this chapter with the recognition of another recognition. And this is the recognition that I was a really lucky bastard – one who could travel to wherever I wanted to in the world, and at the same time contemplate a very early retirement. And even better, I wasn't a blasted Mennonite and I never would be!

Population and Papua

Well, 2001 dawned, and it didn't feel very Stanley Kubrick. It just felt like the year that followed on from 2000, and it probably reminded some of us that when writing about the future, it is as well to write about the far distant future – so that your imagined future isn't overtaken by the mundane reality of the actual future. I mean, had George Orwell still been alive in 1984, he might have been hugely embarrassed to witness not a dystopia populated by perpetual wars, omnipresent government surveillance, incessant government propaganda, rewriting of the historical record and an all-powerful brigade of thought police – all of which would not arrive for another thirty years – but instead a dystopia populated by Torvill and Dean, *The Price is Right* and women's shoulder pads.

Anyway, to return to 2001, why don't I start with a reference to yet another overseas excursion, if for no other reason than to reinforce the impression that my life had become nothing more than a succession of exotic holidays – when the truth was that it was a succession of increasingly arduous work demands, where I had to come up for air occasionally to retain my sanity. (And that statement is only a mild exaggeration. Being a partner in Deloitte – now with a responsibility for something called Rover – was definitely not getting any easier.)

OK, with the record now set straight, I'll first of all tell you where in the world we went on that overseas excursion. It was to Mauritius again – for a slice of genuine do-nothing R&R over Easter. We stayed at a resort called Le Touessrok, a fairly sumptuous resort where we could easily convince ourselves that we were 'off grid' and I could forget all about Deloitte for at least ten days. Or so I thought…

It happened on our first day there – when Sue and I were soaking up the sun on the beach. There, walking towards our loungers, was one of my Deloitte partners together with his wife. And five minutes later another one arrived – with his wife. Now, whether or not this congregation of so many Deloitte partners in one tropical location was connected with Le Touessrok sounding suspiciously like an exotic rendering of our firm's former name, I do not know. But what I do know is that we all agreed to ignore each other for the entire duration of our stay. After all, none of us had travelled 6,000 miles to spend even more time with our work colleagues. It was, of course, just a coincidence, but it did encourage Sue and me to think about where it might be safe to go in the world for this sort of coincidence not to recur. Somewhere a little less sumptuous possibly, and a little more off any beaten track. Somewhere like Papua New Guinea for example…

OK. Lecture warning. Because I think I am now obliged to use that reference to 'off the beaten track' – and what this generally implies in terms of a paucity of other humans – to reveal my thoughts on the more normal situation of an abundance of people. And what I mean are those thoughts alluded to already and, by 2001, now firmly established in my mind, concerning the world's excessive population, and how it might be just a tad problematical. Indeed, how it might be much more than a tad problematical, and so much so that for many years now, I have regarded it as the single greatest problem facing every representative of life on this planet. Essentially, most of the shit going on in the world just now is down to there being far, far too many people, with only the promise of more in the pipeline. And I will now elaborate, not on the 'shit' aspect of that statement (that is scheduled for later on), but on just how far, far too many of us there are, and where our prodigious profusion will almost inevitably lead. So, you have been warned…

To start with I am going to invite you to imagine that you are one of the strange-looking inhabitants of that far distant planet of Priapismia (you know, the one that Mark Zuckerberg came from). If you can then also imagine that you and your fellow Priaprismians have, through your advanced technology, been observing the development of human life on our planet for the last ten millennia, what do you think would be the one aspect of this 'development' that really stood out? Would it be the abandonment of our hunter-gatherer existence for a more settled one? Would it be the unfortunate Teflon qualities of certain religions? Would it be the adoption in so many cultures of the concept of outerwear and underwear? Or might it be a more recent aspect of human development, like the desire to eliminate all unwanted body hair or to eliminate any vestiges of common sense with the aid of social media?

Well, I strongly suspect it would be none of the above, because first and foremost it would be the exponential growth in the human population. And it has been exponential. How else can one describe a population of *Homo sapiens* that has grown from maybe four million 10,000 years ago to one approaching 8,000 million now? And to reinforce the exponential flavour of this growth, may I point out that to get to the first 1,000 million (now referred to as a less worrying 'billion'), it took us all the time from when we emerged as an identifiable species right up until when Napoleon Bonaparte was proclaimed Emperor of France – in 1804 – and may I then ask you to compare that length of time to the mere dozen or so years it took us to add our latest billion. Or… another way of getting a handle on just how fast we're adding to our numbers is to consider that the number of babies now born every ten days is equivalent to that entire world population just 10,000 years ago. And that's an awful lot of babies to add to that huge pile of humanity that now carpets the world. Indeed, one is almost tempted to make a reference to shag carpets. But that would be indelicate, and instead I will make a brief reference to where this exponential growth is now largely being fuelled.

Yes, I hardly need say this, but there are certain countries whose indigenous populations have worked out that for life to be good, its womenfolk do not need to be continuously popping out more humans. That having one, two or even three children per family makes for a desirable existence not only for that family, but also for the entire nation. After all, stability in numbers more often than not creates a path to sustainable prosperity. On the other hand, there are (many) countries where the male of the species still appears to measure his worth in his ability to inflate both his wife's tummy and his country's already burgeoning population. Anything up to five is good but, especially if you're trying to outbreed your antagonistic neighbours, ten is even better.

I won't name any of these clearly culpable countries, but I will direct you to consider the nationality of all those poor wretches trying to make their way into Europe, and you then won't have too much difficulty in identifying the countries I have in mind. Or… if you are encountering any difficulty, may I advise you to look at Pakistan, the population of which has increased five-fold since I was born, or Iraq, the population of which has increased eight-fold (!) in the same short period. And that, incidentally, is to discount all the natives of those countries who have moved generally northwards to various other countries.

Anyway, this focus on how individual countries might be contributing to the expansion of humanity is probably counterproductive, because it detracts from the main point I'm trying to make, which is the point I attempted to highlight by asking you to adopt the dispassionate perspective of a distant alien. Only by doing this, I believe, will you be able to see the real calamity of what is happening in our world. And I say that because I am convinced that most of us are far too close to this calamity to see it as a calamity at all. We might all be aware that 'the world's population is growing', but how many of us have got to grips with the speed of that growth? Tripling our numbers in just my lifetime (as of now) is fucking scary. And it's just a pity that we haven't all been scared into celibacy for the foreseeable future.

Well, the good news is… this can't go on forever. Indeed, various pundits have claimed that the world's population will soon plateau out at somewhere around ten billion, at which point the world will probably hold a party. I mean, if we can keep our numbers down to that modest total – while at the same time raising the standard of living for all to what is currently enjoyed in the West – the world will only have to find another five or so worlds to provide us with all our needs. So, that should be OK then, shouldn't it? However, there is always the possibility that those various pundits are wrong, and that the population will just keep growing and growing – until it collapses into either a remnant population or no population at all…

Much as we would like to, we cannot deny that we are animals. And, as animals, we are susceptible to animal phenomena. Such as what inevitably follows the explosive increase in numbers seen in animals such as locusts, rats or mice – which is a dramatic plunge in their numbers as they exhaust the resources on which they depend. (Which might just ring a few bells.) Of course, if this happens to us, it won't be because we have eaten every available leaf or every available lump of cheese, but because our out-of-control numbers will have precipitated some other sort of population-slimming or population-eradication event.

I won't give you specific odds, but grilling ourselves with some super worldwide fission or fusion event always remains a possibility, and with the ever-increasing number of megalomaniacal leaders in the world, it's a possibility that is not decreasing. Alternatively, we might just screw up our planet so well that it can no longer support us, and we will just end up with a giant squabble over the remaining scraps that leads to our extinction. Or – and this is where I'd put my money – we can rely on the assistance of pathogens, all those millions of bacteria and viruses that we think we've overcome, when all we've done is win a few skirmishes with them. And already they're regrouping – and our only response is to do everything we can to help them when they come back to finish us off...

I mean, not only are we assisting them by overusing antibiotics, dosing our food animals with the stuff, and providing pathogens with air transport all around the world, but some of us (mention no names) are encouraging them to jump from other animal species to ourselves. And we're doing this by scoffing any wild animal that holds out the promise of an interesting new taste – whether this is a very rare species of armadillo or a nearly extinct species of bat. Covid-19, my friends, will prove to be not at all unique, but just the harbinger of yet more 'presents from the East', some of which will be only mildly problematical, and some of which will be absolutely deadly. Right up until the winning, deadliest-of-all pathogen spoils it for all those still to come by wiping us out entirely.

I know this sounds melodramatic or even Jeremiah-ish in the extreme – depending on your individual perspective. But, in my defence, there is no denying what is the indelible hallmark of all these pathogens, and this is their resilience. Unlike us, they have been around for millions of years, and over those years they have learnt to endure. That's why they're in that regrouping mode, organising themselves with mutations and overproduction, so that when they make their final push, we won't stand a chance. Their resilience will come to the fore, and our lack of resilience – and our hubris – will finally be exposed. Just before we're wiped out in our millions...

But now for the punchline, the line of words that will give away the fact that I've been intentionally over the top, and that the idea of our organising our own extinction, rather than our going on to build a world that is better in every possible way, is as nonsensical as a week-long course of unconscious bias training. And this is... Ah, wait a minute, there doesn't seem to be a punchline. Maybe I wasn't being over the top at all, and we are all doomed. Aye, all doomed, ah tell yee. All doomed. An' yers only get yersel' to blame...

Uhm, sorry about that. I seemed to have slipped into a bit of John Laurie there, and I'll try not to do that again. Even if we are all bloody doomed. Instead, I'll leave you to chew over all my words on overpopulation and where this will lead – sometime later – and meanwhile invite you to join me in that place that triggered all those words in the first place, the remarkable nation of Papua New Guinea. Or I will, just as soon as I've made a few choice remarks about a particular handful of our abundant humanity – a handful that proved beyond doubt that there are creatures on this Earth that are comparable to excrement, but only in the sense that, in comparison to excrement, they are infinitely less desirable.

We're now in September 2001. So, no great surprise that what I'm talking about here is that gang of evil bastards who thought that flying jet airliners into the Twin Towers – and into the Pentagon – might in some way lead them to a distorted form of enlightenment, but not, of course, any of us who hadn't yet bequeathed our minds to a medieval brand of superstition. Who cannot remember where they were when they heard the news of this horrendous event – or saw it revealing itself in all its grisly detail? I can certainly remember where I was. Just as I can remember the bravery on show that day, the shock and grief so apparent on so many faces – and the dancing for joy in the streets of Gaza, along with the subsequent revelation that many of those noble warriors were spawned in the easy-going kingdom of Saudi Arabia. What we'd witnessed on that fateful day was, it appeared, not just the destruction of some valuable real estate and the murder of a multitude of innocent people, but also the erection of a signpost, a signpost to where the world was inexorably moving. And all these years on we are still moving in that divisive – and regressive – direction…

But to return to that trip to Papua New Guinea, which was undertaken just a couple of months after the US attacks, I have to say that the only obvious immediate consequence of those outrages was that the aircraft making its way to Port Moresby, the capital of PNG, contained plenty of empty seats. Understandably, many Americans had suddenly lost a taste for getting anywhere near a plane, and certainly one that might be on its way to a part of the world that has nothing in common with America. Indeed, it was undeniable back then – and it might still be now – that PNG has very little in common with anywhere else in the world. It is the one place on this planet that I have visited that could well be on another planet. Or, if one accepts that it is on this planet, then not on the one we experience today, but on another that existed in the long distant past.

This first became apparent when, after a long internal flight from Port Moresby, we arrived in PNG's tree-covered highlands. Because, waiting by the side of the grass runway to greet our plane were hundreds of men who were either from a planet seven light years away or from the dim distant past of our own. Or maybe they had just dressed that way because they thought David Attenborough was on the plane. You must have seen his programmes – from a time when the colour balance on your telly was between light grey and dark grey – and you must therefore have seen the Papuan natives in their elaborate headdresses and their un-ironed loincloths, all sporting large strings of beads about their chests. Well, they are real, and they don't dress like that simply for the visitors; they just dress like that full stop. Largely, I think, because they have little to do other than ensure that the women in their societies look after the pigs properly and do just about every other job. But that might be a little unfair, and it would, after all, be really peculiar to encounter a society anywhere in the world where the men did everything and the women did very little. Furthermore, it would be to ignore that the men most certainly did do their bit when there was any beer in the offing…

We were staying in a lodge in the highlands, which was really rather pleasant, except it didn't stock any beer. This was due to the fact that the locals went all Dick Turpin when a supply lorry from Port Moresby (having spent a laborious three days on the 'road') finally arrived in their neck of the woods and was in some way identified as carrying any of this particular brewed beverage. Then they simply relieved it of its cargo of canned beer and lager without first asking permission to do so. However, they had no taste for spirits or wine. Accordingly, these were the only alcoholic drinks these supply lorries now carried. And this really worked. It meant that there was no longer any more of that Dick Turpin behaviour – but also no refreshing lagers for the lodge's patrons. And quenching a thirst after an excursion in tropical heat with a glass of red or a glass of whisky just doesn't work. And one really might want to do this after one has conducted a very rewarding birdwatching foray in the company of a local bird guide and a man with an AK47...

I don't want to disparage these Papuan chaps more than I have to, but they did add a certain frisson to our stay in this highland area, and that AK47 wasn't entirely for show. Indeed, I well remember one night in our insubstantial reed and grass lodge cabin (when we were the lodge's only guests), hearing what sounded like beer-induced revelry not that far away, which at the time was a little unnerving to say the least. Then there was the fact that our next scheduled destination in PNG had to be replaced with another at the last minute because the locals there had either hijacked a whole convoy of beer-carrying lorries – or had got their hands on some recently matured home brew (I can't remember which) – and it was considered far too dangerous for us to get anywhere near them. Nevertheless, it is incumbent on me to point out that however threatening these highland folk might appear to have been, it was not 'foreigners' who had to worry, but their highland folk neighbours or the local officers of the law. A month after our return to Britain, I read of an attack on the police station next to that grass runway, where for some reason, probably not unconnected with the scarcity of booze, a group of the locals had actually hacked to death four of its unfortunate resident constables. An act which invites no irreverent remarks whatsoever.

Instead, I shall restore some balance to this commentary on the menfolk of PNG by saying just a few words about those we encountered in villages along the country's Sepik River. This was our revised destination – not the series of villages themselves, but a wonderful riverboat called the *Sepik Spirit*, which transported a dozen or so of us along the river to visit these villages. Well, all the men – and all the women – in these remote settlements were absolutely delightful. Just like the villages themselves, which were made up of huge traditional houses, all built from timber, bamboo and coconut leaves, and all beautiful enough to pass for some Hollywood romanticised version of a 'tropical native dwelling'. They were that exquisite. And their inhabitants... Well, they were polite, engaging, very friendly, and one of them had a brother at Oxford University. Oh, and another of them had something he wanted to show us. He was the chief in one of the villages, and in a corner of his vast longhouse into which we'd been invited, was a small wooden tray. And when he pulled out the tray, it became apparent immediately that it was the tray on which he kept his cache of two shrunken heads...

Our Papuan guide, a splendid guy called August, was traumatised. He had never seen shrunken heads before, and even though the chief assured him that they were a relic from the past, and that his family had long since abandoned the practice of miniaturising the noggins of their neighbours, he was only really happy when he was out of the longhouse and using the odd local bird to provide both us and himself with a suitable distraction. Maybe he had a family ancestor who, at some point in the past, had suffered a similarly dramatic reduction in his hat size, and it wasn't a cherished recollection. In any event, he soon got over it, and in due course we were able to discuss not only the less desirable aspects of PNG's former cultures but also some of the more commendable ones that still existed. Because August was accompanying us to our next destination. This was a fairly conventional hotel on PNG's north coast, with a less than conventional hornbill that lived in its restaurant – and with just three patrons: Sue, me and August. Those monsters in New York really had dissuaded a lot of Americans from flying...

Anyway, this is where I need to emphasise that, despite those scary aspects of the highlands, Papua New Guinea is populated by a lot of very amiable, very capable people, and in 2001 it was still something of a paradise and certainly a country like no other in the world. Its geography and its remoteness had held it back in economic and Western terms, but those same features had preserved what is now a growing rarity in this world: a land still covered in its native flora and occupied by diverse groups of people still enjoying the certainties and the reassurance of a traditional life.

It isn't, of course, a real paradise, and many of those people living that wholesome traditional life might readily swap more than just their traditions to get a working clinic less than three days' walk away. Furthermore, a country filled with so many different tribes speaking so many different languages is a bit of a breeding ground for the abuse of power by those who rise above their tribal roots and end up with regional or national responsibilities. The 'big man' culture was very much alive and well in PNG in 2001, and this meant that those powerful 'big men' were almost expected to use their power for their own benefit rather than for the common good. (Just like in the rest of the world, only more overtly.) However, I still think PNG is a remarkable reminder of what we have lost in our headlong rush towards 'progress', and it has much to admire. And I don't just mean ribbon-tailed astrapias (the birds of paradise in PNG are genuinely paradisiacal) or the dedication shown by so many of its inhabitants to their favourite pastime: the chewing of betel nuts. I mean more… well, the retention of a way of life and the attitudes that go hand in hand with this way of life, which would never persuade any of them to fly an aeroplane full of people into buildings full of other people. There are heritages that contain qualities that should be preserved; there are other heritages that contain no worthwhile qualities at all.

And on that sombre note, I should end this chapter. But not before mentioning that 'Papua' is derived from a similar Malay word meaning 'frizzy-haired'. Which is the sort of fact that can prove really useful in bringing to an end a conversational hiatus at a dinner party. And in this respect, it's probably a darn sight better than embarking on a full-scale diatribe about how there are far too many people in the world, and how we are all now inevitably doomed…

The End is Nigh

OK. I'd like to ask you a question. And it is this: have you ever been at a party, one that you've really enjoyed, but where, at some stage, you've come to realise that you'd now rather be somewhere else? You've had a great time, but you know that if you stay any longer you won't have even a moderately good time. The whole thing is just on the point of becoming sour, and the prospect of a settling Armagnac and a packet of peanuts back at your own place is far more attractive than just one more minute of unbridled revelry in the company of some of your closest friends?

Well, I hope you have. Because then you might begin to understand how I was now feeling about my position in Deloitte. My thirty-plus years with this firm had been constantly demanding but they had also been really very enjoyable. Now, however, the prospect of much more time as one of its partners filled me more with dread than anticipation. And it wasn't just because all the best wine had been quaffed and the Twiglets had run out; it was because most of the fun had drained away.

I have already alluded to the remorseless advance of tick-box mentality – and its detrimental impact on our troops' mentality. And I have also referred to the fact that my role was becoming that of a high-paid rewriter of reports. But my disillusionment went far deeper than this. And it was not completely unconnected with two... well, with two completely unconnected developments in my day-to-day work.

The first of these was my role within the small team of partners that was now servicing Rover – which was that of the audit partner responsible for signing off on this company's financial statements. This was quite a challenge, but, in itself, not an insurmountable one. What was much more of a problem was who else was within this same team, and here I have to be super careful, because even a defanged snake can still do you harm…

I will have to proceed with just a series of short statements, starting with 'the Phoenix Four were not Rover; they owned Rover'. Then, how about 'the team partner with whom I was having real problems was the lead partner and very much the Phoenix Four partner'. (He was also, in my mind, not a true Deloitte man, and I detested him, probably more than he detested me.) Then 'because of his behaviour and his actions, I could see that it was all going to end in tears'.

Well, in due course, it did. Fortunately for me, well after I had left the party and was back with my Armagnac and peanuts. And if I've been talking in too many riddles there, may I just direct you to the internet. There, you will have no problem at all in finding a suitable précis of the events following the eventual collapse of that long-established car business, which involve Deloitte being fined £14 million as a result of the advice it gave to the Phoenix Four, and a certain individual partner of Iranian ancestry being fined £250,000 as well as being banned from accounting for three years.

None of this was very funny. While I was still in harness, and before this miserable outcome, I was having to endure a terrible relationship with… well, with a man who was not doing the right thing, and whose manner made him one of the most objectionable people I have ever met. Just think of receiving a phone call from somebody, and that somebody ranting on so much that you are able to leave the phone on your desk, go and get yourself a cup of coffee, and come back to find that the rant is still very much alive and well. This guy had so little regard for other people that he didn't even need them to be there when he was abusing them. Of course, it wasn't just the personal animosity that was wearing. It was the knowledge – without actual proof – that what this man was doing was wrong, but because he wielded so much power (on the back of fees earned that had yet to be applied to the payment of fines) he was being indulged by the firm's management. That's the firm to which I had devoted my entire working life, and for which I still had an unshakeable devotion. I think I've just mentioned how things could become sour. Well, for me, 'sour' was definitely the taste in my mouth, and I knew I had to do something about it before this 'sour' turned to 'bitter'.

Now, I did say that there were two 'developments' within the firm that contributed to my feeling that the party was very much over, and the other was as an indirect result of something naughty having gone on at a company in America called Enron.

Enron, you might remember, was an American energy company based in Houston Texas, which went into bankruptcy in 2001, leading, in turn, to the dissolution of Arthur Andersen, which was then one of the *five* largest accountancy practices in the world. However, whilst 'AA' was dissolved, its partners and people didn't disappear into thin air. And it wasn't too long before many of them found themselves absorbed into one of the remaining *four* largest accountancy practices in the world. That is to say, into our accountancy practice. And in Birmingham, that meant not just a significant increase in the size of our office, but a sort of reverse takeover of their own office, a glitzy new palace in the glitzy new development of Brindley Place – which was open plan!

I don't know who thought up the idea of open-plan offices, but he or she deserves a special place in hell. Or maybe just an open-plan part of hell, where his or her suffering can be witnessed by all for the whole of eternity, and any ability to focus on pain management – or on anything at all – is as unlikely as ever being able to encounter any sort of privacy ever again. I mean, what on earth are the benefits of these office prairies? They may save money – from doing away with lots of walls and doors – and they may look 'right on' in the same way that *Grand Designs* houses without any curtains do. But the reality is that they are no more sensible than those curtainless homes. Just as one might naturally wish to shield oneself from a dark winter evening, so most people, given the opportunity, will want to shield themselves from the constant distraction of close-by work colleagues. And there is just so much a waist-height partition can do, which is considerably less than an internal office wall can do. Especially if the office worker seeking some shielding has spent a lifetime with an internal office, even if for most of this time he has kept its door wide open.

I hated it. Just as I hated what had been built as unisex loos (which soon succumbed to a bit of cross-gender common sense). And this intense distaste for my new physical surroundings, combined with an even more intense distaste for somebody I just could not avoid, ultimately made me take a life-changing decision. I would stop being a partner, and instead I would become an ex-partner – a retired person who no longer had to try to concentrate in a noisy chicken coop and who no longer had to anguish over the egregious behaviour of a prize-winning cock.

I am still in 2002 here, and my parting with Deloitte would not take place until April 2003, but the decision had been made. Furthermore, in my mind, I was already on the road to an early retirement, something that was very easy to contemplate because, perversely, at fifty-five years of age, I was already one of the older partners in the firm. If one hadn't been elevated to the ranks of the firm's top management, it was more likely than not that one would have been ejected well before one was even fifty, and I had lost count of how many of my colleagues had been 'set aside' over the years. Many of them far short of reaching fifty. Anyway, my advancing years meant that nobody was going to stand in the way of my going. Far from it. And somebody might even have relished the thought that he would get as a replacement somebody who would stay on the other end of the phone while he vented his spleen. Not that it's likely that he would ever have noticed…

OK. Point of information here. And it concerns the impression I may be giving that severing my ties with Deloitte was all to do with the negative, the arresting of an untenable situation – in an untenable physical situation. Because this would be the wrong impression, in that it ignores entirely the significant positives of finally being able to do with my time precisely what I wanted to do with my time, foremost of which was a lot more travelling and, quite likely, a lot more writing. And the travelling, of course, wouldn't involve travelling into and out of Birmingham every day, and the writing wouldn't be the rewriting of other people's reports. It would be more of what I actually *wanted* to write…

Some of this I have already mentioned: namely the Renton Tenting trilogy of intergalactic adventuring. But there was other stuff knocking around in my head that I hadn't yet started but that I wanted, at some point, to get down on paper. I had, for example, an idea for three books on my 'pet hates', and I also had an idea for a short book dealing with the scourge of bureaucracy. This, I hoped, would demonstrate the contempt I had for bureaucrats, a contempt that had taken root in the mid-'70s and which, by the end of the millennium, had blossomed into glorious full flower – and which even now is still as fresh as ever.

Yes, I didn't mention them before, but there were two specific examples of the nature of bureaucracy that made themselves known to me early on in my career. The first was connected with the close-down of the Channel Tunnel. Not the one that eventually got built, but the earlier one that got cancelled in 1975, when, on the English side of the Channel, we'd drilled just about as far as my dentist ever has. Well, when projects get abandoned, they have to be closed down. And this close-down process can be an absolute goldmine for bureaucrats, particularly if they know that their political masters want nothing to do with a 'failure'. 'Just leave it to some functionaries, and they can sort out whatever needs to be done.' Which in this case was to compile a summary of all the costs incurred and still to be incurred to bring the whole thing to a final conclusion, and then to establish how 'our' costs and the similar costs incurred by the French should be apportioned between these two affably inclined nations.

These functionaries operated out of some very expensive offices off Piccadilly and, for some reason I cannot recall, they had to endure my presence as part of a team of reviewers of their work. This proved to be quite a tricky assignment, in that it was quite difficult to locate any such work, and not instead be mesmerised by how a whole officeful of people had done so little of anything over so many weeks and months. Their work rate had been almost geologically slow. Which point brings me to the other specific example of the indisputable characteristics of bureaucracy.

This was what my first wife (the tenacious barrister one) had experienced a little earlier than 1975 when she'd taken on a temporary role at Birmingham City Council in one of its vital departments (I think as a stopgap between her lecturing and her starting work for her bar exams). It was again to do with the work rate of our essential public servants, and it took the form of her being admonished by the department head for working too fast! For any particular task, she was apparently taking about a third of the time taken by the permanent members of his taxpayer-funded social club – and this wasn't going down too well with these well-established 'fixtures'. It didn't make them look very good. And she would just have to slow down.

And no. I'm not making that up. No more than I'm making up my feelings for that whole army of individuals we all have to support, and for which, in return, we receive all the interference, incompetence, insouciance and insufferability we might ever need.

I will try not to dwell on this deep-seated antipathy to bureaucrats for too long, as I am aware that if it were they who were describing their distaste for me, they would take three years to do it, at the end of which there would be a 2,000-page preliminary report and a request for further staff to expedite the completion of the final report within an additional two-year time frame. So, I'll just set out the charge list: the principal aspects of our bureaucrats' behaviour that demonstrate why they deserve no more than a gold-plated promise of our enduring opprobrium.

First, there is that work rate. Which sometimes is actually negative. Because if one is operating a system where a workforce expands not to meet an increased workload, but where work must be found – or fabricated – to occupy an ever-increasing workforce, it is sometimes difficult to keep the workload and the workforce in balance. And one can end up with individuals who cannot even give the appearance of working. And if you doubt that the workforce in question is ever-increasing, may I direct you to the 4,000 civil servants who used to run the whole of the British Empire from Somerset House, and ask you to compare that number to the modern-day constellation of bright things that fail even to run a small island off the coast of Europe. There will probably come a time when everybody in Britain is a civil servant, after which we will have to resort to importing the devils…

Anyway, number two. Rank incompetence. I could write a whole book on this. Everybody could. But I will restrict myself to making the observation that if one breeds generalists with no real-world skills, you can't expect much more than a succession of bugger's muddles. I rest my case – other than to observe that ubiquitous incompetence is neatly paired with 'dodging any responsibility'. And this latter aspect of the pairing is achieved by sustaining a system where bureaucrats are moved to a new post before the last post they hammered into the ground falls over because they didn't hammer it in properly. Many hyper-successful careers in the Civil Service have been formed on the back of an ability to time one's dodges to perfection, and never to be around when the next consignment of ordure makes contact with the apparatus with rotating blades designed to create a current of cooling air.

OK. Number three. They look after themselves very well, don't they? They are better paid than those of us who have to toil in the private sector, and their pension arrangements – compared to ours – are outrageous. In fact, just about as outrageous as implying in any way that there is some sort of equivalence between the public sector and the private sector, that they are just two sides of a single economy. They are not. The private sector produces; the public sector consumes – usually a great deal more than the private sector can produce. And too often, the reliance of the public sector on the private is forgotten or even actively denied. Which is little short of abominable.

So is the last item on the charge sheet: the unwarranted arrogance of bureaucrats, born of a misplaced belief in their importance and reinforced by their success in establishing a long-standing, self-serving, superficially respectable racket for which others are obliged to pay. In fact, it might soon occur to them that we should pay extra for the arrogance. No point in giving it away. That's just a waste. And we all know how bureaucracies hate waste...

Well, I may have gone on a bit there. And rather than running the risk of producing more unread words than are contained in the first draft of a white paper on the new regulations for de-genderising flower arranging, I will abandon my 'critique' of bureaucracy – and the theme of writing, from where it sprang – and move on to that other aspect of retirement I had in my sights, which was more travelling. However, fear not. This will be just a brief reference, and nowhere near the length of even a very short story. And it will concern my second trip to Namibia and Botswana, this time with not just Sue but also with her mum – and with a replacement guide.

When we landed at Windhoek International, we were expecting to find Uanee again, but there, waiting to greet us, was somebody who I knew immediately was not Uanee. This was probably because it was not a very tall, well-built black guy, but instead a not-quite-so-tall, nicely built white girl. Her name was Penny, and in due course, she would become a dear friend, and an even dearer friend of Martin, our safari man – when he eventually got round to marrying her. However, that was for the future. For now, Penny was 'just' one of his employees, and our very agreeable guide-cum-chef for our trip around Namibia. She even forgave us very quickly for manifesting some obvious disappointment at discovering that Uanee was not to be our companion.

It proved a great trip. And not just because Penny had long legs and always wore shorts. There was her wonderful prepared-on-the-spot food as well – and her ceaselessly charming nature. Oh, and there was also some wildlife to enjoy.

Our trip involved a slightly different itinerary to that of our first visit to Namibia, and this meant we encountered, amongst other things, a pair of bateleur eagles that dive-bombed us (in a friendly sort of manner) as we were being driven around in an open vehicle on a private 'safari farm'. Then there was the cheetah on the bonnet of another open vehicle we were occupying as we made our way around the previously visited, private nature reserve of Okonjima. And worth mentioning as well is the enormous python we observed defying gravity by sliding up the trunk of a tree when we were on a game drive out of Little Vumbura. Yes, when, at the end of our Namibia tour, we returned to the Okavango Delta, we returned to the same camp as well. And to complete this brief review of memorable wildlife spots, I should just mention something else we saw on an excursion from Little Vum, and this was a leopard eating a baboon he had just relieved of its life. I recall vividly that the screams from the baboon's close relatives, who were witnessing their Uncle George being chewed away, were a little disturbing. But not nearly as disturbing as the grating and splitting noises made by leopard teeth on baboon bone. We were only feet from the leopard – in a vehicle – and this grisly sound was only too obvious. I remember thinking at the time that in all those African wildlife programmes I'd seen on the telly, the programme makers had not included this off-putting soundtrack. And I could well understand why.

Anyway, as well as those long legs and any number of wildlife encounters, this particular trip was memorable for two other reasons. One was the reluctant acceptance that Land Cruisers are rather more comfortable than Land Rovers. (Penny had driven us around Namibia in one of these lovely leviathans.) The other was that we could probably drive one of these vehicles ourselves – without the need for long legs. I mean without the need for a delightful guide. Namibia and Botswana are the two safest countries in Africa, with some of the most underpopulated roads in the world. Next time we visited them, one of us would be literally in the driving seat – of a Land Cruiser or a Land Rover – and the other one would be just to his left. And with that period of life called retirement hoving into view, there would certainly be a next time and, in all probability, a few more next times after that.

And all without the company of a single bureaucrat or a singularly unpalatable partner…

Freedom and Finniegill

Where does one go to celebrate one's new-found freedom? To where in the world would one travel to mark the inauguration of one's privileged emancipation from the onus of work? Well, there is only one place isn't there? Bulgaria!

Yes, Eastern Europe's answer to South America's Bolivia, and the only nation on the planet that is named after a Womble. And there's more. A country that is to sophistication what a flat fish is to philosophy, and one with a reputation for 'brawn'. Because, after all, if, in the old Soviet Union, you wanted to recruit a few bruisers to bruise some of your enemies or even to poison them with a deadly umbrella, you would look to Bulgaria rather than to anywhere else. Here, after all, was a nation that might not be noted for its contributions to the advancement of science – or the arts or… well, to anything at all really, but its performance at numerous Olympic games clearly demonstrated its prowess in disciplines such as weightlifting and wrestling, just the sort of things that made it the ideal source for heavyweight hitmen. And, no doubt, for some heavyweight hitwomen as well…

However, I am getting a little ahead of myself here, because I should first explain that whilst my official retirement date was 31 March 2003, I was already enjoying quite a lot of gardening leave when this new year was still in its infancy. I therefore had lots of time to make some progress with my planned writing, oodles of time to do the 1,001 jobs in and around the house that I'd not had time to do before, and even time to explore the possibility of finally taking up a proper sport (of which more in just a little while). And then there was still time over to plan some holidays, the first of which would be to the country I have just so egregiously maligned. And with barely any compunction, I am now going to malign it some more by giving you a brief rundown of what Sue and I found in this ex-communist state when we visited it in May of 2003 – starting with our organised transport...

This was a very old coach, and it was late picking us up from Sofia's international airport because it had broken down. When it finally arrived, it became apparent that so too had its air-conditioning (and it hadn't been repaired). This was a pity because the ambient temperature in Sofia was thirty degrees, which meant that aboard the coach it was nearer thirty-five degrees. Indeed, it was even hotter at the back of the coach near its rear-sited engine. Which was not really the problem it could have been because the diesel fumes that filled this hindmost part of our conveyance precluded its use by anybody who did not wish to see his or her life prematurely curtailed...

Out of Sofia – which was characterised by ugly communist-era apartment blocks – was ... more ugliness. But this was in the form of ugly rural dwellings, the estate agent's details for which would have to strive to avoid the terms 'broken down', 'threadbare and/or shabby', 'seen better days', or 'just about standing'. And then there was the country's management of rubbish and litter, which was more to do with 'dispersal' than with 'disposal' (which, by no means, made Bulgaria in any way unique). And then there were its various tourist hotels, which ranged from the brutally stark and the just plain unappealing to the indescribably primitive (in a place called Krumovgrad [really]).

Why then had I organised a trip to such a dreadful destination – and indeed why were Sue and I reliant on a coach to transport us in a large anti-clockwise loop around this destination nation? The answer, of course, was 'birds' – and some other stuff like flowers and trees. Yes, this was our second Naturetrek excursion – as part of a group – and one where it was our intention to immerse ourselves in a big bathful of avian and other natural delights in the far east of Europe. And this is where I start to redress my impugning of Bulgaria by commending it for some of its outstanding qualities, virtually all of which concern its avoidance of what had already befallen Britain and most other countries in the West.

Put simply, under its communist rule, Bulgaria's economy was not the most advanced, and its agricultural practices were some of the least advanced – in the whole of Europe. Indeed, if you saw a tractor in a field, it was more likely that you had ingested a skinful of vodka than it was a real tractor going about some ploughing or the like. It was horses and humans that still did most of the work. And with an absence of tractors and most other agricultural equipment came an absence of what is the Western farmer's essential helping hand: tons and tons of harmful chemicals. So, while here in the west of Europe, all sorts of wildlife, and birds in particular, had been almost snuffed out of existence, in Bulgaria, they were in genuine abundance. The natural world was still very much in evidence – and the country therefore constituted an irresistible magnet for a band of British birders. I won't flog this point to death, but as an example of this nation's bounty, I will simply mention that I don't remember hearing a single cuckoo in the distance – which is now a notable event in modern-day Blighty – but I do remember *seeing* a whole gang of them in just one place, all cuckooing loudly. I wonder, now that Bulgaria has sucked on the teat of EU largesse for so long, and has thereby been able to 'modernise' its farming practices, whether such large gatherings of cuckoos – or of any other birds – are still to be found anywhere within its borders. And have its prostitutes suffered a similar decline?

They were all along this main road, at about 500-yard intervals, all, on this Sunday morning, displaying their chemically red hair, their tight tops, their indecently short skirts, and their availability for a dose of stipendiary stuffing. It was a surprise to most of the dozen of us innocents on the coach, but in the words of our laconic Bulgarian guide, 'everything is possible in Bulgaria', and that appeared to include a session of Sunday-morning in-car/in-truck/in-coach (?) paid-for nooky, should one desire this. Although nobody on our coach actually took up the offer…

Well, I have clearly been very mean about Bulgaria, and it is only fair that I should say that as well as the banquet of birds we were able to savour, Bulgaria also provided us with a couple of half-decent hotels, some good food and a fair helping of some very hospitable people. Furthermore, it also provided Sue and me with an insight into the sort of people who are tempted to go on group birding holidays. And no, they are not all nerds and weirdos, but instead just some fairly normal, fairly sane individuals who simply have a healthy interest in birds and nature in general. That had been apparent on our trip to Venezuela and it was even more apparent in this bigger group that had accompanied us on our circumnavigation of Bulgaria. That said… as we would go on to discover, there would quite often be… well, a real weirdo, somebody in the group who was regarded by the rest of the group as a weirdo. And we certainly had one on this trip.

This poor chap shall remain nameless, but how he earned his weirdo status will be briefly explained. It was in part due to his inability or unwillingness to participate in a conversation, but more to do with the fact that for the entire trip – in sub-tropical temperatures – he never once shed his heavy woollen jacket, his slightly less heavy under-jacket, his shirt, his tie or his tiepin. This practice had obvious consequences, and Sue and I could only think that his legal practice in the Wirral (yes, he was a solicitor) operated in a niche market, focusing on all those people who needed legal advice but had no sense of smell. Sometimes those traces of diesel fumes finding their way from the back of the coach could prove a real godsend…

OK. It's now, as promised, time for me to say a few words about my taking up a proper sport, always assuming, that is, that archery can be considered a 'proper sport'. Yes, ever since my rifle-shooting days in Jersey, I had always had a yearning for aiming at something – which, with the necessary acquired skills, I might then succeed in hitting with a projectile. (Just as long as the something came without fur or feathers and was as inanimate as Putin's smile.) Furthermore, I was all too aware of the derivation of my surname, Fletcher – as a person who makes and sells arrows. It therefore seemed more than appropriate to discover whether, with the help of a bow, I could persuade any of those arrow-type projectiles to end up in a reliably inanimate archery target. And whether I might be more successful in this endeavour than I was with a rifle and bullet-type projectiles twenty years previously. I would, of course, need to join an archery club to stand any chance of achieving this goal, and this is what I did. Enthusiastically albeit a little nervously. Oh, and I also equipped myself with a surprisingly expensive bow and some rather more reasonably priced arrows. I was therefore properly set up to become a *bona fide* sportsman – and, in due course, maybe an Olympian. After all, age is a minor consideration in any sport requiring concentration rather than say Bulgarian brawn. Or so I thought before my training in the art of archery got underway…

I very soon discovered four much-less-than-attractive aspects of archery, of which I was not aware before my induction into this (demanding) pastime.

The first was that, just as in that Jersey shooting club twenty years before, everybody else in the archery club was much better than I was, and it looked likely that this would be the case indefinitely. The second was that even putting one's bow together was quite a trial (they come in bits and, of course, the bowstring is unattached). The third was that using the bow was even more of a trial. Even if one avoided damaging one's fingers, one was almost guaranteed to bugger up one's shoulder. The pull required to launch an arrow is immense, and when one has done this a few dozen times, one's 'pulling' shoulder starts to object very strongly and, after the event, goes in for a long-lasting painful sulk. How those Amazon ladies got on, I cannot imagine. And they would have had no access to a metal detector either…

Yes, this is the fourth drawback to archery – if one is doing some archery homework back on one's home patch, and one is trying to land an arrow in the middle of a target that one has set up in the middle of one's yet-to-be-cut field. This is because a number of one's arrows will not only fail to find the middle of one's target, but indeed any part of one's target, and they will instead disappear into the grass somewhere beyond the target. And when I say 'disappear', I mean 'disappear'. They don't conveniently stick up from the ground – ever – but instead they slither their way along until they have concealed themselves in the turf, and so effectively that one can be standing above them and still not see them. So, one has to buy a metal detector, and spend a good deal of one's practice time searching for arrows rather than dispatching them from one's bow. Which, by way of compensation, is a lot less taxing on one's shoulder.

Anyway, ultimately – after having had to visit my doctor for treatment for a chronically painful shoulder – it was not the metal-detecting, the bow-assembling or my comparatively poor performance with the bow that dissuaded me from continuing along the road to the Olympics. It was, of course, that bloody shoulder. As a Fletcher, I clearly needed to stick to making and selling arrows, and give up any thoughts of actually launching them from a bow. That I would leave to the ancient English archers, to the other stalwart members of the Droitwich Archery Club – and to all those Amazon lovelies. I, meanwhile, would occupy myself with the preparations needed for a trip to Iceland, a country named not after a Womble but instead after a chain of British supermarkets specialising in the sale of frozen foods. (And also, for the sake of accuracy, in the sale of non-frozen grocery items such as meat, dairy and dry goods…)

Well, the necessary preparations were few, and consisted principally of Sue and I equipping ourselves with some warm clothes (even in July, Iceland can be a little chilly); equipping ourselves with a pile of Icelandic krona (this was pre-financial crash time in Iceland, and we had been warned that everything was dauntingly expensive); finding a good map of Iceland (we would be driving around its perimeter); and reminding ourselves of the salient points of the previous century's Cod Wars between Britain and Iceland, in case we encountered any Icelandic fishermen who still resented our futile attempts to fish in Icelandic waters (albeit we thought this highly unlikely).

In due course, all these preparations (other than our brushing up on the Cod Wars) would be put to the test. We certainly needed warm clothing – even though, when we arrived in Reykjavik, its happy inhabitants were experiencing a heatwave (it was a scalding nineteen degrees). We also needed all those krona. (An ordinary meal for two with a bottle of wine was the equivalent of about £120, and some of the food was very ordinary indeed.) The map was also essential. We had flown from Reykjavik to the north of Iceland, in order to be able to drive ourselves in a clockwise direction around the island, stopping at various pre-booked hotels until we were back in the capital. And even though Iceland is not overendowed with roads, we often needed to refer to our map.

It proved to be a very enjoyable expedition, during which we saw quite a few birds and even one brazen roadside prostitute. She was at a remote petrol station and, despite Sue arguing that a woman in her sixties, selling vegetables from a stall, was unlikely to be selling her body as well, I think she could well have been a *grande horizontale.* There was even a suggestion of red in her hair. However, I suppose Sue could have been right. Just as I was right in suggesting that Iceland might be likened to a slab of the Moon dropped into the Atlantic Ocean, and then furnished with an abundance of water and ice. It really is like that. A huge expanse of rock, some of it bare and some of it covered in either glaciers or moss and, here and there, enlivened by an impressive waterfall that simply demands one's attention. Indeed, in retrospect, I can more easily recall our progress around Iceland by reference to the torrents of Gullfoss Falls, Dettifoss, Skógafoss, etc, etc than I can by reference to the places we stayed overnight. In a way I found them more memorable than the odd geyser we saw or the close-up view we had of the front of a glacier. That simply looked as though it could have done with a clean. Although, there again, I suppose if you grind your way over rock for years on end, you are very likely to pick up quite a lot of dirty-looking grit. And cleaning it off would probably be entirely impractical…

Anyway, Sue and I were both very happy to have visited that chunk of Moon and, for me, it now holds a very special place in the list of countries I have visited as, along with Western Australia, it is a place to which I doubt I could ever return. I didn't, as I did south of Perth, commit a driving offence, but I almost certainly *gave* offence – to the Icelandic ambassador to Britain. And I did this, soon after our return from Iceland, by sending him my recently purchased Icelandic T-shirt together with an intemperate letter, in which I made plain my disgust at his country's decision to resume whaling. I think, incidentally, that 'intemperate' in this instance might qualify as a euphemism for 'abusive'. But, in any event, the letter's contents were certainly strong enough to cause the ambassador to put in place a bar on my re-entry into his country. Not that he really needed to, because I have no plans to go back there, and would not do so even if they had a special offer going on gin and pepperoni pizzas. Or am I thinking of that chain of supermarkets there…?

Maybe I should move on – to Extremadura. This, as I didn't know until 2003, is an inland region of Spain, situated in the south-west of the country and bordering its neighbour, Portugal. Sue and I were not planning to take a holiday there, but we were considering buying a house there. Our home in Worcestershire provided us with all the peace and privacy we really needed, but for some time we had in mind a place where we could really flex our reclusive muscles and effectively go off-grid – completely. And where better than an area of Spain, so thinly populated that it constituted one of the best Dark Sky areas in Europe? Well, Dumfries and Galloway actually…

Yes, with a dog to consider, along with the difficulties in harnessing the services of an estate agent in a region of Spain shunned by ex-pat Brits, it soon became apparent that it might be better to seek a bolthole somewhere in Britain, somewhere like the east of Dumfries and Galloway, and specifically an area of this huge county where the trees outnumber the residents by about a million to one. And lo! We sought and we found. And what we found was a small wooden cottage (born in the same year as myself), sitting in a valley that led into the Southern Uplands, and that could only be reached by a four-mile drive up a terrible forestry track. Oh, and it came with a modest barn and a modest stable block, and its three acres were bordered on one edge by the beautiful Dryfe Water, a small, rushing river that ultimately drains into the River Annan. This was a place where we could be not just normally reclusive but monastically or even hermetically reclusive – despite our Wood Cottage being part of the village of Finniegill…

And this was because Finniegill comprised just two houses – set about 700 yards apart – and it had a population of just three when we were in residence and… yes, just one when we weren't. And that one other resident was an enigmatic Dutch lady who we would see only very occasionally or, on some visits, not at all.

A little more will be written about this Scottish hideaway in due course, but for now I will just mention that I viewed this place on my own (Sue was not able to join me because she was recovering from some medical interference), and I put an offer in – as agreed by Sue – before she had set eyes on the place. Indeed, she would not confirm the wisdom of her rash agreement until we were back from a holiday in the Seychelles. Here we had gone just a few days after putting in that offer, and it was here that, in due course, we would learn that our offer had been accepted. In one of the hottest, driest situations we had ever experienced, we would be informed that we had been successful in acquiring a property in one of the coldest, wettest parts of the British Isles. It was very welcome news.

Anyway, I have mentioned the Seychelles there, and that is all I will do other than report that our lazy-days holiday on three of its islands was punctuated by an unexpected helicopter flight. Halfway through this holiday, we were due to fly to the far-northern Bird Island on one of the local Twin Otter aeroplanes. However, following the collapse of an undercarriage on one of these planes, the entire (small) fleet was grounded, and we therefore had to switch to a shiny, intensely noisy, made-for-four Whirlybird. I had only ever travelled in one of these machines once before – when I was 'shuttled' between Heathrow and Gatwick in a rather larger helicopter. And I enjoyed this unplanned trip just about as much as I did that first one, which was not at all. It wasn't just the noise, but also the knowledge that helicopters rarely glide very well when things go wrong. And I don't think they float…

OK, 2003 is rapidly coming to an end, and so too is this chapter. But not before my telling you that I was very aware in this year of what was going on in the world around me. My new-found freedom and the way I was using it to travel, to write, to acquire property and to generally enjoy myself hadn't blinded me to events here in Britain or overseas. So, I, like many others, was concerned not only about the way the natural world was being shredded beyond redemption, but also about messy wars, the disconcerting growth of terrorism, the increasingly porous nature of borders, and the consequent development of an asylum industry. Then there was the general malaise that seemed to be overtaking our own country, as it struggled under the stewardship of the muppet and the messiah: the Brown muppet constantly busy demonstrating that he didn't really understand the first thing about his oft-referred-to 'prudence', and the Blair messiah busy leading his people into the desert of decline, too self-obsessed to realise that he didn't have a clue as to how to lead them back out.

It felt to me as though we were approaching a vortex above a plughole. And what was down through that plughole was far from inviting. All the more reason then to get on with more travel plans, more scribbling to my heart's content – and a good bit of putting in order a wonderful retreat in the soggy, miserable, rain-drenched uplands of Scotland. And maybe, at some point, to put an advert in a paper for a little-used, first-class, high-powered bow, complete with a quiver of arrows…

One Test Track and Two Testing Tracks

It was 1 April 2004. So, when the guy in Manchester Airport who was checking my passport as I joined the check-in queue asked me, 'Have you recently had an operation, *Mrs* Fletcher?', I assumed that this was his attempt at a rather lame April Fools' joke. I therefore smiled obligingly and waited for my passport to be returned. But it wasn't. It remained in the hands of the very nice man from Virgin who, I now noticed, wasn't, himself, smiling at all. Instead, he was preparing to ask me another question, and this one was, 'Do you know your passport is showing you as a woman?' I didn't need to answer this question because my open mouth and my staring eyes did this for me. He therefore went on to tell me in an unadorned statement that 'this could be a problem'.

It was a new passport. I had used it only twice before – to get to and back from the Seychelles – and on neither of those trips had anybody spotted what this young man had: that after issuing a lifetime of passports confirming my status as a man, the 'operatives' at the passport office had decided on this occasion to present me as a woman. It was, according to Mr Virgin, not an uncommon error, but one that could still have serious consequences. Like the immigration guys who would be dealing with my arrival in Orlando might deny me entry into their country and send me back to Britain on the next available flight. Or, of course, that outcome might be avoided – if Virgin decided that they would not even let me onto their aeroplane in the first place. However, in either case, it would be a bit of a bummer. It would mean that I would not be able to enjoy a visit to Orlando's theme parks with Sue, her mother, her brother, her sister-in-law and their three very young kids...

Now, I know what you're thinking. But Sue and I would be unhitching ourselves from this family funfest after just a few days and then making our own way down to the Everglades and then all the way down through the Keys to Key West. And we were looking forward to that aspect of our holiday even more than we were looking forward to the close company of all those relatives for more than just a few hours. In fact, for a lot more than just a few hours...

Well, the man from Virgin decided that he would have to debate my case with more senior colleagues, and he therefore soon disappeared – with my bothersome passport. Quite some time later he reappeared to inform me that I would be allowed on his company's Jumbo, but only on the condition that I accepted that I might be on another of its Jumbos very soon – on my way back to Manchester when I had been refused entry into Orlando. This wasn't very encouraging news, but at least I'd be given a chance to get through American Immigration, and that was better than not even being allowed on a plane. And it all worked. About twelve hours later, looking and sounding as manly as I possibly could, I slipped into America without attracting any unwanted attention. Now I would be able to get on with my holiday and simply worry about whether I would ever be allowed to fly back home.

Needless to say, I was. And just to complete this tale, I should mention that, when back in Britain, I of course phoned the passport office in order to discover how I might furnish myself with a new passport that actually matched my gender. They were unfazed by my enquiry (their error was clearly an everyday event) and they simply asked me to return my offending passport with some proof that I was a man. Well, this was in the days when gender was a matter of a penis or no penis. So, I asked the lady at the passport office whether an explicit photograph might constitute appropriate proof – to be then informed that a birth certificate would be preferable, even though most of the ladies in the passport office were always ready for a good laugh. And that was really good to hear. Because now that they presumably have to cope with the pick-and-mix approach to gender, they probably need all the laughs they can get. I can only wish them well.

Anyway, I suppose I should say just a few words about our time in Florida, and what it said about my character. You see, as I have already made pretty clear, the natural world, with all its wildlife, all its wild places, all its remote places and all its empty places, was where I liked to be. And 'manufactured' environments full of 'manufactured' entertainments – and lots of people – were just not my thing. However… I had been to a couple of Orlando's theme parks before – in the cause of developing work for Deloitte, as you might remember – and I had quite enjoyed them. So, it could just be that my character harboured some hidden shallows; that I could indeed be captivated by some fabricated frivolity in much the same way that anybody else could. Especially when there was such a variety of frivolity on tap.

Neither Sue nor I held back, and, with that pack of relatives, we visited a different theme park every day and tasted as many of the treats on offer as we could. Some were exceptionally good, but one in particular stands out in my mind. This was 'Test Track', an 'experience' that was designed to illustrate how General Motors conducted its evaluation of automobile prototypes and, of far more importance, culminated in a high-speed ride in an open car on the roof of a building. This was a 'slot car', just like the sort that came with a Scalextric race track, only much bigger and a lot less likely to fly off the track. So, it wasn't in any way dangerous, even if it felt as though it was, and much more so than many of the other rides. I would have gone on it twice – if there had been time, and if it wasn't for the size of the queue…

And that reminds me, Orlando's theme parks are places to go not only to experience thrills and amusements, but also to witness tenacity – in three very different manifestations. The first is the tenacity on show in those queues. For what could be more tenacious than being prepared to wait for up to an hour – or, in some cases, even more – just to experience a particular ride? That is determination/tenacity taken to the highest level. Then, at a similarly high level is the determination/tenacity required to ignore entirely any of the sartorial demands of clothing. Almost without exception, the theme parks' patrons go out of their way – with shapeless or bulging attire –

to avoid any appearance of elegance or even plain old dignity. Which brings us to the third form of tenacity on show: the tenacity to pursue a diet over one's lifetime that must contain enough calories for four or five lifetimes. The results are only too obvious: legions of punters who are too large to go on many of the rides or even to walk between the rides. Instead, they thread their way through the theme-park grounds on some sort of motorised buggy, often in the company of other family members who together, if dropped into the sea, would constitute a danger to shipping. I know that 'volumetrically unrestrained' people are now a common feature of many Western societies, but for whatever reason, some of the most extreme examples of this posse of the portly seem to congregate in Orlando. And if they're denied most of the rides, they will never be denied their next helping of fast food. Indeed, anybody attempting to stop them would need to be a veritable master of tenacity…

Unsurprisingly, there were none of these super-tubby types in the Everglades – only lots of birds and lots of alligators (on which one was advised not to tread while watching the birds) – and there were not that many of these tubs in Key West either. Instead, here, in the key furthest from the mainland, were lots of 'cool dudes' and a good number of gay dudes, and a feeling that it wasn't really part of America at all. Or, if it was, it was part of an America sometime back in the late '60s/early '70s, when you might be advised by Scott McKenzie to wear some flowers in your hair. It was a lovely place, and our stay at its Southernmost Hotel will not easily be forgotten. Nor, for entirely different reasons, will our stay on Sanibel Island. This was our next stop after the Keys, a small island off the west coast of Florida, supposedly famous for its wildlife reserves. What it should really be famous for, however, is its mediocre, rather sterile accommodation, its overrated restaurants staffed by offensive waiters, its success in locking away virtually all of its coastline behind private property, and its closed or inaccessible wildlife reserves. We would have had more fun sitting in our Chrysler Sebring convertible for two days playing Scrabble. And if we'd parked it somewhere back in Orlando, we might even have seen more wildlife. I know we will never go back there. Nor probably to Florida. That said, our American excursion had given me – and Sue – a welcome respite from our labours in Finniegill.

Yes, Wood Cottage had already consumed a lot of our time, and after our return from America, it was set to consume even more. It still needed a lot of work to get it into the condition we wanted, just as it still quite often needed nerves of steel…

Our hideaway, you might recall, was four miles up a forestry track, and it was a track that not only contained Scotland's national collection of potholes, but also an alarmingly steep section with an even more alarming drop to one side. This had been merely thrilling when we'd first encountered it, and not even as disconcerting as that ride on Test Track. But then winter had arrived, and this stretch of track – complete with a nasty turn towards its bottom where it skirted the rushing waters of Dryfe Water – would either be covered in snow or slicked with ice. And to say that this track was testing would be an understatement. Especially when one was in white-knuckle mode on the way down. (Coming up was more a full-throttle dash with teeth firmly gritted.)

Anyway, with the help of a newly acquired 4x4, we did manage it – every time – but it did tend to set the heart racing, and it also made us think of how the hell we would get the furniture and carpets we'd ordered delivered to the cottage. Even if a removals van could cope with the potholes, it might never get down that track. Or, if it did, it might complete its trip in the river rather than at our cottage. It was quite a concern.

Well, I wonder whether, like me, you've discovered over your lifetime that things rarely turn out as bad as you fear, and so it was with the removals van – and the carpet van and various other vans – that did, in the summer of 2004, arrive to provide us with what we needed to fill our now newly decorated and generally tidied-up retreat. It did, of course, help that there was now no snow or ice. Nevertheless, not one of the drivers of these vans failed to remark on the challenge provided by our most testing of tracks. And most of them had a look of concern on their face when they set off to make their way back to tarmacked civilisation. They also, I imagine, when they rejoined their families, were eager to tell them how they had just met a couple of nutters who had bought a house where there just shouldn't be a house. And one only had to experience the track to this house to decide beyond doubt that they really were a couple of nutters…

Anyway, however mentally unstable we were, we spent maybe a week every month on our new Scottish country estate. We soaked up the beauty and the solitude it offered, and one of us got on with some writing there. This was me, and the writing consisted of my finally committing to paper that trio of books I mentioned a little while ago – on my pet hates. This, I realised, wouldn't constitute Booker Prize material, but it was just something I'd always wanted to do, principally to explore the humorous potential of my pet hates, whether these hates were described in prose or in verse. It was a very satisfying undertaking, and particularly satisfying were those hates put into rhyme. I'm not sure that any of these would ever have been classified as a legitimate poem, but unlike lots of what are now presented as legitimate poems, my efforts did at least rhyme. And frankly, what's the point of a poem that doesn't rhyme? It's no more than a bit of prose where the layout function on yer PC's gone on the blink. Heck, if there are strict rules concerning what constitutes a limerick, why aren't there strict rules concerning what constitutes a poem? And rule one should be that the perishing thing rhymes…

OK. A very quick word about what I was doing with my literary output. This was essentially nothing, until, that is, I decided to get my pet-hate books printed, with the intention of selling them through a website. This I did towards the end of the year, and I was about as successful in this endeavour as I would have been if I had tried to use all three books as currency in Madagascar. Which is a sort of lead in to where, in September 2004, we went on our next Reef and Rainforest-organised trip – a trip lasting three weeks that proved to be a trip to remember.

I could write a book about it. But fear not. I shall serve up just a few of its tastier moments, starting with our arrival at Antananarivo – known to its friends as Tana. Immediately, Sue and I could see that we had arrived in a unique destination – and a poor destination. The airport was shabby, and it was full of young Malagasy boys desperate to earn just a few pennies for carrying luggage no more than a few yards. And talking of money… its *bureau de change* should have provided its patrons with wheelbarrows. For when I equipped myself with enough of the local currency for the entire trip, I had a stack of notes that I could have used as a stool. Then there was the trip into the capital, passing shacks, rickety wooden stalls – and rice paddies. The whole place had the feel of an enormous village rather than that of a country's capital. Nevertheless, the country's former colonial masters, the French, had bequeathed to the centre of this unconventional metropolis some rather handsome architecture – and a tradition of fine food. Our Hotel de Louvre was modest but handsome, and its food would not have been out of place in Paris. It was superb.

However, we were staying in this haven for just one night, and in the morning, we would be confronting the reality of rural Madagascar. This we would be doing by driving south from the capital to start a giant J-shaped itinerary that would see us eventually travelling north for a while up the island nation's west coast. We would not, of course, be doing this on our own. We would have the company of a guide called Kenny and a driver called Harry, who were both black, both quite small and both the owners of long, unpronounceable Malagasy names that caused them to adopt the two much smaller monikers of Kenny and Harry. However, despite these three similarities, there was one unmissable difference between our two travelling companions. For whilst Kenny could easily have passed for a Mauritian, Harry had a face that was unmistakably that of a (very black) Chinese gentleman. This, on first sight, was quite arresting. But it was no more than an extreme example of what would prove to be a common feature of many Malagasies: an element of the oriental in their appearance. This was hardly surprising. Many of them had ancestors who had arrived from places such as Indonesia and China, and the result of this is that the present indigenous population of the island has an unmistakable Asian flavour. And this is not just in its appearance, but also in its habits. Rice-growing is common, for example, and so is the use of rickshaws in Madagascar's towns. And this all means that, whilst Madagascar is unique in many ways, its most distinctive uniqueness is that it is more Asian than African. And citizens with black Chinese fizzogs are not exceptional in the least...

Anyway, we were now almost out of Tana – in Harry's ancient Isuzu Trooper – but not before observing a river lined with ladies doing their washing (Tana really was like a big village) and not before being exposed to the first of many retail opportunities available in Madagascar in the form of roadside stalls. I think this one was selling models of 2CVs made out of Coke cans. Then we were out of Tana, and the countryside looked... denuded. I've never seen any of the *Madagascar* animated films, but I strongly suspect that they don't quite represent the reality of this poor, overpopulated country, where not only has much of the vegetation been removed, but quite a lot of the actual country has as well. Everywhere were great pits where clay had been excavated for brick-making, and all over the place there were the clear signs of serious erosion: great cracks in the ground that made it look as though one day most of Madagascar will end up in the Indian Ocean, with no more than a big bare rock left behind.

Oh dear. I'm not so sure I'm keeping to my promise to serve up only the tastier moments of our trip. So, I will now try to redeem myself by providing you with just a brief list of some of the possibly more 'unforgettable' episodes of our progress south – in chronological order. These are:

1. Mandatory visits to a gemstone workshop, a zebu-horn workshop, a wood-carver's workshop, following on from which was a dance performance (just for Sue and me) – involving almost an entire village, some unavoidable audience participation and lots of tipping.
2. A further mandatory visit to a 'rustic' paper-making factory, where Sue was required to make some paper – and did.
3. Yet another mandatory visit, this time to a winery where the obligatory wine-tasting of its reds, whites and rosés was from glasses rinsed under a tap that certainly did not deliver safe, bottled water…
4. A couple of days in the Ranomafana National Park where we saw our first lemurs and our first leeches. There were so many of the latter that we could not remove them from our boots as quickly as they were arriving on our boots. Even our local forest guide couldn't cope, and we eventually had to return to our lodge. That's when we found a blood spot on Sue's stomach and one on my leg. Two of the little blighters had managed to get through.
5. Met an American scientist working at a research station in the national park, whose area of interest was 'environmental sociology', which, he explained, is the study of how people interact with their (protected) local environment. I wished him lots of luck with that…
6. Arrived in Andringitra National Park to take up residence in what was referred to as a '*gîte*' but was, in fact, more like a multiple-occupation hostel, the unique selling point of which was 'appalling squalor'. We were due to spend two nights there. We managed only one.

7. Left the '*shît*', passing droves of locals interacting with their protected environment with the help of axes (although most of the vegetation was just alien, partially dismembered eucalyptuses) and made our way over muddy tracks (the main road) to an attractive hotel next to the Isalo National Park. Here, squalor was completely absent, even if prawns in a dreadful custard-tasting Pernod sauce were not.
8. Saw our first ring-tailed lemurs and our first massed tourists today. The canyon in the national park that housed these increasingly rare animals was like Clapham Junction. I wonder whether it still is.
9. Drove east to Toliara passing through a 'sapphire town' – without stopping and where Kenny advised us to avoid eye contact with any of its inhabitants and not even to think about taking photos. It was little more than a spread of metal shacks, with a road running through its centre, and on either side of this road, a series of tumbledown shops, a few tumbledown eating places, a few brothels and quite a few Lebanese sapphire merchants. These were the guys who were making the real money out of all the illegal mining in the surrounding area – at the expense of the poor local bastards who were risking their lives doing the actual digging. According to Kenny, this place was now a no-go area for the authorities, and I suspect it still doesn't have a page on Wikipedia.
10. Drove north from Toliara to a place on the coast called Ifaty, to stay in a beachside resort called Le Paradisier. Beautiful chalets, but frightful and inattentive staff and frightful and inedible food. Although clearly a French enterprise, what emerged from its kitchen was literally impossible to eat. It wasn't so much its taste, but more its impenetrability. Each of the two meals of vulcanised chicken we were presented with defeated the sharp prongs of a fork and even the serrated edge of a knife. Think 'hard rubber plaything for a dog', and that was Le Paradisier's version of a chicken leg. It was so bad that Sue and I had to hoard buns from breakfast and use these as a replacement for other meals. The only redeeming aspect of this terrible cuisine was our being able to watch the expressions on the faces of a group of newly arrived French guests when they began to tackle their own doggy playthings. Most of them managed both 'amazement' and 'horror' at the same time…

11. Visited a nearby expanse of rare spiny forest, where more locals were interacting with their environment by hacking it down in order to make some spiny enclosures for their cattle and goats. It made us both cry.

Well, I think that's quite enough in the way of a list of vignettes, so I will now describe what happened when we left the less than paradisiacal Le Paradisier and travelled further north up the west coast of Madagascar. Because this involves first the second testing tracks of this chapter – and then an insight into where such tracks can lead…

The track we took was longer than the four-mile track to Finniegill. It was 200km long. And in the eight hours it took Harry to negotiate this incredibly testing track, we saw just one distant village, no other vehicles and, ultimately, we even ran out of track. It was then just a matter of following the coastline over sand and rock – until, in the middle of the afternoon, we arrived at our destination: the 'simple beachside resort' of Laguna Blu. Here, Harry and Kenny would leave us (and in due course ruin only two of the Isuzu's tyres in taking it back down that track and then all the way back to Tana), and we would indulge ourselves in some serious relaxation before somehow flying back to the capital, so avoiding any further dealings with sand and rock.

However, the resort appeared to be empty. Nobody was there to welcome us. And it wasn't until Kenny had located and then awoken the resort manager from his siesta that it became apparent that the resort was indeed open for business, even if it was staffed by just that single Italian manager and two pretty local girls. Not that there was a great deal of business of any sort…

On the first evening, and having established that there were no other guests, we were having a drink in the resort's rather cavernous dining room waiting for our evening meal (which, like all our meals in this place, would be prepared by the Italian manager and be delicious), when, suddenly, two people walked into the room. And they both looked at us as though we had just arrived from Mars. Their expressions were ones of acute surprise. However, when they had satisfied themselves that we were not really aliens, they joined us and immediately informed us that they were not actually guests of the resort. No, they were both geologists. One was an Australian and the other was a Mauritian, and they were here in Madagascar prospecting for some sort of metal ore in the close-by interior. Indeed, they had been busy doing this for the past few months and, there being no town anywhere near – or indeed anything anywhere near – they had got into the habit of visiting Laguna Blu every fortnight for a meal and to get their laundry done. Oh, and as regards their look of surprise, for which they were very apologetic... well, they had never before seen anybody in this resort other than Mr Italy and his two helpers. We were the first visitors they had ever seen...

The resort is extant. I've checked. Although whether it gets more than two visitors a year I do not know. I still suspect it is part of an international tax scam or it has something to do with the Mafia. How can anywhere that is not connected to anywhere else ever be successful? And it really is in a part of the world that is pretty well inaccessible other than to the resolute or the foolhardy. Indeed, to get out of the place and back to Tana, we first had to climb onto the back of an old army truck and then be driven some way further north over another non-track to a dirt airstrip where a four-seater aeroplane was awaiting our arrival. That then took us to Toliara Airport to the south (which had just hosted an armed attack that had left two dead), where we then were able to catch a scheduled internal flight back to the capital (and to the welcoming arms of a very relieved Kenny).

After that there was still an excursion to be made to another small wildlife reserve to the east of Tana. However, you will be relieved to know that I have no intention of describing any aspects of this last wildlife reserve, but instead I will attempt to sum up what had impressed both Sue and me most about the remarkable island of Madagascar. And first and foremost was not the friendliness of its people – although that was unmissable – but instead the poverty that these people were having to endure, and how their poverty was in turn impoverishing their environment. Too many of them were cutting down what was left of the island's vegetation and too many of them were digging up what remained of its land – because there were too many of them, full stop.

Of course, Madagascar is by no means unique in having to bear an overload of *Homo sapiens*, but the impact of this overload was just so much in evidence everywhere. Even the country's national parks were not beyond degradation, and the only truly pristine places left, of which there were very few, were in the hands of those old colonial masters: a few French people still keeping at bay the pressures of overpopulation by retaining a hold on their old estates. But how long this would last and how long it would be tolerated by the Malagasies was by no means certain. And all the time ring-tailed lemurs and all Madagascar's fabulous endemic wildlife will become increasingly under threat. Indeed, I hate to think how much more of it has been swept away in the last few years…

So, our visit to Madagascar made us more determined than ever to see the world's natural wonders while they still existed. Which might sound a little pessimistic, but is in fact no more than frighteningly realistic. I wish it were not. Just as I wish that I could end this chapter with other than a miserable conclusion. And I will. Or at least I will try – by abandoning Madagascar in favour of… Mark Zuckerberg. Because it was in February of 2004 that this gentleman created Facebook. And has it ever occurred to you that Mark Zuckerberg has the same initials as 'Moronic Zombies'? And I cannot believe that this is just a coincidence…

Ruining, Reading, Writing and (Not) Rolling Over

Now, those of you without a failing memory might recall that when I delivered a lecture on the world's burgeoning population a few dozen pages previously, I threatened to address the excremental consequences of this abundance of humanity. Well, taking account of the observations I have just made about Madagascar and its 'consumption' by its resident humans, I think this is a suitable juncture at which to carry out that threat. And just to be clear, I have in mind here not the wars, the pandemics, the increased flow of refugees or any other impact on our own lives caused by there being too many of us, but instead the impact we are having on every other living thing on this planet. So please buckle up or, if you don't believe an autobiography is a suitable place to condemn the behaviour of the dominant species on the planet, you might want to skip to the second half of this chapter where I will no doubt have returned to my normal sunny self in the reporting of my life.

OK, for those of you still with me, I would like to take you back just 40,000 years – and to the continent of Australia (well before it had Castlemaine XXXX or even a single barbie). Because back then, the first *Homo sapiens* backpackers had made it there from Africa – where all the large animals were only too used to our predatory habits – and had found lots of new megafauna that was ignorant of our dastardly ways, and consequently would soon succumb to them. It wasn't long before species such as Diproton, Quinkana and Megalania – and probably a few more we don't even know about – could safely be classified as extinct. (And incidentally, a Megalania was *not* a giant president's wife, even though there might be a passing resemblance between the former and the latter.)

Well, fast forward 30,000 years, and another load of ramblers had made it to the New World, where they soon got on with the job of dispatching a whole new range of megafauna. Which is why we no longer have giant sloths or giant tapirs or saber-toothed cats or American lions or any number of other animals. Just as in Australia, we had taken on the role of an invasive species, and that meant the death knell for all those resident animals that we saw as a threat or a meal. Which, in my mind, is more than just a little sad.

Well, we didn't stop there. As we carpeted more and more of the world with more and more of ourselves, we continued to obliterate mere 'animals', having, of course, convinced ourselves that we were anything but mere animals. No, we were something very special, something that had the right to do as we pleased – and to kill as we pleased. So, onto the list of disappeared species went some of the smaller stuff – like dodos, thylacines, quaggas, various tortoises and indeed a whole list of other poor buggers who were too slow, too friendly, too nourishing or just too inconvenient in their habits. In fact, it's reckoned that in the last 500 years, we've tidied up more than 800 of these tardy, soppy, tasty and bothersome species, although the true figure is probably significantly higher. After all, if you're not really focused on eradication *per se*, you're not necessarily going to be too concerned about keeping a record of what you've eradicated, even if you've actually noticed that it's gone.

Neither might you have noticed that whilst you may have failed to tidy up every last member of a particular species, you have put a serious dent in its total population. And ultimately that you will end up with lots of animals, birds, fish and even insects who have in their Wikipedia entry 'extinct in the wild', 'critically endangered', 'endangered' or 'vulnerable'. Of which there are now far too many to list, and of which there will soon be many more.

However, we can't take all the credit for this miserable situation ourselves. There is, after all, a limit to how many creatures we can annihilate through our own efforts. Fortunate then that we have always been indifferent or careless in the way we have allowed so many mere animals to mimic the behaviour of our forebears in taking on the role of a devastating invasive species. Because they almost certainly won't concentrate on just megafauna, but instead they will bugger up the lives and take the lives of anything of any size with which they can successfully compete. Just think of cane toads, rats, pythons, grey squirrels, possums and about 10,000 other critters we've let loose in foreign lands, and you get the general idea. And what they get is the chance to wipe out great swathes of the resident critters by eating them, or eating their food, or killing them through their introducing alien pathogens or parasites against which the residents – or their food sources – have no defence. It's the same with flora as well. Thanks to us, the world is now full of the wrong plants in the wrong places, screwing up the natural vegetation and often the lives of the fauna that depends on this vegetation.

It is, I'm afraid, not a happy situation, and our proliferation and our sloppy habits have been good news for only a handful of our fellow creatures – such as tapeworms, ringworms, hookworms, pubic lice and, of course, belly button bacteria, none of which is ever likely to be regarded in the same way as say a cheetah or an elephant. Even if one day, they may be all we have left.

Yes, obliterating our fellow life forms is very much a work in progress, a job we are now tackling with renewed vigour in the shape of forest clearance, intensive farming, overfishing, mining, logging, indiscriminate hunting and, of course, stocking the planet with more and more people who need more and more land and more and more of everything. And there is a limit. It is called the Earth. And the more we take, the less there is for everything else. And you know when this is getting serious when the weight of all human-made materials in the world exceeds the weight of all its fauna and flora combined. (As it did at the end of 2020 when, at 1.1 trillion tons, it was measurably heavier than *all life* on this planet – which, I think, is pretty damn scary.)

Right. Now at this stage I was going to say a few words about how extinctions are just part of the natural process, and that it is reckoned that 99% of all species that the world has hosted are now extinct. I would then have gone on to talk about how we humans are so destructive that the 'background rate' of extinctions is now off the scale, giving no time for replacement species to develop. And therefore, at the current super-rate, we are on course for a full-blown 'Holocene extermination' event that will lead to the extinction of up to half of all the plant and animal species that presently exist by the end of this century. Although I'm not entirely sure whether our sterling work in support of climate change might mean that this outcome is achieved even earlier. But in any event, I am not going to harangue you any further, because I suspect that you have now got the message, and that you will well understand why my life was now set up to be increasingly devoted to my relishing the natural world while I (and Sue) still could – and why my writing would reflect both my fascination with the natural world and my despair at its unavoidable fate. Instead, I am going to treat you to a poem from one of the books I would get around to writing in about ten years' time. Because I think this poem might more eloquently portray what I was already thinking in 2005 than my maundering on any further in my questionable prose. It might also make you think of how lonely it will be when we've finally cleared all our neighbours away. Oh, and it does bloody well rhyme as well!

The chimpanzees have had their time
The pangolins have too
And polar bears, although they're cute
Well, they're now overdue

And so it is with turtles green
And rhinos white and black
And as for ellies brown and grey
They too have trunks to pack

We've worked so hard for many years
To clear these beasts away
And some were slow to see our point
That we alone should stay

But in the end they understood
That on this ravaged Earth
It's just ourselves and nothing else
That's blessed with any worth…

Not bad eh? For an accountant. Or should I say for an ex-accountant. Although, of course, in 2005, I had only recently become an ex-member of the Institute of Chartered Accountants in England and Wales – which wouldn't, incidentally, let me leave and therefore relieve me of paying my annual membership fees, until it had satisfied itself that there were no actions pending against me from my time in practice. I mean, what a bloody cheek! Me, a paragon of virtue, and a paragon who was now in need of a bit of a rest after that demanding trip around Madagascar. Which is why, in early April, Sue and I returned to East Winds in St Lucia for an essential spot of doing not very much of anything at all. Except maybe some reading...

I still have a record of what I read in the two weeks Sue and I spent there, and I therefore have a record of a number of books of which I have very little recollection at all – if any. So, I could tell you hardly anything or nothing whatsoever about what is written on the pages of *The End of Oil*, *The Plague*, *Hard Times*, *Jeeves Takes Charge*, *Decline and Fall*, *The Catcher in the Rye*, *The Picture of Dorian Gray*, *The Inheritors*, *Animal Farm* and *Yellow Dog*. Actually, that is not quite true. I do remember quite a lot about *Animal Farm* (which would go on to influence the writing of my own work on the curse of bureaucracy) and I also remember that Martin Amis's *Yellow Dog* was a pretentious waste of paper, ink and its readers' time. Indeed, I strongly believe that there should be a generous award for anybody who actually gets to its end.

And talking of books that are of questionable merit, I should here put on record that in 2005 I was doing quite a lot of my own writing. To begin with, I undertook a time-consuming rewrite of *Dumpiter*, and towards the end of the year it was a rewrite of the second Renton Tenting book, *Ticklers*. And sandwiched in between was that *Animal Farm*-inspired book on bureaucracy, to which I had given the title of *Crats* (probably on the basis that it would be less off-putting than a book with the title *Bureaucrats*). Anyway, it wasn't quite the short story that I'd had in my head for some time, but instead it borrowed from George Orwell's approach to his masterpiece. And it did this by revealing itself to be the tale of the gradual degeneration of a small South Sea island, seen through the eyes of one of its inhabitants over his lifetime – which was designed to be an allegory of Britain's own degeneration within the European Union at the hands of its own and the EU's self-serving bureaucrats. It might not have been up there with George's allegory, but it certainly reflected my own thoughts at the time, not only about bureaucracy in general but about the European Union and our position within it – thoughts, incidentally, that would never change but only harden over time.

However, the EU and all the millions of bureaucrats in Britain and in Europe were, by no means, successful in capturing all my thoughts in 2005, especially when, with Sue and her mum, I was making my way around the perimeter of Scotland, something I did in May of that year before the midge season had got into its stride. It was a trip I had always wanted to do: up Scotland's east coast, across its north coast, and then back down its west coast – so barely ever turning the steering wheel of our 4x4 Rav in other than an anticlockwise direction. It proved to be a very rewarding trip – even if the weather insisted on remaining very Scottish for almost its entire duration. And two aspects of it stick in my mind. One was the acute narrowness of the 'main road' that follows that north coast, which, for much of its length, is single-track with frequent passing places. And the other is to where one is delivered by that road: the tiny village of Tongue. This place sits not that far from the north-west tip of Scotland and, at a stretch, it could be considered to be a sort of western John O' Groats. Well, it could be in my mind anyway. Because, as we sat having our lunch in the Tongue Hotel, it occurred to me that John O' Groats, together with Land's End, had for too long monopolised the north to south measure of the British mainland. It was between these two extremities of our island that those with bucket lists to tick off or charities to assist, made their way. No other two places were ever considered.

But what if they were? What if, instead of John O' Groats, one set off from Tongue, and made one's way not to the extreme south-west of England but to somewhere near its extreme south-east? So, somewhere in Kent, say, somewhere like Sandwich, for example? And then one could claim to have done the 'Tongue Sandwich'!

Maybe somebody already has, and maybe, one day, I will. Because, that thought in the Tongue Hotel wasn't just about an alternative north to south route, it was also about the possibility of this route providing a unique theme for another of my books – particularly if it took in any number of villages and towns that shared a name with a foodstuff. That way, I could be the first person in the world to write a travel book that dealt exclusively with food-associated places in Britain – such as Wensleydale, Ham, Leek, Fryup (North Yorkshire) and Pease Pottage – and which, of course, would be given the eye-catching title of *Tongue Sandwich.*

Well, as I say, maybe one day I will make that north–south, food-associated journey – and write a book about it – but meanwhile, back in September 2005, the only trip I had in mind was one to Namibia and Botswana. This would be visit number three to these two countries, but the first where Sue and I would be travelling around Namibia without a guide. Yes, it would be yours truly who would be behind the wheel of our very own safari vehicle, and our drive would be entirely unaccompanied and with not a safety net in sight. We wouldn't even have a mobile. We could hardly wait.

Martin from Sandyacre was reckless enough to provide us with one of his own pukka safari vehicles, a lovely white Land Rover with all the trimmings: bullbar, all-terrain tyres, heavy-duty roof rack, heavy-duty jack, two spare wheels, toolkit, fridge, *The Complete Works of Shakespeare* and an inflatable au pair. Oh, and a map. Yes, no sissy sat-navs for us, but just a single map of Namibia with our destinations marked in red, and the assumption that we could read road numbers and signposts and not get hopelessly lost. Indeed, one would have to be a dummy to get lost in Namibia. There are so few roads in the country with so few turn-offs that one would have to make a conscious effort to do so. And even then, one would probably manage only to run out of fuel. As even now there are very few petrol stations in the country, and back then, some of these fuel stops were shown on one's map as 'unreliable'.

Now, at this point, it is probably worth elaborating just a little on the paucity of roads – and working petrol stations – in Namibia. Because this isn't a function of the country's desperate lack of infrastructure, but simply a function of it being sparsely populated. I have referred to this before: 2.6 million people occupying a patch three times the size of Britain. And this means that not only is its road system similarly sparse, but so too is the traffic on these roads. It is quite common to find oneself the only one using a particular road for mile after mile. Which, for someone who is more used to grappling with the M6 car park and similarly clogged roads in Britain, is a cause of delight. I loved it. Even though I knew I had to be careful...

Martin had given me a few tips on driving in Namibia before we had set off from Windhoek, and he had explained to me the dangers of driving on gravel roads. This was an essential briefing, as many of the country's roads lack tarmac and are just graded strips of Namibia's rocky surface, where traction cannot be guaranteed, especially when negotiating bends in a top-heavy Land Rover. One therefore has to be aware of one's speed at all times, and moderate it accordingly. I did, and was therefore able to arrive at the Etosha National Park without mishap, and drive around the park without mishap. I was even able to reach our next destination – over a number of gravel roads – without incident. Unlike someone we encountered there whose driving had not been quite so circumspect.

This was at a place called Mowani Mountain Camp, a rather nice lodge in the Damaraland region of Namibia, an area famed for its beauty – and for its winding gravel roads. We were at the reception of the lodge, probably just passing the time of day with one of the lodge's staff, when a young woman and an old man appeared – on foot. This was unusual. Everybody normally arrives in a vehicle at this place. But what was more unusual was that both the woman and the man were injured, the man more so, which was why he was being supported by the woman. She then announced to her startled audience that she was a safari guide who had just rolled her Land Rover, injuring herself and one of her clients (the man) and killing her other client (the man's wife).

I am not able to report what happened to the young woman subsequently, as she and the man were quickly assisted by the lodge staff and soon thereafter evacuated to a hospital. We never saw them again or received any news of their condition. However, I would guess that if she ever again got behind the wheel of a car on one of Namibia's gravel roads, she would be just as careful as I'd be. And I'd now be super-careful. After all, killing one's passengers through an ill-judged piece of driving would make for a memorable holiday, but only for one with all the wrong sort of memories. And, in view of the fact that a woman had died, I hope that doesn't sound flippant. It's just that I want to emphasise that driving in Namibia is one of the country's greatest attractions, but it can so easily be a fatal attraction. And not an on-screen one but a real one.

OK. I suspect I've dwelt for far too long on the appeal and the perils of Namibia's road network, and I should now take just a little time to make clear that it wasn't just the pleasure and the thrill of the driving that, in due course, would bring us back to Namibia (and Botswana) again and again, but what Namibia and Botswana offered in terms of scenery, wildlife, excitement and challenge. And to give you just a taste of what I am talking about, I'm going to set out a short list of some of the other events on this first 'solo flight' to these two countries – starting with a challenge…

1. Whilst still at Mowani, I discovered that the Land Rover had a flat tyre. This I dealt with by using one of the spare wheels on the roof rack, at the cost of only a ricked back.
2. At our next destination, Okonjima, Sue and I witnessed a young leopard catching a… mouse.
3. At Okonjima, we got close up and personal with a cheetah.
4. After flying to Maun in Botswana, we got flown into the Okavango Delta in a small plane piloted by a schoolboy. (At least, he looked like a schoolboy.)
5. In the Okavango Delta, we saw a whole host of different animals, including a hyena, who rounded off our evening meal in a lodge called Savuti by walking into the dining tent and raising himself up to place his paws on the dining-room table. And he hadn't even made a reservation.
6. We installed ourselves in a redoubt made from dead tree trunks adjacent to Savuti's pumped waterhole, there to be surrounded by a herd of (very close-by) elephants.
7. One evening, we observed ten of these same elephants organising themselves into a perfectly in-line phalanx behind the herd's matriarch, in readiness for a charge towards a hyena who had three days previously killed one of their very young – and then the charge itself. (Back then, if we hadn't witnessed this ourselves, we would have said such discipline – and thought – was just not possible. Although we now know that elephants are capable of just about anything.)

So… Namibia and Botswana would be seeing us again – and again. As would Finniegill. On which subject I should end this chapter by saying that the track to Finniegill was not getting any better (remember), and we therefore swapped our Rav for a much beefier Touareg. And this proved a wise decision, as nature seemed intent on making our journeys to Wood Cottage more and more exciting. As when, in November 2005, we arrived in our valley to find that the river had moved about fifteen feet to the west, demolishing its far bank near our house, but providing us with a noticeable amount of new land in the form of a huge pebble 'beach'. Oh, and it appeared that the deluge that had given rise to this rerouting of the river had cut off our neighbour for three days. None of which, I discovered, had she used to read Martin Amis's *Yellow Dog*...

Dining in Spain and Guyana

I talked a little while ago about the feeling of approaching a vortex above a plughole, and that whatever was down through that plughole being far from inviting. Well, we now seemed to be in that vortex, in the sense that so much of what was happening in the world and in Britain was not what an enlightened, country-loving, nature-loving, fair-minded, still relatively prepossessing, English Baby Boomer would welcome. And I have in mind here not just the unappealing Eton Mess we were making of the whole world – which by 2006 could be taken for granted – but some of the other less important features of life. Like, for example, music…

Well, thanks to a myopic commercialised music industry and a generation of artistes whose style of music might best be described as either immediately forgettable or embarrassingly indistinguishable from any of that of their contemporaries, the general standard of popular music had become lamentable. And if you doubt my word, I challenge you to name any of the top ten hits in the UK in 2006 – or any hits in that year (and you don't even need to be a Baby Boomer to find that challenge impossible). Of course, there was still some good stuff around – being sung and played by little-known artistes in modest venues – whose chance of being presented to a wider audience was minimal, unless, of course, they learnt to shriek or maybe submit themselves to one of the ten electronically produced soundtracks authorised by the aforementioned music industry. Or, if they were black, they were prepared to dishonour the fine tradition of soul music by joining the great deception that 'rapping', in some bizarre way, constitutes 'music', when clearly it constitutes no more than a tuneless celebration of all things unpleasant. Indeed, its only worthwhile use is as an alternative for white sound in the torture of political prisoners. For who the hell could stand more than just a few hours of uninterrupted 'rhythmic speech' and 'street vernacular'? I'd be begging for mercy within minutes. Unless I could really focus on that vortex…

Which reminds me. I haven't mentioned women's and men's fashion yet – which had become… well, either somewhat scruffy or somewhat uninspired. Or the output of the film industry, which had become simply pathetic. I mean, if it wasn't serving up stuff to keep the kids happy like *Happy Feet* or *Ice Age: The Meltdown*, it was feeding us a load of reheated garbage, which I think is the only way one can describe such 'squeeze another one out of the franchise' offerings as *Pirates of the Caribbean: Dead Man's Chest*, *Mission: Impossible III* and *Superman's Return*. Not quite up there with *In the Heat of the Night*, *The Day of the Jackal* or *Deliverance*, are they? Their only redeeming feature is that they were just make believe, and not another aspect of the real world that was spinning that vortex ever faster all the time – like fundamentalism, terrorism, race riots, terrorism and more terrorism. All of which were alive and well in an England that was now rapidly and radically changing its complexion…

So… it was just as well that there were plenty of distractions in my life to maintain my unbounded *joie de vivre*, one of which kicked off in April when, for the first time in my life, I visited Spain. This wasn't going to be a Blanca, Brava, or del Sol type of holiday, but instead it would entail an overnight ferry to Santander, a long drive south, taking in a handful of *paradors*, a stay in a cottage near Ronda, and then a return trip to Santander, sampling just two more of those splendid *paradors* on the way. And indeed, the *paradors* were splendid, as was the journey down through Extremadura (remember?), and there were just two Spanish flies in the ointment. Although, not of the literal insect variety, as a Spanish fly is, in fact, not a fly but an emerald-green beetle, and the source of a blistering agent once used as an aphrodisiac. Probably unsuccessfully.

Anyway, the first Spanish fly was the cottage, which was in an elevated position in a national park – and was… well, quite parky. The weather was not great, and the nights were really very chilly. However, this we could just about manage. Which was not the case with the second Spanish fly, because Sue and I could simply not convince our bodies that eating in the very late evening was a sensible way to go about providing them with sustenance. This late, late dining was a feature of all the *paradors* and of all the restaurants we explored around Ronda, and it is still a mystery to me why a whole country would adopt such a perverse habit. After all, what happens when all those recently stoked stomachs get put to bed – or taken to bed? How can it possibly be conducive to sleep, rest or play? And what's more, has this dilatory dining habit been the cause of even greater harm, as evidenced by this Iberian nation's performance outside the bedroom – in the New World?

I'm talking here about a pet theory of mine, which seeks to explain why, in colonising the Americas, the northern Europeans made such a success of it – in economic terms – while the southern Europeans, represented predominantly by the Spanish, made only an economic balls-up of it. I mean, in very simple terms, the current wealth of the English-speaking USA and Canada is significantly greater than the combined wealth of all the Spanish-speaking countries to their south. Furthermore, those two North American countries have been more 'sorted' throughout their entire histories than any of those South and Central American nations, some of which are still languishing in the banana-republic league, with no hope of an imminent promotion – or a promotion ever.

There are, I am sure, all sorts of reasons economists might put forward to explain this glaring disparity, but I doubt any of them would postulate that a delayed dining regime is the chief culprit. Even though it could be. Especially when one stops to consider how lethargic and ineffective one can feel the day after a late-night blow-out. And if this was the normal condition of all those Spanish conquistadors, and this lethargy and ineffectiveness was then passed on through subsequent generations, it seems to me quite conceivable that it could lead to endemic dysfunction and chronic underperformance, most notably but not exclusively in economic terms.

However, my pet theory does have a flaw. It is called Portuguese-speaking Brazil. Because my personal experience of both that giant South American country and its coloniser, Portugal, is that they share the sensible eating habits of most of the rest of the world, which means their people sleep well and awake feeling refreshed and revived rather than bilious and tired. And if so, why is Brazil not another USA?

I think I know. It just possibly might not be those Spanish eating habits after all, but instead the fact that, through the centuries, northern Europeans had to work hard to assemble enough food to keep themselves alive during long, cold winters, whereas their southern counterparts could play the lotus eaters and still survive what would be a far less demanding time. The northerners therefore developed an ingrained work ethic and the southerners did not – and have not even now. Mildly racist, this view, and probably just as invalid as my eating hypothesis. But I have yet to hear a rational explanation for the huge difference in fortunes of the south and the north of the New World. Just as I have yet to hear a convincing defence of the commonly held belief that 'worth' is synonymous with economic success. However, I begin to digress, and I will now draw to a conclusion my pseudo-philosophical musings on the supposed shortcomings of the Spanish by conceding that their Rioja wines are undoubtedly some of the best wines in the world. And this probably more than makes up for a whole load of anybody's shortcomings.

Talking of which, there were still some shortcomings to deal with in *Lollipop*, my third Renton Tenting book. And the task of dealing with these took up the first part of the year, after which I then spent quite some time distilling some of the best bits from my three pet-hate books into a single book called *Eggshell in Scrambled Eggs.* Its title is, I hope, self-explanatory, in that I cannot possibly be alone in loathing the presence of unwanted eggshell in my nicely cooked *oeufs brouillés.* I might, however, be in a distinct minority in now having five books that I planned to get printed in the naïve belief that, with the right website in place, their quality would ensure that they would be eagerly snapped up by an impatient reading public. And what I'm talking about here is *Dumpiter*, *Ticklers*, *Lollipop*, *Crats* and *Eggshell in Scrambled Eggs*, all of which you should recognise if you have been paying attention. And in due course I might check whether you remember that it was in September of this year that all five books, complete with my very own cover artwork, arrived in proper book form from the (Hong Kong) printers. I will not, however, be testing you on how their sales went, because I'm not going to tell you. I am going to let you guess that for yourself…

Anyway, between sorting out these five books and sorting out how to catch mice humanely in Wood Cottage (they had turned it into a maternity hospital), I did manage to do some other writing. Not of another book, but of a TV comedy series in six parts. It was called *The Lodge*, and it was set in a private southern-African wildlife reserve, but one that was deficient in one important ingredient: wildlife. This had been around in abundance when the lodge of the title was first established, but a tectonic plate movement had caused the reserve's river to disappear entirely, and the wildlife had then upped sticks and disappeared as well. This had caused the owner, with the help of his staff (all of whom were involved in various internet scams) to assemble a collection of fibreglass, cardboard, inflatable and mechanical animals, which, at a distance and with the right 'management', could look like the real thing. Particularly if being observed by a clientele who were predominantly middle-aged and who had less than perfect eyesight. That might sound like a stretch, but from my experience in Namibia and elsewhere, I knew it wasn't a stretch too far. Certainly not for a comedy series.

The six episodes of the series dealt with new owners of the lodge arriving to find that what they had purchased was not quite what they had expected, and soon realising that they had to carry on with the elaborate deception – to stand any chance of offloading the property onto another gullible buyer. And to do this they needed the assistance of the lodge staff – and they therefore needed to allow their staff to continue with their own personal scams. Sounds promising, doesn't it? And I even reckoned it could be made on the cheap in somewhere like Norfolk – on those few days in the year when the sun put in an appearance there. I think I made that point when I submitted it to the BBC. But it made no difference. When I received the nice letter from the nice Asian lady, rejecting my efforts out of hand, I found no reference in it to Norfolk and indeed no reference in it to the fact that the BBC wasn't especially interested in comedy programmes anymore. Even though, as we all know, they were already in the process of consigning comedy to the 'might offend' bin, and replacing it with riveting competitive baking and knitting shows and 'extravaganzas for the lobotomised' productions. I can at least take some comfort from the fact that, if submitted in 2006, *Monty Python's Flying Circus* would almost certainly have suffered

My first cultural appropriation.

Me (second from the right) – with lots of hair and thirteen other articled clerks.

Smoking in Fiji.

Me with the Touche Ross Cerbera and a rather nice tie.

Keeping the staff happy.

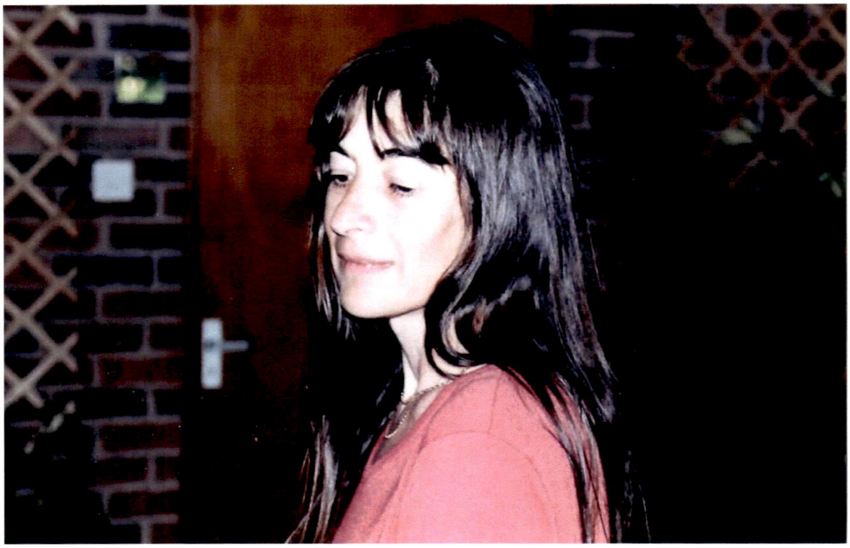

Sultry Sue.

'They're behind you…'

A muster of meerkats.

Somewhere in Namibia or Botswana.

Not a bad pic.

Wood Cottage and a few trees.

Our Galápagos floating home.

Medallion man!

My delicious DB9.

Sue at the wheel.

Awesome Antarctica.

the same fate as *The Lodge*, even though the Pythons' offering might have had marginally more merit than my own. Albeit no blow-up elephants and no cut-out giraffes.

It was similar in Guyana. Not one elephant and not one giraffe. Possibly because Guyana – to the surprise of many – is not in Africa, but at the top edge of that other continent hosting predominantly Spanish and Portuguese-speaking nations that goes by the name South America. Sue and I went there in September 2006 and, in doing so, we probably constituted a measurable percentage of its tourist trade for the whole year. Guyana, after all, is essentially an empty country, with a population that even now is no more than three quarters of a million, most of whom are clustered around its coast, and less likely to venture into its interior than a couple of pale-faced visitors from Britain. No surprise then that we had chosen to go there.

We started off in Georgetown, which had a similar reputation to that of Port Moresby in Papua New Guinea. That is to say, it was not a strolling-around-at-night sort of place. Instead, in between arriving there and making a small-plane flight to see the country's famous Kaieteur Falls (the world's largest single-drop waterfall by the volume of water flowing over it) we strolled around only the interior of the wonderful Cara Lodge Hotel. This is where we were staying: one of the oldest and grandest structures in the city built in 1840, and visited over the years by such notables as King Edward VIII, Prince Charles, Prince Andrew (!) and, just the previous year, Mick Jagger (!!).

I suspect Mick and his then partner, L'Wren Scott, made use of the same 'room' that we did. This was the incredibly inexpensive Quamina Suite at the top of the hotel: a suite of three rooms, all of which epitomised 'Georgetown's colonial elegance and bygone charm'. I wonder, though, whether they found their stay there quite so exciting as ours. Because on our last night in these elegant surroundings – and in the very middle of this night – the lights came on in our bedroom, causing me to wake and immediately bring to mind that we were on our very own isolated floor of a hotel in the middle of a city noted for its sometimes-deadly antisocial behaviour. But, so what. I was an English Baby Boomer, and in the face of adversity, our sort don't just whistle and smile, but instead we get out of bed, equip ourselves with a nearby hand-carved *objet d'art*, and creep purposefully (and stark nakedly) into the adjoining also-lit sitting room, there to confront whatever foreign Johnny has inserted himself into our accommodation. Well, needless to say, there was nobody there. And, as we would discover in the morning, our illuminating incident was all down to the actions of a careless security guard who, following an overnight power cut, had switched on our lights using the switches next to the suite's entrance in the corridor below. So, all was well, other than whoever ends up making the film of my life, if he or she wishes to portray this scene as faithfully as possible, will have to resort to some clever camera angles or maybe a touch of pixilation. He or she will also have to do some filming at Karanambu Lodge...

This was our primary destination in Guyana: a tiny as-simple-as-they-come eco lodge, sitting in the middle of 110 square miles (!) of savannah, marshy ponds and riparian forest, with a thirty-mile stretch of the huge Rupununi River running through it. We flew there in a small plane, and soon realised we again might be sleeping in a bed recently occupied by Mick Jagger, himself a lover of wildlife who, we were told, had made the same journey from Georgetown to this wildlife-rich idyll in the middle of nowhere. It really was stuffed with all manner of creatures – including giant anteaters, red howler monkeys, sun bitterns, purple gallinules and far too many others to mention. And, incidentally, I do mean 'stuffed'. We made a couple of early-evening excursions to a large ox-bow-type lake, and not only was this lake covered in the giant round leaves of giant water lilies, but beneath its waters were caimans of all sizes, and above it were hundreds if not thousands of bats and nighthawks – and on its edge was a bustling heronry filled with boat-billed herons, whose young are able to do a passable impression of large, peach-coloured, bird-shaped powder puffs. It was overwhelming, and an insight into how rich the natural world can be when we aren't let anywhere near it. Unless, maybe to help it out. Which is what the lodge's matriarch, a lady by the name of Diane McTurk, had been doing for years.

She deserves a whole chapter of this book to herself. But I will restrict myself to recording the fact that she had become renowned not just for maintaining a rare slice of paradise, but also for rescuing orphaned giant river otters and releasing them back into the wild when they were capable of looking after themselves. And there was actually one in residence when we were in residence, one who could be observed waddling around the grounds of the lodge, or following our boat when we ventured out onto the river, or playing and swimming with Diane in the river – or taking fish from Sue's hand, being careful with its awesome teeth not to take fingers from Sue's hand as well.

Karanambu is seared into my mind, and one aspect of it is seared into that part of my mind that hosts the 'amusing stories' files. It concerns the evening dining arrangements at the lodge, which involved Diane and her nephew and niece hosting all the lodge's guests at a single table in a big, open-sided, thatched-roofed building at the centre of the lodge. This wasn't difficult, as there were rarely more than four guests, and the table was quite large. It was also situated under that thatched roof, which in this part of the world was always going to provide an ideal roost for bats. One wasn't aware of them during the meal, especially when one was listening to Diane's cut-glass tones as she gave an account of her life in Guyana – and British Guiana. (Her family had been associated with this former British possession for 200 years, but had packed her off for schooling and 'finishing' in England. Hence the voice – and her ability to engender the feeling of a country-house gathering around the table.) However, towards the end of the meal, it was a different matter. This was when the bats would begin to wake and, like many other mammals when they wake, they would pretty soon go to the toilet. Which meant that during coffee and liqueurs, the evidence of their toilet behaviour would begin to land on the table. It did every night. Which might explain why Diane was able to continue chatting amiably while there were droppings arriving from above – and then so deftly employ her used napkin to clear any nearby droppings from the table, without losing eye contact with her guests or even pausing for a second in her discourse. She had apparently once worked at the Savoy hotel, a time she had clearly used to hone her hosting skills, even if that London hotel had not been able to furnish her with the appropriate etiquette for the removal of bat poo. That, she must have worked out for herself.

Karanambu Lodge was a splendid place, made even more splendid by the remarkable Diane McTurk, a 'don't make 'em like that anymore' character, who finally left Guyana and the world in 2016. It was certainly a place that would be a hard act to follow, and although they tried, our remaining destinations in that part of the world didn't really come close – either in wildlife terms or entertainment terms. Our next destination, the Iwokrama River Lodge, did manage a little on the wildlife front, but as this was mostly in the form of sandflies, it was never going to be a serious challenger to Karanambu. The Asa Wright Nature Centre in Trinidad did rather better (this was a two-country expedition), and this 'top birdwatching spot in the Caribbean' certainly lived up to its billing. One was almost overwhelmed with close-by hummingbirds, orioles, honeycreepers, manakins, tanagers and various other little gems. Unlike at the Coco Reef Resort and Spa in Tobago, where all one was overwhelmed with was the indifference of its staff and their overtly surly attitude.

I mention this briefly because it wasn't our first choice for our end-of-exhausting-holiday rest (our first choice had cocked up our booking), but also because the attitude of the hotel's staff was so at odds with the attitude of the 'Trinbagonian' taxi driver who had found for us this replacement hostelry. He was as nice as pie, and in our extended ride around the island, he was very chatty and very forthcoming about how it was in what was now an independent Trinidad and Tobago, and how different it had been when it was still a British colony. And he was unequivocal in his opinion that 'things had been better under British rule'. It wasn't, he explained, that he wanted to ingratiate himself with us, but he just wanted to tell us that since we had packed up and gone, corruption had moved in to take our place. And he, like many of his fellow Trinbagonians, looked back longingly to the time when the rules and conventions of our colonial embrace meant that endemic corruption couldn't find a foothold on either Trinidad or Tobago.

Of course, even recounting this factual story will send a whole brigade of liberal numpties into absolute apoplexy. But it is true. And it even echoes similar views Sue and I have heard in other ex-colonial nations. Well, absolute apoplexy is all very well, but I have in mind to see whether I can go one better and burst any liberal blood vessels – by expanding on this non-woke view of colonialism, probably in the next chapter. But for now, I will simply remind you of a quote made by the ultra-perceptive American essayist, H. L. Mencken, who said, 'The average man does not want to be free; he simply wants to be safe.' He could not have been more right.

Freedom, in my mind, is a much more nebulous concept than safety. Safety is something tangible, and something that everybody can recognise – and that everybody wants. In the same way that virtually everybody wants a corruption-free environment, and a lot of them would choose this even if it meant tolerating a bunch of whities up at Government House – a bunch of whities who are highly likely to have only a minimal impact on their day-to-day lives…

So, there you have it. Spaniards already worked over – with probably zero justification – and now apologist liberals in my sights, who, in contrast to the inhabitants of Spain, deserve everything that's coming their way. I mean, apart from anything else, there's no way they'd ever buy even one of my quintet of wonderful books. I just know it…

The Nastiness of Man and the Isle of Man

Have you ever become aware, in your journey through life, that you haven't packed every item of general knowledge that you probably should have packed? That left behind in various unopened cupboards and drawers, there is all manner of stuff, the like of which others have remembered to bring along with them, but you haven't? I don't mean something like a total grasp of the classics or even a working knowledge of the great English authors. I mean instead some of the specifics – like where did the Jews come from or how did Islam capture and retain the adherence of so many people. Well, I had this awakening around this time of my life, and I therefore decided to consume Paul Johnson's *A History of the Jews* and Karen Armstrong's not very good *Islam: A Short History*, and I would then go on to read Darwin's *On the Origin of Species* and a number of other equally demanding, albeit not necessarily illuminating, tomes.

Anyway, I suppose what this all amounted to was a little dose of delayed education, where the method of teaching was a few bouts of intense self-study. Or, in the case of British history, the writing of my very own *British History* – with images of all the British kings starting at King Aethelwulf (who was actually only King of Wessex) and ending with our present long-serving, long-suffering wonder. This book was, of course, never intended for publication, but just to clarify in my mind the outline story of Britain, and to give me at least a tenuous grip on the order of all our British monarchs

– and how their reigns came to an end. Richard II did come after Edward III, didn't he? And it was Charles I and not Charles II who lost contact with his head, wasn't it?

Well, this burst of principally historical elucidation did have an interesting by-product. It reinforced my view that humanity was a little like alcohol, in that if its deleterious effects had been known before it was let loose on the world, it would never have been let loose in the first place. I mean, (mostly male) humans, throughout the ages, haven't only been abusing the natural world, but they've also been (consistently) abusing their fellow humans – in every place they've ever set foot in the world. If they haven't been 'raping and pillaging' them, subjugating them, or enslaving them, then they've simply been murdering them or sometimes obliterating them in great swathes in an organised programme of genocide. Our record is appalling, and essentially we've always been pretty damn nasty whenever it's taken our fancy. And it seems that it's very often taken our fancy. Indeed, ever since we first stood upright, when, soon thereafter, we probably hit over the head someone else who had also stood upright, who... well, who just ruddy well deserved it...

OK. I'll come clean. What I have just written is a sneaky sort of introduction to what I threatened to do in the last chapter, which was to be a little less than respectful to that powerful coterie of precious uber-liberal halfwits who seek to control our thoughts. And, as indicated, I will be doing this by setting out my less than conventional views on colonialism – and on Britain's role in this abominable practice. And I will begin by repeating what I have just said: we are a pretty damn nasty species, and that means, amongst other things, that we are not noted either for our forbearance or for our hesitation in exploiting others for our own reward. That's why history is full of ruthless men leading other men to get the better of their neighbours in any way they can, and sometimes with the result that they create full-blown empires full of subjugated people, who, incidentally, given half the chance, will probably display a similar disdain for life and liberty by in turn becoming empire builders and subjugators themselves.

So... if one arrives at a point in human history where technological advances in one part of the world mean that the inhabitants of that part of the world can travel all over the world – armed with their clearly superior technology – it would be perverse in the extreme if they didn't use their advantage... to their advantage. And before going on to consider how they exploited their technological superiority, let's just admit that if the boot was on the other foot, and let's say it was the Bantu peoples of Africa who, through enlightenment and science, had been able to produce sea-going ships (and guns), we would now be talking about the 'shame' not of the British Empire but of the Bantu Empire, and how the colonisation of Europe was an unforgivably heinous act without parallel in human history. Which, of course, it wouldn't have been, any more than what actually happened was an unforgivably heinous act. It was just our very imperfect species doing what our very imperfect species does whenever it's given the chance: making the best of that chance. Hell, here we were, in Britain, with the chance to exploit not just our neighbours – most of whom had similarly advanced technologies – but people in faraway lands whose cutting-edge armaments were in the shape of... well, armaments with cutting edges or maybe with sharp points. But nothing involving rifled barrels and fast-moving metal projectiles.

Furthermore, we didn't set out to be unduly unpleasant. We initially set out to make money out of trading – in spices and in all those other commodities that might brighten up the dismal, rain-sodden existence of all those in this dismal rain-sodden island. Quite simply, there was never a monarch in our history who one day woke up and decided at breakfast that he'd rather like an empire. No more than there was a bunch of courtiers who one day sat down for an illustrated-on-parchment presentation on empire-building, and concluded that this would be a shrewd investment for the future. It was all much more *ad hoc,* with the state's involvement in acquiring overseas possessions very much following in the wake of the traders, and never, it seems, with much in the way of pre-planning. Indeed, it could be argued that the British Empire and the whole associated process of colonisation was much more benign than any of the empire-building that had gone on before, in that it was a passive rather than an active process. It was just that more and more places in the world were ending up being painted pink on the map as part of some sort of spontaneous and irresistible natural phenomenon. And at the time, nobody in Britain saw this as other than a 'good thing'. After all, it was adding hugely to our prosperity, and it was also 'civilising all those natives' and 'bringing some much-needed order to the world'.

I have put those last two observations into quotation marks because even I can't swallow the idea that our motives were always quite so noble, and our treatment of those 'natives' clearly left a lot to be desired. We could be, as I hope you have not forgotten, just as nasty as our kind has always been, and even our laudable-at-the-time attempts at 'civilising the natives' – often with the help of a bible – were pretty damn reprehensible. But probably not up there with what Genghis Khan got up to…

And now a word on slavery. Or maybe a statement. Which is that we didn't invent it. We just plugged into a system that had been in operation in Africa (and in lots of other places around the world) for centuries, and was just part and parcel of that being-unpleasant-to-your-neighbour syndrome. As in, when you defeated your neighbours in some sort of serious bust-up, you would be expected to enslave those you had defeated. And if a new market opened up for these slaves in the shape of white guys with ships looking for a new product out of which they might make money, you were hardly going to change your ways. You were instead going to supply them with all their needs until such time as a few heroes like William Wilberforce in a land far, far away convinced his fellow Brits that trading in humans was just too awful even for horrible humanity. Indeed, it's only a pity that he and his colleagues aren't still around today to deal with an upsurge in modern slavery that seems to be getting on very well without a British Empire or an active programme of colonisation.

So, as you will see, I am the antithesis of an apologist for colonialism or the British Empire, and in many ways the Empire was not a bad thing. At least not in the way Nazism or the Chinese Communist Party are undeniably bad things. Just think of the comments that taxi driver in Tobago made, and also think of the infrastructure and governmental and judicial structures we introduced into many of our colonies, whilst at the same time we were expunging some of their egregious habits such as cannibalism and suttee. Indeed, our record could not have been that appalling when one encounters the welcome one receives in these ex-colonies, or when one compares it to what, in many cases, their peoples now have to endure. Not just corruption, but also out-of-control nepotism, presidents for life, brutal police forces, acute poverty, economic stagnation, and, of course, private jets and lots of Mercedes limousines in the hands of the very few. Oh, and the plebs might well end up being shot, blown up or macheted to death.

I still find it difficult to understand why my Britain is singled out for particular criticism when our colonisation of so many countries was no more than an inevitable act, given our technological edge and the natural beastliness of our species. The British Empire was just one of the later examples of the age-old practice of abusing one's neighbours if one could, albeit on this occasion, the neighbours in question were not just next door. Furthermore, it is interesting to examine the definition of colonialism, which is 'the policy or practice of acquiring full or partial control over another country, occupying it with settlers, and exploiting it economically'. Which, I humbly submit, might not be a million miles away from what this country is now the subject of itself. With some of those settlers (participating in our ill-gotten wealth) being the most vocal of all the critics of colonialism. Other, of course, than those damn liberals, many of whom are now probably frothing at the mouth. Which can't be a bad thing.

Right. That's got all that out of my system for the moment. So, it must now be time for me to recount some of the less provocative aspects of my thinking and my life in 2007, starting with a trip to Crete. This was meant to be a laid-back birding expedition, with maybe more of the lying-back element than the birding element, to which end we had rented two villas (to be visited in turn), one in the west of the island near a place called Chania and another, attached to a hotel, near a place in the east of the island called Agios Nikolaos – known to its friends as East-end Nick. Well, we did manage quite a lot of nothing and, when we managed to abandon nothing and got ourselves into bird-spotting mode, we did find quite a few different birds. So, in that sense, the holiday was a success. And furthermore, it is beholden on me to mention that there are parts of Crete which are really beautiful, and the island can certainly pride itself on its cuisine and its hospitality. Nevertheless, we had soon decided that it was not a destination that would ever be seeing us again.

It was windy. All the time. It was also very messy, not just in terms of the abundance of uncleared litter or the number of uncleared rocks on the smart, unused, EU-financed roads through its mountains, but also in more acute terms in those parts of the island given over to tomato production. Because in these areas one could find some of the most abused and unkempt tracts of land one could possibly imagine. Then there was its north coast – its tourist coast – which, with its unbroken crust of various sorts of holiday accommodation, was distinctly more con-crete than attractive-Crete, and about as inspiring as an Ed Sheeran ballad. Oh, and then there was Heraklion airport, the gateway to this island idyll, but something of a barrier to anyone wishing to catch a plane to get out of the island. With its chaotic, under-resourced systems and its surly uncaring staff, it still ranks in my mind as the most disorganised airport I've ever encountered. And that's saying something. Especially when one remembers that I have travelled to Tanzania and various other places in Africa. Sue and I were both very happy when we did manage to make our flight despite the best efforts of this worst-of-all airport, and not at all unhappy that we would not be gracing the shores of Crete ever again. Even if they managed to turn down the wind.

Instead, we'd take ourselves off to a cottage in Cornwall to have a nose around this end-of-the-road county and to have a look at the Eden Project. It was June now, which meant that it rained for most of our stay there – and that the outlook for smokers was even gloomier than the skies. Yes, horrors upon horrors, Sue and I were both regular puffers back then, and we were both very dismayed that another bit of what we regarded as part of our life – puffing while drinking in a public house – was soon to be chipped away and thrown onto that growing pile of what was now not allowed. Indeed, this dismay was so intense that on hearing on the BBC News that, as from 1 July 2007, the Isle of Man would be the only place in the British Isles where one could still have a fag with one's pint in a pub, I immediately announced that we would be acquiring a property on that island as soon as was practically possible. Not as somewhere to live – permanently – but just as some sort of 'safety valve' property; a foothold on that British Crown dependency that would allow us to evade the regrettable diktats of the British Crown's misguided politicians. Even if, on this occasion, they might be right…

In the event, it took me only a few weeks to turn that announcement into action. And by mid-August, I had visited the Isle of Man, engaged the services of an estate agent and, with her help, had found a suitable apartment on Queens Promenade in Douglas (its seaside esplanade). I had then put in an offer for it – and this offer had been accepted. I would soon be the legal owner of a one-bedroom 'penthouse' on the island, complete with balcony and sea views, if with only a modest amount of floor space. Later in the year, when the lawyers had finally exhausted every means of delay at their disposal and title had passed, I made a further visit to the island to furnish the apartment, and to organise its letting. Hell, this was to be just a foothold, remember – which had to pay for itself while I considered the need to use it, and that meant that I needed to find a tenant. This was not difficult. And to this day, the apartment has barely been without a paying 'guest'. Which, given that Sue and I, some time ago, gave up smoking, is not a bad thing. With no need for a smoking-friendly pub anymore and no real prospect of Jeremy Corbyn becoming Prime Minister, the foothold is now unlikely to be used. Instead, it simply generates a useful cashflow, which I like, and the need to complete an Isle of Man tax return, which I do not. And to finish this particular island saga, I will report that from my brief experience of the island, it is almost as windy there as it is on Crete. But it has much less litter.

OK. Time to make a brief mention of some of the other things that were going on in my world in 2007, and to start with I should report that writing that book on British history didn't really satisfy my 'creative needs', and therefore, during the year, I poured my creative juices into another TV comedy series (which would prove to be dead on arrival), and into trying to become a cartoonist. This latter endeavour was not easy, as it required rather more than a few ideas for the cartoons (I had a whole string of them based on the adventures of God). Yes, it also required an ability to draw the cartoons. And even though I bought a book on how to do this, I found it near impossible. Tapping away at a keyboard to produce words was infinitely easier.

So was sending my books to various 'victims', including journalists, actors, 'well-known people' and a couple of my heroes – one of whom, in common with a fair number of recipients, actually acknowledged my gift. Like most of these well-mannered people, he probably didn't read any of my magic prose, but that didn't really matter. For who would not want a handwritten thank-you letter from David Attenborough?! Answer: probably just as few people as would welcome a sliding stock market or the fact that the Russians were murdering people not just in their own country but also in ours. Yes, towards the latter part of the year, the financial crisis was just getting its boots on, and the Russian secret service was putting the boot in – in the form of radioactive polonium administered to one Alexander Litvinenko. There would be much more bad news to come on the financial condition of the world and, over the forthcoming years, much more in the way of egregious behaviour from rogue Russia. But at the time both of these 'unwanted developments' were really quite disturbing. As indeed was the fact that the pre-Corbyn moron by the name of Gordon Brown had become Prime Minister, and it was now difficult to see how things could get much worse.

Fortunate then, that another trip to Namibia and Botswana would be squeezed into 2007. This would be our fourth visit to the irresistible pair of countries, but the first with the company of two friends, a married couple whom we had known for years and who had a similar interest to ourselves in both birds and wildlife in general. So, on this occasion, I could share the driving of our Land Cruiser (not a Land Rover) with Nick, while Sheila kept Sue company in the back of the vehicle. It worked quite well, and it would be something we would repeat in the future.

We certainly clocked up oodles of birds and more than enough encounters with various animals in both Namibia and Botswana, none of which, you will be pleased to hear, am I going to list now. Instead, I will just mention three memorable-for-me events from this trip, the first of which was Sue and I meeting Puck and Three-and-a-Half. Puck was a rescued cheetah we had been sponsoring, who was being looked after at Africat, the big-cat rescue and rehabilitation setup at Okonjima. And he needed looking after because he had been orphaned when he was very young and had not learnt how to hunt. He was therefore going to be a long-term resident of Africat's extensive facility, where they cared for nearly 200 big moggies. Three-and-a-Half would be there indefinitely as well. Because he was the leopard we were sponsoring, whose name reflected his condition, in that, thanks to a vicious wire trap, he had lost the bottom half of one of his legs and would, of course, never be able to feed himself again. All I will say is that to meet these two guys was wonderful – and we both cried. Although Puck and Three-and-a-Half didn't even get watery eyes...

OK. Second memorable event. This happened in Botswana, where, with our friends, we had first stayed at Savuti (which, with its close-by elephants, had proved as awesome as ever) before moving on to Little Vumbura again. And here we discovered that its new manager was a guy we had previously encountered as a guide, and whose name we thought was 'Dudley'. He, of course, remembered us, and we certainly remembered him. For who could possibly forget a giant black Zimbabwean who was never without a smile on his face? Anyway, in his new role, he would often chat with us, and it wasn't long before one of us asked him whether he knew that he shared his name with a large industrialised town in the 'Black Country' in the middle of England. Well, yes, he did know, because he was actually named after this town, and that was because his (clearly black) father had worked there as a vet in the '60s, and his affection for the place had made him choose its name as the name for his first-born son!

While still coming to terms with a black African working as a vet in '60s Dudley, we were then informed by smiling 'Dudley' that whilst his father had become very fond of the Midlands town, he had not become very fond of the local pronunciation of its name – with its emphasis on a very flat 'Dud'. He had therefore named his son not 'Dudley' but 'Dardley', which he considered would require a much more refined pronunciation. This may or may not have worked, but it didn't stop Dardley giving his own son the same name, or at least a similar name, in that he gave him the genuine, real-deal 'Dudley', with no attempt whatsoever at gentrification. And no attempt at distancing himself or his son from his country's former colonial master (see earlier in this chapter!).

Right. Third memorable event: in returning from this holiday, for definitely the first time ever, I was able to spend my birthday flying over the continent of Africa. Yes, on 26 October, I was in the air and in the process of clocking up fifty-nine years on this Earth. I mean, fifty-nine years! And I still hadn't become a famous writer; I still hadn't driven an articulated truck; I still hadn't seen an iceberg; and I still had loads of places I wanted to see and loads of things I wanted to do. And in just a year I'd be bloody sixty!

Well, I couldn't do anything about deferring that forthcoming sixty – always assuming I didn't pop off in the next twelve months – but I could do something about visiting lots more places and doing lots more things.

And I started as soon as we got home – by beginning to organise a trip to Costa Rica and by reading Christopher Hitchens' *God Is Not Great.* This, incidentally, is a book well worth reading. Despite its title so eloquently describing the graphic quality of my cartoon version of the Supreme One, a quality that never did get any better…

Sixty!!!

2008 got off to a much better start than 2007. Because, on 1 January 2008, I did not receive a telephone call from my neighbour in Finniegill to tell me that Wood Cottage was without power and had sustained some storm damage – as I had done exactly twelve months previously. That meant that I did not have to drive up to Scotland the next day and discover that about four acres of forest had been literally flattened by the storm, as had the power lines that fed the Finniegill metropolis of two houses. In fact, the damage was so bad that the electricity would be out for days, and Scottish Power even offered to supply both houses with a generator while they were conducting the necessary repairs – an offer which was accepted by my neighbour, but one which I declined. I was rather more interested in getting back to an electricity-provided residence in Worcestershire as soon as I'd patched up the storm damage to the cottage. A remote, cold bolthole held out very little appeal in the first week of a Scottish January.

However, that had all happened at the outset of 2007, and at the outset of 2008 there were no such worrying events in our tiny upland retreat. Not that it didn't provide a few more challenges later in the year…

Yes, as most people know, owning any property can be something of a trial. However, owning a second property in an inaccessible, 'challenging' situation can be more like a three-year-long public inquiry, not just in terms of its associated cost but also in terms of the demands it makes on its interested parties. These demands never seem to end. And whether it is merely the need to deal with the constant infiltration of a whole army of mice – and their attendant failure to develop any acceptable latrine arrangements – or gutters falling off, radiators deciding not to work, or plumbing deciding to work when it shouldn't, it can all get a bit wearing. Nevertheless, Sue and I had fallen in love with Wood Cottage, and it would take more than a few domestic irritations to cause us to fall out of love with it. Particularly when we were spending quite so much of our time there, and when, in 2008, we would be using it more and more as a base to see other parts of southern and central Scotland. Heck, not only did we get to places such as the Solway coast and the Mull of Galloway, but we even got as far as Edinburgh to have a nose around the *Royal Yacht Britannia* – the interior of which, I remember, was a wonderful mix of the '50s, the chintzy, the modest and the downright spartan. Indeed, any present-day billionaire lowlife, looking for his next superyacht, would probably have been deeply insulted if presented with such a humble hulk for his consideration. I mean, apart from it having a complete ostentatiousness bypass, there wasn't a single place where one could store all of one's whores...

However, on a more uplifting note, I should also mention that Finniegill was not a million miles away from Eskdalemuir. And just outside this tiny village is the 'Kagyu Samye Ling Monastery and Tibetan Centre', a (very substantial) Tibetan Buddhist outpost that boasts a magnificent gilded temple, a stupa, a collection of statues, various accommodation buildings, some handsome gardens, an absolutely wonderful veg plot, and a greenhouse in which there is what must be the biggest, most productive vine in the whole of Scotland. It is a genuinely remarkable place, capable of inducing a feeling of serenity even in the hearts of a couple of cynical old atheists like myself and Sue. Accordingly, we visited it whenever we could. And on those rare occasions when we hosted guests in Wood Cottage, we would try to convince them that we were not entirely deranged by transporting them from our secluded wooden yurt to gaze in wonder at this most unexpected of establishments. Without fail, they would be amazed when they first spotted those gilded roofs through the pines, and they would then be just as entranced as we were when they went on to experience the monastery's indisputable physical and spiritual charms.

David Bowie and Leonard Cohen (yes, Leonard Cohen) were students at Samye Ling, and indeed David Bowie almost became a monk there. I could easily understand why. It just so much radiated peace and tranquillity, and it seemed to be able to keep at bay all those concerns and troubles of the outside world – even more so than Wood Cottage could. And, of course, in 2008 there were far more of those concerns and troubles than in most other years. Because, of course, 2008 was the year of a quite significant financial crisis...

Yes, this economic disaster that had been putting its boots on the previous year now had them tightly laced up and, with its jacket buttoned up and its loins appropriately girded, it was marching into the lives of millions. (Although I should probably admit that girding one's loins alludes to the practice of those Biblical types tucking up their traditional long robes into a girdle [a belt] so as not to hamper their physical activity. And this might be quite tricky if one was wearing a buttoned-up jacket at the same time.) However, I digress. And the important point to make is that a load of banks full of a load of brainless bankers had set in motion a worldwide financial meltdown that would consume not only huge financial institutions such as Lehman Brothers, but also a lot of everybody's time as they tried desperately to protect whatever financial assets they might possess – often by shifting them from one suspect institution to another. And that was never easy. When it all started to get really scary in about September, I remember spending most of my waking hours on the phone or on a computer, trying to ensure that a lifetime's worth of savings wouldn't evaporate while I slept overnight. And sometimes I even cursed.

Of course, it would be wrong to blame just those brainless bankers. There were quite a few other culprits as well – like all those mediocre, arrogant, greedy, insatiable, unscrupulous, testosterone-fuelled, hair-gelled, waste-of-space bonus-junkies who, together with their hopeless, immoral, even-greedier, unprincipled, incompetent, dead-loss, good-for-nothing, grossly over-rewarded bosses, constituted what was comically known as the finance 'industry'. Because I've yet to hear anybody explaining what this 'industry' has in common with 'the companies and activities involved in the process of producing goods for sale' or indeed 'hard work', which are the only two legitimate definitions of this word. Let's be honest. The finance 'industry' is no more than a gigantic parasite sucking resources out of the genuinely productive parts of the nation's economy, and it is largely of real benefit only to itself. 'Rent extraction' is apparently a term used by economists to describe the process of making money from useless, valueless activity. And given what the finance 'industry' actually does, even when it's not shaking the foundations of our society, it cannot be denied that rent extraction must feature heavily in its make-up. And, indeed, it could be argued that it is what really defines it: making money out of other people's money – for its own benefit and at their expense.

I'd become aware of this 'organised swindling' nature of the beast long before it finally tripped over itself in 2008. Although, I have to admit that initially I'd formed the impression that the swindling was principally achieved by its using the conman's favourite device: complexity. After all, if one has a load of punters whose major concern is to provide for themselves in their retirement out of the income they have generated throughout their lives, as a professional finance 'industry', one should be able to do this on their behalf relatively easily and without much in the way of active interventions. However, for the finance guys, this is a bit of a problem. Because… well, simplicity doesn't pay well, does it? Much better to introduce extensive and confusing choice, non-stop activity and change, contradictory signals with a need for constant 'expert' guidance, and as many other purposeless complexities as one can muster, all of which provide countless opportunities to make much more money – out of the money management process. This is, of course, still an important part of how the finance 'industry' fleeces its sheep; how it shaves off all the woolly wealth it needs to fund all those outrageous salaries and all those obscene bonuses. But it's not the essence of the scam. Or should I say that, by focusing on the working practices of the finance 'industry', one risks missing what is its fundamental flaw (or its major strength, depending on one's perspective) – the one it exploits at the very substantial expense of all those sheep. And this is the 'principal/agent' aspect of its business, and what this means in terms of a devastating misalignment of interests.

You see, the finance 'industry' is run by and populated by people who are not the beneficial owners of the money they 'manage'. They are merely agents, and the real owners are the members of pension funds, endowment policy holders and wealthy individuals, who together constitute those poor innocent sheep alluded to above, and who are merely trying to preserve their capital with a view to providing for themselves an income that might be drawn upon years or even decades into the future. These owners – the principals – are clearly obliged to depend on the people who run and operate the finance 'industry': the agents. And just as clearly, these agents couldn't give a fig about even next year, let alone decades into the future – and all they want is the largest possible cash reward they can get. And they want it now!

Incentives for these masters of the universe are therefore hopelessly short-termist, in that they are rewarded after just one or two years, and not over the thirty or forty years that they have their hands on their principals' cash. Their rewards are also grossly unfair, in that if anything goes wrong over this long period, they are never penalised. Not surprising then that, as well as introducing needless complexity into the investment process, the agents are very happy to take all sorts of risks with this 'other people's money', in the full knowledge that it will not be them who suffer if the risks fail to pay off. And it gets worse…

There have, after all, been attempts to reform the 'industry': stuff like trying to dismantle the toxic bonus systems and replacing them with more reasonable, long-term incentive arrangements, or endeavouring to change the very culture of the 'industry' by making it more collaborative, more conducive to long-term thinking and more tolerant of well-intentioned mistakes. And all this would inevitably lead to a far better deal for all us defenceless, worked-over punters. Heck, they could even introduce a bonus system which would mean that bonuses were deferred until retirement. And at last there would be real convergence between our interests and those of our agents. But guess what. None of this has happened, and it's as likely to happen in the future as my being canonised, an event that stands no chance of ever breaking out of the 'not a chance in a million years' category. Even if either the Pope or I succumb to some well-earned senility.

So, we're all stuffed. The financial world might not be collapsing around our ears as it was in 2008, but we are still getting screwed – by all those malevolent agents. And, frankly, we have to look at some rather more imaginative measures if we ever want to control their egregious behaviour. The most obvious solution would be to replace all those testosterone-fuelled scoundrels who currently infest the 'industry' with 'testosterone-light' women, who might have a little more empathy with their clients and a little less desire to take them to the cleaners. And maybe they could be joined by all those current incumbents who were prepared to be gelded in order to achieve a similar testosterone-free status and therefore something approaching a measurable level of decency in their dealings with the investing public. But there again, we're back into as-likely-as-canonisation territory, and I think what is called for is a much more radical solution. Mine, if I were ever asked, would involve the use of snipers positioned on the top of tall buildings – tall buildings in the City of London and Wall Street. These guys would then take out as many of the fat bastards as they could. And I am reasonably confident that this 'shoot to reform' strategy would soon bear fruit and, under a white flag of surrender, the leaders of the world's finance 'industry' would announce – quite eagerly – that they were now prepared to join the real world – in terms of their conduct and their rewards – and we principals would finally get something like a half-reasonable deal. And no, just the threat of being shot would not be enough. They'd either ignore it or they'd somehow securitise it and then chop it up into some sort of complicated financial 'product', and sell it on at a profit. Whereas I'd like to see them try to turn a speeding bullet into some new form of derivative...

Yes, shooting is the only remedy. And no, I'm not being entirely serious, but just a little bit serious. And would the world really miss a bunch of greedy grifters who, back in 2008, allowed their excessive greed to threaten the wellbeing of so many people around the planet? If they didn't look quite so similar to ourselves, we might have treated them like a virus. And maybe next time we should. Because I have very little doubt that there will be a next time, and I just hope that this next time arrives too late for this book – but before we've all forgotten what happened in 2008. The financial crisis, that is. Not Sue and her husband going off for a birdy holiday in birdy Costa Rica...

This was in April of 2008, and not long after our second best-dog-in-the-world, Max, had to be euthanised to save him from what was quickly becoming a life of distress. It was as awful as our losing Freddie ten years before, and it made us think that as much as we loved dogs, we could no longer cope with their eventual demise. Quite simply, most dogs are a lot more lovable than most people, and to lose one of your own is to lose part of your life. It hurts, and it hurts so much that one can hardly wait to take oneself off to somewhere like Costa Rica to lose oneself in the charms of what sells itself as a virtual aviary, just bursting with all manner of tropical birds.

Well, it proved to be very much like what it said on the tin, and I could now fill the next five pages with a neat list of the birds Sue and I encountered on this trip. But I suspect that would not be a wise move. Instead, I will provide you with a flavour of this country and the treasures it contains by describing briefly one or two of the aspects of one or two of the places we stayed.

Our first port of call was the Casa Corcovado Jungle Lodge, which is situated on the Osa Peninsula in south-western Costa Rica, next to the extensive Corcovado National Park – and which is a bit of a place. Not only does it sit on a hilltop overlooking the sea – within its own 107-acre private reserve – but one cannot reach it by road. Instead, one has to fly south from Costa Rica's capital, swap one's small aeroplane for a truck, and then abandon this truck in favour of a small boat when the truck encounters a river. In this boat, one is then transported down the river through a mangrove system and out into the Pacific Ocean. There then follows a sixty-minute trip south along the coast until one eventually arrives at a beach – a beach that is guarded by some threatening-looking rocks. Here the boat is backed in, to be grabbed by three able-bodied men standing in the surf, so that one can disembark and join them in the surf. With wet legs, one is then shepherded to the shore, and there loaded onto a tractor-pulled trailer to be taken up a steep track to the hilltop lodge itself. I don't think we have ever been to anywhere else that has had quite such a dramatic means of access to its hidden-away charms. And it certainly did have some charms…

Corcovado is the last remaining Pacific lowland rainforest of sustainable size in all of Central America, and has been called 'the most biologically intense place on Earth' – beating even the Glastonbury Festival by a comfortable margin. And all this intense biology was in evidence all around. The place was not just stuffed with all sorts of birds, but there were bats, there were various sorts of lizards, plenty of agoutis, a few stupefyingly endearing sloths, and more than enough of what I regard as the most awe-inspiring of all monkeys: howler monkeys. Though small in size, these agile tree-dwellers have a voice that King Kong would be proud of, and to hear their booming, almost unearthly calls as they approach through the forest is to experience a mix of awe and some sort of primeval dread. For even though one's brain knows that this sound is that made by a harmless primate, one cannot expunge the feeling that something monstrous and menacing is heading one's way. Quite simply, there is nothing to compare with this 'vocal thunder', and I would advise anyone who hasn't heard it to put on his or her bucket list an opportunity to get a full-blown blast of it. He or she will not be disappointed. Any more than we were when we ventured into the forest around the lodge – to encounter more birds, more agoutis, a deadly coral snake – and a crocodile.

This crocodile was lazing in a pool in a river. Indeed, in the pool situated right above the pool in which we had just swum, a fact known to our guide but only revealed to us when, after our swim, we walked from *our* pool past *his* pool – and didn't stop for a chat. Not only did we not think that a wise move, but we also had other things on our mind – like coping with the extreme heat and humidity of the forest. And I'm not talking about sticky underpants here; I'm talking about a constant stream of sweat into one's eyes. Corcovado, we decided, wasn't just the most biologically intense place on Earth, but one of the most perspirationally intense as well. But still bloody wonderful.

The Arenal Volcano was pretty good as well. This was the third place we visited in Costa Rica (after a stay at a cloud forest lodge where we saw some magical quetzals). Our hotel accommodation was at the foot of the volcano, and our room gave us a panoramic view of its constant activity – which was no less than dramatic, particularly at night. Not spurts of lava or rivers of this stuff, but just a constant cascade of rocks tumbling down the volcano's sides, which, in the dark, glowed red as they rolled and bounced their way down. They were even more entertaining than the crusty old American in the hotel bar who, one evening, sitting directly below the sign that informed the bar's patrons that they could neither smoke nor bring with them their prostitutes, was chain-smoking and making idiot talk to a heavily painted, lightly attired local lady, who was clearly not a member of the Neotropical Bird Club. She undoubtedly belonged to a much longer-established institution than that.

Well, I could go on – about 'lava burgers', orphaned howler monkeys being cared for at our final seaside destination, and the woman on the tiny plane that took us back to the country's capital who had a dog in her handbag (and whose unauthorised presence was happily tolerated by the plane's pilot). But instead I'm going to jump forward five months to when Sue and I were on another plane, a very special plane; indeed nothing less than a genuine World War II Lancaster!

Sue had given me one of my sixtieth birthday (!) presents early. It was a VIP day out at an aviation museum in Lincolnshire, with the highlight of the day being a taxi ride around the aerodrome in *Just Jane*, the museum's venerable and 'drivable' (but not flyable) Lancaster. It was, of course, a VIP day for both of us, and after the event we both decided that the promised highlight of the day would probably qualify as one of the highlights of our lives. Just being in the plane and being allowed to sit in all the different crew positions was pretty exciting in itself. But to hear those four Merlin engines bursting into life and then to feel the plane moving was about as exhilarating as it gets. If, of course, one ignores the almost orgasmic thrill of then hearing all four engines being taken up through the revs to achieve the sort of roar that even a whole army of howlers couldn't manage. It was a riveting experience. Indeed, just as riveting as the entire day had been sobering, in that one was constantly reminded not only of the cramped, cold conditions that bomber aircrew had to endure – for hours on end – but also of just how many of these guys didn't make it home. In fact, over 57,000 of them were killed, representing a barely credible 46% death rate in the bomber service. And it doesn't get any more sobering than that. Unless one starts to dwell on what they gave their lives for, and to question how many of them would willingly have boarded one of those remarkable machines if they could have looked into the future and seen who exactly, in eighty years' time, would be relishing the delights of their green and pleasant land. Was any crewman's life worth sacrificing for that? I do have my doubts.

Anyway, having hosted a slightly premature 'Survival of the Fifties' party to acknowledge that I really was on the threshold of Victor Meldrew territory, on the actual day of my sixtieth birthday, I was boarding yet another plane. This was bigger than a Lancaster, because it was one of those absolutely gigantic Airbus A380s – those massive double-decker aeroplanes that look as though they've been built with the aid of anabolic steroids. And on the Singapore Airlines A380, I think the business-class seats had no less than overdosed on these steroids. One could have entertained in them; they were that big. And even with a six-foot-two frame, I felt I was hardly doing them justice. However, I soon reconciled myself to this opulent accommodation. In fact, very shortly after some sort of starter-motor truck had been brought in to start up the A380 – because its own starting system had decided not to work! Fortunately, that was the only teething problem with this machine, and in due course, all four engines worked all the way to Singapore, where we then boarded a marginally smaller plane to fly to Auckland.

Yes, we were making our first expedition to New Zealand, a visit that would involve a self-drive 4x4 trip around the country's North Island, before a self-drive 4x4 trip around its South Island, the two trips together designed to consume the first three weeks of my sixty-first year. We had an itinerary and a couple of maps, and an expectation that we would encounter little in the way of excitement in this faraway land, but instead just a great deal of delight and quite a big dollop of 'niceness'. And we would not be disappointed in this expectation. New Zealand was just as we'd been told it was: full of nice people, considerate drivers, lots of sheep, lots of stunning scenery, lots of British birds (but few endemics), lots of space, quite a lot of rain, more than enough amazingly clean public loos, and people saying 'Divin' when what they're trying to say is 'Devon'. (This last feature of this wonderful country can be the cause of acute embarrassment – such as when the owner of one of the many B&Bs we used introduced herself as 'Divin', and I had to repeatedly ask her to repeat herself. I hope I didn't give her any sort of complex.)

I can't say that New Zealand influenced my views in many ways – other than it made me yearn for Britain in the '60s (because that is what it is like) – and I'm therefore going to do no more than set out a very brief list of one or two things that have stuck in my mind. And this list is:

1. Seeing our first ever morepork, which is a small brown owl with one of the best bird names going.
2. Seeing our first wrybill, which is a small plover, and the only species of bird in the world with a beak that is bent sideways (always to the right).

3. Travelling on a ferry between North and South Islands, the painted-out name of which was *Pride of Cherbourg*.
4. Going to a *very* ordinary restaurant in the *very* ordinary town of Hokitika on the grim west coast of South Island that revelled in the name of *Café De Paris* (but without the acute accent over the e). Brilliant!

Well, that more or less wraps up the year of the financial crisis, but it would be wrong of me not to be mention something that lifted my spirits greatly right at the end of the year – even though you'll think I'm being a mean-minded bastard by doing so. But sorry, I just can't help myself. Because when you've observed somebody in public life who you've concluded is an extremely dim prat, and he then goes and confirms this on national television, it cannot fail to be a cause of great delight. And the guy I'm talking about is David Lammy, Labour's very own village idiot who, to intellect, is what Winston Churchill is to a nine-banded armadillo: not even distantly related. He revealed his towering ignorance and stupidity on a *Celebrity* (!) *Mastermind* on 29 December 2008, when, although soon to become the Minister for Higher Education in Gordon Brown's dysfunctional government, he finished in a very firm bottom place behind three others who were never to be elevated to ministerial roles.

He did this with a stunning combination of ignorance and ineptitude, which involved him identifying the married name of Marie and Pierre who won the Nobel Prize in Physics in 1903 for their research into radiation as... Antoinette, and suggesting the monarch that succeeded Henry VIII was... Henry VII. He also sought to educate us mere mortals by informing us that the blue cheese commonly served with port was, of course... (Red?) Leicester. Which, to be fair, if left out in a warm room for two months, may indeed turn blue, and might then require some port to mask its rank taste.

I have been mean, haven't I? But I include this brief tale of inadequacy writ large simply because it casts a blinding light on the quality of those who seek to rule us. David Lammy is still an MP and may one day be a minister again, with the power to make decisions that affect our lives. And the really bad news is that he is by no means unique in his heroic limitations – either in terms of his intellect or his knowledge (of kings, cheese and probably most everything else). No wonder then that we all hold our politicians in such low regard when some of them haven't even the sense to conceal their shortcomings by first of all turning down invitations to appear on a TV quiz show. And no wonder our democracy is in such a poor condition when it is run by no-brains such as D. Lammy MP.

Yes, I was now sixty, and now more aware than ever that incompetence wasn't the sole preserve of the finance 'industry'. It was everywhere. In politics, in many of our established institutions, and possibly even in our very DNA. And, for ministers of state, it was often in there along with hubris, arrogance, self-delusion and possibly even an unfamiliarity with the many different varieties of English cheese...

At which point I am going to wrap up this chapter, just in case I'm giving the impression that I'm not just on the threshold of Victor Meldrew territory, but that I'm already slap bang in the middle of it, loudly extolling the virtues of the past over the present, as exemplified by the work of such great people from the past as Marie and Pierre Antoinette, Nobel Prize winners for their study of the radioactive qualities of Camembert and Roquefort...

India, Indictments and Inebriation in Namibia

On 1 January 2009, Alistair Darling, the Chancellor, was probably looking forward to a less hectic year than 2008. After all, one financial crisis is quite enough for any Chancellor to have to deal with. And, what's more, another one would probably have turned his eyebrows white. Unless, of course, the rumour was true, and for years he'd been using Just for Men hair dye – but only on his eyebrows and not on the hair on his head, as that sort of extravagance by a Chancellor would have been seen as imprudent. There again, if they were genuinely black, while the hair on his head was uniformly silver-white… well, what colour were his… other hair clusters? I actually ended up reading his book on the financial crisis, called *Back from the Brink*, and I can tell you that this was one insight he did not provide within its pages. Which was a pity really, because it was so dull, it would have benefited greatly from a revelation of that sort. And it might even have helped its sales.

Anyway, *this* book is supposed to be about me, not about a politician with suspect eyebrows. So, I will move quickly on to the subject of sounds. That is to say, sounds of the musical variety and sounds of the spoken variety, and it is those of the musical variety I will address first.

You see, I do love music. I have very catholic tastes (as in 'all-embracing', not in the other sense), and I enjoy not just music from the golden years of the '60s and '70s, but also a wide range of classical music, 'world music', blues music and all sorts of folk music. Indeed, by 2009, Sue and I were already fairly frequent patrons of a small music venue in Worcester where we would be constantly amazed at the virtuosity of performers who were either quite old or, because they didn't conform to the commercial music world's mandatory mediocrity standards, not very well known. However, a critical feature of all this music was that it was my choice (or our combined choice). It was definitely not somebody else's choice; not somebody else's idea of what might enhance my shopping experience in a retail outlet or what might, if played really loudly, aid my digestion in a pub or a restaurant. This stuff, I hated. However, by 2009 it was already a well-established aspect of modern life, and one I have never been able to understand – unless, of course, it's really for the benefit of the people who work in these places and not for the punters. Although that, of course, assumes that they're even aware that there is 'music' playing, which I suspect they are often not. Anyway, it's a curse – possibly a curse that intensifies when one passes the age of sixty. And I've lost track of how many shops I've had to eschew in order to avoid its worst manifestations and how many times I've had to plead with pub and restaurant managers to maybe just turn the curse down – so that I and my fellow diners can actually hear what each other is saying. And don't they know that the best possible sound in a pub or a restaurant is the hubbub of other people chatting and laughing? It is not Kylie Minogue bashing out another instantly forgettable exercise in nasal warbling. God, she's bad enough to be employed by the BBC...

Yes, it's time to address sounds of the spoken variety – and how they were well on their way to becoming a real scourge back in 2009. Particularly if they were spoken by a woman. I don't know quite when it happened, but the BBC – and other broadcasters – used to employ people whose voices did not get in the way of what they were saying. They were soft, rather anonymous voices that allowed us to concentrate on what was being said – and they didn't 'grate'. But now... well, over the past decade or more, a particularly unpleasant 'little girl' voice has found favour with those who know better, and we are therefore constantly informed of the state of the economy or the next jihadist atrocity by someone who sounds as though she still needs stabilisers on her bike. Now, I know that may sound sexist, so let me quickly move on to a further problem with voices – often heard on broadcast news – that is not the province of just women. Men are equally guilty. And what I am prattling on about here is all those 'children' who sound as though they are addressing other children – by emphasising every second or third word they speak when no such emphasis is required. It's a 'tabloid' approach to speaking, and somebody should really tell them that they would do a lot better if they spoke as they might speak at the breakfast table. That is to say: normally, without the repeated injections of a faux dramatic effect that doesn't ever work. It just makes them sound stupid – and childish. Which maybe they are…

However, enough of this old man grousing, because I need to get on and tell you about my experience of somewhere that was the antithesis of our normal holiday destination, in that it was not off the beaten track and thinly populated, but instead it was (and still is) as busy as it gets – and it was (and still is) simply teeming with people. Yes, in April 2009, Sue and I made a three-week visit to India…

This wasn't going to be a 'Golden Triangle' visit, and nor would it attempt to take in as many of the 'must-see' places that would inevitably be being seen by thousands of other visitors at the same time. No, it would be a cruise down the Brahmaputra in the far north-east corner of India, taking in the local wildlife (and culture), thereafter followed by an excursion to the Sundarbans – the mangrove-covered islands at the top of the Bay of Bengal – to take in a *soupçon* of their culture, but mostly their wildlife. And to get this two-part visit underway, it was first necessary to fly to Calcutta (or Kolkata, if you're that way inclined) and overnight in a five-star hotel…

That hadn't been the original plan – on what was a reasonably priced Naturetrek group holiday. However, an unexpected by-product of those Pakistani monsters attacking the posh Oberoi hotel in Mumbai five months previously was that its sister hotel in Calcutta had virtually no business, and had clearly offered a deeply cut-price deal to the Naturetrek guys to get at least some custom through its doors. Not that these doors were that easy to get through. When we arrived at the hotel, all two dozen of us in the party had to file through an outer barrier, and then make our way past a sand-bagged machine-gun post to the hotel's steps, there to be searched (twice) before we were allowed through the hotel's elegant portals. And that would be the routine on three occasions. Because on three occasions we used Calcutta as our central staging post. Which meant that on three occasions we encountered not just the opulence of this grand hotel, but also the couldn't-be-further-from-opulence of Calcutta itself. I could be very rude here, but let me restrict myself to describing this city of fourteen million souls as… ghastly. I couldn't imagine living there for much more than a day. (And, incidentally, it was so noisy that any music-infected shop or restaurant would serve as a welcome retreat, even if populated by girlie-voiced announcers and reporters.)

The *Sukapha* was infinitely better. This was the riverboat that would serve as our home for our journey down the Brahmaputra, and it was superb. Not opulent like the Oberoi, but comfortable in every way and top class in terms of its food. (It even did chips.)

We joined this vessel near a place called Jorhat, to where we had flown, and from there it gradually made its way down to a city called Guwahati. On the way we would visit a couple of national parks to observe animals such as one-horn rhinos and birds such as fabulous pied harriers, and we would also visit a number of villages and a couple of temples – to get our promised dose of local culture. Having then returned to Calcutta, a smaller number of us would be bussed down to the Sundarbans and spend five days seeing more animals and birds, and a little bit of Sundarbans life as it was lived – and perspiring a lot. The Sundarbans are very sticky – as well as being very vulnerable to cyclones and the like. That said, if I had to make a choice, I'd definitely choose to live on any one of the Sundarbans islands rather than in Calcutta. Apart from anything else, there were no half-starved skeletal 'sacred' cows in the Sundarbans, trying to exist on a diet of rubbish and spoil – an unmissable feature of this great country to which I will return after listing just a handful of 'magic moments' from this memorable holiday. These are:

1. Having an *al fresco* fry-up breakfast in a gibbon sanctuary while a leech was breakfasting on me.
2. Chatting to a fellow member of the group who was a recently retired Concorde pilot, and who, after three days of the *Sukapha*'s passage west, was under the impression that it had sailed a long way *east.* (I assume

these aeroplanes must have had equipment that sorted out automatically which way you were going.)

3. Seeing a Bengal florican (top bird!).
4. Being subjected to a white-river, white-knuckle ride on a river in flood – on what was no more than a big rubber inner tube with a plank laid across it.
5. On a remote island in the Sundarbans, being subjected to a truly death-defying ride (with six others) on a 'kerosene-powered three-wheeler', a vehicle of sorts that had ridiculously cramped accommodation, absolutely no safety features, and a deranged speed-loving driver.
6. On this same island, being designated by its isolated residents as Indians from Bihar, because, as explained by our guide, they had not heard of England and had no concept of where it was.

That last item in the list may seem a little insensitive or even a little cruel, but it was true. And I have to stress that, like all the people we met in India, these 'disconnected' fellows on this out-of-the-way island were all entirely charming and as friendly as the language barrier would allow. Which I think is my cue to get properly insensitive and cruel. And I'm going to do this by providing you with my thoughts not on the people of India, but on its state, which in all sorts of ways is pretty grim.

As I've made clear, Calcutta is really grim, not just because it is overwhelmed with all those millions of people – and noise – but also because it is more than a little scruffy and more than a little filthy – as in littered with all sorts of garbage and waste. And I'm afraid to say that this ubiquitous rubbish in the city is mirrored by ubiquitous rubbish in the whole of the country (save for in the poorest villages in the Sundarbans and on the Brahmaputra, whose residents haven't the means to generate rubbish – particularly of the plastic variety). It seems that nobody notices or cares about this abuse of the environment, and I well remember seeing a woman on the river bank in Guwahati making some sort of ritual offering – first taking from the offering its plastic protection, which she then threw into the river. Worse was a temple on a small island in the Brahmaputra, reachable only by boat, which sat above an entire escarpment of rubbish. They must have last cleaned the place when Gandhi was in nappies.

So… India didn't have much in common with New Zealand, and there is no way I would want to go back there. It's too crowded, too noisy, too dirty and too litter-strewn (much more so than littered Britain). And even though it's full of lots of charming, hospitable people, too many of them now make a practice of phoning me to tell me that I have taken out a subscription to Amazon Prime or that my computer needs their Microsoft expertise – in order to get money out of me. And I don't like cheats and scammers. And they are the worst possible people to make you want to visit their home. That said, India is, of course, not in the same league as Russia or China when it comes to being truly odious. As I will now take a little time to explain.

Yes, I think I have taken enough of your time in making disparaging remarks about India, and I will now proceed to making some much more disparaging remarks about these two other giant countries. Starting with Putin's Russia, Putin's rather malevolent Russia…

To understand why this country now behaves as it does, I believe it is first necessary to understand its history and in particular the significance of serfdom in its history. You see, the serf system arrived early in Russia, and it remained in place well after similar systems had been abandoned elsewhere. So, for centuries, the Russian masses had essentially been made to think like slaves. Instilled into them was the belief that they were little more than chattels; the human property of their master, there to do his bidding and to have no life of their own. This meant that the serf mentality became very deeply embedded in the national psyche, and so much so that even when serfdom was abolished in 1861, the serf mentality endured – and endured. Indeed, so much so that when Stalin decided to return his people to serfdom by driving them in their millions onto collectives and state farms, it was far easier than it might otherwise have been, and it also had the effect of reinvigorating a serf mentality that had never really disappeared. And, of course, it still hasn't.

This is very good news for any Russian leader who might want to exploit his people, people who might best be described as socially infantile and barely bothered by the concept of personal responsibility or personal initiative, and who are instead much more comfortable with what might be described as hard-edged paternalism. This, needless to say, brings us to

Mr Putin, a man who is regarded by most of his serf-minded citizens as a kind though strict father, one who has to fend off all sorts of malign forces on their behalf. And the fact that he is not the product of a real democracy, as operated in a real, modern civil society, is inconsequential. People don't care, and nowhere near enough of them care that this acceptance of what is much closer to an autocracy than a democracy is being hugely abused by the country's elite – under the leadership of 'Tin ov Pu' ('Putin' is, in fact, just the diminutive of his proper name – and not many people know this).

Anyway, with this ready-made supine society, Putin and his clique of acolytes and supporters have been able to construct the greatest mafia state that the world has ever known, and in doing so they have been able to enrich themselves obscenely at the expense of all those gullible peasants. Indeed, Russia can be accurately described as 'a corrupt, autocratic kleptocracy, centred on Putin's leadership, in which officials, oligarchs and crime lords are bound together to create the sort of gangster state in which it is impossible to differentiate between the activities of the "legitimate" government and those of organised crime'. And all that is required to maintain these mafia conditions is the belief in the minds of the masses that now, more than ever, they need a strong and ruthless leader, somebody who can deal with all those malign forces, all those mostly external malign forces that threaten mother Russia like never before. And here is where we find the source of all that malevolent behaviour…

I mean, it's no good just to point a finger at all these supposed malign forces. One has to confront them. Even if they don't exist, and your confrontation has more the character of uncalled-for belligerence, possibly involving your snatching part of your neighbours' territory or something a little more subtle like assaulting them in cyberspace. Oh, and why not try to undermine and generally unsettle any other country you choose by interfering in their elections and flooding them with disinformation? In fact, by doing anything that helps to portray you in the eyes of your sheepish plebs as Russia's home-grown Superman, and not as the Godfather-in-chief of a worm-ridden, third-rate, can't-even-make-a-decent-toaster state, which only excels in the appalling standard of its driving. (And in terms of incompetent roadcraft, sozzled drivers, badly maintained vehicles and badly loaded vehicles, there isn't another country on the planet that comes anywhere near Russia.)

There is no easy way to bring to an end Russia's malevolence, because that would entail overcoming the legacy of serfdom in millions of Russian minds. But one could at least fight back a bit. Hell, Russia can't even manage to poison Putin's enemies very well, and it's not unknown for it to shoot down planes it didn't intend to. So, it's hardly likely to be invulnerable to a bit of judicious 'interference' – something that might hobble its gas production, for example. Or maybe even its doping regime. Or... how about a direct attack on Vladimir Putin himself? Why not draw attention to his small size – probably apparent in all his component parts – by henceforth referring to him as 'Vlad, the not-so-great impaler'? It's no more than he deserves. And for all I know, it might be a very well-deserved title. And, furthermore, how could he (decently) disprove it?

Anyway, you now know why I never considered a career in the diplomatic service. And while I'm still in full spiteful mode, I'm now going to have a crack at a country that is an even greater threat to us than Russia – and an existential threat to most of the natural world. I mean, of course, China.

For this menace, I am not going to dwell on its history, other than to observe that throughout its entire history it has seen itself as the greatest civilisation on the planet and, more recently, the most wronged civilisation. Principally at the hands of all those inferior specimens in the West. It has therefore been seething with resentment for years, and has been directing all its energies to returning to its rightful place in the firmament of nations. That is to say, as the world's number-one power and the world's undisputed number-one master. And we, of course, have gone out of our way to help it. Not only have we gifted it most of our manufacturing and then let it into the World Trade Organization to act as it chooses, but we have also let it walk off with shedloads of our technology and knowhow, so that there is now no way we can stop it becoming dominant in any sphere it chooses. And, at the last count, it is choosing more than just a few of them and more every year.

Russia might be a very serious irritation, but China is the real peril – a peril with a capital P. It already has its fingers in just about every other country in the world, and it will very soon *own* much of the world. And it won't be the most benign or enlightened of owners. Forbearance, fairness, decency and propriety have never been its strong suits, and one only has to look at what its attitude to the natural world is to see how it will do whatever it takes to get what it wants. Even if this means leading the charge in the extinction of so much of our fauna and flora.

I know I've been here before, but it is impossible not to mention China's culpability when it comes to the elimination of so much wildlife, a culpability which in my mind far outweighs its deplorable behaviour in so many other fields. It just doesn't seem to care that it might erase any number of iconic animals from the Earth's surface. Although it's more than likely to be aware of the increase in market value of any of those species that are on the point of being erased completely. Some are already there, and there are plenty lined up to join them. There might now still be millions of sharks in the oceans, but how long will that be the case if you're butchering them – in the cruellest way possible – at the rate of 100 million a year? And just for some fucking shark's fin soup. I mean, how can they be so barbaric?

Well, I don't know. But I do know – as we all now know – that their habits, and particularly their distasteful omnivorous eating habits, threaten not just the lives of wild creatures, but also our lives. Covid-19 might as well be China's subtitle, because it's truly its own doing and it will truly be associated with that country for generations to come, however much it tries to claim it came from elsewhere. The only mystery surrounding its source is where in Wuhan it came from – a market or a lab. And despite the gruesome aspects of China's 'wet markets' – and taking account of how much damage has been conveniently done to the rest of the world – many will opt for the lab origination. Although, of course, with the help of China's open and transparent approach to resolving this mystery, we will probably never know, and certainly not before the oceans can finally be declared shark-free.

Golly, I've gone on a bit there, haven't I? And without much to relieve the diatribe nature of my… dispassionate review of the two evil empires on the planet. Or should I say two of the greatest nations on the planet which are much misunderstood and much unfairly maligned? Even if they're not. No, I think I'll stick with the evil-empire tags, and quickly take a little of the steam out of this chapter by moving on to some rather less polemical issues – such as what I was writing in 2009. Because this was something of a groundbreaking book – and it was called *Brian on the Brahmaputra.*

It was, of course, an account of our holiday in India, but seen through the eyes of my alter ego, Brian, accompanied by Sue's alter ego, Sandra. And the purpose of having those alter egos was so that I could 'embellish' the story of our trip – generally for comic effect – and I could also, more easily, give vent to some of my grievances and prejudices (which will, I am sure, not surprise you in the least). Yes, this was to be a whimsical but accurate-where-necessary exposition of our Indian travels, and it would prove to be the first of ten such expositions, nine of them covering holidays yet to come, but all of them graced with the presence of Brian and his long-suffering wife, Sandra. They were all bound to be a resounding success. Obviously.

And talking of holidays to come, there was another towards the end of the year: another expedition to Namibia, this one to last over five weeks, with the first three weeks being shared with our friends who had accompanied us two years previously. It was, as you might imagine, another immersion in a huge bathful of natural wonders – of both the inorganic as well as the organic kind. And I mention the inorganic element because our itinerary took in not just the normal mix of beautiful Namibian scenery, but also some of its truly dramatic scenery. First, this was the red, sandy expanses of the Namibian Kalahari in the south-east of the country, then the exposed-geology scenery of the far south – including the Fish River Canyon – and then the stark scenery in the hinterland of Lüderitz on the southern Namibian coast. And then, of course, on the organic side, there was a whole pile of animals and birds to observe and enjoy.

The bad news is that, in 2010, I wrote a book about this holiday. But the good news is that I am again going to restrict my references to the holiday in *this* book to a handful of memorable moments – just as I did with the Indian excursion above. And these 'most memorable' moments are:

1. Standing on a viewing point on the edge of that Fish River Canyon, the second biggest canyon in the world after the Grand Canyon – in a group of six people. (It was a busy day.)
2. Visiting a place called Diaz Point, just below Lüderitz, to see penguins, and discovering that it was so incredibly windy there that there was a real (upward) hazard in using its nearby open-ended, long-drop loo.
3. Getting inebriated with sherry and wine on a dolphin-watching

catamaran out of Walvis Bay well before lunchtime.

4. Getting entirely inebriated at a place called Huab Lodge with the help of a pineapple liqueur that came in a bottle wrapped around with (real) barbed wire.
5. Being provided with the 'Bush Suite' at Okonjima, a 'chalet' on steroids that came with its own swimming pool and its own waterhole – and that had recently been occupied by Joanna Lumley!
6. Meeting Puck again at Okonjima – and then our new sponsored leopard, Pickles.
7. Meeting, face to face, a fortunately well-fed hyena at Okonjima.

That's not too bad for five weeks, is it? And there was so much more I could have listed. But all good years have to end at some point, and that point will be now. Other than to note that I wish to apologise unreservedly to Alistair Darling for those personal remarks I made at the outset of this chapter, and will do so as soon as he and his muttonhead boss at the time, one Gordon how-the-hell-did-he-get-the-job Brown, apologise for their role in accelerating the ruination of this country during the first decade of the new millennium. And Blair ought to say a bloody big sorry as well...

Syria to Sabah via Despots

As you will no doubt recall, in the not-too-distant past, a whole string of evil bastards and deluded tosspots made their way to Syria to join something called ISIS (which, as you may not recall, stands for 'Incredibly Savage Imbecilic Scum'). However, when Sue and I made our way there in April 2010, the nearest we got to ISIS was an 'ibis', as in a bald ibis, which, even back then, was one of the rarest and most threatened birds in this troubled country. This may give you a clue as to what we were doing there, which was nothing to do with the worship of barbarism, but everything to do with the enjoyment of wildlife, especially wildlife of the avian variety. Yes, our friends at Naturetrek had organised what would be a pioneering group birding holiday to this 'questionable' destination, and Sue and I were part of a dozen-strong group of (guinea pig) pioneers who had signed up for the trip. Not surprisingly, it would not only be the first time that any 'Naturetrekkers' had visited this country, but also the last…

Of course, Syria is not famed for its wildlife, and certainly not for its birdlife. It would certainly never feature near the top of any birder's must-go-to list. However, it is in fact home to quite a number of desert-living birds. And furthermore, its position at the east end of the Mediterranean means that it acts as a corridor for a very large number of migrating birds. It certainly has enough to keep a party of visiting birders very happy, and that's even without taking account of what it has to offer as side dishes in the form of its many monumental ruins, its admirable cuisine and, of course, its status as something of a police state in the hands of a not very nice person. Neither Sue nor I had been to anywhere quite so 'despotic' before, and to have an opportunity to see what despotism looked like close up – from within the safety afforded by a group – made the decision to join this particular birding foray very easy indeed. Oh, and so did the fact that in 2010, tourists of any sort in Syria were only slightly less rare than Syrian bald ibises. Although now, of course, they have become essentially extinct.

OK. I have to warn you that this is one overseas trip that I cannot simply gloss over with a list of interesting events. And that is because in so many ways it was a trip full of experiences and observations that together made this one of the most memorable trips ever. Albeit some of those initial experiences and observations weren't necessarily those one would have chosen. And here I'm talking about the pile of dumped hardened concrete (complete with wheelbarrow) blocking the external fire-escape stairs at our first hotel in Damascus; the less than scenic scenery on the way out of Damascus; and the widespread use of litter to decorate the countryside outside Damascus, which would in due course prove to be a nationwide habit and one that was a really quite depressing aspect of this god-fearing country. (I have got a bit of a thing about litter, haven't I? But it's such a wonderful litmus test of people's attitude to their environment. And all too often, it indicates that their attitude is somewhere between non-caring and actively disrespectful. I wish it were otherwise.)

Anyway, our coach and its complement of passengers and Syrians was now out of Damascus on its way to Palmyra, and it is probably incumbent upon me to say just a few words about the onboard Syrians. They were, after all, so much a part of our excursion. There were three of them. One was Ali, a short-haired, smart-looking guy of about fifty, who drove the coach (very well), but who spoke no English. Then there was Houssan, a Fonz-type character who was half Ali's age and who could speak a little English, but whose principal job was to assist the third Syrian, Adib. And Adib was a tall, middle-aged man with a splendid hooked nose, extravagant drooping moustache, and a shock of black wavy hair, and, in Syria, was even rarer than those much-referred-to ibises. Because he was Syria's one and only ornithologist. And, with his Central Casting looks and his Central Wardrobe red and white scarf and indeterminate crumpled clothes, he would lead our party – and our party leader, Chris – around his not very bird-aware country. Oh, and he would also act as the third participant in the on-board three-sided conflict with his two fellow citizens. I still have no idea whether this was a bit of Shia/Sunni/can't-quite-decide antagonism in play or something to do with tribal or family feuds, but these three guys were, for most of the time, at each other's throats, and maybe represented a microcosm of the sort of relationships that have led the whole of the Middle East down such a tortuous and unrewarding path. I mean, if three Syrian nationals had this much trouble with each other, how must most Syrians get on with their Arab neighbours – or with Israel? No wonder discord is woven into the very fabric of this part of the world, and no wonder that Syria would so easily go on to rip itself apart.

Nevertheless, we were all spared actual fisticuffs or stabbings (although only just), and we would soon begin to appreciate how Syria could provide us with rather more than just a display of overt antagonism. This was first apparent in our initial scheduled destination: Palmyra. All I need say here is that Palmyra's ruins – before they were really ruined by ISIS – were stunningly beautiful, and our first proper Syrian meal – in a Palmyra restaurant – was superb. Who would have thought that flatbreads, dips, finely minced, spiced lamb – and various other aspects of Syrian fare – could so easily challenge the ambrosia of the gods on the way-past-delicious scale? And I won't keep going on about the food in Syria, other than to say that it was consistently some of the best food I've ever eaten. Even if, sometimes, it couldn't be accompanied by anything alcoholic.

Yes, Syria did have a few drawbacks, and one of these was the absence of booze in some of its eateries. Another was the call to prayer at four in the morning – when you were trying to sleep for a six o'clock start to your birding day. Then there was the proliferation of images of Assad, the current ogre, and Assad senior, the passed-on ogre, which were to be found all over the place. And without exception, all those (very large) images were looking directly at *you*. *You* were not going to be allowed to forget who was in charge here. And lest you should, there were some burly guys in awful suits who might arrive in an anonymous-looking car to remind you that Big Brother was watching you. And that is not supposition. It happened to us when we attempted to conduct some birdwatching at a remote lagoon outside Deir ez-Zor in the east of the country. Clearly a group of Westerners –

with binoculars – was a reportable event there, and they certainly merited a visit from what were either the secret police or members of the Deir ez-Zor Tourist Board. And, despite their charming smiles, my money wasn't on their being from anything other than one of Assad's enforcement brigades.

You may, of course, recognise the name 'Deir ez-Zor' from the coverage of the war in Syria that kicked off twelve months after we left the country. It was, after all, soon taken over by ISIS. And given that it was one of the more cosmopolitan places we visited, it is appalling to think how it must have suffered. There again, Raqqa, as ISIS's declared capital, may have suffered a lot more. Even though it would have started off as an irredeemably scruffy place, the only saving grace of which was that it hosted one rather basic restaurant that provided us with an exceptional lunch on our way to Aleppo. It was splendid, notwithstanding the fact that it came without any crockery or cutlery. One ate one's meal off a flatbread. Which is possibly why ISIS established its capital there. Operating a knife and fork without breaking one's plate is a skill probably well beyond the capacity of most of its Morlock adherents. They would certainly have had a problem in the somewhat upmarket hotel we stayed in in Aleppo – which was the hotel in which we first learnt of a certain badly behaved volcano in Iceland…

It appeared that this volcano – which had, as its name, an entire Icelandic saga – had been belching so much stuff into the atmosphere that quite a few flights in Europe had been cancelled or put on hold. This was mildly interesting, but not something to bother a bunch of birders in Aleppo. And anyway, whatever was happening now would certainly have cleared up by the time these birders needed to fly back to Britain in six days' time. No question about it. And meanwhile normal birding and normal nosing around the country could be resumed. And it was. We visited a very bird-full lake outside Aleppo. We travelled south through a remarkably clean Idlib province to explore some remarkable 'Dead Cities' sitting in the middle of some genuine Mediterranean scenery. (These were the well-preserved ruins of some very long-abandoned villages.) And we ended up at a gruesome jerry-built hotel that in due course would provide us with a dramatic fly-past of hundreds of migrating cranes, and also act as a base from which we could explore the even more dramatic fortress known as Saladin's Castle. (Even though the Crusaders built it and all Saladin did was evict them without compensation and then use it as an occasional holiday home.)

I have to admit that a little historical inexactitude might have crept in there, but the fact remains that Saladin's Castle is one of the most splendid and most well-preserved castles I have ever seen. Its construction – involving a huge man-made defile and, within this defile, a twenty-eight-metre-high needle of rock to support the castle's drawbridge – is barely credible. And of course, we were its only visitors. It was like going to a souped-up Warwick Castle during a Covid lockdown – in really warm weather. And although we would go on to visit the arguably more famous Crusader castle of Krak des Chevaliers further south, it will be Saladin's Castle that sticks in my mind. I just hope that it hasn't got knocked around by ISIS or by any of the other dismantlers of Syria's precious heritage.

OK. I think you may have had more than enough of Syria by now, but to draw this account of our stay there to a close, I want to say a few words about smoking, and I will start by pointing out that, in early 2010 Syria, one was almost encouraged to smoke. Not only were ashtrays made available everywhere – and used everywhere by the smokers of 'regular' cigarettes – but every restaurant was always ready and eager to bring out the 'hubble-bubbles'. So, if one wanted to round off one's meal with a draft of apple-infused tobacco or maybe a melon-infused mix, a suitable, already-lit sheesha would be produced and puffing could commence at will. Almost half of our group indulged in this practice, and I well remember one evening where I was required to tackle a sheesha that was no less than six-foot tall – with two electrically powered, tastefully illuminated fountains adorning its vertical shaft – and on top of which was a whole melon. However, the point I really want to make here is not to do with any aspects of Syrian smoking *per se*, but instead to do with the fact that our last day in Syria (which was the day after our last scheduled day in Syria) was also the first day of a national smoking ban in Syria…

Banning smoking in this country, we all thought, was akin to banning sex in a brothel. It clearly wouldn't work, and it would be more than just deeply resented. In fact, I recall very well that I suggested at the time that it would lead to a revolution in the country! I now wish I hadn't. Even if an absence of nicotine may have played a microscopically small part in the country's meltdown. But, of course, nothing like the lead role that a volcano in Iceland would play in our spending more time in Syria than we'd planned. Yes, this unpronounceable geographical upstart was just about settling down, but on our return to Damascus, we were first informed that it had already caused so much disruption across Europe that our flight home would now take place in two weeks' time! We would be devoting more time to waiting for our flight than we had so far devoted to travelling around the entire country.

This news caused quite a bit of consternation in the group, and this consternation only dissipated when, after a delay of just twenty-four hours (which enabled us to witness the locals' consternation as a result of that smoking ban), we were informed that a return flight to London had been cobbled together by grabbing an aircraft that had been stranded for days in Cyprus. There was huge relief when we were finally aboard this aircraft – a relief shared with the plane's stewardesses, who, having expected to be on a return flight from Cyprus on the same day as they had arrived there, had not equipped themselves with five days' worth of toiletries or underwear. In fact, I got the impression that they were rather more relieved than we were...

Well, a few days of my life spent in Syria has taken up rather more than its fair share of this book. However, my time there made a great impression on me, as it contained so much... interest, stimulation, enjoyment, and even some excitement mixed with just a *soupçon* of apprehension. It was also spent in the company of a particularly great bunch of people, all of whom, like Sue and me, must now look at what has happened in Syria and weep. An evil descended on that country shortly after we left it – an evil that would destroy much of what we had relished – and, of course, the lives of literally millions of Syrians. And it was an evil that had nothing to do with smoking bans but everything to do with a shedload of religious fanatics and a bad person who had created the space for these fanatics to wreak havoc and cause immense suffering. And, unfortunately, he, Assad, is not the only bad person in charge of a country these days – a feature of our current world that I think warrants one of my brief, albeit didactic, commentaries...

You see, I am of the firm opinion that over the past decade or so, we have been witnessing the emergence of more and more national leaders who are not renowned for their wisdom, their statesmanship or their empathy, and certainly not for their innate good nature. Instead, they are leaders who can be variously described as demagogues, autocrats, despots, tyrants and even monsters. I will leave it to you to decide which title best suits which leader, but I have in mind here not just President Putrid and his odd-looking counterpart in China, but also the aforementioned Assad, that Duterte chap in the Philippines, the tonsorially challenged Kim Jong-un in North Korea, the po-faced Erdoğan in Turkey, the murdering MBS in Saudi Arabia, the thuggish Lukashenko in Belarus, the incompetent Maduro in Venezuela, the brainless Bolsonaro in Brazil, that jumped-up soldier in Burma, whose name is not even worth mentioning, and then of course that guy who hasn't quite gone away even if he's been banned from Twitter. Lump this lot together with two dozen 'presidents for life' in Africa, a clutch of beastly clerics in Iran, and a raft of totalitarian tossers in central Asia, and you've got virtually your entire cigarette-card set of the world's least desirable head honchos, none of whom would regard decency other than as an impediment to his rule.

But why? Why has the world equipped itself with so many out-and-out rotters? Well, here's the didactic bit. Because I think it's all down to there being far too many of us on this planet (a point I have possibly made before). And with too many of us now having to share too little space, we are beginning to behave like rats that are exposed to similarly cramped conditions – conditions in which they soon become aggressive and openly violent. We might not have reached the openly belligerent phase (everywhere) just yet, but we are certainly becoming more combative and more protective of our own space – and certainly more ruthless and even more brutal in our outlook. And what better way to display this shift in our character than to elevate into a position of leadership someone whose character reflects these qualities above all other qualities, and someone who exercises both his ruthlessness and his brutality in the conduct of his role? Quite simply, our current crop of nasty-bastard leaders is the first very obvious symptom of our rampant billions running out of space and out of something called common humanity. And short of finding some suitable euthanistic rat poison, I've no idea what one does to stop it getting even worse. And I'm more than certain that there are more nasty bastards waiting in the wings. Few of whom will ever sit down to write a book…

Yes, time to again turn down the polemics and to report that in 2010 I was writing more books than all those despots put together. Because, at the start of the year I was penning something called *Namibia's Worst Restaurants*, which was the account of my 2009 Namibia trip (with a title that was a scurrilous play on 'Namibia Wildlife Resorts', the government-run lodges in the country that served the worst food imaginable). Then, having returned from Syria, I wrote *A Syria Situation* (before, of course, knowing what was about to happen in that country). And finally, towards the end of the year, I started on *Sabah-taged*, which was a shortish account of an October expedition to the Sabah province of Borneo. Which inevitably means that this chapter has yet to include a few words about our time in the company of orangutans and other similarly remarkable creatures. However, before then, I just want to make the observation that in 2010 I really was a busy boy. Three books being written, three holidays taken (there was also a short expedition to the west coast of Ireland), various places closer to home visited, Wood Cottage maintained – and repaired as necessary – Spindlewood kept in order, and even the local church's graveyard mown. (And me a raging atheist.) How I fitted it all in I don't know. And how I ever found time to be an accountant a few years earlier is a mystery I have still to solve. Maybe the days were longer in those days…

Anyway, it's now time to provide those few words on the delayed celebration of Gordon Brown's ejection from Downing Street in the form of Sue and I going off to the jungles of Borneo – on our own. This would be another Reef and Rainforest-organised trip, and one that will not now be recounted in detail but by way of a few edited highlights. Or, if not highlights as such, then 'experiences' – experiences that have seared themselves into my mind rather more successfully than… other experiences.

The first was a jungle walk in the company of a guide at a splendid jungle lodge called rather unimaginatively the 'Borneo Rainforest Lodge', where we had been strongly advised to wear heavy-duty leech socks to protect us from the attention of the zillion or so leeches who called this place their home. It was good advice. There were more leeches than there were drops of sweat from my brow. And in the hot humid forest there were frequently enough of these drops to coalesce into a stream. Anyway, at one point we stopped at a forest pool and were invited by our guide to take a dip to cool off. On then being told that there were fish in the pool that would nibble our flesh, we decided to refuse this invitation and just stand and sweat instead – and provide an opportunity for a particular leech to have himself a meal.

I still don't really believe it, but you see, in this stretch of Borneo rainforest, there are not only ground leeches, which can be successfully kept at bay with those impervious socks, but there are also arboreal leeches, which have the near-magical ability to drop onto a likely meal by detecting the heat emitted by that likely meal – in the middle of all the ambient heat of the forest. And that's how one came to arrive on the back of my hand! I hadn't felt it at all, and it was only good fortune that I spotted it before it made its way up my arm to its favourite destination: a wet, clammy armpit. Needless to say, I immediately dissuaded it from this course of action by rolling it up and flicking it into the undergrowth. Following that I suggested to our guide that, as we had seen all the forest birds that we wanted to see, and that as, in addition, we were now drenched in perspiration, it might be a good idea to make our way back to the lodge for some refreshment. However, the real reason for my eagerness to return was not being satiated with birds or saturated with sweat but the fact that, unlike Sue, I was not wearing a hat, and the thought of another leech landing on the top of my head – unfelt – was appalling. Fortunately, this didn't happen. Although, having walked no more than fifty yards from the pool to make our way back, arboreal leech number two landed on exactly the same spot as leech number one – on the back of my right hand! Now, how can they do that? How can they be that heat sensitive and that accurate? And do the Americans use them in heat-seeking missiles? I think we should be told.

I also think I, in particular, should have been told about the conditions in the Gomantong bat cave before our guide led me – and Sue – into its cavernous interior. There again, I should have suspected the worst when I picked up that smell as I approached it: that unmistakable smell of poo.

You see, this cave is home not just to bats but also to those diminutive swiftlets whose nests are harvested to satisfy yet another strange dietary demand of the Chinese (in the form of bird's nest soup). These nests are very very high up, and their harvesting is both demanding and dangerous, albeit less dangerous if there is a six-foot-deep bed of bat poo beneath one's ladder, which will cushion one's fall should one come un-rung. Consequently, the bat poo is never cleared, and it now completely covers the floor of the cave – and it reeks. Well, I say completely, but in fact down the side of the cave is a wooden walkway that leads to the back of the cave and then returns on its other side. And this is substantially poo free. There is just a slick of it on the walkway underfoot – which makes every step along it an exercise in not slipping over and soiling one's trousers – externally. And this outcome is more than possible because the walkway's handrail is entirely unusable because it too is covered in a slick of poo – together with literally thousands of large scurrying cockroaches (which are also on the floor of the walkway).

I had never before seen so many of these delightful critters – or so many of the large venomous centipedes that occupied the walls of the cave. And frankly, I have never before been so relieved to be out of a cave – without having slipped into the ordure and without collecting any of it on my head from a passing bat (there were plenty flying about). And whilst what I have just described could legitimately be called a little slice of hell on earth, worst was to come. Because, on completing this ordeal, Sue reported that she had enjoyed it! And then made the unwelcome observation that I was clearly being a wimp! She then repeated that observation when I began to complain of having been bitten by four flies that were probably carrying some poo-cultivated infection that would see me hospitalised within days. And I still suspect it was just good luck that this didn't transpire, and instead I was able to witness some Darwinism in action when, a few days later, we had lunch in a place called Sandakan…

This is experience number three, and it is a very different experience to the two that have gone before. Its setting was the pool restaurant of a swanky hotel in Sandakan, where we had been taken by our guide for some necessary lunchtime refreshment before making our way to the Sepilok Orangutan Rehabilitation Centre. The restaurant had an *intérieur* and an *extérieur*, and, as we had arrived early, we had the opportunity of choosing either that air-conditioned *intérieur* or the hot, humid *extérieur* to partake of our meal. It was no contest. No alcohol was served in the *intérieur*, whereas in the poolside *extérieur* it flowed freely and invitingly. Accordingly, we were soon seated outside, and there, as the restaurant began to fill up, we were able to observe that it had two very distinct varieties of patrons. Joining us for alcoholically accompanied dining were Europeans and Antipodeans, largely dressed in swimming shorts and bikinis, while, making their way into that cool *intérieur*, were some of the wealthy Muslims of Sandakan, kitted out in rather more modest apparel. Indeed, most of the Muslim women had about as much skin on show as was being covered by the bikinis of all the infidel women seated outside. (Though not the same bits of skin – obviously.)

It was a fascinating division of diners, and it made me think of… Darwin. For what I was observing here were two groups of the same species that (a) have a dramatically different appearance, (b) display radically different behaviour, and (c) by and large, do not interbreed. And if one provided this information to any evolutionist, he would conclude only one thing: that under the laws of Darwinism, what was being witnessed here was the evolution of one species into two. For what in nature defines a species if not its appearance, its behaviour and its reluctance to interbreed? And if the answer to that question is its DNA, who is to say that this might not be changing as well? I won't. And I will leave it to you to decide whether you would or not.

I could write a lot more about Sabah after these three specific experiences, but I will restrict myself to saying that what Sue and I found there was very different to what we'd found in Papua New Guinea. And the biggest difference was the obliteration of the forests with endless expanses of palm-oil plantations. Sabah – along with the whole of Borneo – is disappearing under a barren monoculture. They might just as well pour concrete everywhere. It would provide just as little in the way of a usable environment for Borneo's animals and birds.

That's a bit of a bummer to end on, isn't it? And it also ignores the fact that, despite leeches, cockroaches and scary centipedes, both Sue and I enjoyed our trip to Sabah very much. And we also enjoyed being reminded of the fact that if our species does evolve into two, we will always be associated with the one we regard as being infinitely preferable…

Lost in Cape Verde, Bitten and 'Stung' in Botswana

When I was at university, the Cold War was still very much a feature of life, as was the possibility of a nuclear conflagration. Everybody was therefore very receptive to a joke form of contraception that was then doing the rounds. This took account of the radioactive fallout from nuclear testing, and postulated that so much radioactivity would have been absorbed into one's pubic hairs that if they were brought into close contact with someone else's similarly contaminated pubic hairs, a critical mass would be achieved, and there would then be a small nuclear explosion – which would probably take the edge off the thought of any planned copulation. And I suppose I should just add that we are talking here of a time before pubic hair had become an endangered species, and the likelihood of two clusters of it coming together was a great deal higher than it is today.

This has nothing to do with my life in 2011 – which is where we are now – but everything to do with my reluctance to set out what happened at the beginning of this year. Yes, it is no more than a delaying tactic, and unfortunately a delaying tactic that cannot delay indefinitely. Which means that I am now obliged to set out the two less than agreeable events that marked the beginning of this second prime-number year of the twenty-first century. The first was a communication from Her Majesty's Customs and Excise, received in that dead period between Christmas and New Year, 'asking' me to pay them a little over £50,000 by the end of January – to settle an outstanding tax liability. I was not impressed, and I was even less impressed when I visited my local tax office – to inform them of the error of their ways – and there had to deal with a 'customer (?) liaison' lady, whose knowledge of any aspects of tax was less than my knowledge of the gynaecological problems of Herdwick sheep. To this day, I still think she thought she was working in a 'tacks office'. Anyway, after a number of subsequent phone calls with a few people who could probably spell the word 'tax', the issue was resolved. They finally admitted that they had made a mistake, and that my tax demand was overstated by… a little over £50,000. I think the correct figure I was due to pay was about… £120. However, my relief was soon to be overtaken by a big dose of grief, and this was due to the second even more disagreeable event of the new year – concerning my fish…

It had been a particularly cold winter, with snow and freezing temperatures characterising not just the run up to Christmas but the whole of December. This meant that our pond (which we'd had excavated shortly after moving into Spindlewood and that covered more than 1,000 square metres) had been frozen over for weeks. This freezing-over wasn't a unique event, but it had never before lasted so long. And never before, when the thaw caused the ice to retreat from the edges of the pond, had there been so many dead fish. There were hundreds of them, many of them quite sizeable chaps who could easily have withstood the attention of a whole gang of herons, but who were now kaput and fit only for the attention of the local foxes. It was a real loss: for Sue and me, (just) our long-term acquaintances who'd lived in our pond; for them, their very lives. And for those of us still around, it was a quite emotional experience. And who would have thought that some 'dumb' denizens of the not very deep could cause such a reaction? Well, I can assure you, they could, and I still regret their passing to this very day. Even if I happily eat their distant cousins, wrapped in batter and served with chips and peas. But *our* fish… well, they should have lived longer.

Anyway, Sue and I both needed something to drag us out of our sense of bereavement, and very soon we had exactly what was required: the 'live birth' of a muntjac deer in a rose bed just outside our utility-room window. It was both captivating and inspiring, and it would prove to be the first of a number of such maternity events in this sheltered part of our garden. And even if muntjacs are something of a bloody nuisance, and gobble anything green that dares put its head above ground, who cannot be entranced by the sight of wobbly new life and the way that a mother cares for her vulnerable offspring? Well, it really did help us to get over the very poor start to the year. Although probably not quite as much as our early-March trip to Cape Verde did – which involved no tax demands and no suffocated fish whatsoever. But quite a lot of wind…

This was to be a combined birdy and lazy holiday, taking in three of Cape Verde's little clutch of islands. First, it would be Santiago, the human-rich principal island, housing Cape Verde's capital, Praia. Then it would be Boa Vista, the human-light pancake of an island that housed little other than a collection of rocks and a lot of sand. And finally, it would be Sal, the country's holiday island that offered a combination of sun, sea, sand and… sod all else.

Santiago, one of the geologically younger islands, was quite mountainous but, with that superfluity of humans, it was all a bit threadbare. And the only remnants of its endemic flora were clinging on to life on a small number of inaccessible-to-humans-and-even-to-goats peaks, and any endemic fauna had just about lost its grip entirely. The island did, however, provide us with a couple of guided walks that would require more goat than human capabilities. Albeit I doubt that many goats have to slide down precipitous mountain tracks on their bottoms to stand any chance of avoiding the potentially lethal properties of gravity. Oh, and our hotel in Praia was first class. Helped to no small degree by the fact that 99.9% of Cape Verde's sun, sea and sand seekers never visit this island. That might sound a touch elitist, but it's a fact. And so too is that our visit to Sal, for the really lazy element of our visit, needs no comment whatsoever other than to say that this was where we experienced not only more of the unavoidable wind that blows strongly and incessantly throughout all of Cape Verde's islands, but also one of the worst restaurant meals we have ever encountered. This, the meal, was 'enjoyed' in the restaurant of our hotel, a hotel, I might say, that thought itself a cut above the ubiquitous 'budget accommodation' found elsewhere. Which only made the restaurant's performance that much more deplorable. It involved waiting thirty minutes at our table to get a drink, and then another sixty minutes before we were confronted with any food at all, none of which merited any waiting whatsoever. It was appalling, and the restaurant itself was arguably more disorganised than Tracey Emin's knicker drawer. (Although I should say immediately that I have no first-hand knowledge of Ms Emin's knicker drawer or any of her drawers, but I make that comment based on the condition of her 'bed' so-called artwork – and her general… 'arty ambience'. I will willingly provide her with a profuse apology if she informs me that, contrary to my supposition, she keeps a reliably tidy knicker drawer and that I am mistakenly confusing art with life.) However, the fact remains that the Hotel Morabeza – for that was its name – caused us to find other sources of sustenance and to downgrade our marking of our stay in Sal to just one very tarnished star.

Boa Vista, on the other hand, merited four properly shiny stars – at least. This was the island we visited between our visits to Santiago and Sal, and in many ways, it was the most memorable of the three. It is no more than a flat disc of nothing in the Atlantic that has yet to be 'developed', and both its paucity of humans and, rather perversely, its paucity of even a few geographical features, made it very attractive indeed. As did the rather chic converted-fishing-village resort we stayed in, together with a genuine bit of excitement-cum-terror…

We hired a car in Boa Vista's minute capital, Sal Rei (which incidentally and intriguingly is an anagram of 'Israel'!), and I then attempted to drive this car around what was shown on our simple Boa Vista map as a track that ran around the circumference of the island. Well, it didn't. It just sort of fizzled out. And then matters hardly improved when an improbably steep incline appeared in our (indistinct) path, causing my underpowered Daihatsu 'jeep' to have an immediate fit of the vapours, and I was obliged to turn back. I was not obliged, however (after I'd turned back), to discover a whole multitude of other indistinct paths, and then to get lost. But I did. And I mean seriously lost, the sort of lost where a mental review of our water supply was undertaken, followed shortly thereafter by a mental review of the resilience of our relationship. (Sue would definitely have preferred it if I hadn't got lost.) But… well, I did get lost. And for quite some time.

No matter. I did eventually find my way out of nowhere. Furthermore, on the next day, by discovering another track through the middle of the island, I was able to pick up that fabled circular track – beyond that insurmountable incline – and was therefore able to pursue the completion of my circumnavigation of Boa Vista. And frighten myself to death at the same time. This was because the mere suggestion of a track that I'd found soon turned into an endless field of rocks and pebbles, with no tracks whatsoever, but with just a series of seemingly bottomless crevasses, many of which could easily have swallowed a Daihatsu jeep whole. Furthermore, many of them were only passable by my driving my inadequate vehicle with two of its wheels on one side of these terrifying fissures and two on the other. It was like negotiating a succession of car inspection pits, modelled out of mud, and likely to collapse at any time. Oh, and with nobody around to come to our aid should my vehicle miss its footing. After all, nobody else on the island was foolish enough to stray into these demanding stretches of rocks and cracks. Indeed, if we had come to grief, we would have stayed in grief. And maybe I wouldn't now be around to tell you about one other experience in Cape Verde which made an even bigger impression on me than all those daunting rocks and gruesome gullies, and which involved our guide on that first island of Santiago: a chap by the name of Napoleon…

Napoleon was a well-built black guy, who, he informed us, had represented his country in international boxing tournaments, one of which had been a whole-of-Africa event, hosted, I think, in Kenya. In recounting his experience of this coming together of African athletes, he was at pains to tell us how much he had detested the event – because of the racist attitudes to which he'd been exposed! It seems that he and his fellow Cape Verdeans, together with other 'off-shore' boxers from Mauritius and the Seychelles, had been regarded by the mainland Africans as not proper Africans, and had therefore been shunned.

Sue and I found this amazing, not least because we had both been well enough indoctrinated to think that racism was the province of just white people, and that, along with slavery, it had never existed before our malevolent forebears had willed it into existence. And whilst that might be a slight exaggeration of our view of 'nasty racism', it was still quite a shock to hear a black man accuse other black men of this deplorable behaviour. After all, it wasn't anything that Napoleon had done that had earned him this treatment, but just the fact that he was seen as an outsider; somebody who didn't belong. And, of course, this difference between attracting opprobrium from 'being' rather than from 'doing' is all important.

Now, I have in front of me at the moment a huge expanse of thin ice, because I believe that, to be true to the ethos of this book, I need to set out my less than orthodox views on racism – and that means skating out onto that ice and waiting to hear the sounds of ice cracking. You see, racism has two definitions. One is 'the belief that different races possess distinct characteristics, abilities or qualities'. And the other is all about a display of prejudice, discrimination and antagonism against a particular racial or ethnic group – and is now regarded as something comparable with spit-roasting one's grandparents or forcing one's attentions onto an adolescent panda in front of an audience of nuns. It is at the apex of 'stuff that is wrong'. And, of course, it should be – because it is the sort of 'nasty racism' experienced by Napoleon. But here comes the real skating-on-thin-ice bit. This second common-usage definition of racism has virtually eclipsed the first – which is not a good thing. It has made any legitimate discussion of genuine, cannot-be-denied racial characteristics, abilities or qualities essentially toxic. Even if that discussion might focus on commendable characteristics, abilities or qualities such as ingenuity, dependability, hospitality or prudence.

Of course, in many instances, such a discussion will not focus on what is commendable but instead on what is reprehensible; what about a particular race – through its conduct or its culture – might render it 'less attractive' than one's own race. And to the sound of cracking ice, I might suggest that this could include stuff like the widespread practice of child marriage, domestic slavery, female genital mutilation, industrial levels of corruption or so-called honour killings, none of which fill me with anything but revulsion, and an absence of which might point to a more enlightened way of living. And even though these 'racism' observations are the antithesis of the unwarranted sort of racism aimed at Napoleon, they are regarded as taboo, and therefore all these abhorrent practices cannot receive the full blast of condemnation that they truly deserve. Which, in my mind, is hardly helpful in the crusade to eliminate from the whole human race, a bunch of 'traditional customs' that are not only medieval in their nature but also despicably cruel. It's only a pity that my skin colour means that my attempts to introduce some rationality into the fraught arena of racism will be judged to be both ignorant and despicable, and I will be left to flounder in the icy water until I am either dead or have seen some right-on sense. Even if, meanwhile, girls get married off at thirteen or have their genitals cut with razors – because racism is much, much worse, even if it isn't in fact 'nasty racism', but instead its almost benign brother 'observational racism based on behavioural traits' (such as that in which I have already indulged when talking about my experience of Deloitte partners from the USA and Japan). But anyway, please now excuse me while I attempt to drag myself out of this freezing water, and maybe go off and flagellate myself until teatime...

No. Bugger that. I'd rather tell you about how I spent the summer of 2011, which was to enjoy Spindlewood, Wood Cottage, various places in Britain such as the South Wales coast and Durham – and to write another book, this one called *Cape Earth*. It was, of course, an account of our time in Cape Verde, a nation that, despite its undeniable charms, hosts too many people with too few resources, and one that can only exist with the help of international aid and remittances from Cape Verdeans living overseas. (There is a large community of Cape Verdeans living in New England, who are the descendants of the many Cape Verdeans who worked on the whaling ships of the past, based in that part of America.) Anyway, I saw the clearly 'exhausted and unsustainable' nature of this island nation as a pointer to what was happening all around the world, and in the book, I considered what would happen when the whole planet was in the same threadbare and barren state as Cape Verde – and from where it would then receive the external support it would so dearly need. Hence that *Cape Earth* title, and, in the book, the conclusion that, in the absence of civilisations on Mars and Saturn making themselves known, there might be no external assistance at all. And we'd all be completely screwed. And no, I never have been invited to contribute to the CBBC Book Club. And, in any event, back in 2011, I would have had other demands on my time, such as another trip to Namibia and Botswana, this one for a full five weeks and scheduled to take in a little slice of Zambia...

This was to be quite an expedition, and it would be conducted in another of those beefy Toyota Land Cruisers. Heaven indeed. And our first stop on our heavenly progress was the incomparable Etosha National Park, where we again encountered an abundance of wildlife – and, this time, a

Scottish traveller with whom we are still in contact to this day. This was Ted, who, with his wife Dorothy, shared a table with us at our first lodge, and who, it transpired, had been to just about everywhere in the world that Sue and I had been – and would continue to do so over the coming few years. Although who was following whom, we have never quite established. What I can report, however, is that when we left this lodge to make our way further north, Ted's own vehicle did not appear in my rearview mirror. Nor, for that matter, through the Land Cruiser's windscreen. However, what did appear through this windscreen was a Namibia that Sue and I had not witnessed before. It was neither the rather 'tamed' and organised Namibia nor the super-scenic barren Namibia that we had become used to, but instead what might be better described as the 'typical African rural Namibia', with all that means in terms of simple huts, roaming goats, virtually no vehicles and some all too obvious but not desperate poverty. It was quite an eye-opener.

This set the tone for what we would experience over the next few days – as we made our way to our next lodge on the Okavango River and then to another one over the border in Botswana. And that tone was still there as we returned to Namibia to make our way further east along that narrow corridor which is the Caprivi Strip to our next lodge – which is where my stomach had a brief revolt. However, that soon settled down, and this was just as well, because we now had to steel ourselves for something that we had been warned might take that 'genuine African experience' up by more than just a few notches: crossing into Zambia at its notorious Sesheke border crossing – with a vehicle and little understanding of what we would actually encounter…

Imagine, if you can, a set for a new Terry Gilliam dystopian movie, and that might give you an inkling of the physical appearance of the interior of this border post. It might even assist you in going on to form an image in your mind of the decrepit nature of the outside of the post and the moribund nature of its two 'outbuildings'. That is to say, the 1950s micro-caravan, with a big hole in its floor, that housed both a small man with a beard who issued the road insurance certificates and a larger woman with an impressive cleavage who issued the carbon tax certificates – and then the freight container, with a hole cut in its side, that housed the issuer of transport tax certificates. There again, it wouldn't necessarily paint a picture of the various middens of beer cans and other assorted rubbish that surrounded this fifth-world border post – nor the more substantial 'detritus' found here in the shape of the dozens of ancient, overloaded lorries that might wait here for up to three or four weeks to be allowed over the border into Namibia. Furthermore, Terry Gilliam's movie set wouldn't convey the fact that all those certificates – and another one issued in the main building – had to be paid for, and in three different currencies (South African rand, Zambian kwacha and US dollars). And that to acquire all four would take well over an hour, despite the fact that we were the border post's only vehicle-equipped customers, probably for the entire day, and that we had conveniently to hand every one of the many documents that we were required to produce. And we also smiled all the time.

I have dwelt on what was involved in this border-crossing exercise because it so well exemplified the sort of badly organised, under-resourced bureaucracy which is still strangling much of Africa, and which is probably endemic in Zambia. And I say that because in our short stay in this country we encountered it two more times. The first time it was in the form of a man with a clipboard (?) who stopped us on our way out of Livingstone to demand proof that we had entered his country through Kasane (another border crossing into Zambia), and who continued to demand this proof even when I was able to show him that we had entered through Sesheke – which wasn't Kasane! (He only backed off when I raised my voice and got red in the face.) The second time it was in the form of a man with a departure stamp (at Sesheke) who stamped our passports but without checking that there was any ink left in his ink sponge. In fact, it had none. Which is why we then had to experience a worryingly long hold-up on the Namibian side of the border. You just couldn't make it up. That said, it was all part of the rich tapestry of our expedition and, in retrospect, all highly enjoyable. And far more memorable than our stay in Livingstone and our visit to the Victoria Falls.

Which reminds me. I should stick to just the very memorable on this trip, or I run the risk of rewriting the book I subsequently wrote about the whole five weeks (cryptically named *Strip Pan Wrinkle*) – and that ran to 286 pages. So, moving quickly on through a stay at a lodge near the Chobe region of Botswana, I can report that we embarked on a very long drive south along one of the most potholed roads in the world (with potholes so deep, any ears seen poking up above their rim are apparently more likely to belong to a giraffe than to a rabbit), and eventually arrived at a wonderful, completely mad lodge in the middle of Botswana called Planet Baobab – to pick up a guide to lead us to a very different sort of wonderful, completely mad camp called… Jack's Camp.

This is situated in the middle of the Makgadikgadi Pan in central Botswana, which means it might as well be situated in a remote part of the Moon. There is very little there, other, of course, than Jack's Camp itself and, more recently, a couple of small sister camps. Nevertheless, as 'Jack's' is presented as a taste of old-world safari glamour – with touches such as Victorian fittings in its four or five tents, an enormous tented swimming pool and an equally enormous dining tent, complete with a billiards table and a small museum – it is a place well worth visiting (if one can ignore its astronomical cost, which, with a more recent upgrade, is now, I believe, somewhere in a next-door galaxy). Of course, despite the salt-pan sterility, there is wildlife about. (There is always wildlife about.) And at Jack's, we saw quite enough of it to keep us very happy indeed, and our wildlife encounters included not just elephants (who we had to shoo away from the dining tent one evening) but also meerkats; lots of charming, quite adorable meerkats.

What happens… is that you are taken out in the very early morning by your guide, and he parks his glamorous safari vehicle within walking distance of a very low mound in which there are a couple of holes. You then walk to this mound, and when you've arrived there, he then instructs you to lie down near the holes – after you have first given him your camera. Then you wait. And after only a few minutes, a large number of meerkats appear from the holes and, as their first job of the day, they get on with checking for circling birds of prey or any other dangers. And to do this, they use whatever convenient high point they can find – which is you! Sue and I were like children, but calm, delighted children, with meerkats on our legs, our backs, our shoulders and even on our heads. And then, when they'd done with us, they were off – and we could have our breakfast out of the back of that glamorous safari vehicle, and feel very good to be alive.

This was going to be a hard act to follow. But our next lodge, Leroo La Tau, with its handsome chalets set above the Boteti River, and with its zebras, elephants, hippos, lions and a generous assortment of birds, gave it a good try. And furthermore, it provided Sue and me with another unforgettable experience. However, in recounting this, I should first say that it had taken us hours to find this place, and we had also nearly become stuck on a sand track. This was not an uncommon experience in locating lodges and camps in either Namibia or Botswana, but in Leroo La Tau's case, with an absence of sign posts and a pretty daunting, grade-one sand trap, it was as though the lodge just didn't want to be found at all. Indeed, its hidden-away/inaccessible nature was possibly not unconnected with the fact that we were its only guests – until our third night in the lodge, when we were asked if we might be prepared to have dinner with Botswana's Minister of Youth and Culture! He was apparently opening a new village library somewhere in the region, and he and his driver would be arriving in the lodge for an overnight stay, and, of course, the minister would need to be fed – and, if possible, provided with some erudite company. Or failing that, with Sue and me for company.

It was all set up, and in due course we attended at the appointed time to act as companions for a government minister. And then we waited for the government minister to arrive – and then waited some more. Finally, it was decided that we should start our meal without him, because his driver had just phoned the lodge to report that he could not find the lodge! He was having just the same difficulty that we had experienced three days before. However, there was a minister at stake here, so the lodge quickly dispatched two of its staff to find and lead the minister's car to its destination. Which they would have done if they hadn't themselves got lost! Accordingly, more staff were sent off to bring the minister and the lost staff back to the lodge, and the poor guy – and his unhappy-looking driver – made it into the dining room just as we were finishing our meal. We had to settle for a nod and a smile in place of a shared repast. Pity in a way. But what would we have discussed with the minister? Not the state of that potholed road, nor the racial observation made by one of our earlier lodge hosts that Botswanans were not naturally 'ebullient' and, when employed in lodges, had to be taught how to smile and laugh. No, certainly not that...

Anyway, the one and only real problem with this particular holiday is that there was just so much going on that I have not nearly enough room to give you a report on all of it – in what is supposed to be an autobiography and not a travelogue. But I do have to mention – very briefly – just a few more unforgettable elements of our giant loop through three southern African countries. And I will start with what we found when, having 'dumped' our Land Cruiser in Maun, we flew into the Okavango Delta to return to Savuti Camp, the camp at which we had stayed two times before. Because what we found was that this camp, which had previously been perched on the side of a huge dry channel, was now perched on the banks of a huge very wet river! Tectonic plate movements were responsible for this dramatic change, and for providing a new home for numerous fish, numerous waterfowl and quite a big helping of riparian vegetation. It was barely credible.

I should mention that we also found Iris at this camp, a 'slightly elderly' American lady who would become an email pen friend for life – and a real friend with whom we would spend time in London. She was and still is a star. However, no such relationships were sparked at our next camp in the Delta, but it nevertheless furnished us with two (again memorable) surprises. This was Vumbura Plains, an opulent version of Little Vumbura where we had stayed before, but which on this occasion could not accommodate us. And surprise number one was the standard of opulence in this place. I will say no more than an opera could have been staged in our luxurious chalet. It was that large. And after the opera, the audience and the cast could have had a dip in our private plunge pool. That surprise, we of course managed. The second surprise was more difficult to deal with. It was my being bitten on my back by an ant and subsequently suffering a very painful allergic reaction that went on for days. Even now, after ten years, a hot bath can transform my back into a fleshy form of sandpaper.

And one very last thing. I got caught for speeding in Botswana – within sight of its border with Namibia and after spending three weeks driving very carefully around its deserted roads – and after spending a lot of money in the country. It was a 'sting' designed to catch unwary tourists, and a 'sting' that caused me to write a letter of complaint to the Botswanan ambassador in London on my return to England. His name was Mr Blackbeard (really), and he never replied.

Well, that just about wraps up 2011, other than to say that a year that had started out so badly – with erroneous demands for tax and a dispiriting loss of fish – ended up as one of the best years of my life – and of Sue's life. And there hadn't been even a threat of a thunderbolt all year – from my expounding my 'toxic' thoughts on the subject of racism. Probably because they are, in fact, not in the least bit toxic at all…

Tajines and Tsetse Flies

At the beginning of 2012, I was still writing *Strip Pan Wrinkle*, the curiously but thoughtfully named account of my journey with Sue around Namibia, Botswana and just a little bit of Zambia. In due course, and in common with all the other accounts of our shared travels around the world, it would be submitted to a whole raft of literary agents – to be either rejected or ignored by these agents. Which is probably my cue to say a few less than kind words about this particular genus of parasites.

You see, it is essentially impossible to approach commercial publishers directly and then expect them to do anything more than huff in indignation before turning their attention to their next celebrity writer or their next tried and trusted, albeit dull-as-ditchwater, 'safe bet'. After all, they are in the business of making money. It's not as though they exist to take risks. And indeed, that is why they have, as a rank of vigilant gatekeepers, a bunch of overwhelmingly London-based ladies and gentlemen who are equally interested in making money and avoiding risks – who call themselves 'literary agents' and who present themselves as the essential route to publication. Which, very irritatingly, is what they are. If you don't get past the agents, you don't get published. Full stop.

I have to concede that this arrangement works very well for the publishers, very well for the literary agents, not so well for the reading public, and not at all well for most authors. And especially those authors who have not before been published. This is possibly because, not only are these agents risk-averse in the extreme, but many of them are really only interested in attaching themselves to the next J. K. Rowling so that they can retire from actual agency work and devote the rest of their lives to making trips to the bank. I kid you not. If you equip yourself with the latest edition of the essential-for-budding-authors *Writers' and Artists' Yearbook*, you will discover within its pages lots of agents who are 'taking on no new work' – probably because they have fastened themselves so tightly onto one or two super-productive teats in the shape of a couple of best-selling authors that all they need do each day is trim their toenails and congratulate themselves on choosing to become one of those exploitative souls otherwise known as agents. Not low-life football agents, or questionable theatrical agents, or even sometimes useful estate agents – but *literary* agents, the very *crème de la crème* of agents, who are showered not just with (a big share of somebody else's) wealth, but also with standing and a degree of almost unimaginable admiration. For who, at a dinner party, would not be impressed to find him or herself in the company, not of a couple of common-or-garden estate agents, but instead in the company of a couple of those rarest of rare beasts, otherwise known as literary agents? Their very presence would cause an involuntary squirm. And to be allowed to talk to them would probably bring on a serious dampening of one's neatly pressed georgette top, if not something involving an even greater amount of 'moist'.

OK. I suspect you might now be scenting the unavoidable whiff of some slow-cooked resentment topped off with a crust of bitterness and pique. And I can tell you now, your sense of smell would be working fine. Because by 2012, I had made so many submissions to literary agents – including manuscripts, extracts of manuscripts, covering letters and various other pieces of required guff – that, if bound together in hard copy, they would have needed a forklift truck to have been returned. Of course, most were in the form of digital submissions, so nothing so cumbersome would ever be required. Instead, each agent could simply either press a key on his or her computer to send me a 'Dear John' email, or another key that would simply delete what had been sent without generating a response of any sort. Indeed, I think the no-response deletions were already in the ascendancy over the polite 'no thank yous' well before 2012.

This was quite dispiriting. Not necessarily because it made me think that my stuff was trash. Because it wasn't. But more because it made me think that

I was up against a system that was heavily and inexcusably stacked against me. After all, these literary agents were overwhelmingly youngish, metrocentric, lefty-liberal types who knew as much about my world as I knew about theirs, but who were probably even less interested in mine than I was in what they posted on their Facebook page. Of course, that would not have been such a problem if they were keen to identify a book that might have an appeal to, let's say, people born in the '40s and '50s who wanted something interesting and amusing to read. But, by and large, they did not. As they freely admitted on their own websites, they were much more interested in finding a work that appealed to them personally (even before it might appeal to a hard-nosed publisher). And I can only suggest that if, say, they were vegetarians whose job it was to procure food for a supermarket, and they adopted this same 'this is what I like' approach to their buying choices, they would very soon have the customers of that supermarket leaving it in droves. Put another way, they were never going to be attuned to the cynical outpourings of a jaundiced Baby Boomer, and no matter how well I wrote, I was never going to get my literary masterpieces past these literary border guards and anywhere near a commercial publisher – who, in any event, was probably already being distracted by the prospect of a shedload of sales from that latest ghostwritten slice of celebrity pap to land on his desk.

So… if one wants to get into print, one can do this oneself – as I had already done with the Renton Tenting books, along with *Crats* and *Eggshell in Scrambled Eggs*, or one can go not just for some self-printing but also for some full-blown self-publishing. One can sign up with a self-publishing house, and buy its expertise and know-how to generate a 'proper' book, and, by parting with just a little more cash, get this book marketed – at least to the trade. And that, I decided in 2012, is what I would do. And, as a first step, I would revisit all the books I had already written to give them a final polish before they were submitted for self-publication – just as soon, that is, as I'd finished writing that *Strip Pan Wrinkle.* And not surprisingly, all that polishing and writing would take more than a couple of weeks. I would not be visiting my chosen self-publisher until late July. And meanwhile, I would just continue to seethe with resentment – but also find some time to take Sue on a Naturetrek group birding holiday to southern Morocco. Well, we all make mistakes…

To be fair, it wasn't a complete disaster. There were, after all, sightings of wrynecks and blue rock thrushes and a good many other birds. But... the weather was dreadful (cold and wet turning to hot and windy); the accommodation on our trip through the 'desert' south of the Atlas Mountains was mediocre (and some of it was laughable); the food in this 'desert' area was third rate (the tajines were reliably awful and none of the food came within a million miles of the excellent stuff we'd experienced in Syria); the company of our fellow Naturetrekkers was uninspiring in the extreme (and, like the food, in sharp contrast to that we'd enjoyed in Syria); and that 'desert' was not nearly deserted enough and instead full of ribbon development along its roads, acres of filth and litter next to its roads – and some of the most unwelcoming locals we'd ever encountered. I mean, why, when all you have on show through a narrow slit in a black shroud are your two eyes, would you want to hide even this glimpse of yourself by pulling up more of this black shroud at the approach of a bus-full of middle-aged men and women? What are you fearful of? What do you think they will do if they catch a fleeting glimpse of your eyeballs at fifty yards? And how can normal human thinking and reasoning be so bent out of shape as to bring about such extraordinary behaviour? And is this really what the husbands and brothers of these women want: their wives and sisters to be buried under a combination of needless sensitivity and joyless caution – with little or no interaction with the world around them? Maybe it is. But I can assure you: I don't intend to find out. At least not by going back to Morocco, a country where uninhibited or even demonstrative conduct seems to be frowned upon, and where even the window-deficient design of its buildings reinforces its inward-looking and inhospitable character. Or maybe, just possibly, we caught it on a very bad day – for ten days in a row...

Fortunately, Sue and I soon found an antidote for our Moroccan malaise, and this was a very welcome sojourn in Provence, well away from tasteless tajines and wary women, and in the company of four of our longstanding friends. And I should say that all four of them had been through a very demanding selection process to ensure that they would be up to the rigours of the planned food and excessive booze fest. Jim and his wife, Fran, friends of twenty-five years standing, had, only the year before, helped us sink nine bottles of wine at an extended lunchtime nosh-up. And Phil (of American exchange fame) and his wife, Heather, had both, on more than one occasion, slipped into slumberland at a Spindlewood gathering of mates with the help of some liberal lubrication. There was no question that all six of us would be pulling our weight in assisting the French wine industry to thrive and prosper. Of course, we did do a little more than behave badly on this holiday, but our behaviour would definitely have been frowned upon in Morocco, if not punished with a strict diet of tajines until we had seen the error of our ways. And one can only think what the authorities in that country would have done had they seen me parading around in my tight Speedos, my long blonde Rod-Stewart-alike wig, and with a large plastic gold medallion around my neck (as shown in the photo section of this book). My only defence was that this was conducted within the privacy of the property we'd rented in Provence, and I was far too sober when I did it. I think…

However, all too soon, this terrific holiday was at an end – and I was presenting a eulogy at the funeral of one of my friends from my days at work, a larger-than-life fellow by the name of Alan, who, with the help of a bad doctor, no longer had a life at all. His death had saddened me greatly, and it had also reminded me of my mortality and of the need to make the most of my life while I still had it. So, I was soon cramming into the summer as much as I could, including, to recognise the 2012 Summer Olympics, two Spindlewood 'Olympicnics', mini versions of the excesses enjoyed in France – but with medal ceremonies. That is to say, during each Olympicnic, there would be gold medals awarded to the winners of such (imaginary) events as the women's fencing and hedging tournament, the men's 74kg freestyle weight-losing competition, the 200m unwarranted breaststroke race, the women's synchronised sinking competition, the men's arthritic gymnastics, and the men's 1,000m canoodling challenge. And no, there was no question of my behaving like an adult in putting together this sort of stuff. That I saved for when I was writing to politicians to bring to their attention that they were behaving like pusillanimous invertebrates by continually avoiding the need to address the law surrounding assisted dying and euthanasia. And while I am in the middle of jumping from one topic to another, I might as well now jump to Troubador Publishing Ltd, which was the self-publishing setup to which I would now be entrusting my recently polished jewels, otherwise known as my first five travel books – along with those five other books I'd had printed and which would now be converted into ebooks. I'm sure you remember the titles of all ten of these books, so I will not list them again here, but instead just make the point that with such a large delivery of literary magic, it wouldn't be until 2013 that any of these books emerged from the publishing process to take the book-buying public by storm – and thereby propel me to stardom. Not surprisingly, I could hardly wait...

Meanwhile, however, there was another trip to Africa to undertake, this time to the bureaucratically challenged Zambia, which, despite its obvious failings with border crossings and men with clipboards, held out the promise of some absolutely scrumptious wildlife – wildlife that was just waiting to be observed. We went there on yet another Naturetrek holiday – with just three other souls – but, through a different holiday company, we then extended our stay by taking on the role of 'independent travellers'. And what we found there not only vindicated this extension but also elevated this country to a 'must-go-back-there' destination, no matter how slowly it might get to grips with its bureaucracy. It really is a wonderful place, with some national parks that compare well with any other parks anywhere else in Africa. And we first became aware of this when we arrived and then began to savour the delights of the South Luangwa National Park – 9,000 square kilometres of some of the most wildlife-rich woodland savannah in the world. Complete, unfortunately, with a few full-strength battalions of 'insects that bite'. But more of those later. First, I want to mention another delight of a safari holiday, and not just one taken in Zambia, but one taken anywhere on the giant continent of Africa. And that is the shared conversations with one's fellow travellers over a delicious meal in the warmth of an African evening. They were often as memorable as the wildlife one had observed during the day.

However, you will be pleased to learn that I am not about to recount a whole collection of these conversations to reinforce my point that they are an essential and often delightful feature of the holiday experience. Instead, I am simply going to touch on three topics that I seem to recall established themselves as suitable subject matter for regular dinnertime discussions – largely because it was I who introduced them at the table...

The first was – and I'm sorry to say this – all to do with national traits (as in the non-nasty version of racism). And it stemmed from an over-dinner revelation by the South African manager of a lodge at which Sue and I had stayed in Botswana. And what he revealed was that if any lodge had a slightly imperfect chalet – with, say, a loudly dripping tap or a temperamental cistern that flushed only when it chose – it would be assigned to a pair of... Brits. This was because if it was assigned to a pair of Americans, they would demand that the fault was fixed immediately – or else. And if it was assigned to a pair of Germans, they would simply demand to be moved to another chalet that had no such imperfections. On the other hand, the pair of Brits would soon agree between themselves that 'well they're such very nice people, it just seems awful to make a fuss – and, after all, we're only here for two nights, and I'm sure we can manage'. And so they would soon reconcile themselves to the imperfections and 'not make a nuisance of themselves' – unlike those demanding Americans and Germans. And the world would continue to turn smoothly on its axis and the lodge manager and his staff would sleep peacefully in their beds. Even if the pair of Brits were kept awake all night by a loudly dripping tap. But that's just how they were. And all those who ran African lodges knew it. Which... well, kind of makes you proud to be British, doesn't it? We might be wimps, but we're very agreeable wimps. And lots of us love cheese...

Yes, this is the second topic: cheese. And it often featured over dinner because I often challenged my fellow diners to suggest what might be the greatest achievement of mankind. And, almost without fail, they found it difficult to answer this question, and would come up with what were clearly just a number of the also-rans, such as the invention of the wheel, the invention of the steam engine, getting a man on the Moon (!), human rights (!!) – or, believe it or not, democracy (!!!). Only when I prompted them by drawing their attention to where they were – at a dining table – would it occur to maybe one of them that mankind's greatest achievement might concern what we put in our mouths. Not wine or any other alcoholic beverage, which as a group, come in at a laudable number two, but the pinnacle of comestible delicacies, otherwise known as cheese! Yes, just think about it: the aggregation of human imagination and human skills at their very best, that over centuries has provided so many humans with so much pleasure through the creation of a veritable pageant of remarkable cheeses: blue cheeses, soft cheeses, hard cheeses, sour cheeses, sweet cheeses and even smoked cheeses. Every taste and every texture contained within the bounds of just one foodstuff, against which nothing can compete. And furthermore, unlike the wheel or the steam engine, this greatest of all achievements has only ever given pleasure, and has never been harnessed to do damage or cause harm. Nobody, as far as I know, has yet weaponised a wedge of Wensleydale or a chunk of Cheddar. And I am pleased to say that nobody – whether dining at a safari lodge or anywhere else – has been able to dislodge this creamy delight from the number-one achievement spot. Cheese still rules supreme. It even beats the physical design of *Homo sapiens*...

Yes. Topic number three. Again, almost exclusively or indeed completely exclusively as a result of my introducing it at the dinner table. And what I'm talking about here is how the development of the human body has failed to keep pace with the demands now made upon it. How evolution is far too slow a process to equip both men and women with the physical attributes they need to operate efficiently and safely in our modern world. And if only we could put evolution onto fast-forward, we could equip ourselves with stuff such as... well, let's say super-hard skulls with some sort of internal webbing – to obviate the need for hard hats when we were riding, cycling, climbing or doing anything that posed a threat to our heads. Or maybe a stylus-thin index finger that would allow us to avoid hitting the wrong tiny key on our tiny electronic devices. Or... how about internal earplugs to protect us from the assault of unwanted muzak and the noise of tartrazine-fuelled children? And then, for the male of the species, there might be the possibility of furnishing oneself with retractable genitalia to allow one to play rugby or cricket without fear of an excruciatingly painful injury – and, to aid one's performance in another 'sport', a natural easy-to-use, switch-it-on-when-you-want, switch-it-off-when-you-don't, libido-independent, internal stiffener. And not to forget the ladies: inflatable boobs. These could be completely deflated when one wanted to go jogging, inflated a little when bouncing was no longer a hazard, and then inflated a lot when one wanted to... well, impress a prospective mate. And don't tell me that however sexist that suggestion might be, most women wouldn't sign up for this ultra-fast Darwinian enhancement before you could say 'pimp my bosom'. Anyway, nobody actually left the table when presented with this idea...

Which reminds me that Sue and I and others were only at a table because we were on safari – and that I should, before I end this chapter, say just a few words about our safari in Zambia and our time not just in the South Luangwa National Park but also, after we'd left this park, in the Lower Zambezi National Park to its south. I could just say that we saw more animals and birds in both these parks than we'd seen since we were last in the Okavango Delta, and that the Zambian guides we encountered were absolutely excellent. But I do feel I should say a little more than that, and to avoid replicating what I went on to write in a book about this trip (entitled *Marmite, Bites and Noisy Nights*), I will restrict myself to listing just a few of its many highlights – as I have done elsewhere in this book. Starting with an interaction with a baboon – just after I had educated my companions at an outside breakfast table on the method used to produce Marmite... So:

1. Nearly losing my Marmite-covered toast to a fast-moving rampaging baboon, who I managed to scare away with a roar, while, at the same time, catching my toast in my lap, Marmite side up.
2. While being driven at speed in an open Land Cruiser through a mopane forest, being assailed (and occasionally bitten) by countless randy tsetse flies who could not distinguish between a moving Land Cruiser and a moving water buffalo (on which receptive lady tsetse flies usually await their suitors).
3. Waking in the middle of the night in an unlit cabin and, despite the local hyenas, venturing out into its open-to-the-world bathroom, to dislodge with a twig an insect that had settled down for the night in my left ear.
4. Remaining very quietly in our tent while Dixon, the naughty elephant, together with his three mates, pulled up and ate the rain trees just behind our tent.
5. Having a Mongolian meal – really – in a lodge, while being observed by two close-by lionesses and their three cubs.
6. Having to hide in our open-fronted chalet in this lodge when one of the lionesses decided to approach it one morning – before deciding to go elsewhere.
7. Hoping that the wild dogs we were shadowing at speed wouldn't actually catch the antelope while we were around to see it...

8. Having to wait for quite some time for our Land Cruiser to be dug out of a sand trap, having been placed there by one of our excellent guides who proved to be less than excellent in choosing where to drive.
9. Becoming quite concerned at one lodge where we were the only guests – staying in an elevated open chalet served by a wide staircase, of the same design as that used in a nearby lodge that was now closed because the local lions had learned how to climb the stairs.
10. In this same chalet, having to be careful in its open-topped bathroom in order to avoid stepping in the urine or the faeces, kindly deposited overnight by the troop of baboons who had taken to roosting in the branches of a large overhanging tree.
11. Discovering – in this same lodge – that the laundry tent had been squashed during the night by a couple of elephants in search of some ladies' underwear.
12. Being worked so hard at one lodge – with very, very early rises, little free time in the middle of the day, and very long afternoon/evening drives – that we had to ask for cheese sandwiches to be eaten on the afternoon/evening excursion, to remove the need to eat dinner when we returned and wanted only to go to bed (after a quick gin and tonic).
13. Encountering more barely credible, wholly pointless Zambian bureaucracy when we passed through Lusaka airport on our way, in a small plane, to the Lower Zambezi.
14. In our first Zambezi camp, our tent being surrounded by elephants, so requiring us to use a walkie-talkie to be 'rescued' by one of the camp's Land Rovers and taken to the dining tent (on more than one occasion).
15. On our last evening in Zambia, choosing to have a gin and tonic on the banks of the Zambezi, rather than driving to see a leopard that had been spotted a couple of miles away – because we had already seen so many leopards elsewhere on our trip…

As I write this book, Sue and I have yet to take ourselves back to Zambia, and the only reason for that is our finding too many other places to visit first. But we will get back there, despite the presence of those troublesome tsetse flies and those worrisome lions, and indeed the not insignificant number of mosquitoes we encountered, which will have to make do with this passing reference, as in no way could they be regarded as a highlight of our visit and thereby included in the above list.

Anyway, 2012 is running out of road here, and all that remains for me to say is that Sue and I decided to spend our Christmas of this year estranged from Sue's dearest and nearest relations. Instead of yet another Yuletide family gathering, we would take ourselves off to Scotland. Not to Wood Cottage, but to a splendid small hotel on the Mull of Galloway by the name of Knockinaam Lodge. It was a delight in all sorts of ways – with not a tajine or a black shroud or a biting insect in sight. And with surprisingly few lions around…

SAS Training and a Bit of Thieving

The beginning of 2013 was all about books. That is to say, all about *my* books. And you will no doubt be delighted to learn that this is what the beginning of this chapter will deal with. I am going to say just a little about the books that would be written in this year and maybe a *soupçon* more about the books already written – and how I used them.

OK. At the very beginning of the year, I was busy writing that travel book about my experience of Zambia, called *Marmite, Bites and Noisy Nights.* This would take me some time to finish, after which I would start writing aspects of my next travel book – one that would be based on a further trip that Sue and I would undertake to Namibia and Botswana – before we had actually undertaken that trip. That wouldn't happen until September. How I was able to take such a novel approach to writing a travelogue will all be made clear in due course. Although, I will make clear now that I am using the word 'novel' here in the sense of 'unusual' and not in the sense of 'fictitious prose'. It wouldn't be until 2018 that I would embark on the writing of a thriller inspired by two of our overseas adventures...

However, I am really getting ahead of myself there, and I now want to tell you about those already written books that Troubador had been busy bringing out as hard-copy published works and/or ebooks. Well, the first to make it into the arms of an eager public were the Renton Tenting ebooks together with the ebook versions of *Crats* and *Eggshell in Scrambled Eggs*. And I am able to report that, whilst the eager public must have been looking the other way or were maybe in some other way distracted, this vanguard of literary brilliance did pick up some really good reviews. These were on something called 'NetGalley', which is a (well-known to those who should know) website, where book reviewers and other professional readers can read books in their digital form, and then report their opinion of the worth of these books and also give them a rating. The Renton works generally earned some kind words – and even a 'must read' review – and generally netted four out of five stars. It was a similar story with the hard-copy versions as they began to emerge, with *Brian on the Brahmaputra* earning some encouraging comments, and even *A Syria Situation* getting a pretty good reception. Oh, and about as much interest from the buying public as those original ebooks, even with the employment of a little bit of marketing and a wonderful new 'David Fletcher Books' website. Perhaps my books weren't going to take the book-buying public by storm after all...

In fact, there's no 'perhaps' about it. The lack of interest in my books in 2013 was not an ephemeral phenomenon. There would be more and more of it in the years to come, no matter what I wrote and how well it was received by reviewers. I was not going to make a living out of writing. However, that had never been my objective. And whilst it would have been 'nice' to find a wider audience for my work, I was very content to find a string of friends and acquaintances who did relish my outpourings of humour and grief and who did provide me with all the encouragement I needed to carry on writing more of the same stuff. Inevitably, however, there were others who were not nearly so 'motivating' in their response, or who provided no response whatsoever...

I have had two friends who have written books themselves. When they gave me a copy of their works, they were read assiduously, and I provided them with very complimentary feedback. I thought this was the least I could do as an acknowledgement of both their efforts and their generosity. I was therefore surprised – and very offended – when certain recipients of my own books had not the courtesy to tell me whether they had even read them. There wasn't so much as a 'what a load of old rubbish'. Now, I know that not everybody wants to read about the way we are mutilating our world, even if this constant theme in my books is served up with a generous helping of entertainment and humour. But haven't they got any soddin' manners?

I've even had no-response responses for a couple of my travel books from 'friends' to whom the books were dedicated! You know, on the flyleaf. And I only wish now that I'd got the printers to use disappearing ink – not just for the dedication but for the whole damn book. I also wish that I had never given my books to anybody under the age of thirty, which I did indeed do by giving them to a few of the children of my friends and to a few of my younger relatives – who I thought might welcome an informative and amusing read. How stupid was that? I mean, what is the point of giving someone a book if he or she gets out of breath towards the end of reading a long Twitter post? The whole idea of their making their way through 300 pages of print – when they have the attention span of an amoeba with Alzheimer's – is preposterous. They'd have trouble with the synopsis on the back cover. And they'd certainly have trouble with a word like 'synopsis'.

Oh dear. I seem to have laid bare my... let's say my dismay at the behaviour of some of my so-called friends. And that's on top of my exposing my feelings for literary agents and my disappointment at not being able to produce anything that the buying public wanted to buy in measurable numbers. However, I do need to stress that not only was I very happy just to write, no matter who might or might not read what I'd written (and that is still the case), but I have found the whole process of attempting to get published, and the negative/no-response reactions to my self-published efforts, a very positive experience. It has been like SAS training for the mind. And what I mean is that I am now impervious to rejection and disappointment, when these two gifts are laid at my door by people whom I don't know or whom I don't care to know. Anonymous literary agents and failed acquaintances can now do nothing more than arouse a slight interest in my mind – as to how they can be so blind or so rude – but they can do no more than this. In fact, it occurs to me that if we really are breeding a snowflake generation, all we have to do to toughen them up is get them to write a book and attempt to get it published. If they do this, I can guarantee that in no time at all, they will have equipped themselves with all the resilience and all the fortitude they will ever need. I won't, however, suggest that, in taking on this challenge, they give their work to their friends to review, as we all know that if they did this, they wouldn't get past the first (minor) hurdle. Because after half a page of reading, their friends would get distracted by their need to re-engage with Twitter or TikTok or with any one of a dozen other time-sinks into which they empty their lives. And, consequently, the poor little sausage authors wouldn't even get started on the process of growing up into sunny, well-balanced people such as myself – whose thick skin, incidentally, isn't impervious to the feelings and actions of those he cares for. Which, I think, is an important point to make...

But just to round off this wallow in self-commiseration, may I please emphasise again that writing is a pleasure in itself, and I would continue to do it even if the whole world was reduced to the reading and communication level of Donald Trump, and it regarded a hard-copy book as an interesting but obsolete relic of a past generation. Possibly because I myself was quickly becoming an obsolete relic of a past generation – who would become ever more obsolete if only he could survive the slings and arrows of outrageous misfortune...

The first serious threat to my continued wellbeing happened on my way back to our house – from our greenhouse. I tripped over – before the first drink of the day – and gashed my hand 'comprehensively'. It was a hospital job, and I had soon been delivered into the arms of our ever-ready NHS where, after a rapid session of triage in the Aargh! & Eek! department, it was decided that I needed a whole line of stitching. That was when it got interesting. To start with, a trainee (lady) doctor cleaned up my wound in preparation for her needlework, but then she disappeared. This, I subsequently discovered, was because somebody had jumped the queue by injuring himself quite seriously through crashing his car. In fact, he'd crashed it because he was a Slovakian gentleman who held very firmly to the Slovakian habit of driving on the right, even when in a country where everybody else drove on the left.

I wasn't aware of his misfortune at the time, but I did become aware of why I was pushed even further down the queue. Because the reason for this was another gentleman who just happened to be in the curtained-off cubicle next to my own. And his problem wasn't so much that he was an inmate of one of Her Majesty's local prisons, but more that he had used a biro to shove a ball of aluminium foil from a packet of cigs – up an artery in his right arm.

This is not something you should try at home. But if you are in prison, it's well worth giving it a shot. Because you are then immediately taken off to a nice hospital, probably by two very nice prison warders, where you will first have the aluminium extracted from your arm, and then be given two or three nights in a comfortable hospital ward before being sent back to your slammer. And there, no doubt, you can, if you want, shove another piece of aluminium up your arm and start the whole process all over again. And I have indulged in that little dose of mean-minded cynicism because this was indeed this bloke's second visit to the hospital to have metal mined from his arm. And I suspect it wouldn't be his last.

So... one taxpayer left waiting, while one non-taxpayer (in this country) was treated, and another non-taxpayer (who was already being kept at the expense of said single taxpayer) was given a real treat. It wasn't ideal. And neither was the stitching, as this was performed by that trainee lady doctor from the sub-continent, whose mother had clearly not forced her to apply herself to embroidery in her youth. And the icing on the cake with this story is that my local GP practice could subsequently not find the three minutes in its busy schedule that would be needed to remove the stitches during the following week. I had to have them removed at a private hospital at my own cost. Which leads me to conclude with the rhetorical question: 'Who, in his or her right mind, would choose to be a law-abiding taxpayer?'

Anyway, this wasn't the only threat to my life in 2013. A little while after the gashed-hand episode, I was mowing part of our field with my sit-on mower when I heard a noise that made me think that I had just run over a sheet of metal. Maybe even a sheet of aluminium. I therefore stopped my machine immediately, looked around – and saw that within inches of the back of the mower was the top twenty feet of a nearby crack willow. That noise had not been as a result of my running over metal, but it had been the noise that is made when the trunk of a crack willow cracks – leading, of course, to a large weight of timber being subjected to the force of gravity and quite possibly landing on the head of a passing unsuspecting mower-driver. I had just skipped death. Albeit without the involvement of any Slovakians or inmates of British prisons. Nor were these disparate types involved in my getting caught for speeding...

Yes, it wasn't a sting and an on-the-spot fine in Botswana this time. It was a sting and a bureaucratic money-making process in England – starting with a note through the post ten days after the event. This informed me that I had been driving at a reckless 34mph on a 30mph stretch of road – through a hamlet in Shropshire that had last recorded a pedestrian in 1947 – and that I could either pay a fine and have my licence decorated with three points, or I could attend a 'speed awareness course'. Not wishing to spoil the clean, minimalistic lines of my licence, I opted for the course – and whatever this would cost me. And in due course, I attended this… course.

What a waste of time! And what a con. In fact, what a dreadful money-making con that has as much chance of improving road safety as I have of improving my chat-up lines after half a century of neglect. All these courses do is alarm any of their 'normal' attendees by exposing the lack of intelligence of all those other people with whom they are sharing the roads – as well, of course, as filling somebody's coffers with piles of ill-gotten loot. And I mean the loot taken from the pockets of a hefty proportion of the British population who might possibly have exceeded an arbitrary speed limit by the sort of speed managed by an arthritic pensioner hobbling his way downhill. And who is this somebody – or somebodies? I believe the courses are run – and charged for – by private companies. But who owns these companies? And do they pay commission to anybody for supplying all those unfortunate not-very-boy-racers? I would love to know. And I would love to know just how much of this is an unexposed racket and who are the racketeers. (And whether the setting up of speed traps is a completely unconnected matter.)

Anyway, the good news was that I passed my speed awareness course, and I then managed to drive around Mallorca without falling foul of even a single speed trap. This was very good news, as was the fact that Sue and I had gone there with Phil and Heather (of drinking and general socialising fame) and had secured for ourselves a very nice villa in which we would all indulge in an extended period of self-indulgence – with the odd drink.

There is not too much to report on what indeed proved to be an extended sybaritic session in the sun, other than to make a brief reference to thieves, animals and tennis balls – in that order.

So, thieves first. And this was the warning from the holiday rep who visited us in our villa that we should always make sure its windows and doors were locked – even when we were just outside it by its pool – because the Romanians were very active this season. In fact, as fast as the authorities could catch them and kick them out, they were back with a new name and with the intention of making off with as much stolen property as they could – snaffled from all those wealthy Brits who couldn't even bother to lock up their villas. This warning, I found very interesting – as well as alarming. Because it wasn't swaddled in layers of political correctness. It was just factual. It told us what we needed to know. That we should be on our guard against people not with Asian or Amerindian Indian features, but people with Eastern European features; and, if we were able to identify them, specifically people with Romanian features. Because it was virtually exclusively Romanians who were doing the thieving. I remember wondering at the time whether an ardent advocate of anti-racism, who might have chosen to stay in this same villa, would have been appalled or relieved to have received this accurate (racist) warning. My suspicion is that he or she would have responded to the information supplied with just a weak, if not feeble, smile, and have felt an understandable mix of both guilt and relief.

And so to animals – in the shape of the three dogs, six sheep, nine hens, one cockerel, one pig, one mule and four cats, all of which were in the care of the owner of the villa, who, together with this impressive menagerie of not-very-wildlife, seemed to spend most of his time in a small windowless building at the rear of the villa. They were all a constant source of pleasure, but one of them, one of the dogs, whose name was Drac, was more than a source of pleasure. He was a highlight of the holiday. He visited us every day, and soon adopted me as the one most willing to throw a stone for him to chase – repeatedly. Indeed, I did this so often – in the field to the side of the villa – that I became concerned that he would get damaged in some way or, as a minimum, he would break his teeth. After all, stones are hardly the best thing to grasp in one's noshers. So, Sue and I bought him four tennis balls – each of which he destroyed as soon as he'd chased it and retrieved it. We were soon back to stones – and soon enjoying each other's company immensely. He was a really good guy. Although his Spanish was even more limited than mine.

Anyway, it had been really hot in Mallorca. Which was quite a good preparation for that next trip I mentioned earlier in this chapter, which was to be yet another driving holiday around Namibia and Botswana. It would last for five weeks, and for the first three of these weeks Sue and I would be accompanied by Nick and Sheila again. Although to start with not by our luggage…

British Airways had failed to exceed our expectations (or maybe had met our expectations) and had managed to get all four of us to Frankfurt for our onward flight to Namibia, but with only the luggage belonging to Nick and Sheila. Ours would follow in our wake. Which meant that our first twenty-four hours in Namibia were not the best in terms of 'feeling fresh'. It was a great relief when our bags finally arrived, and we were able to embark on our planned safari in, needless to say, another great Land Cruiser. This one came in a nice shade of 'parched sand', and was kitted out with the obligatory two spare wheels, monster jack, spade, toolkit and modest fridge. (After all, one has to have all the necessary toys to make it a proper safari.)

Our first destination was the huge, privately owned NamibRand Nature Reserve in the south-west of the country: an immense swathe of breathtakingly beautiful desert, in which there have been built just three camps. These make up the 'Wolwedans collection of camps', and we would be staying in two of them. First it would be the Boulders Safari Camp and after that the Dunes Lodge, and it would be the former that outshone the latter without even trying – as I will explain.

'Boulders' is no more than four exquisitely presented 'tents' situated at the base of a big-boulder-strewn hillside – with an opulent dining 'tent' to cater for the nutritional needs of its patrons. And those 'tents' are in inverted commas, because they are not the sort of tents one would find being used by the 1st Worcester Scout Group on its annual pilgrimage to Borth, but more the sort of tents that might feature as a backdrop for an advert for Bentleys. They are really very plush indeed. This, all four of us could deal with. Just as we could easily deal with two of the other guests in the camp: a pleasant Norwegian couple who lived in Angola, and who had come to Namibia for a bit of vital R&R in non-threatening surroundings. However, the other two guests were more of a problem. They were an English couple who lived in Switzerland, and they took every opportunity they could to tell us how wonderful Switzerland was and how shitty England was. I didn't like this, and I came very close to reminding them that Switzerland's enviable everything might just be built on it having a parasitic nature within the body of Europe that was surpassed only by Luxembourg. And did they not remember that while the rest of the continent of Europe was fighting for freedom, Switzerland was keeping its head down and simply working out how to evade the need for financial transparency for the next sixty years? It was hardly a place to admire.

However, I should not be dwelling on this Anglo-Swiss fly in the ointment, and instead I should be making the point that our stay at Boulders was thoroughly enjoyable. We were looked after very well, and we were shown all sorts of desert wildlife and some stunning desert scenery. And we weren't robbed…

Dunes Lodge is a little more basic than Boulders, and houses maybe twenty guests. Needless to say, it was still a delightful place to stay, and it had a very inviting bar. So inviting, that when we arrived there, the first thing we did, after we'd been taken to our chalets, was to assemble in the bar for a drink before we sat down in the camp's restaurant for lunch. Following this, the four of us returned to our respective chalets, and I set about working out how to use the chalet's built-in safe. This was, after all, the very beginning of our five-week stay in Africa, and I was carrying quite a lot of currency with me. And, whilst we were in the middle of nowhere, one can never be too careful. Or, in this case, one could have been a lot more careful, and not left one's wallet, bursting with large-denomination notes, in one's holdall in the chalet, while one had gone off for a beer and a bite to eat.

Whoever the thief was, he hadn't taken it all. In fact, he'd taken just US$250 and 2,200 South African rand, which was barely enough to alert me to the fact that my wad of notes had become marginally slimmer. But it was just enough to alert me. And when I'd conducted a count, and had worked out how much I'd unwittingly contributed in international aid, I had to report it to the camp management. Nothing happened, of course, even though I knew the identity of the culprit. It was one of the camp's staff – a guy who had provided us with a very offhand greeting when we'd first arrived, and had then been seen skulking *beneath* the bar when we had been making our way there for that initial drink (the whole camp was built on stilts). Inevitably, even though we were exposed to more delights during our stay at this second retreat in the desert, it left rather a bad taste in our collective mouths, and we were not sorry to leave and make our way north – with every intention of staying as close as possible to our paper wealth.

Anyway, I am happy to report that we encountered no further criminal activity, which I think means that I will not impose a detailed account of the following month of our circumnavigation of Namibia and Botswana, but, instead, just provide you with the very heavily edited highlights, which are, in chronological order:

1. Encountering Namibia's 'coastal chill' arising from the cold Benguela Current – first at Walvis Bay and then at Cape Cross.
2. Entering the Skeleton Coast National Park through a pair of gates decorated with a skull and crossbones – when eventually we had found the gatekeeper to unlock them for us. (I don't think he'd seen a car in weeks.)
3. Getting delayed by a group of unapologetic French Canadians in our attempt to get to the remote and wonderful Etendeka Mountain Camp (long story).
4. Experiencing the slowest safari drives in the world at the enchanting Huab Lodge (another long story).
5. Being harassed (and I mean seriously harassed) by a truculent warthog at Okonjima.
6. Getting uncomfortably close to a couple of rhinos in the Etosha National Park.
7. Staying in a barmy chalet at a lodge on the banks of the Okavango River, which came equipped with a view of Angola through its windows and a sparkling LED light canopy above its capacious bed.
8. Being overwhelmed with a profusion of elephants, wild dogs and some really dumb Canadians in Savuti Camp (after we'd moved from Namibia to Botswana – obviously).
9. Chatting with the executive chef at Little Vumbura (a black man) about his time working for a prince in Saudi Arabia, and his giving us his opinion that Saudis were all either mad or ignorant. (His opinion; not necessarily mine.)
10. Meeting a guy at Motswiri Camp (another middle-of-nowhere establishment) who was an agricultural student from Harper Adams

University, working on the practical experience part of his course – and whose parents ran a post office in Rugby!

Well, I think that's quite enough of all that, other than to say that this particular Land Cruiser cruise through two countries led to my writing yet another book, this one given the informative title of *The Country-cides of Namibia and Botswana.* And when I say 'informative', I mean, of course, 'tantalising' or 'confusing'. Because without reading the book one would not discover that within its pages, I'd set about committing a 'country-cide' on thirty separate nation states by painting a not particularly glowing picture of their less than laudable behaviour. Some would get away with little more than a light admonishment, but many others would get the full-blown 'murder treatment' reflected in the book's title – and which they so thoroughly deserved. And, of course, this is why I was able to write great chunks of this book before I had stepped into that Land Cruiser. I had been able to compile thirty indictments of thirty countries in the months leading up to our trip, all then ready to slot into *The Country-cides* as I began to write it in the latter part of 2013. After all, there's nothing wrong in introducing a bit of tactical pre-planning into the creation of a work of literary genius…

However, back in the real world, I can report that we again missed out on a 'family Christmas' by taking ourselves off at the end of the year to spend our Christmas in… the Gambia! We stayed at a wonderful riverside eco-resort called Mandina River Lodge, which not only housed some interesting Christmas escapees, but also some more permanent residents in the shape of rescued dogs. The owner deserves a medal. And his lodge deserves to thrive. I hope it does. And I hope that I haven't dwelt too long on a year that saw thirty-nine international workers killed at a natural gas facility in Algeria, two bombs detonated at the Boston Marathon, Fusilier Lee Rigby butchered to death in London, and nearly 1,500 people killed in a chemical attack in Syria. Yes, the world was becoming ever nastier all the time, something I might return to when I compose the next load of nonsense to fill this book…

A Very Big Bump in the Road

I celebrated the beginning of the new year with a visit to my GP for an abdominal aortic aneurism screening. It's what people who are getting old do: get various checks on their ageing jalopy of a body in order to keep it roadworthy for as long as they can. And, in this case, the mechanic's diagnosis was good. I was told that I would never need another abdominal aortic aneurism screening – because I would never die of an aortic aneurism. Brilliant! The clinical mechanic was no less than a soothsayer. And she – for she was a she – assured me, without any reservations, that I would not be departing this mortal coil through a burst in my main blood vessel. Unfortunately, her soothsaying powers were rather limited, and she could not assure me that my life wouldn't end as a result of a shark attack or by my being trampled to death by elephants, and she wouldn't even give me odds on the likelihood of it coming to an end by my being struck by lightning. But I couldn't complain. One route to the underworld had been ruled out, and that was really quite enough. It was a very good start to the year.

Anyway, having established that I had a robust, fully functioning aorta, it was time to immerse myself in what I liked to do best in winter, which was to get down to some more book writing and, in this winter, to indulge in a bit of shameful hypocrisy. Yes, despite my former claim to be indifferent to how well my books might sell, I had decided to have one go at supercharging my marketing efforts by employing the services of a publicity and marketing guru in London who specialised in broadcasting the brilliance of any author prepared to pay for his services. Although, of course, what I found was that it is the author who is left to do most of the broadcasting. The paid publicist just sets up the platform from which you then shout your wares.

I have to admit that it wasn't a great success. If success is measured in terms of book sales. However, if it is measured in terms of the number of articles I had to write and the number of appearances on not-quite-mainline radio stations, it was an absolute triumph.

Some of the stuff I ended up writing, I have now thankfully forgotten, but there are a couple of pieces that, as much as I try, I cannot forget, and that ended up in some worthy (not-quite-mainline) journals. They were written to order. They were certainly not my idea. One was 'The top five places to visit to avoid tourists' (and that couldn't include places like isolation hospitals and Wigan; they had to be proper 'world destinations'). And the second was 'The top ten ways not to upset the locals' (and again, that couldn't be stuff like not burning their houses down or not showing them a clip of a Frankie Boyle performance; it had to be something realistic, like not suggesting they organised a litter-pick).

The radio appearances involved rather less work. For example, I could think of nothing to prepare for my planned interrogations on Radio Jersey and Radio Guernsey (conducted remotely from a studio in Coventry). I wouldn't even get to ask the daytime presenters any questions myself. So, no possibility of formulating an incisive enquiry into the current state of hostility between the two islands. All I was there to do was answer dumb questions – from two presenters who clearly and understandably hadn't read any of my work – and then make a reasonable observation when one of them expressed a desire to visit Iran. Which, as I distinctly remember, was to express my personal view that it would require the un-banning of booze in that country before I'd even consider going there. And then, after that consideration, I wouldn't go there anyway. Because I really wasn't very keen on repressive theocracies that murdered and imprisoned whoever they chose. I'm not sure that the lady presenter in question appreciated this observation. Maybe I should just have told her about what was planned for Wood Cottage and Spindlewood...

Yes, getting old doesn't entail only visits to have one's aorta checked over. It also entails deciding what might be turning from a pleasure into a burden – the sort of burden that is susceptible to storms and tempests in the uplands of Scotland and that needs constant attention to keep it in good order. And that was Wood Cottage – a bolthole that we'd enjoyed greatly for ten years, but one that was now becoming too demanding in a variety of ways, and one that we knew we had to dispose of. Accordingly, we began to seek the services of an estate agent in Dumfries and, at the same time, those of a builder close to home. And that was because Sue and I had decided to replace our bolthole in Scotland with a sort of bolthole attached to our house in Worcestershire. This would be built as a fully serviced 'granny flat' – not for any grannies, but for visiting guests and for us or our carers in later life, should the need arise. And it would be of just the right size to accommodate all our furniture from Wood Cottage. It would also be built at the extreme end of what currently constituted our home – in place of what was an exterior swimming pool that was also quickly turning from a pleasure into a burden. (Maintaining a swimming pool at the correct pH and chlorine levels in the British climate is as difficult as finding a worthwhile number of days in which to use the blasted pool in said British climate.)

So, we had set in motion two projects that would inevitably require a lot of our time – to which we then added a third: the construction of a large raised deck that would straddle the wall between our garden and our field and give us an unhindered view of our pond. It wasn't in the *Grand Designs* league, not by a long way. But it did involve a great deal of preparation, a large amount of design input, and ultimately a bit of a battle with its builders to lower the height of the handrail that ran around its perimeter. In fact, I think that battle took place just before or just after I sold my beautiful green Jaguar (which, in all honesty, had already become another 'more burden than pleasure' aspect of my life). It was the third of the green XJ6 Jaguars that I had owned for over a quarter of a century, and letting it go was quite painful. Even more painful than the paltry sale proceeds I was forced to accept from its buyer. But with two other cars in the family, including a recently acquired Golf GTI and a recently acquired VW Touareg, it was just too much to deal with – and likely, very soon, to become far too costly to keep on the road. Its aorta was OK, but its skin and some of its vital parts were not quite so healthy. And it did go to a good home: a guy who was buying it for his eighty-five-year-old granddad who had always dreamed of running a Jag. And who may well, very soon after receiving it, have run it into a ditch. But even if he did, I'm sure he would still have been very happy, right up until he realised he was going to part company with the tarmac. And even in the ditch, he would still have been able to smell that fine supple leather...

Meanwhile, back in my own life, it was time for Sue and me to take ourselves off to the Congo. And I'm really sorry to go all didactic here, but I really do need to make it clear that we were not planning to visit that permanent war zone, otherwise known as the Democratic Republic of Congo, but instead its smaller, not quite so unstable neighbour to its west, which rejoiced in the rather more honest name of 'the Republic of Congo'. It is actually a democracy, but... well, its head honcho was first Numero Uno between 1979 and 1992 – when this Congo was a single-party state – and, in 1999, after a short interregnum, he resumed the top job in the new democratic Congo, and is still in that top job to this day. So... not what you might call a model democracy. More a sham democracy under which lurks an autocracy. Which has at least avoided the pitiful fate of the DRC – and which, in 2014, provided a safe enough environment to convince ten intrepid Naturetrekkers to visit it, in order to observe some of its lowland gorillas.

We would be the first Naturetrekkers to go there (without a leader, incidentally), and, as we would discover when we got there, we would be some of the country's very first tourists, full stop. The Republic of Congo had just been through (another) rather turbulent period, and its tourist industry consisted largely of two very small jungle camps in the north of the country – in its largely untouched Odzala-Kokoua National Park. That was where we were going. And it would be those two camps in which we would be staying. If, that is, our Dornier 228-200 made it through the storm clouds and its pilot could find the diminutive grass runway...

We had arrived in Brazzaville from Paris, and had stayed overnight in one of Brazzaville's very pleasant hotels. Here, all ten of us had got to know each other a little, and had discussed, amongst other things, Brazzaville's airport, Brazzaville's general ambience, and Brazzaville's name. They were all interesting topics. And to start with, there was that international airport, the one that failed dismally to meet everybody's expectations. For not only was it not fly-blown and generally rundown (which is still a popular style of airport in certain African countries), but it was smart, clean and its design and fittings made it appear to be a distant annex of the airport from which we had just flown in: Charles de Gaulle Airport in Paris. This was very telling, as was the city's general ambience – which was distinctly French. It wasn't just the *boulangeries* and the *patisseries* at the side of the road, but even the signs *on* the roads – all unmistakably French in appearance. Oh, and of course, in this ex-French colony, everybody spoke French as well. And not much English.

We would subsequently discover that whilst the country was now being courted by China (where in Africa isn't?), it is still very much wedded to its old colonial master – right down to receiving four planeloads of edible goodies from France every week in order to keep the capital's better-off residents supplied with all the French cheeses, chocolates and other delicacies that they might ever require. None of which would be happening at all if a certain bloke, by the name of Pierre Savorgnan de Brazza, hadn't visited this part of Africa in the mid-nineteenth century – and claimed it for his adopted country. (He was originally an Italian.)

Now, I might be going on a bit here, but this guy is really interesting. After all, most colonists – in whatever period they were busy colonising countries – were not noted for their excessive humanity or even their restraint in dealing with 'the natives'. But de Brazza was. His approach was not in the least oppressive or coercive, but rather to employ the concept of what he termed 'association', which was to encourage local tribes to come together voluntarily under the French flag. And this worked! Helped to no small degree by a desire on the part of these tribes to have a genuine authority in the area – an authority that had been absent ever since the demise of the local kingdoms that had once provided it, namely those of the Kongo and the Loango (details of which are somewhat beyond the scope of this book).

Anyway, this isn't just fanciful nonsense. Because not only is de Brazza the only African colonist to still have an African capital that bears his name, but he is properly revered in the Republic of Congo. Why else would the inhabitants of this country, in 2006, have had his body – and those of his wife and four children – disinterred from their ill-chosen resting places in Algiers (a long story), and then placed in a newly built, rather plush mausoleum in the centre of Brazzaville? This guy had clearly been something special, albeit in a very different way to the resident primatologist at Ngaga. Yes, I really ought to move on to recognise that Sue and I hadn't come to the Republic of Congo to study its colonial history, but to observe its wildlife. And given that our Dornier's pilot had indeed found his way from Brazzaville to that vital grass runway, and had successfully landed his plane on it (even bringing it to a stop before the grass ran out), I will now say a few words about our time in the two delightful Odzala-Kokoua National Park camps of Ngaga and Lango. To do this, I will once again employ the economical format of bullet points – to record what were its most memorable aspects, starting with that resident primatologist. So…

1. Encountering the (Spanish) resident primatologist at Ngaga Camp, whose twenty years of work had saved the local population of lowland gorillas, but had done nothing for her manner or her manners. She was both odd and rude.
2. Discovering that in tracking these gorillas one has to commit to dig a one-foot-deep hole should one require a pee, and to make a three-foot-deep excavation should one want to make a more substantial deposit. (In order to protect the gorillas from unwanted infections.)
3. Discovering that, to further protect the gorillas, one must wear a face mask when one has successfully tracked them down, together with a head-net to protect oneself from the attention of zillions of inquisitive sweat bees.
4. Concluding that when all these protective measures are combined with the necessary brisk route march through a steamy jungle in order to locate the gorillas, gorilla-tracking is not for the fainthearted – or the infirm.
5. Discovering – in Lango Camp – that forest elephants are an entirely different species from the 'common' bush elephants, and that they sing – beautifully – in the middle of the night.
6. Undertaking a walk down the shallow river that runs past Lango – by walking down the river. (There are no paths, and one simply reconciles oneself to wet feet and the odd awkward encounter with a water buffalo or an unthreatening snake.)

7. Remembering, on a boat ride down a more substantial river, that tsetse flies are attracted to blue, and that wrapping one's ankles in a blue cagoule in order to prevent their being bitten is therefore almost certainly counterproductive.
8. Finally conceding defeat in our attempts to extract a Land Cruiser from a mud trap – by sharing two bottles of champagne between the six people aboard this vehicle, before accompanying our driver and guide back to Lango on foot.
9. Witnessing – on the telly, back in our Brazzaville hotel – the recently introduced tactic designed to reduce the incidence of illegal parking in this fine city – which was for the police to use very sharp machetes to slash the tyres of the offending vehicles – intentionally and in full sight of a television camera. Honestly.

Yes, Congo was interesting, exciting and fun. And, whilst my recollection is not perfect, I think it was where, around the dining table, I was able to ride a couple of my very favourite hobby horses, two little chaps whose saddles had been worn paper thin by their constant use. One of these fellows was called 'international aid', and the other was 'the responsibilities of government'.

In accord with my desire to shed a little light on what was going on in my head as well as in my world, it will be no surprise to you that I intend to mount these hobby horses again – now. And I will start by parking my bum on that international-aid filly, in an attempt to illustrate how the whole concept of international aid should be put out to pasture as soon as possible and never employed again.

OK. There are so many aspects of international aid that are wrong, that it is difficult to know where to start. But how about the fact that a great deal of the aid that our country dishes out goes to some of the most corrupt and least competent governments in the world? So, it would be just about as effective (and we would also save on the postage), if we simply turned this aid money into compost, back here in England, and ploughed it into the ground. Nevertheless, I will admit that some of this loot doesn't just disappear into the unfathomable black hole of 'budget support' for these governments; some of it goes into identifiable programmes – such as health programmes. So that's OK then, isn't it? Only it isn't. Because it wasn't that long ago that the World Bank reported that half of all funds donated to health programmes in sub-Saharan Africa did not reach the intended hospitals and clinics. This was mostly due to that already mentioned corruption – the one that guarantees that oodles of cash will be diverted into lining the pockets of numerous officials and paying for their business-class shopping trips to London.

Anyway, not all international aid money just disappears. Much of it stays around and does positive harm. One only has to observe how politicians in some countries distribute aid to their own tribes – and to nobody else – to see the damage it can do. Or how about the fact that using large amounts of Western cash to purchase the local currency, as well as stoking inflation and forcing up interest rates, inevitably drives up the exchange rate in the recipient country, and makes life difficult for that country's exporters. And this isn't just an academic consideration. It actually strangles one of the principal methods by which poor countries have become richer over the past fifty years. In fact, it is not an exaggeration to say that international aid can actually add to the instability of a recipient country, and it can even increase the likelihood of rebellion and civil wars. But never mind… because at least these conflicts can be funded! Yes, it has been estimated that as much as 40% of all military expenditure in Africa is financed by overseas aid…

I could go on to compare the amount given in international aid to the vast amounts spent on protecting the West's agriculture – to the detriment of poor countries around the world – but instead I want to conclude this diatribe by introducing you to just two more irredeemably negative aspects of this misguided 'worthy endeavour'. The first is that giving money to 'developing nations' reinforces the idea of 'us' and 'them', and it undermines the self-worth of 'them'. It has to. The second is that it is totally wrong in principle. This last point I cannot stress enough. Because, however it is dressed up, international aid is charity, and charity is – or should be – the province of the individual. You and I should choose to whom we provide any sort of charity. It should not be done by any institution – and by that, I mean any government – on our behalf and with our money. It is just wrong. If people running Western governments – such as Blair and Cameron – felt the need at a G7 or a G20 meeting to indulge in a bit of 'my dick is bigger than your dick', then they should have done it for real and not with truckloads of their taxpayers' money. Which brings me on to my second hobby horse, which is what our governments *should* be doing with our money – otherwise known as 'the responsibilities of government'.

This is simple. They should be using it to keep us secure. After all, the world is full of shits, and many of these shits are potentially dangerous shits. We do need protecting from them. And it is just unrealistic for individuals to try and organise this protection themselves. Few could afford a ballistic missile, and even fewer could find the funds for an aircraft carrier or for their own personal GCHQ. We have to accept that only by pooling our resources and getting the government on the job can we acquire the security we need.

Quite simply, the first duty of any government is to look after its citizens, and it should discharge this duty by spending whatever is needed to ensure that it is discharged properly. Let's have the best armed forces, the best intelligence service, the best border force, the best police force and the best 'cyber army' money can buy. And to those who would say that we cannot afford this, I would say that we can – if we accept that security is not just the first duty of government, but also that it should be the *only* duty of government. If we didn't pour unmeasurable amounts of loot down the plugholes of welfare, health and education – and international aid – all areas of spend that could be addressed by the individual or by charity, we would have no problem whatsoever in securing that security we need.

I do accept that the state might want to move into other areas beyond security, and I would accept this, just as long as it was just two areas, and it didn't involve spending any of my money. So that would be 'education', where it would restrict its duty to ensuring that any manifestation of religion came nowhere near the classroom (children would be protected from the superstitious beliefs of their parents). And it could also be 'India', where all that the government would need to do is cut off all telephone links with that country. This would ensure the repatriation of countless call-centre jobs, and it would also relieve a grateful nation of approximately 100 billion scam telephone calls each year. Why this hasn't already been done, I've no idea. No more than I have any idea how seriously you have taken those two canters on my two treasured hobby horses. Maybe they weren't revealing what was going on in my mind back in 2014, but they were more what I regarded as good material for an after-dinner debate in the middle of an equatorial jungle. Or possibly for an after-dinner debate back in Spindlewood – before all such dinners had to go on hold…

Yes, it's time to address the event that prompted the title to this chapter, and which would put much of my life and even more of Sue's life on hold for the rest of the year. It was indeed a very big bump in the road because it was Sue being diagnosed with cancer. This happened in July 2014, and it wouldn't be until Christmas of this year, after submitting to a fairly arduous regime of cancer care, that Sue was declared cancer-free. It was not an easy time – for either of us. But it was made that much more bearable by the support of relatives and friends. Some of them were award winners – people who were far from being close relatives or friends, but who made every effort to ease Sue's passage through chemotherapy and surgery. It was very humbling, and it certainly made up for the indifference displayed by Sue's two sisters-in-law, the wives of her two brothers who I have been mean enough to mention in this book because they justly deserve to be mentioned. Six months passed without a note, an email or a phone call from either of them, and there was a similar silence in the New Year. I still find it difficult to believe. And impossible to forgive.

Well, that wasn't a pleasant interlude, was it? So maybe I should reinforce the point that, even though it had undoubtedly been the biggest bump in the road that either Sue or I had ever encountered, the overwhelming support of *most* of the people we knew helped us enormously to keep a firm grip on the steering wheel and to keep our life on track. And matters were further helped by our builder and his four grade-A workmen, who arrived to build our extension in September, and who provided us with a constant distraction as they first conducted an exercise of devastation before initiating one of construction. Furthermore… we'd found somebody who was prepared to buy Wood Cottage. And, in October 2014, we ended the period of our hardly noticeable colonisation of Scotland. Dumfries and Galloway would have to make its own way in the world without us.

(That's one of us cured of cancer and one of us with a perfect aorta…)

Failing Nations and Falling Doctors

Now, assiduous readers of this *magnum opus* will recall that the last *itinerantur opus* I was working on was *The Country-cides of Namibia and Botswana*, based on our 2013 excursion to those two countries. Well, it was still not quite finished by the beginning of 2015, and my first job of this new year was to bring it to a conclusion before I could then start on my next *itinerantur opus* – based on our 2014 Congo expedition. This I managed to do by the end of January, enabling me to commence work on the snappily titled *First Choose Your Congo* by mid-February. As far as I was concerned, this particular title underlined the fact that there were two Congos, and that it was very important to select the correct one to visit. Making the wrong choice could easily result in a most undesirable outcome, involving something as serious as being in no condition to make use of one's return flight other than in a coffin. A trip to the DRC might not guarantee one's demise, but it definitely constituted a serious risk to one's continued enjoyment of life. Whereas, a trip to the Republic of Congo was barely above the 'unknown risk' level.

Anyway, I do still wonder whether I try too hard sometimes. That snappy title was an obscure take on Mrs Beeton's apocryphal start to one of her recipes of 'first *catch* your rabbit'. And not only did she never use this term in any of her recipes, and not only was the substitution of 'catch' with 'choose' probably an obscure step too far, but who, under the age of sixty-five, has even heard of Mrs Beeton? She's not on Twitter and she's never trended on any social-media platform, and is never likely to. So, it's just as well that back in 2015, as now, the only person I really had to please with my writing – and with my choice of book titles – was me. If anybody else shared in this enjoyment, then that was a bonus. And at least I wasn't doing anybody any harm.

That, however, could not be said of the loathsome creatures who attacked the offices of the *Charlie Hebdo* satirical magazine in Paris, killing twelve people. Or of the evil sod who held people hostage at a kosher supermarket in that city and ended up killing four Jews. Nor of the scum who murdered people in Tunisia or of the scum who, later in the year, visited yet more atrocities on Paris. Nor of any of that pile of *merde du diable*, otherwise known as ISIS, who were busy building their caliphate by destroying everything in their path, including people's lives, often in the most barbaric manner possible. Oh, and I suppose we shouldn't forget the excrement within our midst, examples of which were responsible for the resignation of the entire cabinet of Rotherham Borough Council, following the publication of a report into the town's child sexual exploitation scandal.

Yes, this book is an autobiography. It's supposed to be about me. But how can I ignore what was going on in the world around me – when it seemed to be getting uglier and nastier by the day? Even if little of it was affecting me personally, it was colouring my view of my fellow man and making me wonder what had gone so wrong with humanity over my lifetime that a world of mystery and enchantment was being turned into one of horror and hate.

When I was very young, I was given a big book called *The World's Greatest Wonders*. It was probably published about the same time as I was born – and I still have it. Within its pages are lots of black-and-white photos of 'wonders' from all around the world, all with an often-unnecessary explanation of how they have earned their 'wonder' status. Some are natural wonders, such as natural rock bridges or great waterfalls. Others are engineering wonders, such as impressive bridges or colossal dams. And many more are 'built wonders': the ancient ruins of past civilisations or the exotic, elaborate buildings of more recent and very much extant civilisations. What they all have in common, however, is a celebration of what nature and what we, as a species, had bestowed on this world (before we became aware that we might be bestowing rather too much on the world to the detriment of nature). It was and still is a fascinating book. And when I first absorbed its contents, I was thrilled to learn just how marvellous the world was, how much it had to offer, and how many colourful and mysterious cultures it contained. Out there was a world very different to Warwickshire, and one that held no real menace, but instead… well, just an endless catalogue of wonders – wonders that one day I might see for myself.

But now… Well, not only are lots of those wonders out of bounds – especially if one is a son of Warwickshire or much of the rest of the Western world – but the planet is simply seething with menace or with its trusted travelling companions, brutality, repression and persecution – three associates who plague the lives of much of the world's population. In fact, it is no exaggeration to say that many of those formerly colourful and mysterious cultures have now mutated into something despicable: a series of regimes which, if they're not spawning or inspiring terrorists, are busy making the lives of many of their own citizens a living hell. Or they might be doing both.

I can't provide a definitive explanation for this metamorphosis, but I suspect that it is not unconnected with the burgeoning of the human population of this planet, and it more and more having to fight for space and resources (a point I know I have made before). Nor, I suspect, is it unconnected with this population being infested with an unconscionable number of numpties – idiots who defy their own intellect by still embracing the discredited superstitions of the past, otherwise known as organised religions. And by doing so, and by taking their beliefs to the extreme… Well, not everybody would put a downed Iraqi pilot in a cage and burn him alive, but literally hundreds of millions would certainly take a very dim view of what I and my friends would regard as a normal, liberal life. If they could, they would bring it to an end. Just as it's been brought to an end or strangled at birth in so many of those hateful regimes.

Now, I could move on here. I've probably already made the point that, in my eyes, the world has turned rather sour. However, I am not about to move on yet. And this is because, back in 2015, I was already distinctly peeved at how my country's heritage was being belittled, in part by an equivalence being drawn between its merit and the merit of those of clearly much less accomplished nations. Not only was its vast store of achievements in science, technology, medicine and many other areas being largely discounted (and other nations' empty stores being ignored), but even its values, developed over years and in which there was much reason to take pride, were now being attacked, often by people who had settled and made a life here. So, by way of a counterattack, I am now, first of all, going to run through a few countries that, for me, represent some of the worst curdling of the human spirit (some, but not all of which, have as their leader, one of those tyrants I berated several chapters ago). And because I have already been less than complimentary about China and Russia, why don't I start with Afghanistan and then work my way through the rest of the list in alphabetical order? So:

1. Afghanistan: a country slowly approaching the Middle Ages, whose chief exports are pomegranates, apricots, melons, opium and refugees, and whose belligerent, tribal culture provides the ideal conditions for the practice of misogyny and a persistent form of internal terrorism, marketed under the brand of 'the Taliban'.
2. Burma: a country run by a sizeable cadre of complete shits, who have developed the novel belief that a nation's army and police force do not exist to protect its citizens, but to harm them or even kill them. (Unfortunately, this belief is not that novel and certainly not unique to this country, just enthusiastically embraced there.)
3. Cuba: a country with an Orwellian regime that has lots of doctors but no free citizens.
4. Egypt: a country where female genital mutilation has supplanted pyramid-building to such an extent that about one in five of all cases of FGM in Africa is now in Egypt.
5. India: an anthill of a country where female foeticide, a caste system and sexual attacks on women should probably merit more attention than its space programme.
6. Indonesia: a country well on its way to becoming the biggest palm-oil plantation in the world – and nothing else (other than a repository for some rather primitive beliefs).
7. Iran: a country run by a bunch of very holy men and a Revolutionary Guard, who together conduct diplomacy through hostage-taking, and their internal affairs through violence and intimidation.

8. North Korea: not so much a country, more a compound for the clinically insane – where bad haircuts are revered.
9. Libya: not so much a country, more a large stretch of sand that has proved surprisingly fertile for the (almost exponential) growth in dysfunctionality.
10. Nigeria: a country known for its bad taste, its bad bookkeeping (in the oil sector), its bad telephone habits, and its bad-ass Boko Haram terrorists.
11. Pakistan: a country that successfully blends feudalism with failure, topped off very nicely with the shameful treatment of women and those who try to pursue minority faiths.
12. Saudi Arabia: a country that, whilst to be commended for its recognition of the potential dangers of allowing women drivers on the road (only kidding), needs to be condemned for all sorts of other things, including its willingness to murder its opponents – if necessary, in overseas embassies – and its unwillingness to let any 'fun' enter its territory.
13. Venezuela: a country awash with oil, corruption and a stupendous amount of incompetence that has proved, beyond doubt, that bus drivers do not make good presidents.

I could go on. I could list quite a few more countries that, through their treatment of women, animals, minorities, prisoners of war or the truth, deserve nothing but contempt. But I hope I don't need to. I hope, by providing this far-from-comprehensive list of countries, which, taken together, reflect the appalling nature of so much of our human affairs, you might begin to understand why I believe we have so much to be proud of in this particular country. We are far from perfect here, very far from perfect. But we're not going to dispatch a bunch of fundamental Christians to attack a mosque in Dubai. We're not going to ask the Household Cavalry to carve its way through a column of demonstrators on London Bridge. And we're not going to overrun most of North Africa and the Middle East with thousands of our citizens fleeing repression and poverty in our green and pleasant land. We're not even going to pursue our enemies in foreign parts and then poison them with some home-brewed Novichok, or attempt to make the Scots just like the English by incarcerating them in 're-education centres' before deploying them on farms and in factories. Yes, please don't forget Russia and China.

Anyway, I have gone on a bit here, haven't I? And with barely a quip to relieve the vehemence. However, the dire state of so much of the human world was something I could not possibly ignore, and my concerns were so great in 2015 that I sought an explanation for its deterioration wherever I thought I might find one. Like for example in the pages of *Mein Kampf*...

It was now late summer of this year, and with our extension completed and with *First Choose Your Congo* written, I had some time to get stuck into some serious reading. And where better to pursue an understanding of the diseased nature of so many human societies than in a book written by a guy who virtually single-handedly infected one such society, and turned it into a rabid monster that eventually had to be contained and then killed. Furthermore, Hitler wasn't unique, but just a very accomplished example of the sort of people who often end up running some of the sickest societies on the planet. So, surely, somewhere within the many pages of his 'My Fight', I might get an insight into the nature of the beast – in more than one sense of that term.

Well, I did. Sort of. You see, Hitler was undoubtedly a great orator and rabble-rouser, but as a writer, he was completely shite. He wasn't helped by the turgid, rambling nature of his prose, but what really made his writing stink was that it was riddled with arrogance, delusion, misunderstanding and hatred, and it completely lacked any logic, rationale, humanity or even basic common sense. How the heck he got away with *Mein Kampf* as some sort of manifesto for Nazism is something I will never understand. But the very fact that he did maybe suggests something of significance, and this is that societies have to be receptive to infection before they become sick. It's not only the leader at work in poisoning a society; it's also a receptive population, one ideally marinaded in an irresistible blend of resentment, ignorance and stupidity. Indeed, one only has to look at the recent experience of 'the greatest country in the world' to see how a fat Hitler with piss-stained hair, together with millions of resentful, ignorant and stupid people (known appropriately as his 'base'), came very close to infecting it with a terminal dose of redneck fascism, one that still has the capacity to lay low its fragile democracy if given half the chance.

Anyway, encouraged with this finding, I then decided to extend my studies by reading *The Koran.*

Well, what can I say about this – safely? Maybe I'll just say that I would actually read it again in 2016, to confirm in my mind that what I had read in it first time round was indeed what was in it – and leave it at that. And I will also leave the whole subject of the souring of the world, and pay just a brief visit to another subject that had finally gained the attention of our own MPs in September of 2015: namely the 'right to die'.

It will be of no surprise to you that I am an advocate of the right to die (because I have already made that clear in this book). I own me, and that should provide me with the right to do with me whatever I want – just as long as it doesn't harm anyone else. (So, no ending it all by jumping off skyscrapers and landing on passers-by.) However, there is a problem, isn't there? It is the power of a pseudo-liberal, self-indulgent elite in this country, which is determined to impose an indefinite period of care onto a whole load of people who want nothing more than to be allowed to sign off and disappear with a modicum of dignity. Through some peculiar interpretation of 'humanity' – buttressed, no doubt, by some strange belief in the sanctity of human life – the people making up this elite successfully eliminate 'humaneness' from any end-of-life considerations in favour of righteousness and 'feeling comfortable with themselves'. It is an absolute scandal that this situation is allowed to persist, and that it does even now despite the opportunity given to our politicians back in 2015 to do something about it.

Of course, like the wee timorous bastards they are, they 'searched their souls' and then they chickened out. They left their constituents to suffer in a way that a pet dog or an injured horse would never be left to suffer. And, what's more, this ending-of-life stuff should never be their business in the first place! As I made patently clear at the outset to this diatribe, I own me, and no authority of any sort should attempt to stake a claim in me. Which is exactly what our elected politicians are still doing by preventing me from choosing when I want to guarantee that I'll never see any of them again – on account of my being dead. And frankly, even if I wanted to top myself when I was not ill or suffering, that is just my business (and, of course, that of Sue), but certainly not the business of any self-satisfied parliamentarian, who, in any event, is probably more interested in my vote than in my life.

Anyway, I just hope that if they still insist on making it their business, then, very soon, we catch up with some of the more civilised countries in this world, and take at least some tentative steps towards recognising that the most important choice we should all be allowed to make ourselves is the choice to live or to die. Whatever that Archbishop of Canterbury might say, and whatever anybody might say is our responsibility to society. The former is poppycock; the latter doesn't exist…

OK. Probably time for a bit of light relief, and this will be provided in the form of a very brief account of the trip that Sue and I undertook to Tanzania at the beginning of October. This would involve a return to where we had been twenty years previously: the Rufiji River in the Selous, followed by a visit to the Ruaha National Park a little further to the west, before finally travelling back east for a spot of R&R at a small coastal resort in Zanzibar. Again, it would be another Naturetrek excursion, this one shared with just half a dozen cordial and congenial characters, two of whom, Richard and Sue, would become real friends – and dedicated readers of my books!

Well, the very brief account could consist of 'saw lots of interesting wildlife in both the Selous and Ruaha, and had a very agreeable rest in Zanzibar at the conclusion of our safari exertions'. However, you're not going to get away that lightly, and, as before, I am going to describe just a handful of events experienced on this holiday that will stick in my memory for all time. In fact, four of them.

The first two were experienced in the lodge in the Ruaha National Park – which was a favourite hangout for quite a few elephants. Number one involved these elephants, and a significant number of them threatening to interrupt our walk from our chalet to the dining room for lunch. Well, I am ashamed to say that, even though in the company of most of our party, my stiff upper lip drooped rather more than just a little when one of the adolescent ellies embarked on a mock charge in my direction. Even though I knew that 'ears back' means a serious charge, and 'ears out' (as his were) means just a warning or, in the case of a stroppy juvenile, just a bit of showing off, I abandoned where I'd been standing very quickly and sought shelter by a wall. So much for my 'cool'. Number-two event wasn't much better, even though it took place in the privacy of our chalet…

You see, safaris involve getting up very early. If one is doing this in a lodge where the generator is not switched on much before eight o'clock, this means that one is getting up in the dark, and one is having to dress oneself in the dark. Accordingly, one sorts out one's clothes the previous evening, and has them disposed around one's room, ready for them to be pulled into place when required. This system works quite well, but it does leave one's clothes exposed to the attention of nocturnal beasties. So... when, one morning, in pitch darkness, I drew up around my legs my favoured black underpants, it wasn't until they were almost completely *in situ* that I became aware that, in just the wrong place, they were harbouring a denizen of the night. And it wasn't a small denizen. It was a big denizen: nothing less than an improbably large armoured bush cricket – with improbably impressive gripping powers. Removing it – safely – from its overnight nest – in the dark – was by no means easy. But it did ensure that I was completely wide awake by the time I mounted our safari vehicle for our morning expedition. And it also ensured that all items of underwear would be guarded at all times for the remainder of the holiday.

All too soon, it was time to fly out of the Ruaha National Park, and for our small plane to deposit just Sue and me at Zanzibar's airport, before taking the rest of our party on to Nairobi to make their way home. And it was as we were physically leaving our diminutive aeroplane on the apron of this airport that event number three got underway. It started with our observing an uncomfortably close-by Ethiopian Airlines Dreamliner taxiing out to depart the airport – with apparently nobody aboard it. This minor mystery was then soon solved. In fact, just as soon as we had made our way into the cramped arrivals hall – which was jam-packed with lots of gentlemen, all dressed from head to toe in long white 'shrouds'. The penny dropped immediately. These guys must have been late returners from the 2015 Haj in Mecca, who had been deposited back in Zanzibar, with no one to take their place on the flight back out of the island.

It was all mildly disturbing. But before we had a chance to work out how we might possibly extract ourselves and our luggage from the throng, a local guardian angel appeared out of nowhere, and fast-tracked us through the whiteout. And before we knew it, we were in a taxi and set up to be conveyed to our little seaside resort. However, we were not out of the shrouds just yet...

The front of Zanzibar's airport faces a natural amphitheatre. On this particular day, none of this amphitheatre was visible, because it was completely covered with the wives of the white-shrouded gentlemen – clearly awaiting their partners – and all of them were almost entirely hidden under *black* shrouds. This was a little more than just mildly disturbing, not least because this phalanx of black sentinels was not just obscuring the amphitheatre, but it was also blocking the exit from the airport, and it seemed disinclined to move. Only when our taxi driver made it clear that he would continue his departure from the airport, whether the ladies in black approved of it or not, did they allow him through. It was a very strange 'welcome' to somewhere we had visited on two occasions previously – and it left me feeling that Islam and individualism are at the two extreme ends of quite a wide spectrum. And I know at which of those ends I'd definitely like to stay…

The resort at which we had chosen to stay was not like the airport. It was all shorts and swimming costumes rather than all-enveloping clothes. And it was very small. It was made up of less than a dozen chalets, and when we arrived, only three of these were occupied. We would have the place almost to ourselves – until the arrival, the following day, of a party of German doctors. They had apparently been conducting an inspection of Tanzania's hospitals, and had now come to Zanzibar for an end-of-visit relax – as we had – and to provide us with event number four.

The main buildings of the resort were situated on the top of a cliff overlooking the sea. Below the cliff was a small ledge, just big enough to take a few dining tables. Sue and I learnt this, because on the first evening of the German occupation (no slight intended), we and the only other English couple staying at the resort were invited to take our meal on this ledge, so allowing the Germans to occupy the main dining area, and presumably make as much noise as they desired. This worked very well, not least because the other couple were extremely pleasant and quite prepared to share with us their enjoyment of their meal by suggesting that we convert our two tables for two into one table for four.

Much eating, drinking and chatting ensued, until, towards the end of the meal, all four of us thought we'd heard a dull thud. However, in the half-light of the evening, we could see nothing untoward, and so we continued with our meal – until this drunk appeared from around a corner further along the ledge. He appeared to have imbibed a healthy skinful of booze, and he could barely keep his balance as he staggered slowly towards us. In fact, his emergence from the semi-gloom was such a protracted affair, that it took all of us an embarrassingly long time to realise that he wasn't a drunk after all, but one of the German doctors who had unwittingly swapped his situation on the cliff edge for one on the ledge ten feet below. Indeed, as we would subsequently discover, he had left his companions at their shared dining table to undertake some star-gazing, and had been so absorbed in the night sky above that he had simply walked over the cliff, falling very badly onto the hard rock beneath

Not surprisingly, we rendered some assistance immediately, and made sure that the nearby squadron of doctors was made aware of his need for some urgent attention. And he really did need some attention. He had, I think, concussion and a broken or dislocated something or other. Interestingly, the contingent of German doctors, having spent the past two weeks observing the conditions in Tanzanian hospitals, soon decided that he would not be availing himself of any of the local medical facilities, but instead he would be whisked off to Frankfurt as soon as possible the next morning. And it was during that morning that we met his (doctor) wife, who thanked us in not-perfect English for our minimal assistance the previous evening, and who, in response to our commiserations, informed us in very clear English that 'shit happens'. I can only hope that her husband got back to Germany safely and there received all the medical attention he required – and that no more shit has happened to either of them ever since.

I also hope that the Queen never has to host Xi Jinping on another state visit to Britain. He and his repugnant security detail had arrived in Britain shortly after we had arrived there back from Tanzania. Inevitably, his presence set off my thoughts about tyrants and undesirable regimes again. Which wasn't all bad news, because it reminded me that it wasn't healthy to dwell too long on the unpleasantness in life, and that instead it would be better if I got down to writing my next book. This I did – in November. It was to be a compendium of wisdom (what else?), and it would revel in the title of *The A–Z of Stuff*. More will be said about it in the next chapter, and for now I will close this one with a final observation. And this is that not only had Jeremy Corbyn been elected the Labour leader in 2015, but millions of people were actually taking him seriously. Maybe, I thought at the end of that year, it wasn't completely impossible that we might end up in a similar mess to all those countries that had so easily earned my disapproval…

Sharks, Shaking off Migraines, and Shakespeare

Sue and I were staying in Quito's Hilton *Colon* Hotel. Its name was not, as I'd fleetingly thought, some acknowledgement of the *passage* to the New World forged by those early pioneers 500 years before, but merely the recognition, in Spanish, of one of them. Yes, the guy who we know as Christopher Columbus, is known, in the Spanish-speaking world, as Cristóbal Colón, and the hotel had been named in his honour. This revelation did head off any potential embarrassment in the future, but it also sparked a thought in my head. It made me wonder whether colonisation, as in the creation of overseas colonies, had any connection with the name of this earliest of colonisers, and, if it did, why then were we not anglicising these two words into respectively 'columbusisation' and 'columbusies'. We could then talk of a country's columbusial past, when it was chock-full of arrogant, plundering columbusials from somewhere in Europe. If nothing else, such stupid words would relieve the monotony of our being continually pilloried for Britain's dark, satanic past, a time when we had apparently taken on the role of a monster in our attempt to make the whole world just one giant columbusial possession. Without even any attempt to achieve a gender balance in the pursuit of our wicked ways…

Well, maybe it was jetlag or maybe it was elevated Quito's thin atmosphere that caused me to have such ludicrous thoughts. Who knows? Because, as all good grammar school boys should have remembered, the word 'colonisation' actually has a Latin root and therefore has nothing to do with old Cristóbal. So, I should probably quickly draw a veil over that aberrant episode, and promptly move on to explain what Sue and I – and a dozen other Brits – were doing in that Hilton Colon Hotel. It was simple. We were catching our breath before we embarked on a Naturetrek group holiday to the Galápagos Islands. After a couple of days taking in the delights of Quito, we would be flying out to that promised magical environment, and there we would board a small motor yacht called the *M/Y Beluga*, in order to conduct a full two-week voyage around the entire archipelago. We could barely wait to get started.

After the event, I would write a book about this voyage. Obviously. It would be called *Absolutely Galápagos*, and it would contain 257 pages of text. Clearly, I do not intend to devote quite as many words as were ultimately contained on those pages to an account of the visit in this book, but I will devote a few. After all, our trip to that sanctuary in the Pacific Ocean was rather special. It provided Sue and me with lots of memorable sights, lots of memorable experiences, and a number of memorable companions – in addition to the two companions we already knew quite well. These were Nick and Sheila, who featured in three of our Namibia and Botswana trips, and who, like us, ended up with a cabin on the main deck of the *Beluga*.

I think that is my cue to say just a little about this handsome vessel, which was by no means capacious, but very well appointed and just... well, just very nice indeed. On its top deck was a sun-lounging area and a single, stand-alone cabin. On the main deck below was the bridge, the captain's cabin, a shrunk-in-the-wash galley, a dining room, a lounge-cum-bar-cum-further-dining-area, and, right at the back, two compact cabins, which, as indicated above, housed Sue and I and Nick and Sheila. Then, on the deck below, were another five passenger cabins and the minimal space made available for the yacht's crew of six. Now, those amongst you who are arithmetically inclined will have worked out that fourteen Naturetrekkers could only possibly occupy what was a total of eight cabins if two of the fourteen were single travellers. However, there were no single travellers on this trip, and that eighth cabin that was unused when we embarked on our voyage was, after two days, filled by a couple of non-Naturetrekkers: a pair of Americans from California, who certainly added a new feature to the shared experiences of all those on board. As will become apparent in due course.

OK. To reduce those 257 pages of words in *Absolutely Galápagos* to the much smaller number that will fit into this tome, I am again going to resort to bullet points, each of which will provide a brief description of one of the highlights of a trip that in many ways was just one continuous highlight. However, I am also going to reserve the right to conclude my commentary of this trip with just a short passage of proper prose. It will deal with one very high highlight, and also with what might be regarded as the trip's 'lowlight'.

So, without further ado, what will stick in my mind forever about our voyage around the Galápagos archipelago has to include:

1. Being very hot and very sweaty. Probably something to do with the Equator clipping the top of the archipelago.
2. Snorkelling with fish, turtles, sea lions and reef sharks – on numerous occasions. This was simply mesmerising.
3. The American couple, Randy and Suzy, arriving, and demonstrating very quickly that they were not quite such rewarding company as many other Americans we have met on holidays. Think 'delusional', 'ill-mannered', 'inconsiderate' and 'too loud'.
4. Being impressed by the ability of the *Beluga*'s diminutive cook to produce such large amounts of such varied and tasty food in his equally diminutive, not to say tiny, galley.
5. Being impressed by the athletic abilities of our Ecuadorian guide, Darwin (whose name had been chosen by his parents because he had been born on the same date as Charles Darwin). He used to do standing-start backflips on any available beach, or backflips into the water from the roof of the forward part of the top deck (which meant a disturbingly long drop to the sea).
6. Being highly amused to see Darwin entering the dining room looking pale and wan, after having backflipped into the sea, only to land on top of a three-metre-long shark (probably an oceanic whitetip shark, known for its opportunistic and aggressive behaviour). Thereafter, he restricted his backflips to beaches.

7. Observing, at close quarters, male magnificent frigate birds, using their inflatable, red-coloured throat pouches, to attract the... birds.
8. Celebrating with booze, crossing the Equator (four times).
9. Observing, at very close quarters, all sorts of boobies, mockingbirds, other birds, iguanas and tortoises, all of whom demonstrated an admirable incurious attitude to the presence of any nearby representatives of *Homo sapiens*.
10. Snorkelling with hammerhead sharks and turtles – and learning how to deal with Suzy's spatial-awareness bypass, at its worst when snorkelling in a group. (She spent most of her time barging into other snorkellers.)
11. Tasting home-made hooch on Santa Cruz (the principal island in the archipelago).
12. Visiting the biggest volcanic caldera I've ever seen – on Isabela (the largest island in the archipelago).
13. Observing an entire carpet of marine iguanas on Fernandina (the youngest island in the archipelago).
14. Snorkelling in one-hundred-metre-deep water off Isabela, while being dive-bombed by boobies.
15. Realising that what had been thought to be a sunfish was in fact Randy – who had gone swimming on his own off Isabela (without telling anybody) – which was good news for him, because it meant that he wasn't left behind when the *Beluga* set off for its next destination.
16. Relishing the motion of the *Beluga* as it raced across the sea.
17. Relishing the sight of feeding-from-the-surface-of-the-sea storm petrels in the wake of the *Beluga* as it raced across the sea, and not being able to comprehend how such a small bird can live out in the open sea and survive by employing such a high-energy feeding technique in the pursuit of such little food.

OK. With so many points clocked up, I definitely deserve the bonus of now being able to indulge in a spot of conventional prose – as threatened. And what I want to write about first is some snorkelling I indulged in off the coast of an island called Floreana. This is an island in the south of the archipelago, and one we had visited to post a postcard in its post barrel. (This is a literal barrel in which one places one's postcard – to be discovered by subsequent visitors to the barrel, who will then deliver it if they live close to the address of the intended recipient [and it works]).

Anyway, off the coast of Floreana, in deep water, is something called 'The Devil's Crown'. This is the residue of a long-dormant volcano: a (crown-shaped) ring of jagged rocks, jutting out of the water, that has now become home to a multitude of fish, and therefore a must-visit for any passing, sufficiently foolish snorkellers. Yes, this is not beginner-snorkeller territory, and when offered the opportunity to taste its delights, only a handful of the party (including me) accepted Darwin's invitation to join him. When we then approached the aforementioned coronet, I suspect I wasn't the only idiot in the inflatable who was beginning to regret his or her decision. The water out near the protruding rocks was more than lively, and having already been warned by Darwin that the currents around these rocks were challenging, it might have been better if we had all stayed on the *Beluga* and attended to our toenails. I, for one, was certainly… well, almost terrified. There was therefore only one course of action. When, after the inflatable had reached the Crown, and Darwin had given the go-ahead to go over the side and commence snorkelling, I went in within a nanosecond, knowing full well that, with just two nanoseconds of thought, I would have stayed on board our tiny raft – which was now being tossed about in the swell…

Then, pure magic. As I plunged into the water – and immersed myself in this water to get my bearings – there, below me, was a ten-foot-long hammerhead shark. It was just me and him (or her), and I still believe that he (or she), at that moment, was as indifferent to my presence as I was stunned – and enchanted – by his (or hers). If anyone had told me before my visit to the Galápagos that, not only would I willingly share the ocean with sharks, but that I would experience one of the most uplifting and inspiring moments of my life by sharing it with just one of these (bigger-than-me) creatures, I would not have believed it. But it's true. That encounter was one of the pinnacles of my life, and it so reinforced my belief in the equivalence of 'animals' and ourselves, that I wish every other human on this planet could have a similar experience. That way, apart from anything else, we wouldn't have fleets of boats roaming the oceans, full of unthinking bastards killing literally millions of these wonderful beasts just to 'harvest' their fins. We might also defer the Holocene extinction event – possibly indefinitely.

However, back to reality. Hammerheads are not particularly dangerous, and I doubt I was in any real danger. So, after absorbing the thrill, I embarked on my snorkel of the Crown, and I saw more varieties of fish than I could ever have hoped for. Indeed, the ocean bed within the Crown was barely visible; there were just so many fish above it. Oh, and I did soon appreciate why this was not a snorkel for beginners. The currents were evil, and they obviated the need to propel oneself through the water – entirely. This was OK when one was pursuing one's directed anticlockwise navigation of this mid-ocean ring of rocks, but not so good when one was then trying to make one's way back to the inflatable against the current. Never before have I remained stationary in water while swimming vigorously. It was just as well that Darwin in the inflatable was aware of my plight. And 'plight' is the perfect word to begin this final passage of prose on the Galápagos. Because the plight of this entire archipelago is all too worryingly obvious...

Now, if you don't want another dose of gloom and doom, then you might want to skip to the next paragraph, because this one has wall-to-wall doom and gloom. You see, this wonderful collection of islands is under threat not just from Chinese fishermen who come to murder its sharks and generally devastate its marine life, but also from its resident population of humans. This used to be a very small population, and something that the wildlife on the island and the marine life around them could cope with very well. But it has now mushroomed, principally because of the poverty back on mainland Ecuador combined with the opportunities that presented themselves on the islands as a result of the large influx of eco-tourists – such as me and my fellow *Beluga* adventurers. Yes, all of us had been appalled by the squalor of the three principal settlements on the Galápagos (and they were all squalid) and by stories of the locals adding to the Chinese assault on the islands by fishing illegally and generally ignoring the islands' invaluable status. But it was because of us and others like us that these people were here in the first place. Someone has to import, store and distribute all the food and other materials required by the (large) local fleet of tourist vessels. Others then have to look after the needs of these people. And all these people combined then start to have children. And they need teaching. And everyone needs medical facilities – and maybe some administrators and some police – and houses, and places to shop, and places to exercise, and places to socialise.

And before you know it you have the same problems of a burgeoning population as you have in the rest of the world, and you're well on the way to buggering up everything those eco tourists came here to see in the first place. I may be exaggerating here, but only a bit. The Galápagos Islands are super-fragile, and once we've broken them, no amount of vinegar and brown paper is going to put them to rights. And that's why, although I will remember my visit there as one of the high points of my life, I will also feel more than a little guilty that I went there at all. Indeed, the only redeeming feature of my indisputably damaging visit is that it will assist Ecuador in resisting China's claim that, like those distant-from-its-shores islands in the South China Sea, the Galápagos Islands are its own and should revert to Chinese control forthwith. And that's not as daft as it sounds, believe me. There's even a small island in the group called Chinese Hat!

Well, I did promise less than 257 pages of words, and I will now make no further mention of the Galápagos, other than to note that after a post-Galápagos visit to the jungles of Ecuador, KLM flew us back to Amsterdam, just clipping Newfoundland airspace in the process. This route had been chosen to avoid bad weather elsewhere, and I mention it simply because a very old bugger like me finds it very difficult to conceptualise the impact of a globe-shaped world on the choice of international flight routes. And with that Mercator projection of the Earth fixed firmly in my old brain, there is no way that Newfoundland should be anywhere near a flight path between Ecuador and Holland. But it is...

Anyway, the bad news is that we're only just into February...

But never mind. I will employ my powers to précis to the best of my ability to rattle through the remainder of 2016, and I will do this by first mentioning what I was doing before Sue and I went to the Galápagos, which was to press on with the writing of *The A–Z of Stuff*. So that when we returned from the Galápagos, I was able to finish this by the end of March. I still think it is one of my best works – not just 'a compendium of wisdom' as already referred to, but an enlightened compendium of wisdom that still manages to bite the ankles of all those who are deserving of a chunk of flesh being removed from their lower legs. I suppose I should explain that it is an A to Z of topics where I have given the world the benefit of my studied opinions on each one of the twenty-six chosen – in much the same way as I have done throughout this book, only in much more (entertaining?) detail. I just can't work out why it didn't become a best-seller.

And now a medical bulletin. It concerns my having a consultation with my doctor – in late March – to discuss my over-reliance on a drug called Imigran to control my chronic migraines. Indeed, I had long used this drug – in pill form – as a prophylactic as, without it, I could never be certain that I wouldn't wake up with a debilitating headache – not something one would want, especially when one was doing something like travelling around an enchanting archipelago in the Pacific Ocean. Anyway, he prescribed another drug – to be taken daily – to (possibly) reduce the number of Imigran pills I would need. I was not impressed. Two days later I went back to see him and to announce that I would not be taking this new drug, but that instead I would do two things. The first would be to join a gym to enable me to swim – a lot – and the second would be to tell myself that I was done with migraines. Having had them since I was in my twenties, I was completely fed up with them, and they could just sod off.

Well, I did both the gym thing and the self-instruction thing, and after that return visit to the doc – and before my first swim – I had just two more migraine attacks, and I have not had a single one since! This may be an odd piece of information to put in an autobiography, but for me it was life-transforming, as I was now able to go about my life without the constant threat of the sort of crippling pain that only other migraine sufferers can really understand. And to those of you who *are* still suffering, I can only suggest that telling oneself that one has had quite enough ruined days and nights *might* just do the trick. I should also mention that, despite this early success, I did carry through with my promise to swim and then swim some more. Indeed, for almost the rest of the year, I generally made two visits to the gym every week, and each time, in its outside pool, I swam a complete mile. I only stopped when, in winter, I had to retire to the indoor pool and thereby submit myself to the screams of toddlers in their nearby paddling pool. That I could not stand. It threatened to bring back my migraines…

May saw me starting that *Absolutely Galápagos* book, first of all by gathering information on all the nations of South America. This was because I had decided to give its readers a special treat by presenting them with various interesting facts on each of these countries, if possible in a humorous fashion. After all, I didn't want to be accused of shortchanging them, and I knew how most people were simply thirsting for knowledge on any aspect of the South American continent. Just as many people, back in 2016, were thirsting for their freedom, and therefore wanting desperately to throw off the shackles of the European Union...

What joy! I stayed up all night to watch the referendum results, and was able to greet Sue in the morning with the very good news and with a glass of cognac in my hand. It was a triumph for so many 'normal' people, and a fitting rebuff to all those others who wanted to impose their own misguided opinions on all those of us who had formed different opinions. Of course, the bad news was that loads of these bastards then tried to frustrate the decision that had been made – in the most dishonourable fashion imaginable. And some of them, in due course, would prove themselves to be masters (and mistresses) of dishonour, and none more so than that Bercow bloke and that Miller woman. Bercow was dreadful – someone who would subvert the role of Speaker of the House to such a degree that his name merits a new use in the English language, as in 'to do a bercow', meaning 'to bring into disrepute to a barely credible degree'. What an arsewipe he was, and probably still is. And I can't say much better about Gina look-at-how-wonderful-I-am Miller. After all, here was a woman who was born in what was then British Guiana, who rather than being grateful for being granted a good life in Britain, did everything she could to overturn a decision made by those who might even have been born here. I can think of no greater manifestation of ungrateful and rude behaviour than what she so arrogantly did. And furthermore, you may recall that I have been to what is now Guyana, and I would like to take this opportunity to remind Mrs Miller that, whatever faults we might have in this country, and however poorly its backward peasants might behave, she might find that in her country of birth, there is still much to do to bring it to a state of Nirvana, and probably quite a lot to do in order to bring all its citizens up to scratch. However, given the state of the wine bars in Georgetown and the miserable level of earnings from investment work in that country, I doubt she will be attending to any of the necessary remedial work any time soon. If indeed ever...

Anyway, on a lighter note, in August, Great Britain came second in the medals table at the Rio Olympics, and soon thereafter, Sue and I went off to France. It was a little less demanding than our trip to the Galápagos, and noticeably less hot and less sweaty. In fact, it was a very lazy holiday, where I finally managed to make my way through *Middlemarch*, so putting myself in a suitably cultured mood for a couple of further doses of culture during the autumn – at the Royal Shakespeare Theatre in Stratford-upon-Avon.

Sue and I went to see a production of *Cymbeline*. It was indistinguishable from a production of this play put on by a Tower Hamlets junior school. Everything about it was wrong, and what was particularly wrong was its casting. While I am able to accept a wide spectrum of people in a wide spectrum of roles, I still have this unfortunate old-fashioned view that siblings should either be all white or all some other colour, but not a mix of hues. Unfortunately, this production was a harbinger of things to come. And whilst the RSC did redeem itself later in the year with a splendid interpretation of *The Tempest*, every other production we saw thereafter – in 2017 and beyond – would be no less than an exercise in diversity indoctrination, combined with an attempt to subvert the original nature – and beauty – of Shakespeare's classic works. Indeed, each director appeared to be intent on subverting the bard's work more than had been done in any previous productions, and distasteful pantomime would ultimately extinguish a classical-rendition approach entirely. It wouldn't be long before we were walking out at the interval and then simply cancelling our RSC membership. Of course, even the pantomime approach will soon be a thing of the past – when the forces of wokeness finally prevent any of Shakespeare's plays being performed. For who could allow the works of a misogynistic, racist, white-supremacist, classist bastard to pollute the virginal minds of a new generation of innocent angels, for whom social justice and racial justice combined constitute the new religion of the age. Even if history tells us that most religions end up as bulwarks against true enlightenment…

Talking of which… and therefore being reminded that enlightenment has a flip side, no better epitomised than in the shape of one Donald Trump Esq, I feel I cannot end this recollection of my life in 2016 without mentioning that it was in November of this year that the awful oaf was elected by a large minority of the American people to become the President of the United States. This was dreadful news. Although, in truth, I don't know whether the news of his success was the very worst thing I heard in that year or whether it was something I heard on a visit to my barbers.

You see, my regular barber was off sick, and I was therefore put into the hands of a young lady barber – somebody who was probably about thirty. She was very pleasant and she asked me about my holidays – which is when I told her about the Galápagos Islands, and discovered that she seemed to know little if anything about them. So, in an attempt to stir in her mind whatever slight recollection she might have had of their whereabouts and their importance, I informed her of their association with the renowned Charles Darwin.

She had never heard of him. She had never heard of a man who, with Winston Churchill and Isambard Kingdom Brunel, vies to be the greatest Briton of all time – and in my mind, is. She had zilch knowledge of the man who worked out how all life on this planet works – and how life evolved to give rise to… life forms such as barbers…

What hope is there? Brainless bullies put in charge of great nations, and people going through life in a haze of ignorance that must take a conscious effort to maintain. And for what it's worth, I think that what came from the lips of that lady barber was worse than what came out of the imperfect American election system. After all, most ignorance tends to hang around for rather longer than four years.

(Incidentally, I did not mention to the lady my misplaced thoughts on the derivation of the word 'colonisation'. I did not think that this would be either helpful or appropriate…)

Melanesia, Misanthropy (?) and Mud

As I stood no more than twenty feet from the volcano's rim, I wondered how much notice one might be given that the volcano's activity was about to move up from level two, through levels three and four, to an abandon-ye-all-hope level five. And even given any notice period at all, would it be possible to get down that dreadful track to the coast, board one of the inflatables, and get back to the ship before the Mount Yasur volcano really blew its top? It might now be indulging in just a series of volcanic belches, throwing up a plume of ash every ten to twelve seconds, but if they were not belches, but more in the nature of coughs designed to clear its throat, it could be getting ready for a real technicolour eruption at any minute.

However, that, I knew, was pretty unlikely. The volcano had been erupting rather lackadaisically for 800 years now, and the chances of it building up a bit of enthusiasm – and a bit of explosive potential – were pretty remote. No, more of a problem was the toxic gas it was discharging. Oh, and the large, hot projectiles that it was burping out along with all that ash – the ash that now coated my shoulders and my head and that was pasted to my face with a film of perspiration. One did have to be wary – and, of course, it also helped to be both ignorant and naïve. Yes, fortunately, it wasn't until I was back in England that I read that by viewing the volcano's activity from its crater's edge, one wasn't just taking a calculated risk, one was actually putting one's life in danger. Especially through the interaction of a descending chunk of half-molten rock with one's entirely unprotected head. Nevertheless, I now look back on that visit to Vanuatu's best-known volcano – and one of the world's most active – as a real highlight of my visit to Melanesia.

That reminds me. I should explain that in February 2017, Sue and I went on a cruise! Now, let me say immediately that this didn't entail our boarding a floating block of flats with 2,000 other holidaymakers, nor would there be a water slide or a floorshow in sight. No, this was an *expedition* cruise, on a pocket cruise ship – called the *MS Caledonian Sky* – in the company of just ninety other passengers and a similar number of crew. And we wouldn't be embarking on a trip around the Caribbean starting and ending in Miami, we would be threading our way through Melanesia, a remote part of the world that some of us had been obliged to look up in an atlas. So, if you think I've just been rather elitist in making those comments about mega cruise ships full of happy punters, then, by way of an apology, I offer up this happily rare example of my geographic ignorance. And just so we all know, Melanesia is a sub-region of Oceania in the south-western Pacific Ocean – which means that it's made up of all those islands off the eastern shoulder of Australia, otherwise known as New Caledonia, Vanuatu, the Solomon Islands, Papua New Guinea and, further out, Fiji.

We had started this odyssey in Auckland, having endured a less than agreeable stopover in Hong Kong, and by the time we had landed on the island of Tanna to observe its wonderful volcano, we had already made a visit to the microscopically small (Australian) Norfolk Island, and the Isle de Pins at the tip of New Caledonia. This meant that Sue and I had been given ample opportunity to identify who, amongst those ninety passengers, might make good travelling companions – and who might think the same of us. Which is why we had now fallen in with four others: Jens and Anne, and Peter and Sylvia, four delightful people who would become not just travelling companions for this trip but friends for life. Indeed, it was these new relationships rather than a visit to a volcano, or any of the other delights of this cruise, that constituted its *real* highlight. And these guys even read my books!

Anyway, talking of books, this trip would give rise to my writing yet another of my humorous travel books, this one called *Melanesia,*

Melancholia and Limericks. The first element of the title explains itself. The second element does not, and you'll just have to buy the book if you want to discover why it's included in the book's title. But I *will* tell you why the third element is there. This is because the ship's expedition team organised a limerick competition during the voyage, as a bit of fun and to recognise that, in Captain Cook's days, composing limericks was a popular pastime for crews who might be at sea for months if not years. I, of course, entered this, and submitted a number of limerick gems – of such quality that I and another entrant to the competition ended up in a quick-death shoot-out in front of the entire passenger complement to establish which of us would be crowned the limerick king. I lost. Graciously but very resentfully. Indeed, so resentfully that, in due course, I would write 366 ribald limericks that I would then publish in a book – just to prove that my limerick-writing abilities were far more extensive than those of the chap who beat me. Probably.

However, I seem to have gone off track there, as my mentioning *Melanesia, Melancholia and Limericks* was designed to reassure you that I am not about to provide you with a detailed account of our cruise, but instead I will mention just a couple of the more obscure aspects of the trip that have really stuck in my mind. The first of these has to be our stop at Honiara, the capital of the clearly impoverished nation of the Solomon Islands. This not only involved a police escort for our three minibuses – to carve a path to the country's national parliament building through the capital's chronically congested traffic – but also a billboard advertisement spotted on this short journey, which would have made any member of the woke brigade froth at the mouth. It was an invitation from the Pan Oceanic Bank 'to make a valuable gift to your child' by depositing some money in a child-specific savings account – featuring a smiling child, with, next to him, a sort of cloud on which was shown the name of this type of account. It was the 'POB Pikinini Minor Savings Account'. Of course, in Melanesia, '*pikinini*' is no more than the usual word for 'child', and may refer to a child of any race. Nevertheless, I am still quite surprised that the Order of Saint Proper hasn't dispatched a batallion of its knights to that poor, misguided region of the planet, to point out to its inhabitants the gross insensitivity of their ways. And furthermore, the advert portrayed only a smiling *male* child.

There was not a girl in sight. Clearly, that crusade should be launched at the earliest opportunity possible. Although, if it were, and the knights stopped on their way to Melanesia anywhere near the town of Cairns in Australia, I have no idea how they would react to what I saw as some fairly despicable behaviour on the part of some of the local aborigines...

It was at the end of our expedition, when we'd left the *Caledonian Sky* in Rabaul in New Britain, and had flown to Cairns for a brief taste of Oz Land before returning to Blighty. Here, having finally recovered from hypothermia in our disappointing hotel (a long story, but not unconnected with aggressive air-conditioning), Sue and I decided to join an organised, *full-day* expedition to Daintree Forest to the north of Cairns – to see some rainforest wildlife. There were about a dozen of us on this trip, and our guide was a very pleasant young Australian chap, who turned out to be quite knowledgeable about wildlife – and sickeningly deferential to his aboriginal countrymen...

It all started to go wrong when, after a fascinating *half-day* in the forest and a dreadful lunch, we set off towards the coast in our minibus – to spear some crabs! We thought our guide was joking. But he wasn't. Whatever morons had set up this trip had decided that the highlight of any visit to a rainforest should be to leave the rainforest and go off and murder a few harmless crustaceans – cruelly and needlessly. In retrospect, one of the worst aspects of this aberration was the willingness of the rest of the party to accept this weird idea. Sue and I, however, did not. And while the spear-equipped tossers went off to thin out the local wildlife population, we retired to the house of the guy who had supplied the spears and who was now leading the death-dealing mission. He was a local aborigine, and his very nice house was also very large, as were his two well-appointed 4x4s on its drive. This chap was the antithesis of the impoverished, ragged-looking aborigine, so often presented as the victim of white colonialism and a living manifestation of the white man's evil ways.

However, good luck to him. If only all Australian aborigines were in his fortunate position – along with his brother, his mother, his other siblings – or any of the scores of his other relatives who, according to his brother, made up their close (and clearly comfortably-off) family unit. And not only did none of these guys have to be too tied down to work – thanks to the support of Australian taxpayers – but they also enjoyed various privileges not available to the majority of Australian taxpayers, such as being allowed to kill protected animals to feed their many mouths, 'because such behaviour is part of our tradition'. And who, in any event, is going to miss the odd dugong or the odd green turtle, especially when they are killed so rarely (just for special occasions) that Mr Spear had only one half-eaten turtle pie in his fridge to offer to his spear carriers at the end of their expedition.

Everything about this miserable afternoon was awful: that it happened at all rather than our being able to spend more time in the forest; the needless spearing of crabs; the evidence of butchered turtles – and the fact that these aborigines were taking the piss. Big time. They were not only enjoying the fruits of a modern Australian society – largely with the financial assistance of that society – but they were also abusing their status as the 'victim' members of this society in the way they were living their lives and in the way they were ending the lives of so much precious wildlife. And maybe worse than all this was the cringing deference shown to these guys by our feeble guide, who was not prepared to answer a single question about aboriginal history, culture, customs or attitudes, lest he offend the turtle-butcher or, heaven forbid, call into question any aspect of this guy's manifest piss-taking. And apologies for what has turned into a bit of a rant, but what Sue and I witnessed that afternoon was not the oppression of a minority people by the majority, but the exploitation of the majority by at least part of the minority, involving quite a lot of collateral damage to any mere animals who might make a good filling for a pie. We were never more pleased than we were when we left that house and the bitter taste of fraudulent behaviour, seasoned with more than just a dash of misplaced colonial guilt. And we wouldn't be picking up any more mosquito bites either…

Anyway, it would be wrong to conclude this record of our trip through Melanesia with a petulant account of offensive behaviour in Queensland – when I could instead round it off with a short dissertation on my firm belief in the 'illusion of progress'. So that is what I will now do, starting with the commonly held view that the lack of infrastructure and all sorts of other facilities in places like Vanuatu and the Solomon Islands clearly points to these countries' 'lack of progress'. For what else provides better evidence of 'progress' than the continuous improvement in our lot, manifest in fine buildings, myriad examples of our technological prowess, and, quite often, a tamed or even subjugated environment? And one certainly doesn't find much of this stuff in poor old Melanesia.

However, the slight problem with this view is that 'progress' is a myth. There hasn't been any in the past and there never will be in the future. I'm serious. What humanity commonly refers to as progress is no more than a series of useful innovations – various discoveries and inventions that have greatly reduced the burden of living for at least some of its members. But that in no way is genuine advancement. How can it be when humanity's history is a long procession of conflicts, abuses, failures and disasters – and continues to be – and when all its institutions and administrations are as much riddled with corruption and incompetence now as they have always been? And with this reality of the human condition staring us in the face, how can we think that the future will in any way be better than the past or the present? How can we fool ourselves into thinking that in some way we will make 'further progress' when we have made none whatsoever so far?

The truth of the matter, in my opinion, is that no species on this planet 'makes progress'. Tigers don't. Worms don't. Pilchards don't. Instead, they either survive as a species or they do not survive as a species. And it's just the same for us. Because, no matter how clever we believe we are, and no matter how many discoveries we make and how many inventions we come up with, we are still just a species; just a particularly smart-arsed animal that's been around for a brief spell of Earth-time, and that may not be around for a great deal longer. After all, not only are we not progressing, but what we are wrongly interpreting as progress is already hastening our demise.

'Progress', with its 'advanced' techniques and equipment, is enabling us to become more and more efficient – in clearing the oceans of fish, the savannah of animals, and whole tracts of the world of their beauty. Of course, some might still regard the emptying of the oceans (and their pollution) or even the decimation of the African elephant as progress. Or how about the loss of the Amazon rainforest, the exodus of people from Africa and Asia into Europe, unstoppable global warming, or any of the other disasters that will soon only get a great deal worse? Well, if they do, they are fools – simpletons who cling to the illusion of progress because it is no less than fundamental to their making sense of their lives. After all, if one takes away progress, then one takes away purpose. And one reveals the future for what it really is: just a replay of the past, but with more apps and more city breaks in Europe. Until, that is, the future hits the buffers; until that time when the penny drops, and mankind not only realises that it cannot 'progress', but also that it can only survive or become extinct – just like tigers, worms and pilchards. And, at the current pace of 'progress', that point in time will soon be reached – along with most of the smart money then being put on extinction...

Well, maybe I should have stuck to being rude about piss-taking aborigines. But this is an autobiography and, as I've made clear before, it has to include what was going on in my head as well as in my world. Even if what was going on in my head bordered on the nihilistic, and probably put me in contention to win the annual, hotly contested 'Worcestershire's Most Ardent Misanthrope' award – for the third time. Or maybe I should just move on very quickly to a trip that Sue and I undertook to Poland, a country that has made a lot of progress over the past few years...

This was a long-weekend, Naturetrek visit to the difficult-to-spell-without-Google 'Białowieża Forest'. I mean, it's even got an 'l' in it that isn't just an 'l'. It's a sort of crossed-out 'l'. And why would anybody want to do that? Or, of much more relevance to this tale, why would anybody want to visit this Białowieża Forest, a large stretch of woodland than straddles Poland's border with Belarus? The answer is simple. The Białowieża Forest is one of the last remaining parts of the immense primeval forest that once stretched across the European Plain. It is a special place, and so special that it has been declared a UNESCO World Heritage Site, in part because of its size and in part because it contains such a rich store of wildlife, including 800 European bison, animals who are now damn sure that they will never progress, but just grateful that they have not yet become extinct...

We did see some. We also saw oodles of birds, including lots of different woodpeckers, and even a couple of these guys mating. Which is something of a fifty-pointer in the I-SPY book of nature-nooky. Indeed, it was a very rewarding trip in many ways. Albeit it would have been better if it hadn't been unseasonably cold (in May!) and Sue hadn't tripped over in the forest, in preparation for tripping over on a concrete path – to provide herself with a bump on her forehead and an optician, back in England, with a sales opportunity for a new pair of specs. I, of course, sympathised with her plight, but did not attempt to point out the difference between a trip *to* Poland, and a trip *in* Poland, and how one was far preferable to two of the others. In this way, I was able to make it back to England with no bumps on *my* head, and ready to engage in a long, idle summer.

Well, it wasn't entirely idle, in that Sue and I went to stay with friends, entertained other friends, visited a couple of museums and a couple of nature reserves (in one of which I saw my first ever 'corky fruited water dropwort'!) and we even made a brief visit to France with Phil and Heather. And… I suppose I should confess that in late August of this year, I took delivery of a second-hand, but still ravishingly beautiful Aston Martin DB9! Now, I could justify this by claiming that my ownership of this six-litre, twelve-cylinder beast would make the world a greener place, because I would prevent anybody else taking it onto the road too often and thereby stoking that global warming already referred to. But who am I trying to kid? I was still in short trousers when I first yearned to own and pilot an Aston Martin, and with that signpost for 'seventy years ahead' just along the road, I thought I would indulge myself something rotten. And furthermore, a polished, black DB9 is a work of art, and I was soon drooling over it as much as I was driving it – if not more. And drooling doesn't add to greenhouse gases in the slightest. I rest my case.

OK, time to distract you from that exercise in gross self-gratification – as it were – by telling you about our next expedition to faraway lands. And you will be either appalled or bemused that we again took ourselves off to Namibia and Botswana. These two countries had not yet lost their appeal, and I doubt they ever will. Not if they continue to provide the sort of experiences we enjoyed on this particular sortie. And forgive me, but there are some experiences worth telling. Not about all the birds and animals we saw, because relaying these experiences in words can never be like the real thing, and, in any event, there would be just far too many to report. However, there are a number of others that should convey a little flavour of this, our seventh holiday to both Namibia and Botswana, and these I will again present as a number of bullet points – and save to the end one special experience that warrants the full prose treatment. So, bullet points first, dealing with twelve 'ordinarily' memorable experiences, and kicking off with three on Namibia's Skeleton Coast:

1. Flying to the remote north of the Skeleton Coast, to stay at a fabulous tented lodge by the name of Hoanib Skeleton Coast Camp, and spending time there with a great Swiss couple by the names of Patrick and Peter.
2. Our guide at Hoanib getting his Land Cruiser properly stuck in a sand dune on a long trip from the lodge to the coast, and discovering his jack didn't work and neither did his radio. We were very fortunate that, by chance, another vehicle eventually arrived and was able to pull our own vehicle out.
3. Due to a cock-up with the booking arrangements, which indicated that I had a birthday at every lodge we were to visit (!), having to go along with the celebrations of my (first) non-birthday – which included a birthday cake and lots of enthusiastic dancing and singing.
4. Picking up our own slightly scaled-down Land Cruiser – a Toyota Fortuna – and discovering that it was as good as its big brother.
5. Discovering at a lodge called Epako that a lady giraffe and her grown-up daughter were extremely sociable, and the daughter, in particular, when she wasn't eating the potted plants in the lodge's terrace restaurant, was very keen to greet one on the way to the restaurant. (She would lean down to have a bit of face-to-face time.)
6. Having a celebration of my real birthday at Mushara Outpost Lodge – courtesy of the lodge's staff.
7. Having arrived in Botswana, being informed at Nxamaseri Island Lodge (where we had stayed some years before) that we would not be charged for any of the many drinks we'd had 'because we had returned there'!
8. As I'd done at every lodge we'd visited since Hoanib Lodge, informing the manager of the lodge we stayed in just outside Maun that, despite what the booking arrangements might say, it wasn't my birthday, but then agreeing to his request to pretend that it was – so as not to upset the kitchen staff, who had already made my birthday cake, and who wanted to celebrate my birthday with some appropriate singing. It was all very nice, and the other guests, who also knew that it was not my birthday, went along with the ruse.
9. Being given the honeymoon tent (complete with outside bath) at Little Vumbura in the Okavango Delta (where we had stayed multiple times before).

10. Being told while we were having a late breakfast that a large tree had just fallen on the honeymoon tent, and that we would have to move to a honeymoon-over tent. The tree had been half-chewed through by elephants, and had eventually succumbed to gravity. Happily, not when we had still been in our tent just a few minutes earlier.
11. Being introduced by our guide at Selinda Lodge (in the Delta) – to his beautiful new bride, who in a very un-Botswanan show of affection, gave both Sue and me a very big hug.
12. Being taken from Maun back to Windhoek in our small chartered plane by a young black bloke, who (like other pilots we had encountered) looked as though he should still have been at school. During the two-hour trip, he was able to show us the ten-house village down below in the middle-of-nowhere-Namibia, where he had grown up. And at the end of the flight he was able to show us that it wasn't just us who thought he looked young. This is when we sought out the lady immigration officer in Windhoek's domestic airport, who proceeded to address me as the pilot, and when I shook my head, then addressed Sue. She looked really bemused that it was the black guy with us who was the pilot, and I will pass no comment on whether this bemusement was entirely due to his young looks or to the fact that he was black and we were white. And yes, she was black herself.

OK. I am now going to do what I threatened, which is to give an account of what was a really outstanding experience on this holiday, and one that concerns our driving out of Namibia into Botswana. It could be argued that it started when we were first planning the itinerary of our expedition. Because that was when I asked 'our man in Windhoek', Martin, whether, rather than using one of the two border crossings we'd used in the past (one near the start of the Caprivi Strip in the north and one on the Trans-Kalahari Highway in the south) we could possibly use one shown on the map that would bring us into Botswana near our first destination: Nxamaseri Island Lodge on the Okavango River. He said we could, but that we might regret our choice. The road away from the border on the Botswanan side was not really a road at all, and it would make for a very demanding drive. Furthermore, the crossing was in a very remote area. Just reaching it would be a real effort. Well, that settled it. That's the border crossing Sue and I would be using!

Fast-forward to 28 October 2017, and our setting out from Mushara Outpost Lodge just outside the Etosha National Park, to make our way to a safari camp next to the Khaudum National Park, a national park that sits against Botswana's border in the empty, north-eastern part of Namibia. This was a drive of 422km, involving 200km along a dead-straight gravel road on which we saw just two other vehicles, and then a 40km sand track to the safari camp itself. This was called Nhoma Safari Camp, and it was worryingly billed as an 'activity-oriented camp', albeit the activities were largely passive, in that they would entail observing how the local San bushmen went about setting traps, making arrows, hunting in general, finding underground tubers to eat, and all the other 'activities' that allowed them to survive in what was a very desolate environment. They lived in their small village right next to the camp, and during our two-night stay there, three of their number would show us many of their skills and a little of what went on in the village, including some inevitable dancing and singing and an active disregard for health and safety in the use of fire. I should add that we were the camp's only guests, and therefore the only guests in the camp to wonder whether their tent might be either blown or washed away in a violent overnight storm. It wasn't, but the precipitation associated with the storm would certainly have an impact on our forthcoming journey.

Yes, it was time to drive back down that sand track and rejoin the straight, gravel road that would take us a further 50km east to the border between Namibia and Botswana – and some genuine excitement.

When we arrived at this border, there was not a great deal going on, but there was a border post, and inside this post were a couple of amiable border police, one of whom asked me whether I was driving a 4x4. When I confirmed that I was, she said something like 'just as well'. Anyway, with formalities completed, I returned to the Fortuna and proceeded to drive towards the border crossing proper, marked here by two pairs of big metal gates set in two tall mesh-wire fences. No sooner had I done this than I was back at the Namibian border post, asking its amiable occupants how I should go about getting through those gates. They were, after all, properly closed, and there seemed to be no Botswanans around to open them. 'Just open them and drive through,' I was told. 'And then somebody will turn up.'

Five minutes later, Sue having opened both pairs of gates (and not having closed them again until I'd driven through them), we were standing next to our vehicle in Botswana, and I was shouting as loud as I could that we had arrived in this country, in the hope that someone would arrive to acknowledge this and then stamp our passports. Eventually, someone did arrive. He was a rather apologetic guy, who took us into his tiny kiosk of an office, stamped our passports and then asked me to fill in and sign his register – a register that recorded all the arrivals into his country through this crossing. I couldn't help noticing that whoever had passed this way just before me had done so about ten days previously! This border crossing, I thought, risked healing up entirely.

Nevertheless, we were now in the country we wanted to be in, with our paperwork sorted, and all that remained was a drive of some 130km to take us back to the world of tarmac. And how difficult could that be? After all, I could already see that the road further east, whilst not actually a road, was a sound-looking sand track, and it would prove a doddle for the Fortuna. And it did. Right up until we approached a very slightly hilly part of otherwise flat Botswana, where the sand gave way to mud…

In a dry condition, this mud would presumably have taken on the character of concrete, but having been drenched by that storm we'd experienced at Nhoma, it was now proper, viscid, gooey, clingy, grade-1 mud – a thirty-yard-wide strip of the stuff disappearing into the distance. And this strip wasn't so much ridged as carved into interlocking troughs of various depths that made the choice of path along its length something that would have challenged a cutting-edge variety of artificial intelligence. It certainly provided me with a challenge, and I can recall quite clearly that in the air-conditioned interior of the Fortuna, I was soon perspiring rather heavily. Then the flow rate of perspiration doubled. I had just spotted that up ahead there was a feature that was as wide as the track and that cut across it completely: a trench. And this trench was full of water!

At this point, artificial intelligence would probably have stopped the car. I, however, did not. Far from it. I put my foot down and built up as much speed as I could before plunging into the trench and hoping against hope that the Fortuna's wheels would somehow overcome the normal forces of nature and take it through the trench rather than just into the trench and what would then have been a very problematical static state (there being no phone coverage whatsoever in mudland). Well, it made it. Even though there was a certain sensation of grip being lost and, as muddy water enveloped the entire vehicle, a distinct hesitation on its part, it did get to the other side. So, relief all around – that lasted right up until the next water-filled trench…

I lost count of them. But for over 40km, I had to battle not just improbably deep troughs through a world of mud but, at intervals, tackle giant water features, any one of which might have 'sunk' the Fortuna and any hope we had that we might make it to our destination as intended. In fact, we would have been in an awful lot of trouble. However, we overcame – or the Fortuna overcame – every soggy hurdle, and eventually we were back onto (comparatively) piece-of-piss sand, and, ultimately, tarmac. The sand track met what was the main drag in this part of Botswana at right angles and, feeling as smug as it's possible to feel, I turned left to take us north to Nxamaseri Island Lodge – and into a speed trap…

I now have the dubious honour of having been caught twice for speeding in Botswana, but the real honour – in my mind – is being one of the nutters who have crossed into this country through a border post that soon delivers its victims to a driving hell. I'm not sure I'd do it again, but I'm so very pleased I did it once. And even Sue was pretty pleased. Albeit, very much after the event. And let's face it, when you're sixty-nine, is it better to be watching *Antiques Roadshow*, having read the inane contents of three colour supplements and Googled 'when to prune hydrangeas', or instead be scaring your own pants off in the middle of a muddy nowhere? I know what I think, and it doesn't involve one, single, overpaid presenter.

Anyway, we're almost done with 2017, other than to record how happy I was to hear that Russia was being banned from the 2018 Winter Olympics because of its state-sponsored doping (of its own athletes and not just those annoying critics of Mr Putin). And how sad I was to hear that Mr Trump had no plans to visit the Mount Yasur volcano, and thereby give the world a very slim chance that he might have his bouffant interfered with by a heavy, red-hot projectile – with providential, terminal effect…

Emberá Embarrassment

Now, I want to say a brief word about my writing. Not of this book, but of all the writing I've done in my lifetime. So, that's all those essays and exercises at school; all those notes and write-ups of experiments at university; all those working papers, memoranda, letters and reports at work; all those emails and letters since I retired – and then, of course, all those books I've already written and published. Add that lot together, and I've certainly written more words than I've had hot dinners by a factor of several thousand, and I suspect I will never stop. And to emphasise just how big a word count I've clocked up, I'm now going to give you a brief rundown of what further words I was churning out at the beginning of 2018.

To start with, there was my annual, handwritten letter to a correspondent in Hertfordshire who, once a year, sends a handwritten letter to me – because he doesn't own a computer and never will. These letters can run to thirty pages. Next, there was the book I was just starting to write: my first thriller! It was set in the Congo and Morocco, and its title would finally emerge as *Darkness.* Incidentally, it is a brilliant story, and if you haven't read it, you should. It's even more exciting than this autobiography. Anyway, as a little light relief from writing this novel, I was also writing those limericks I referred to in the previous chapter, so that by September of 2018 I would have reached my desired total of 366 of these little gems to go into a book with the self-explanatory title of *A Leap Year of Limericks.* All of them were good, and some of them were bloody good. This, you can check for yourself in the first appendix to this book, where I've thoughtfully reproduced just a few of them in order to allow you to confirm for yourself their unquestionably high quality.

What I have not reproduced in any of the appendices is a fourth piece of writing that I was embarking on at the beginning of the year. For this you will have to wait until I am dead. Because it is my funeral proceedings. You see, having witnessed a funeral in 2017 that had been patched together without any pre-input from the deceased and that was consequently… well, not very reflective of the deceased and completely uninspiring, I had decided that when my swansong was sung, it would be with my words – and my orchestration. This was no more than any self-respecting control freak would do when he was that far along the path of life that, at any second, he might step on a medical land mine and be blown into oblivion without warning. So, what better than to compose one's entire send-off, complete with one's music choices and one's curated slide shows, and that way get exactly what one wanted and at the same time relieve anybody else of the need to second guess how one might want to say one's final goodbye? I should say that Sue did the same, having accepted that my Boy Scouts' 'be prepared' approach was nothing more than a prudent preparation for an inevitable event, and not some weird, mawkish exercise that might warrant a visit from a psychiatrist. Anyway, this preparation was not brought to a conclusion for some time – until, for both of us, our respective *adieux* were magically squeezed onto a pair of tiny USB memory sticks, ready for use whenever that curtain needed to be brought down. And, in case you're wondering, our words were spoken by a professional actor, as not only was he going to make a better job of it than we ever would, but also his voice would not freak out the intended audience. After all, narrating one's own funeral would be *really* weird, not to say downright creepy. As I'm sure you'll agree…

OK. So, with all this writing in the first part of the year, a bit of a breather was required by March, and this was taken by Sue and me whisking ourselves off to the most famous breached isthmus in the world, otherwise known as Panama. There we would spend two weeks travelling around this country, staying in eco-lodges to observe wildlife, and then a further week aboard a small catamaran, exploring a little of Panama's Pacific coast, before doing the same on its Caribbean coast, having, of course, sailed through the Panama Canal!

It was a triumph of a holiday. On the eco-lodge fortnight, we encountered lots of remarkable birds, lots of remarkable wild places, (unfortunately) lots of filth and litter while travelling between the wild places (Panama has a big housekeeping problem), and lots of interesting people – quite a few of them interesting, and very pleasant, American people. More of these then found their way onto our catamaran, a beautifully appointed vessel that provided an idyllic temporary home for just seventeen of us, none of whom would be able to find a bad word to say about the *Discovery* – and certainly not about the quality of its catering, which would have made that Ramsay guy curse with envy. It was that good.

Now, I could write even more words about this trip, and tell you in some detail about the tin can we stayed in at the beginning of our expedition (the ex-radar facility known as Canopy Tower); the amount of red wine we drank with two of those interesting and pleasant Americans; the sighting of the amazing three-wattled bellbird; or even the sighting, at a dreadful hotel in Panama City, of some of the 'fashionably' fattest women we had ever seen, who, with the tightest clothes imaginable, were revealing every substantial mound and every disturbing crevice of their overinflated bodies. Or I could even recount a dreadful tale of how we could not get an effing drink in this same hotel, because it was Good Friday, and the Catholic Church in Panama dictates much of what goes on in Panama, and no more so than when it involves robbing people of some of the pleasures of life for no good reason whatsoever. However, I will do none of this, but instead merely give you an account of a visit to a genuine Emberá Indian village in the Darién Gap...

The Darién Gap is the area of east Panama that abuts Colombia and that makes the Pan-American Highway not entirely pan. This is because this 'gap' is filled with impenetrable jungle and improperly behaved drug-traffickers and murdering thieves. If one really wants to drive from Alaska to Tierra del Fuego, then one either has to equip oneself with a few well-armed guards and buy for oneself a fully tricked-out Land Rover Defender (one of which was the only vehicle ever to have made it through this uninviting impasse) or, more practically, one has to put one's vehicle on a boat, and sail around the impasse. But, anyway, on our first full day aboard the *Discovery*, after it had sailed down the Pacific coast of Panama from Panama City, we were scheduled to be taken into this Darién jungle – to visit a village occupied by the endemic indians of the Darién: the Emberá Indians.

This particular excursion started with a long, very fast boat ride up a large river, followed by a much slower ride up a muddy creek into the depths of said jungle. And there we were met by a contingent of very young Emberá girls and boys, who had been dispatched to escort their honoured guests along a *planted*-tree-lined avenue through the jungle that led to the promised village. This was nothing short of an enchanted greeting, and the village itself was pretty enchanting as well: well-ordered, sweet-smelling, and full of a large number of very fit-looking Emberá Indians of both sexes (and probably identical genders). The men wore red loincloths; the women, colourful skirts and lots of beads, but not much else. There was, therefore, quite an abundance of bosoms on display – from, I have to say, the generous pendulous to the prominent perky, with the age of owner playing a considerable part in determining their conformation.

So… after a welcome by the chief, a presentation on village life and Emberá culture, a wander around the village, and a bit of handicraft shopping, it was time for some dancing in our honour – to be conducted first by some of the village matrons, and then by some of its… prepubescent maidens. There were six of them – six young girls between the ages of about eight and thirteen – who had been gathered together in the open-sided village 'rotunda', each of them dressed in accordance with local practice in a skirt and some beads, but without a blouse or even a liberty bodice in sight.

This was a bit awkward – for reasons I need not go into. Although I will say that, as regards the eldest 'budding' girl in the troupe, it was particularly, not to say exceedingly, awkward. Nevertheless, if one focused on their feet and their faces, it wasn't too bad. And if one could then decide to re-tie one's shoelaces, mid-dance routine, one was saved the anguish of even having to look in their direction. This is what I did. I thought it was a brilliant move, right up until I realised it was a terrible mistake. This was when I became aware that, just in front of my now neatly laced shoes, was a pair of diminutive feet. And as I raised my eyes, I discovered that they belonged to that eldest girl in the troupe, that is to say, the one with the most obvious breasts – by quite some way…

Had I been given the opportunity to think about it for a second, I could possibly have prepared some story of an old war wound or just a prosaic hernia, but I was robbed of that second as soon as she extended her hand to invite me on to the dance floor! It appeared that I was now about to spend the next few minutes of my life with a half-naked prepubescent (or maybe pubescent) girl, in full view of the girl's family and friends, my companions from the catamaran – and my wife. And God help me if any one of those companions who had now started to film me had a penchant for putting stuff on YouTube.

A couple of the other visitors had also been recruited into the dance routine, but they were women, which meant that I was now the only man shuffling around the rotunda in the company of eight females – much to the evident amusement of all. And why not? I am six foot two. My dance partner was about four foot and a bit. So, on top of my obvious dancing-with-half-dressed-minors embarrassment, there was clearly a very healthy topping of looking completely ridiculous – even if the disparity in our respective heights did mean that I was very unlikely to have a close encounter with either of her outstanding features. That said, my time on the dance floor was still a little taste of purgatory, and the relief when it ended was immense. Albeit short-lived.

It was as I was recovering from the ordeal and as we were all being gathered up to return to our riverboats. The village visit was now coming to an end, and I would soon be able to return to acceptable Western norms, in which there was no place whatsoever for a young girl's bared bosom, especially the bared bosom of the young girl who had just approached me from behind and had now grasped my hand in an iron grip…

She had clearly decided that she was going to escort me back to the boats, which meant another twenty minutes of her close company, and probably a renewed bout of unrestrained amusement for all my companions. Indeed, they conspired to enhance their amusement, and they did this by dawdling on the way back down that boulevard – to observe birds such as a black-chested jay (honestly) – while I and my diminutive minder strode on purposefully, and thereby quickly found ourselves well ahead of the pack, her with me, and me with her and her… chest. This is when it occurred to me that if I ran into an off-duty sergeant from the Met (unlikely, but not impossible), I would probably have my name taken, to be placed on the sex-offenders' register, and that this would not be an ideal conclusion to the day's excursion. And then I had another thought, one stemming from that earlier presentation on Emberá culture – which had included the information that marriages here were somewhat informal affairs!

Crickey, I thought, I hadn't been married to this girl, had I? By dancing with her, I hadn't effectively proposed to her – and had my proposal accepted? And now we were off on our honeymoon, without even a best-man's speech or a slice of wedding cake. Which meant that I might have to add bigamy to my sexual misconduct problems. This was all preposterous, of course, but when one is walking through a forest with a bare-breasted girl – without a chaperone in sight – one's thinking can become a little distorted. And it wasn't until we were back at the boats, with the rest of the catamaran's passengers – and a grinning wife – that rationality returned, and I was able to reassure myself that all would be well, and that I still had only one wife. And furthermore, begin to relish the fact that, out of all the male passengers on the catamaran, it was me who that young girl had selected – either for my noble good looks or my kindhearted demeanour. Or maybe because she somehow knew that, in due course, I'd write about her in a book. I will leave you to judge which of these reasons caused her to choose me. Although I should say that not only does she feature in this book, but she also stars in *A Man A Plan A Canal Panama*, which is the palindromically entitled book that records our time in Panama and which includes photos from the Emberá village, but none of any breasts...

What it also includes photos of, amongst others, is our passage through the Panama Canal, and it would be wrong of me to conclude this Panama interlude without at least a brief mention of this amazing experience. Because it was amazing. To be on a small catamaran, passing through this gigantic piece of exceptional engineering – in the same lock as a considerably larger vessel – is something that I will never forget and that I will relish for all time. If you ever get the chance, do this yourself. Preferably on the *Discovery* and with a group of amiable North Americans. And preferably after visiting an Emberá Indian village with a bad leg that regrettably prevents you from dancing...

OK. Back in England, two days after him and her became Mr and Mrs Markle, I had to attend Worcester Crown Court to serve as a juror – for the third time in my life. That meant I would have an opportunity, for the third time in my life, to witness, first-hand, the self-serving dysfunctionality of our renowned legal system, and I really wasn't looking forward to it at all. Because, for as long as I can remember, I have held the firm belief that our adversarial system of 'justice', where the focus is on winning, is a very poor second best to an inquisitorial system, where the focus is on searching for and establishing the truth. In my mind, it is much better to have a professional inquisitor to decide somebody's guilt or innocence than a panel of amateurs who have listened intermittently to a couple of bewigged players hamming it up for all they're worth. And I can still think of no better illustration of the reason for my distaste for the adversarial approach than to quote that old exam question, which runs as follows: 'Either I get better justice by paying Sir Timothy Arbuthnot twenty guineas than by paying Mr Bunk two guineas, or I do not. If I do, then justice is bought, contrary to Magna Carta. If I do not, the legal profession is obtaining money under false pretences. Discuss.'

Well, of course, it is the former. Because advocacy – or the power to bemuse, confuse and generally mislead a bunch of jurors – is what really counts in a court of law. Accordingly, if one can afford the services of the very persuasive Sir Timothy, one would always choose to buy his services in preference to those of the not-quite-so-persuasive Mr Bunk. And that doesn't smell much like genuine justice to me. In fact, one doesn't have to give this issue much more thought before one sees that the adversarial jury system principally benefits the lawyers (who can squeeze mountainous fees out of long-running courtroom battles) and, of course, the criminals (who are more likely to get off, either through the efforts of their effective but amoral advocates or through the perverse actions of twelve confused and not-necessarily-very-bright members of the public). So, barristers and toerags are the winners, and victims of crime (and the taxpayers who fund the whole creaking system) are the losers. I really don't know why our legal system is held in such high regard when it achieves so little at such great cost, and when its deficiencies are not even hidden from view. One only has to serve on a jury to be almost blinded by its radiant mix of incompetence, inefficiency, pomposity and self-indulgence. And one will also quickly observe how it has developed rules of evidence that are specifically designed to further line the pockets of lawyers, even if it might mean that it is virtually impossible to secure the conviction of any known guilty party. In fact, the whole system of justice is so flawed and so defective in both its conception and its operation that it might be better if it were replaced with an organised flip of a coin – or, indeed, with anything at all, just so long as it didn't involve a jury. Then I wouldn't have to waste another minute of my life, waiting around in a juror holding pen, before eventually being discharged because the rotten thief had changed his plea to guilty when he'd turned up to court. That, of course, is not going to happen. But I am hanging on to the thought that if I do get called up for a fourth time, I should be able to get myself a good advocate, who will successfully argue that this would constitute one call-up too many. And I'd be very happy to play the hypocrite and pay him very handsomely indeed…

Anyway, our court system is happily pretty peripheral to most people's lives – as even most victims of crime won't come anywhere near it, because neither will the crimes committed against them. And unfortunately, neither will most people become aware of a far more profound problem, one that isn't concerned with the process of justice in this country, but with the very future of that animal called *Homo sapiens*. Yes, it's that point in the chapter when I want to bend your ear on another of my longstanding beliefs – already honed to perfection by 2018 – that essentially our species is entering a period of rapid degeneration, largely as a result of some of our more commendable qualities. So, buckle up, and be prepared to learn of our doom…

OK. Let me start by mentioning eugenics. This, as I'm sure you know, is the process whereby one seeks to improve the genetic composition of the human race through 'interventions'. And it was the sort of interventions contemplated by its sponsors that soon brought this process into disrepute, and such disrepute that it is never likely to be brought back into use – certainly not by any of our modern liberal societies. However, these same societies are in the vanguard of those who make 'interventions' all the time, not to improve our genetic composition, but to keep us alive – and capable of breeding, irrespective of our suitability to do this other than at the expense of the gene pool…

Now, having just read those words, I suspect certain readers might be experiencing a pulse of indignation or even fury. But let me please mount my defence of what they may well see as a completely indefensible observation. And the first point I would like to make is that eugenics, no matter how intolerable a concept, would, if applied widely, produce an outcome, and this outcome would be measurable in terms of the genetic composition of our species. And remember, its application would inevitably involve 'interventions'. The second point is that it is indisputable that countless well-meaning and worthwhile interventions are currently being made – to improve the medical wellbeing of countless individuals – and that these interventions will have an outcome as well – a long-term outcome for the genetic composition of the human race that can only be... well, adverse. To put it bluntly, if one takes any animal species, and one makes constant interventions to protect its weakest members, and one then allows these weakest members to breed, then the whole population of that species begins to degrade. Its members become slower, less agile, less physically strong than their ancestors, and less able in every aspect of their make-up. No longer is it the survival of the fittest, but the survival of the most assisted.

This stuff isn't normally discussed. Who, after all, would want to suggest that in our modern human-rights-for-all, best-available-medicine-for-all societies, we are unwittingly practising nothing less than 'reverse eugenics', and in doing so, we are committing our very species to unavoidable, long-term decline? Nevertheless, just because it isn't normally discussed and it's all rather unpalatable, doesn't mean that it's not true. Furthermore, I am talking here not about our intervening in the world's population of cheetahs, and committing it to oblivion by causing all its members to run more slowly than their forebears, but I am talking about *us*. And our greatest facility isn't our ability to run but our ability to think. Our strength is our intelligence. Which means that it is our intelligence that is at greatest risk from all our continual tampering. Put another way, we are destined to become ever dumber...

Now, I have to be very rude here, and suggest that – from a Baby Boomer's perspective – there are already some clear signs that this process of deterioration is already underway. Think 'mental arithmetic', 'attention spans', 'common sense', 'powers of perception', and that bundle of stuff we call 'maturity', and ask yourself whether any of these seem to be on an upward trend – or in a downward spiral, and I think you'll see what I mean. And if you still have any problem, just compare the normally rather brief time spent by a typical Baby Boomer staring vacantly into the screen of a smartphone compared to the lifetime of time spent by a millennial doing just the same – incessantly. I just hope that I'm not still around when intellect has fallen sufficiently far to see us reapplying for membership of the European Union…

Talking of which (and radically changing the subject), we did venture into its territory in September of 2018, by returning to a farmhouse south of Bergerac where we had stayed twice before. This time, however, we travelled there in that scrumptious DB9, stopping off at some suitable hostelries both on the way down and the way back home – and loving every minute of the travelling. This car does go rather fast when you ask it to go fast. And even faster than most of the cars in France.

Anyway, there was little about this expedition that merits mention in this autobiography, but I will touch on just two events that I will not easily forget. The first happened in a delightful hotel in Normandy, in which we stayed on our way going south. This place is called Manoir de Surville, and among its many delights was a huge ceramic bath in our stylish suite – which had clearly been designed to ambush any perfidious Brit foolish enough to lower himself into its vast, *very steep-sided* interior. With those steep sides being both tall and smooth, and with no handholds available, I couldn't get out of it. And it was only with the help of a handy spouse that I eventually managed to prise myself free from the trap. And I'm over six foot, remember, and slim. I doubt any smaller person or any plumper person would have stood a chance, and the chambermaid has probably had to learn to run in body clearance with her normal cleaning duties. I'm surprised the inevitable high death count at the establishment hasn't made the news. I'm also quite surprised that Famille Moutier hasn't – for entirely different reasons…

This is a restaurant close to our holiday farmhouse, and one which we visited on our first trip to this part of France. On that occasion we had driven there in our car – a car that would need to be driven back to the farmhouse. We would not do that again. Instead, we would use the services of a taxi. And this was because the menu at this rather rustic eatery reads as follows (in English and in abbreviated form):

Kir (for which one is given a bottle of white wine to mix with cassis)
Posh paté (with a bottle of sweet Monbazillac wine)
Lots of posh duck salad (with a bottle of red wine)
One of a selection of main courses (with a different bottle of red wine)
A formidable plate of cheeses (with yet another bottle of red wine)
A choice of desserts
Coffee with mini-desserts
A digestif

On that first occasion, we had, for our kir, a bottle of rosé as well as a bottle of white – which meant that our meal for two had included six bottles of wine (and a digestif) as well as more beautifully prepared food than we could possibly have managed. And what was genuinely remarkable was that the price for all this (per head) was just thirty-eight euros! It still was on this visit in 2018 – although checking its website, I see that the price of this same meal has now been raised to an outrageous forty-one euros. *Quelle horreur!*

Well, I wouldn't normally put a restaurant experience into my life story, but this was such an experience – for the third time – that it just had to feature. It was on a par with the experiences Sue and I had had more than forty years before, when France was full of rural restaurants providing exquisite food for absolute peanuts. Furthermore… by including this particular restaurant experience in this book, I can tell you that if, at the end of one's meal in this place, one chooses something like a Poire William for one's digestif – or, indeed, any clear liquor – this drink will be served in a small china 'glass', which has, on its internal base, a very pornographic picture, brought into sharp focus by the meniscus lens of the liquid above it. The only bad news is that the pornography entirely disappears when one has drained one's surprisingly rude receptacle. Which is probably just as well…

Anyway, returning to life after overindulgence in France, it was just a matter of taking note of the bad Saudis murdering one of the few good Saudis in that embassy in Turkey, before I celebrated my seventieth birthday. I mean, seventy! Shit, when I was young, I thought that sixty was ancient. But seventy? Well, that was positively fossil-like. I would have expected to have resembled a trilobite by then – with maybe just a wisp of greying hair. But here I still was, still looking like a regular human being – more or less –

and celebrating my survival in style at a fancy hotel in Dorset. It was quite a thing to celebrate and, in retrospect, even more so, given what happened just a month or so later…

Yes, our dear friend, Heather, had a stroke and died. She was our age – and the fittest and cleanest-living of us all – and she was suddenly taken from Phil, her husband, and out of our lives. It was a terrible end to the year, and one I will not even attempt to lighten with my acerbic wit. Instead, I will remind you of that odd exercise I undertook much earlier in 2018 – to produce my funeral proceedings. Well, now it didn't look quite so odd. It merely looked prudent. That said, Heather's death did not make Sue or I focus on *our* demise, but, on the contrary, it made us focus on our life to come. More than ever, we realised that we had to squeeze into it everything we could. Starting with a mere four further holidays in 2019…

And we might even, both of us, learn how to drive an HGV!

The Arctic, the Azores, the Amazon and the Antarctic

Who says holiday friendships don't endure? Early January saw Sue and her very old husband travelling down to London to share some special time with an even older (!) lady whom we had met in Botswana quite a few years before. She (as you might remember) was Iris, an American originally from New York, now living in South Carolina – and the mother of two sons, one of whom had captained a couple of those Space Shuttle missions. Oh, and she had – and still has – considerably more marbles than most people half her age. Anyway, we had a great time eating, drinking and visiting Westminster Abbey with her. Although, I have to say, we did have a bit of an issue with the fact that we were assaulted with incessant overloud music in our shared hotel, the rather posh St Ermin's Hotel in Westminster, where they also had an 'overseas' waiter, who needlessly and rudely lectured us on our choice of wine. They really ought to know better. Just as I should move quickly on to what I was doing just a little bit later in this new year…

Well, I was finishing that Panama book, cleaning up that *Darkness* book, and getting ready to go with Sue to the Arctic. This, we were scheduled to do in mid-March, and not by taking a cruise through cold Arctic waters, but instead by travelling first to Finland, and then, overland, to the very north of Norway, to a place called Vardø, well within the magic Arctic Circle. It would be yet another Naturetrek excursion, with, on this occasion, just five other people in our party, one of whom lived only five miles from where we lived, and three of whom I would end up wishing lived five *million* miles from where we lived. But that is another story, and I should now stay with the principal story by saying just a very few words about our brief visit to these two, snow-covered Scandinavian countries.

This involved our flying to Helsinki, then flying north to a place called Ivalo, from where we travelled by minibus across the Finland-Norway border and then nearly 400km to our destination on Norway's north coast. Only, our destination wasn't actually on Norway's coast; it was on an island off this coast. And wouldn't you know it; the Norwegians, at the very end of this great spread of nothing in the very far north of their country, have built a 3km tunnel under the sea to take those wishing to go to a modest fishing village called Vardø onto the small island on which Vardø sits. It was quite remarkable, albeit they have not yet got around to building a tunnel from this island to another close-by island called Hornøya, which hosts 100,000 seabirds, and which was the principal reason for our venturing into this part of the Arctic. And that's probably just as well. It means one has to make a concerted effort to get there – in a boat – and then attempt to withstand the intense, wind-reinforced cold as one observes its multitude of puffins, guillemots, razorbills and shags (while, all the time, trying to avoid the results of their aerial pooing).

Anyway, despite some questionable company on this trip, it was a very good one. And it also provided us with an opportunity to test the suitability of our cold-weather kit for a holiday later in the year – at the other end of the world. Not that we wouldn't, rather earlier than that, have use for our fleeces, jackets and other assorted kit when we reported for duty at a windblown ex-airfield in Devon, just a couple of weeks after returning from Scandinavia – to learn how to drive a forty-four-ton articulated truck!

This was my delayed seventieth birthday present – an opportunity to get behind the wheel of a behemoth, and possibly make a fool of myself. And, of course, Sue would have the same opportunity. She, too, would receive a lesson in how to drive these monsters – and how to reverse them. It was splendid stuff. Although I was moderately disappointed to discover that reversing large articulated lorries is almost impossible. And very much more disappointed to discover that reversing them around a corner is completely impossible – unless your name happens to be Sue. Then you can do it.

Even though I couldn't. Terrible. And entirely irreconcilable with my belief that women have a very poor sense of spatial awareness compared to men – which is true. I can only think that the steering on the truck was in some way defective, and it somehow managed to correct itself by the time it was Sue's turn to drive. Or I was drugged...

I wish I *had* been drugged when, just a few days later, Sue and I went to see *As You Like It* at the RSC in Stratford. I have already mentioned our falling out of love with the productions at this theatre, and this was what killed off our love entirely. After all, why would you make the play's 'melancholic lord' a woman, turn the character Sylvius into Sylvia – therefore making Phoebe bisexual – and not only bring a whole spectrum of jarring inadequates (including an irredeemably Brummy Asian) into the proceedings, but also make Audrey mute, so that she has to employ the services of a signer on stage! They only needed a lesbian with a hearing disorder and a transvestite spokesman for the SNP, and they would have had the full set. Needless to say, that really was the last time we would be gracing that venue with our presence. And I imagine old Bill Shakespeare has long ago forsaken this supposed temple to his works, and instead now just occupies himself with a sustained series of rapid revolutions in his grave.

Never mind. In May, a UN body announced that, through our continued irresponsible actions, we were well on course to witness the extinction of one million of our fellow species – an item of news that was successfully eclipsed by the announcement that Mrs Markle had just given birth to a little Markle. And we wonder why the Earth is in such a friggin' mess...

Well, maybe I should move on to something a little more uplifting – like our next (Naturetrek) expedition, which would see us visiting that mid-Atlantic archipelago, otherwise known as the Azores. This was to see whales. It was definitely not to be seasick. However... after a four-hour flight to this collection of little islands in the middle of the ocean, our plane was unable to land on our intended island, São Miguel, because the wind was so strong. Our Ryanair (!) aerial conveyance had to land on a smaller island, hang around there for a while, and then continue to São Miguel when the wind had climbed down at least one of those rungs on the Beaufort scale. It was, of course, still extremely windy when we finally landed. And this should have informed us of the likely state of the sea, as there is quite often a connection between wind speeds and the size of a mid-ocean swell…

Yes, the following day, the swell – out in the open ocean – was five to six metres – not necessarily ideal conditions for a spartan whale-watching catamaran. Which is probably why half of those aboard it were violently sick, with some of them simply begging for a return to shore as soon as possible. Unfortunately, Sue and I were amongst this unhappy company of chunderers, although we were not in quite as bad a state as one of our Naturetrek companions, who suffered from emetophobia (the extreme fear of vomiting or seeing other people vomiting), and who had to be transported from the catamaran back to our hotel in a wheelchair. All in all, we have had better days. And, indeed, some of these followed in the wake of the extreme-seasick day with barely a pause. First it was a number of days exploring the interior of São Miguel – which is beautiful and which provided us with a number of bird spots – and then it was some further whale-watching trips on a somewhat flatter sea, which enabled us to clock up not just humpback, blue and sperm whales, but also a full pack of different dolphin species and even some flying fish (the first we'd seen since that trip through Melanesia). Nevertheless, there was a real highlight to come, and it came towards the end of our stay in the Azores when Naturetrekker Chris from Barnsley proposed to Naturetrekker Cathy from Milwaukee – and had his proposal accepted! It was a first for a Naturetrek trip: a romantic transaction, and one that would be suitably celebrated by the whole party in a very pleasant Ponta Delgada restaurant, where the owner even presented the assembled company with an early wedding cake.

That was the Azores, but I should just add that, as I write, and because of that effin' Covid thing, Chris is still in Barnsley and Cathy is still in Milwaukee. They are two of the countless millions of casualties of that unspeakable scourge released by China. And I can only hope that very soon they might be able to realise the intentions that were expressed in Chris's proposal and in Cathy's acceptance. Although I suspect they won't be considering a honeymoon in Beijing…

Well, returning to my own more fortunate story, may I suggest that when one has made it halfway across the Atlantic, it is only right that one then makes it all the way across – which is what Sue and I did in August of 2019 by travelling to Brazil (not with Ryanair) in order to embark on a boat ride up the Amazon. I am almost embarrassed to say this, but it was yet another Naturetrek holiday, this time with eleven other souls, who, together with Sue and me, would completely fill the small Amazon riverboat called the *Iracema.* And when I say 'fill' I mean 'fill'. Shoehorns were not provided on this vessel to ease one into one's cabin, but they could well have been. Certainly for the benefit of the more pneumatic members of the party...

Anyway, I should confess that most of our voyage up the mighty Amazon – starting in Manaus – was not up the Amazon, but up the equally gigantic river that joins it near Manaus called the Rio Negro (if that name is still permitted). This is not an insubstantial waterway, especially in August, when it is at its highest level and it floods literally hundreds or maybe even thousands of square miles of riverside forest. Indeed, to convey just how big this river is, at one point of our voyage along it, we encountered the biggest inland archipelago in Brazil, where its constituent islands sit within the river's banks, which, at this point, are separated by several miles. Furthermore, just after this archipelago encounter, we encountered an overnight storm, which was so violent that the boat's captain had to halt its progress. It was like being in the middle of a stormy North Sea, albeit just a little bit warmer.

Anyway, this expedition was mostly about birds (and only a few forest-living animals). And much of it was conducted not from the *Iracema*, but from its two canoes, which were able to thread their way through the flooded forest to either side of the river to bring us into close contact with the wildlife we sought. After all, if lots of the birds live in the treetops, and the trees are inundated in twenty feet of water (yes, twenty), the treetops are almost at eye level and the birds can be easily spotted. Needless to say, one is also staggered at just how big the Rio Negro can become – and just how much bloody water is held within the Amazon Basin at this time of year. Indeed, that might be my enduring recollection of this holiday – along with that of my intimate encounter with pink dolphins...

We had seen an encouraging number of these critters, together with their grey cousins, all along the river. But there was one place, back on the Amazon River proper, where an enterprising young chap had taken to providing them with fish, in order that eco-enthusiasts such as ourselves could indulge in what might not meet the strict definition of ecotourism.

And what I'm admitting to is that we visited this place, and some of us got into the waters of the Amazon – to join the pink dolphins who were turning up for their fill of fish. It was brilliant! They weren't captive. They weren't being forced to do anything against their will. They certainly weren't being fed enough fish to preclude the need for their finding most of their food themselves. And they quite seemed to be enjoying our company! So, my enduring recollection of this encounter is not one of guilt, but instead one of pleasure – and specifically of the image of a pink dolphin's head emerging from the water (just feet from where I was standing chest-high in this water), and seeing it grasp an offered fish with its long, teeth-filled, crocodile-like mouth. And my enduring sensation is of him or one of his chums knocking into my thigh with what felt like a body full of rock-hard muscle. A fish diet clearly doesn't lead to your developing too much fat or flab. Nor, probably, to your brain becoming fat or flabby…

It was on the four-hour flight back from Manaus to São Paulo, where we would then catch our flight back to Britain. And it was a woman across the aisle of the plane who, for most of the four hours, was preoccupied with her phone. Of course, these days, this sort of preoccupation is hardly a novelty. Indeed, as I've alluded to before, what is novel is observing a young person who is *not* preoccupied with his or her phone. However, this preoccupation was 'the next level up', because, presumably, in the absence of a signal allowing her to 'chat' with her fellow halfwits, she was scrolling through a store of photos, and selecting which of these, in due course, would be sent to these halfwits. And I know this because I couldn't help becoming captivated by her seemingly endless endeavour – principally due to the fact that every photo she was selecting was a selfie. Not surprising in a way, taking into account that all the photos on her phone from which she was making the selection were… selfies. She may have been visiting Manaus and possibly its surrounding forests, but she had clearly decided that what was of most interest in this fascinating part of the world was… herself.

I remember thinking at the time that not only was she a fully paid-up halfwit, but also that her actions were a wonderful microcosm of human behaviour in a more general sense. After all, you may have gathered already that I believe *Homo sapiens* to be the ultimate self-interested, self-absorbed and self-regarding species on the planet, and here was proof positive that it is. Putting ourselves at the centre of things, irrespective of the worth or the attraction of everything around us, has become one of our principal hallmarks. And what is now the most obvious manifestation of this dreadful stamp of hubristic narcissism – indulged in by countless millions of halfwits – is the infantile, silly selfie – idiocy made visible through the magic of digital technology. And none of these halfwits has any idea of how they are allowing that technology to reduce them to something far worse than a halfwit, and therefore ideally suited to a new digital age that has barely got underway…

Yes, I seem to remember that I have already taken a single potshot at the spawn of digital technology, otherwise known as social media, by observing how it affects the productivity of all those supposedly working, but who, in reality, are updating their Facebook pages and keeping an eye on what's trending on Instagram. But I think it is now time that I enlightened you on my views on how this new world of technology, with all its billions of little screens, is… pardon my French, fucking us up a treat. Because it's not just selfies that are sucking out our brains; it's a whole matrix of digital offerings, in the hands of giant organisations, all designed to drain our brains dry – and, in doing so, make even more money for these organisations than the super amounts of money they're already making.

OK. I'll start with the alleged benefits of social media. Because that won't take me very long. These are, I am told: its ability to provide people with connectivity; its ability to bring together people with common interests; and its ability to provide a platform on which 'one can share one's life with the rest of the world'. Well, pardon me while I retch, and now please allow me to plough on with my explanation of why these highly questionable benefits are provided at such an extortionate cost – in terms of their effect on poor old *Homo sapiens.*

I will start with that connectivity stuff, and, in particular, that bringing together people with shared interests. Social media does, indeed, provide this. But quite often not to knitting circles in order to allow their members to exchange patterns, or to pigeon fanciers in order to allow them to share their fancies. No, it's quite often to Nazis, paedophiles, nutters like that QAnon bunch, conspiracists, whole batallions of trolls, bullies and bastards, and, of course, quite a few rogues, cheats, tricksters and scammers. Yes, unfortunately, while most of us are not naturally horrible, almost all of us are *capable* of being horrible. And if presented with the facility to be horrible anonymously and without risk of detection, many of us will be only too pleased to be really horrible – or to seek out similarly horrible people, to convince ourselves that we are not horrible at all, but just as normal and nice as all those other harmless Nazis. This is not good. It is giving free rein to some of our worst characteristics, and poisoning the conduct of human affairs – by driving millions of people into their chosen camps, silos and bunkers, there to be picked off more easily by big-tech's instruments of infantilisation…

I am told that lots of young people, when they are not 'sharing their life with the rest of the world', are getting their news from Instagram. Which is a little like inducting them into the realms of gastronomy by repeatedly taking them to McDonald's. And I wonder how they choose which bits of news to absorb. Possibly those bits pushed their way by their internet 'friends', which must be infinitely better than the miscellany of junk that the major news channels and the traditional print press put together. But not to worry, because so much screen time is, I am sure, devoted to 'great purpose', such as the fostering of philosophical debate, the promotion of informed political discussion, and the exploration of ways to make the world a better place, free of injustice and poverty and safe for all our fellow animals. And if, just occasionally, there's a clip of film of a kitten in a teacup or a cat using a lavatory, then there's no harm in that. I mean, it's not as though by spending excessive amounts of time looking at crap like this or recording what one had for dinner or what new shoes one has just bought is ever going to turn you into a socially inadequate moron who can barely converse with another real person and whose idea of a 'good time' is to get stuck into Kim Kardashian's tweets before a serious session of Candy Crush or maybe some Angry Birds. And here, I would just like to point out that infantilisation is defined as treating someone like a child so that he or she starts to behave like a child. And if an adult playing an update of the sort of games that Baby Boomers might have played when they were still children isn't indisputable proof of the widespread infantilisation of more recent generations, I don't know what is.

Anyway, let me just encapsulate in a few words what I think is happening as a result of the ubiquitous presence of 'stuff on a screen'. And those few words are 'young people are not being allowed to develop in the way that our species was intended to develop – through real-life experiences and real-life interactions'. How can they be when one can observe them in, say, a beautiful national park, with their eyes glued to a smartphone, or when, at a large family gathering, their focus will not be on their relatives – and certainly not on their older relatives – but on a few square inches of pixels, and whatever silly images these pixels are forming? And the result of this deformation of their development is already only too apparent. It is there in the shape of a multitude of new adults who think that they are more enlightened, more well-informed, more wisdom-filled and, of course, more 'socially aware' than their forebears, but who are, in reality, more ignorant, more *ill*-informed, more wrongheaded, more childish – and more receptive to technology taking over what were once exclusively human skills – than those of us who came before. Which means that they will make ideal material for the 'inevitable' more-than-ever-digital future.

The more people stare at a screen – and through that screen, conduct much of their life – the more that life comes under the control of those who populate the screens with their digital goodies. It is far from a secret that, in return for availing oneself of these goodies, you are providing 'someone somewhere' with some data – data that will be used to entrap you further, and make more inroads into what once used to be your private life. That 'someone somewhere' will quickly learn all about your habits in intimate detail: what you like, what you don't like, where you go, where you are, and quite possibly, if you've added one of those snooping voice-interaction devices to your stable of digital gadgets, even who you screw. All this information isn't then stuffed into a drawer and forgotten, but instead it is cut, cubed, spliced and diced – and monetised. Your life will have been reduced to a commodity that can be sold to the highest bidder – and, like a stick of rock, embedded along its length you will find the words Facebook, Amazon, Apple, Microsoft and Google. And the word 'Google' will be in bigger print than any of the other four.

If, at this stage, you think that I've become a conspiracist myself, and I have conjured up the image of a cabal of all-powerful corporations intent only on infantilising us and, at the same time, making us less independent and less self-responsible, all in the cause of making money, then let me just say a few words about driverless cars. You know, those vehicles that the whole world has been crying out for since the dawn of time, and that, when introduced in their hundreds of millions, will make our roads even safer than a beige-coloured lounge with beige-coloured curtains.

Well, in reality, the only demand for these cars is the one made by their big-tech promoters and implanted into the minds of young people – all those young people who have not and probably never will experience the unsurpassable joys of motoring. These joys still exist, and one of the greatest is being 'in control'. Even in the constricted and regulated road networks of the modern world, you can still choose where to go and where not to go. You're a free spirit with wheels – and, much to their frustration, beyond the reach of Google and its partners in crime. Or at least, some of us are. Because it wasn't too long before even old people were introduced to the idea of a sat-nav, and how this magic device could relieve them of the need to notice their surroundings. Even if it meant that sometimes they might not take note of their immediate surroundings, with consequent unfortunate results. But, by and large, sat-navs were seen as something to take some of the drudgery out of driving. Because that's what driving is, isn't it? It's not a joy at all; it's a drudge.

This was such a smart move, because this idea that driving was something to be relieved of underpins many more of the technical 'innovations' that have been introduced into cars since, and that relieve us of ever more of our own found-to-be-wanting skills. And here I'm talking about 'advanced driver-assistance systems' that make driving 'safer and better'. That is to say, safer and better than when left to those clumsy old humans – those clumsy old humans who seemed to be losing the ability to avoid obstacles, avoid collisions, join a lane safely, stay centred in a lane – and park! I mean, with a working steering wheel and good, all-round vision, we were apparently still incapable of placing our vehicle in a given space – and our vehicle therefore needed to be called upon to do this for us. It's incredible. But, there again, very credible, because it's just another step along the path of demeaning our own skills and replacing them with machine skills, so successfully that our own skills do indeed begin to wither – to the point where we do become reliant on that 'very helpful' technology. After all, how many new drivers will soon still be able to park a car – or even consider that this is something they should ever be called on to do themselves?

Mmm… that leap to driverless cars now doesn't seem much of a leap at all, does it? After all, we're halfway there with all those enhancements, so we might as well go all the way. And then, completely relieved of the drudgery of piloting a chunk of metal from A to B (what a thought!), we can use the time in our car to be… well, creative – or to relax or even to have a kip. Or… maybe we can plug ourselves into Facebook or look at those latest offerings from Amazon, or hear what's on offer from that new Chinese restaurant that's paid to get its message through our car's intelligent info system – which already knows that we just love Chinese food…

See what's happened? The free spirit has been trapped by technology, and all that time that was once yours is now not yours anymore. Big Tech has found a way to reach into a part of your life that had evaded it for years – and, in doing so, make even more filthy lucre. In plain English, driverless cars are nothing to do with safety or convenience or making anything better. They are simply the next big step in Big Tech's campaign to claim and monetise every bloody moment of a person's life, which might otherwise be left as private and therefore literally unrewarding for 'others' in terms of dollars and pounds. And remember, not only have they already successfully convinced drivers that driving is a chore, deskilled them to the point that they are already overdependent on technology to transport them between two points (and park them), implanted in their heads that driverless cars are *Inevitable*, with a very big 'I', and that not to embrace them is to 'cling to the past' – but over many years, with all those handheld devices, they have reduced many of them to digitally lobotomised dullards, who probably think a torque converter is a new real-time translation app.

So… that's why I think virtually every aspect of applied digital technology is very, very bad. All these consequences of its takeover of the lives of billions – along with quite a few more I haven't even mentioned – make it the most disruptive and damaging development in human history. And rather than trying to tame it – by learning how to use it sensibly and in moderation – the whole human race is already standing with its arms open to embrace yet more of it, and in its turn to be embraced back, or even to be gripped so tightly that it won't be able to breathe. At least, not without the help of Big Tech. And that, of course, is not an entirely true statement. Because quite a few Baby Boomers – such as myself and Sue – will not be caught up in this warped desire to give up their lives, their skills, their minds and their choices – to somebody in California. And the only driverless car they might ever be seen in is a hearse. Albeit, I will be leaving instructions that when my coffin needs shifting, it will be in a device that still requires a driver to handle its steering wheel. And, if possible, its sat-nav will be either disabled or emasculated, in much the same way as Mark Zuckerberg and Sundar Pichai should be. (And as regards Mr Pichai… well, you might want to Google his name…)

Well, that was all a bit heavy-going, wasn't it? So, for a bit of light relief, I am now going to transport you to the Antarctic, where Sue and I were simply transported – with pleasure. This won't take long. Because, even with my unsurpassed facility to paint a vivid picture with just words, I have to concede defeat when it comes to trying to describe the beauty – and the majesty – of the southernmost part of our world. All I am going to do is jot down a few bullet points in the hope that these might give you at least a hint as to why a visit to Antarctica – and to the Falklands and South Georgia – cannot fail to constitute a towering high point in anybody's life. So here goes, a list of some of the things that made this trip so stunningly memorable:

1. Finding ourselves, with ninety other passengers, on the *MS Island Sky*, the sister ship to the *MS Caledonian Sky*, on which we had sailed through Melanesia – and finding it just as superb as the *MS Caledonian Sky.*
2. Having a meal in the ship's outside lido restaurant as we sailed out of Ushuaia along the Beagle Channel, with snow-dusted mountains to either side – and, with the help of very benign weather, repeating this outdoor eating routine all the way down to the Antarctic.
3. Having our first dose of dolphins and assorted birds, including various penguins and albatrosses, when we landed on two islands in West Falkland.
4. Seeing a Waitrose van through the window as we sat in the Globe Tavern in Port Stanley.
5. Hearing an account from one of the expedition team aboard the *Island Sky* of his role in the Falklands War, when he served as a young marine.
6. Becoming adept in dressing oneself in twenty-one pieces of clothing to keep warm and snug when out and about in the lower latitudes.

7. Making a toast with whisky at Shackleton's grave in Grytviken on South Georgia, before running a gauntlet of fur seals to have a look around what was once the principal whaling station on this vast, remote island.
8. Running a gauntlet of more fur seals and elephant seals at a place called St Andrew's Bay on South Georgia to observe an entire landscape of king penguins. There were almost a quarter of a million of them gathered together, the most extreme example of assembled wildlife on an island that is simply smothered in wildlife. One doesn't just observe it; one wanders through a mass of it.
9. A leopard seal's head (and scary mouth) coming within a couple of feet of my bum as I sat on the edge of an inflatable, bobbing around in the ocean just off rugged Elephant Island.
10. Making it onto the Antarctic continent proper at a place called Brown Bluff – to be met by hordes of Adélie and gentoo penguins.
11. Being in an inflatable off the Antarctic Peninsula – very close to a couple of humpback whales.
12. Having a barbeque in that lido restaurant as we sailed down a channel made by the peninsula and a series of off-shore islands, with every piece of land brilliant-white with snow, and a clear blue sky above turning to silver-blue the mirror-smooth surface of the sea all around (albeit that mirror-smooth surface was quite often ruffled by more of those humpbacks).
13. Sailing past countless icebergs, some of them very close, some of them very, very big, and all of them impossibly beautiful.
14. Exploring an unoccupied Argentinian 'research station' in the aptly named Paradise Bay (more brilliant white and blue).
15. Witnessing – from an inflatable – a huge avalanche above an enormous glacier in Paradise Bay, reduced to insignificance by the indescribable grandeur of this part of the Antarctic.
16. Sailing *into* Deception Island in the South Shetlands, and being able to do this in the *Island Sky* because Deception Island was once a vast active volcano, but is now a placid, giant, flooded caldera, with a single gap in its rim just large enough to allow through a vessel of the size of the *Island Sky.* (FYI, the caldera is six miles long by four miles wide, and on its inner rim there are two research stations and a now unused runway!)

17. Getting back to Argentina across the infamous Drake Passage without actually throwing up. I just came very close…

Lots more happened on this trip – and even when not much at all was happening, I was still very aware that Sue and I were in a very special part of the world, still visited by very few people and still largely untouched by people in general. This meant that we were constantly in awe of our surroundings, whether these were of the unforgiving, almost primeval type found on South Georgia or the magical, exclusively blue-and-white type found in the Antarctic Peninsula. It had to qualify as a 'holiday of a lifetime', and when we were finally home, we began to properly appreciate just how fortunate we had been to have made it to the bottom of the world. And in exceptionally good weather!

Oh, and, of course, without much in the way of Mr Google. What more could you want?!

Two Bumps in the Road

Having relished a Christmas at Lympstone Manor with some close friends, the first jobs I got around to in the New Year were sorting out the parking at Heathrow for our forthcoming trip to Namibia (yes, again!), and booking Eurotunnel and a couple of overnight hotels in France in readiness for another trip to Bergerac later in the year. Little did I know…

Then I had my eyes done. From the Court of King Cataract-For-Us, I had received the first warnings that my eyes were likely to become misty even without the assistance of plaintive ballads, and it was therefore decided that I should have a couple of bionic lenses to replace the wearing-out real ones. That way I could get down to writing another long letter to my friend without a computer and also have a go at making balloon animals with the balloon-animal-making kit I had received as a Christmas present. And I should say that the first proved more successful than the second. Take it from me, balloons pop when twisted into impossible configurations.

However, the really big news of the beginning of 2020 was nothing to do with forthcoming holiday arrangements, my eyes, letters, or even attempts to make balloon animals, but everything to do with my starting a new novel – on exactly 18 January of this year. And I do need to record that date in this book, because this novel, which would draw on a certain recent trip to the Antarctic, and which would be the realisation of a story that I'd had in my mind for maybe a year, would be all about a deadly 'phenomenon' originating in China! I'm not making this up. Why would I? But I was already well into the writing of this latest masterpiece when, at the beginning of February, I first heard of Covid-19, and then sometime in March I began to realise that the Chinese had gifted us a New Year present, the like of which I had never seen before. I will add little more to this rather troubling manifestation of prescience other than to say that, as I wrote more and more of *Survival* (the book in question), I began to think that what I was writing was driving what was happening in the real world. That is to say, as I was documenting the progress of a fast-spreading deadly plague and its potential impact on the passengers and crew of a pocket-sized cruise ship in the Antarctic, the real plague was embarking on a worldwide rampage that was already killing thousands – before it would then go on to kill millions. I only wonder whether the possible causes of 'my' pandemic, as I set out in *Survival* (which you will be able to discover only by buying the book), will, in due course, be proved to be equally prescient as my writing of the entire novel. If, that is, China ever sees fit to tell the rest of the world what the real causes of the real pandemic were. Which isn't too likely – as in 'completely impossible'.

Anyway, just before I embark on the consequences of China's generous contribution to thinning out the world's inflated population, I have to make a brief mention of Britain's long-awaited freedom from the European Union. On 31 January, the shackles were finally removed, and we became something like a real sovereign state once again. It was all very fraught and all very messy, and there was all that arguing about how much we should pay them and how both sides should deal with Northern Ireland and its land border with the Irish Republic. I did try to help to resolve this issue – by suggesting to Boris that we pay the EU what they were demanding – in kind, the kind being a very attractive property called Northern Ireland, complete with its population of very lovely sitting tenants. Heck, not only would this relieve us of paying them a large number of billions of used oncers, but it would also relieve us of that troublesome province that should never have been other than part of an Irish nation in the first place. And that's not me taking sides with the hateful Irish Republicans; it's just effin' common sense. Why Boris didn't take my advice, I have no idea...

OK. Time to talk about the first little bump in 2020, otherwise known as Covid-19. And wasn't it a bump that took us all by surprise? One minute we were leading a normal life, and the next minute we were trying to register on supermarket websites for either deliveries or 'click and collects', while, at the same time, ordering deliveries of enough wine to float a Chinese junk. Or, at least some of us were. And I do have to confess that there had never before been more wine in our house than there was at the beginning of April 2020 – along with quite a healthy store of gin, pastis, Tio Pepe, Noilly Prat – and Twiglets. (Just in case.)

It was a strange time – but only for us; only for us housebound humans. For the rest of life on this planet – if our little patch was anything like a reliable indicator – life went on as if nothing had happened, or it even got a little better. The frogs, in particular, seemed to be having a field day, and managed to populate our pond with about as many tadpoles as there are atoms in the universe. And if not quite that many, then certainly with more than enough to form a ribbon of black, wriggling bodies along maybe forty or fifty feet of the pond edge.

Not that the foxes were interested in them – all eight of the charming new cubs who had been installed by their clever mum in a huge coralberry nursery next to the pond, and who would go on to become a continuing source of entertainment for weeks. Not only were we treated to the survival and the subsequent dominance of the litter's runt, but we were also able to catch snatches of the growing family's daytime and night-time lives on a camera trap – and send the resulting pictures and videos to a number of our friends. Which is, I think, a suitable introduction to how relationships were maintained over many months by the use of some of that dreaded technology – not, of course, of the mind-mushing social media sort, but of the more amenable and much more controllable email variety.

Yes, Sue and I did manage a handful of socially distanced foursomes in our garden but, by and large, friends became email friends – and to maintain these friendships, one needed more than exchanges on the misting up of one's specs when one was wearing a face mask or a series of mutual moans about cancelled and deferred holidays. Even if one was pretty well fuming about losing not only a trip to Namibia and one to France, but also a much-anticipated cruise between Tahiti and Easter Island. (Sue and I had still been trying to squeeze in everything we could – while we could.) So… I soon alighted on the idea of sending to a whole list of incarcerated friends, a regular helping of some of the limericks contained in my *A Leap*

Year of Limericks book. I should say that I did check with all the recipients whether they were prepared to admit into their inboxes a succession of not-necessarily-decent odes, and only one pair of friends declined. The rest were only too willing to get anything into their inboxes. And, as my efforts at humour were delivered with an invitation to respond with their own efforts (in the shape of their own disreputable limericks, to be entered into an all-comers' limerick competition) my modest little project soon got air under its wings and became… well, quite a popular project. Indeed, when I'd submitted the twelfth batch of these limericks, and had decided that they had now run their course, I felt obliged to follow up the distribution of the competition's winning entries with a string of more of my own hopefully humorous poems. The first of these were some that I had written over the years. But as the pandemic dragged on, I began to write some new ones – on the subject of the pandemic itself. They were quite well received, and two of them even got published in our local parish magazine – much to the annoyance of the only Chinese resident in our village. And that is why, together with a few of my already-written odes, some of them are reproduced in the appendices to this book. They will hopefully provide you with some entertainment, and they will also underline just how odd life was in 2020, and what straws we all had to grasp at to keep our sanity and at least a little contact with all the other people in our lives. And for some of us, contact with others was very important – after that second bump in the road had been encountered…

This one tried to knock our wheels off in June. It was the confirmation that Sue's cancer had returned, and that she had in front of her another extended period of cancer treatment. This was the worst news possible – of course. But at least the treatment got underway very quickly, despite the medical profession being engaged in battling Covid to the apparent exclusion of all else. And I am very happy to report that by the end of the year, the treatment was successful, and Sue was declared cancer-free, with only some follow-up belt-and-braces stuff scheduled for the following year. Again, she had received not only first-class medical attention, but also the support of a large number of our friends and *some* of our relatives. (But not, as before, *all* our relatives.) And if that sounds mean again, then it's supposed to sound mean again. Shit, they didn't even acknowledge any of my limericks...

Anyway, it wasn't until September that I had finished and 'polished' *Survival*, whereafter I went through the usual futile exercise of offering it to a number of agents before deciding again to opt for the self-publishing route. And having set that process in motion, I then embarked on another book, this one called *I, Baby Boomer.* Yes, what you are reading now started life at the end of October 2020, just a few days after I'd completed seventy-two years of my rather agreeable sentence on this planet. Albeit one that, I might argue, was becoming not nearly so agreeable in a number of ways. Indeed, in certain ways, it was becoming entirely *disagreeable*, and there appeared to be little one could do to make it much better.

Now, I should issue a warning here. You see, much of what I was finding more and more disagreeable was appearing daily on what, for us housebound Baby Boomers, was a vital portal to the outside world – otherwise known as the television. And because of the nature of what I was finding disagreeable, that warning needs to be directed towards any liberal, snowflake, softie, wimp or wet who, against all the odds, has got this far through this book, and will now not only be deeply offended but also pretty well enraged. He or she might even throw a pretty tetchy tantrum, and then share this with likeminded lovies on Twitter, all of whom, no doubt, will be suitably enraged themselves. So, watch out, guys. Wokeness is in for a kicking.

Let me start, not with the substantive stuff on the telly – all the marvellous programmes, whether uplifting reality shows or hilarious comedies – but with what interrupts them: those endless adverts that we fortunately no longer have to endure thanks to the recording power of a Sky box. Nevertheless, one still runs the risk of catching a glimpse of them when one first turns on the telly – or a racing glimpse of them when they are being fast-forwarded at thirty times normal speed. And what does one always see? I think you know. It is an entirely false picture of Britain today, a shameful manifestation of wokeness at its worst, pushed down the throats of all us British citizens by an irresponsible, virtue-signalling advertising industry that should know a heck of a lot better. In the real world, not every snapshot of life in this country would include a black person in the frame, and not every married couple would be a mixed-marriage couple. But in advert-land, that is exactly what is portrayed. And if you think I am now being overtly racist, may I also point out that Chinese and Asian people are somehow mysteriously absent from this representation of purely fantastic Britain, as though black people can serve the purpose of 'anybody but white' and the necessary box can then be ticked. I don't know what black people in general think about their part in this gross misrepresentation of our country, and I wonder whether they might be more embarrassed than gratified by their universal appearance in modern adverts, and even a little concerned that it might lead to a degree of resentment in the minds of their white neighbours, in much the same way that all those actual programmes do as well…

With these, first and foremost, it is the must-be-observed decree – non-observance of which will result in a destroyed career or even one's admission to the BLM Hall of Shame – that every offering on television has to have 'the right mix'. It's the RSC syndrome alive and well on our screens – a woker-than-woke syndrome that puts diversity above any other considerations when putting together something for our illumination or entertainment, notwithstanding that such an approach will often produce not just a second-best product (because of resulting incongruities or deficiencies in required talents) but often a product that is simply unwatchable. Lots of people do not want indoctrination on their screens in the evening. Indeed, they want anything but indoctrination. Not that what they want seems to matter. No, all that matters is that the deity of diversity has been placated. And the feelings of… well, probably quite a number of normally very reasonable Baby Boomers are not worthy of consideration.

It gets worse when trying to watch the news (or, indeed, listen to it on the trusty wireless), because it now seems to be admitted (and celebrated) that other than white people are overrepresented as news broadcasters and news reporters. And the *bad* news for black people – who have more than just an edge in advert-land – is that it is Asians who are in the ascendancy in news-land. There must be more of them in this news line of work than there are in all the pharmacists and opticians in Britain put together. And that is not my being rude, but just a tad facetious to make a point. Which is that overrepresentation of any sort is not a good idea. And for some, it might even be rather disagreeable…

All this wicked nonsense might not seem quite so wicked – to me – if it wasn't accompanied with quite so much white-bashing. And white-bashing is more than merely disagreeable; it's positively offensive. Particularly if you happen to be – through no fault of your own – male, white and old. Because then you at the front of the queue to get bashed.

I know it isn't called white-bashing. It is more commonly described as the struggle to achieve equality amongst the races, the desire to see each race fairly represented in every facet of modern life, and the imperative to remove not only institutional racism from our 'shared culture', but even to eliminate something called 'unconscious racial bias', where it is apparently not enough to be a non-racist, but essential that one is an anti-racist. (And I apologise if I've not been entirely accurate in that summation of the euphemisms surrounding white-bashing, but I have been trying very hard not to immerse myself in the finer details of this whole oppressive business.) However, the point is that these possibly admirable goals should not take as their starting point the (erroneous) assumption that white people are the spawn of past generations of evil white people – who spent most of their time ravaging the world (as discussed earlier under my enlightened look at colonisation) – and therefore, not only should we current whities be desperately ashamed of our entire, formerly glorious history, but we should also acknowledge our inherited communal guilt and our being... well, just very bad people, responsible for everything bad in the world.

You know, I think it may have all started as a thought experiment in a psychology department of a third-rate university. After all, universities are now not just institutions dedicated to high-level education, but they are also the source of all sorts of half-baked and harmful ideas. In fact, some of them have more or less junked the education bit in order to be able to concentrate exclusively on the soppy-idea task. Therefore, it isn't beyond the bounds of possibility that some simpleton professor launched a project to test how far the British population would be prepared to indulge in an orgy of cowedness and self-loathing – just because he could. He put out a rumour – bolstered by its widespread distribution on social media – that all the many achievements of this country counted for nothing, and that we could take no pride in any aspect of our native culture – because it was a 'bad, white culture' – and then he sat back to see whether such rubbish would gain any traction. Well, if this is what happened, that professor must now have been showered with numerous research grants – to establish whether this nation's communal common sense and commitment to ideals such as fair play and justice have also been blown away in the wind to join its lost pride in its heritage and its very self-respect. And, as unlikely as it is, if any of his Twitter followers happen to trip over this chapter, would they kindly tell him that this particular Baby Boomer still thinks that Britain is and always has been one of the greatest countries in the world and, when compared to virtually every other country on the planet, has sod all to be ashamed of and almost too much to be proud of. Not everyone in Britain has bought into the insanity of national shame and national self-hate, and they never will, no matter how forcefully it is promoted by its millions of misguided adherents. And no matter how much it has now become the almost obligatory perspective of the young…

Ah yes, the young. It's what every country hell-bent on obliterating its entire history cannot do without. And the more whining, ignorant, petulant and narcissistic they are the better. Buff them up with a diet of incessant social media disinformation and a grovelling acceptance of their ersatz victimhood, and they are fucking perfect. And that's exactly what we've got: a me, me, me generation, who seem to believe in something called the 'wisdom of youth', when anybody who has experienced and survived youth will tell you that you don't know what you're bloody well talking about when you're young. And rather than wasting your time trying to dismantle everything that is proven and worthwhile, you should just be focusing on having as much consensual sex as you can get your legs around and trying to catch up on the correct use of apostrophes. I can really only speak of my own experience here, but that includes my being more or less aware at the time – up to my late twenties – that I knew very little about anything, and that I was much more interested in my career, my appearance (yes), my bank balance and my voyage of discovery in the bedroom, than I was in imposing my naïve views on my fellow man.

Yes, I know I'm sounding like a prime example of a miserable old git, an antique, wrinkled curmudgeon who has got it in for young people just because he long ago lost his own youth. And I also know that I am indulging in the sort of generalisation that is as unjust as it is egregious. There are, of course, very many young people out there who deserve only our admiration for their conduct and for how they are dealing with a world where everything seems increasingly to be stacked against them. Nevertheless, I still believe there is more than a kernel of truth in my old-git generalisation, and so, at the risk of incurring a whole pile of opprobrium, I will proceed. First, by making some balanced remarks about how the young quite often regard the past...

You see, not getting that plum media job at the end of your demanding gender-studies degree might leave you a little pissed off, but it does not give you the right – or the requisite knowledge – to demand a rewrite of history, and nor does it give you authority to judge all actions of the past by the restrictive, puritan-like standards of the present. And may I just say that this puerile tendency to view what happened long ago through the lens of the present, and thereby to find just about everybody who lived in the past either just plain reprehensible or grossly reprehensible, is based on a premise that is as fragile as it is ridiculous. Because it assumes that our current standards are the zenith of standards and that they will never be bettered; that we have got everything perfectly right now, and never will anybody look back to 2020 and question how we – or, more specifically, our youth – could have been so wrong, and so damn arrogant.

Might generations in the future (if there are any) not question the way that it had become fashionable to close down debate, 'in case somebody's feelings were hurt'; to insist on people conforming to 'the accepted views' on, for example, transgender issues; to take offence on any number of issues on other people's behalf; and to hold in contempt a whole raft of people for the (white) colour of their skin. Oh, and how about Baby Boomers, such as *moi*? Because I have heard a rumour that lots of young people hold us in contempt – just for being Baby Boomers. It doesn't matter to them that all we have done with our lives is what they would have done had they been born when we were – and hadn't been continually bludgeoned around the head with the cosh of social media. Although they seem to believe it, we are not, all of us, 'bad', and not all of them are 'good'. Indeed, in many ways, we were and still are a great deal gooder than they are. We didn't and we don't express our green credentials by smothering parks and beaches under a tide of litter; we didn't and don't make a big issue out of the nonsense of 'cultural appropriation' while ignoring the much more serious issue of 'cultural imposition' (on an endemic population); we didn't and we don't believe that there is some God-given right not to be offended; and we didn't and we don't hold the view that we have only rights and no responsibilities. I could go on, but I suspect I have probably made my point, which is that I do not believe that young people should be quite so assured of their views or their behaviour. Both, in due course, will be found to be sadly wanting.

However, let me leave the young people to their own concerns for now, and return to what I was finding particularly disagreeable about life in 2020. And, whilst this might involve some unavoidable repetition, I do want to emphasise two aspects of modern Britain that were really getting on my upper chest parts. And the first of these was that self-loathing trashing of our heritage. To start with, this is just very wrong in principle. After all, liberty depends on memory. That is why one of the favourite ploys of tyrants is to cut off people from their past and to discredit their ancestors. They know that this is the way they can reinforce their grip on these people, as no society can remain healthy and vigorous enough to withstand them – if cut off from its roots. Then, of course, there is *our* heritage to consider. And all I will say here is that for a small, rain-blown island off the coast of Europe, we haven't done too bad. In fact, taking account of our much-maligned imperialism, our numerous victories in wars, our numerous technological innovations, our scientific and medical achievements, our further achievements in the arts, our formulation of many of the world's sports, our unsurpassed skills in the making of pork pies, and so much more, we have done remarkably well. And we should wear our heritage as a badge of pride, not ever as a mark of dishonour. So there.

The second aspect of modern Britain that I have to address is all and everything that comes with this focus on diversity. I heard recently that I live in a 'privileged white space' – because I live in the countryside. I find this comment not only deeply offensive, but I believe it also betrays a wilful disregard for our recent history, in that when I and my Baby Boomer colleagues were born, the whole of Britain was a 'privileged white space', because overwhelmingly it was occupied by British people – who were white. That is now not the case, which is why we have a diversity 'industry', chomping away greedily on a whole smorgasbord of anti-discrimination legislation, and making quite sure that there isn't the most trivial aspect of our lives into which it hasn't inveigled itself and its onerous demands. In fact, I find it interesting that a country like Japan, for example – which is largely full of Japanese people, and few others – has no comprehensive anti-discrimination laws whatsoever, and is unlikely to have any in the future, unless, of course, it is daft enough to follow us down the path of multiculturalism. Which, of course, might mean that the 'diversity imperative', in reality, is nothing more than the oil we use to ease the passage of the square peg of natural behaviour into the round hole of multiculturalism. And the peg will, in all probability, never sit very comfortably. No matter how much we endemics seek to atone for the sins of our past…

Which leads me to say just a few more words about the new disagreeable Britain – as I might as well get hanged for a sheep as for a lamb, and I have a distinct feeling that the forces of righteousness and wokeness have already been dispatched to hunt me down. And before they find me, I need to say these words, and I will do so in the form of some questions. Which are: 1. Why, if we are such a miserable race with such an egregious past, do so many people want to come to share with us our very limited space? 2. Why are flows of people always from Africa and Asia to here, and not the other way around? And 3. Why are some of these people from faraway places (or their offspring) amongst the most critical of our national culture and our national heritage – and the keenest to throw symbols of our past into docks? Could it be that no matter how they found their way here, they enjoy a far better life here – on just about every measure – than their counterparts in other continents? After all, how many folk in Burkina Faso can afford designer-label clothes *and* a Megaboom Bluetooth speaker, and how many people in Pakistan can contemplate investing their hard-earned funds in a shiny Peloton exercise bike? Answer to both questions: very few if any at all.

This observation can, of course, be made about other Western countries, and about the USA in particular. But it never is – because it's just too uncomfortable, and it smells far too much of overt racism, even though it is no more than a legitimate comment on the situation to be found in a whole string of Western countries. Indeed, its legitimacy stands in stark contrast to the arrant illegitimacy of some of the accusations levelled against the white people in these countries – people who, not that long ago, used to have almost exclusive use of their own territory, but no longer do. And to ignore that fact and to pretend that everything has got better and will only get better still is about as silly as believing that wokeness will ever make the world a better place.

Well, I will now try to put the forces of righteousness and wokeness off the scent by admitting not that all this disagreeable stuff has caused me to become irrational and in no way responsible for my possibly provocative views as expressed above, but that these views simply provide evidence that by 2020, this particular Baby Boomer was well on his way to becoming obsolete. There was no question about it. Life had been changing around me for years – and I hadn't. I was still living in a time forty or fifty years ago, when I felt really comfortable with the world. That was a time when I didn't have to witness – on a screen or, on those rare occasions in 2020, on a street – sights and attitudes that would have been regarded as either alien or even reprehensible back in the '60s and '70s. And to illustrate what I mean – and to move away from all that really provocative stuff into safer waters – I'll just take you towards the end of this chapter with a few examples of how things have changed since I was a young Baby Boomer, and how none of them is a change for the better.

Let me start with tattoos, once found only on the Popeye-type arms of hairy sailors, but now in evidence on any of the body parts of more mutt-heads than you could fit into the Isle of Wight. And most of these mutt-heads are neither *matelots* nor particularly hirsute. Why do they want to do this? Why do they want to offer their skin as a blank canvas, in the full knowledge (?) that when the sags and wrinkles begin to overtake their bodies, that lion on their right arm will look more like a walrus, and that angel of death on their right calf will become shot through with varicose veins? I can only think that, like Pooh, they are people of very little brain. Especially those who have more canvas available than a standard-size person…

Talking of which… how about all those people who haven't quite grasped the significance of clothes sizes, and who, as a result, have something of an issue with their trousers and leggings – an issue that can become an even more serious issue for those of us who have to observe these under-strain items of clothing? In fact, it's just as well that there is often some light relief on hand in the shape of all those folk who have eschewed the use of a dining table in favour of feeding themselves as they walk through a shopping centre, even if it means abandoning their smartphone for a while in order to keep one hand on their pushchair. I'm talking here about that new breed of people who would regard an appearance on one of our new sophisticated reality shows – of the *Big Brother* or *I'm a Celebrity Lobotomy Job etc* sort – as the apogee of their lives. For which elitist observation, I make no apology at all. Programmes like that are no more than a dreadful reflection of our unseemly self-regard and a toe-curling illustration of our growing, comprehensive ignorance – about anything whatsoever. Tripping over a single piece of erudite conversation on such a programme would be as likely as discovering that any of their participants knew that they should not be proud of their comprehensive ignorance. And their poor use of English…

I've nearly finished this coruscating indictment of my younger British brethren, but I cannot end before I have first mentioned not just some of their physical behaviour but also some of their… quite disconcerting attitudes. I speak here of stuff like 'emotions', which once upon a time used to be one's private property, but now seem to be no more than a currency one employs to gather more Twitter followers or more 'likes' for one's posts. An emotion is now only a good emotion if it is shared with as many people as possible, and the more that these people are people you don't know, the better. That proves that they are *forceful* emotions, and well worth the attention of the biggest audience possible. And, unfortunately, there is no shortage of those wishing to take their place in this audience. Ever since the much-parasitised death of Diana, people have been queuing up to identify with somebody else's suffering and grief – even if it is somebody they have never met in their lives. So, when you post the 'news' of the loss of your pet iguana, there will be a stampede of people to empathise with your loss, even if every one of them has not the first idea of what real emotions are all about. Indeed, you will often find these same idiots shuffling along in a great cortege of other indigestible modern attitudes and misconceptions, including such horrors as a complete lack of self-responsibility, a conviction that every mishap in life is somebody else's fault, the interpretation of every manifestation of attraction between the sexes as some form of sexual abuse, and the belief that all that hip hop, grime and drill music is something more than a tuneless expression of hatred, misogyny, crudity and savagery. And my God, don't all the exponents of that shit, with their moves and their grinds, look like a bunch of brain-deficient lummoxes?

Anyway, with that rhetorical question hanging in the air, it is probably time to draw this interesting year of my life to a close. But not before underlining the point that manifestations of Baby Boomer ideals (or maybe, just *my* ideals) in modern Britain seemed to be becoming rarer than an authenticated Stradivarius drum kit. And, on top of Covid and Sue's second brush with cancer, this 'rarity of rationality' tended to make 2020 something rather less than a red-letter year – and, indeed, indisputably disagreeable in so many ways. So, it was just as well that 2021 held out the prospect of it being the start of a new golden age – an age where the world would be put to rights in every way possible, and my own life would become more agreeable than I could ever have imagined. I could hardly wait. And even now, as I write, I can barely believe what I'm writing…

The Real End is Nigh

I did make an effort. I mean, there was no way that 2021 could possibly be as bad as 2020, and so I started the new year in a rare optimistic mood. And, indeed, this mood got a very welcome early boost when that overweight Hitler finally left the White House, even if, in the face of facts, he would not concede defeat to Joe Biden. (There again, I doubt he'll even admit to his own death when he finally falls off his perch.) And then there were a couple of new holiday bookings; 1. our already-deferred-once Namibia trip – which would now take place in 2022 – and 2. a new 'expedition' cruise from Alaska to Norway across the top of Russia (with two friends, Mag and Andrew) – which would also be a 2022 event. And in early February, I even got my first Covid jab!

However, optimism is a fragile creature, and mine was soon having to contend with reports in the news that convinced me that my Baby Boomer salad days were receding faster than ever in my rearview mirror, and that even if we all managed to reach a post-Covid world, it would not, in any way, be a world to relish. And to illustrate what I mean I will now list just half a dozen of the news reports that I just couldn't avoid at the beginning of 2021, and that so well supported my belief that we were on a journey to anywhere other than the sunlit uplands of a bright and appealing future. So, in no particular order, these news reports were:

1. Three men in Pakistan cornered and then bludgeoned to death an endangered Asian leopard – in an area where clashes between animals

and people are becoming more common as 'development' spreads into previously wild areas (a phenomenon not unique to Pakistan).

2. Not content with subjecting Uighurs to mass surveillance, detention, indoctrination and forced sterilisation, it seems that the Chinese authorities had instituted an organised system of mass rape, sexual abuse and torture of Uighur women. And few people outside China were much surprised.
3. Pupils at a school in London, as well as demanding a change to the school's uniform policy that they saw as an attack on Afro hairstyles and colourful hijabs, insisted that the Union flag that flew outside their so-called seat of learning be taken down – because it was a racist symbol. It had apparently been pulled down and burnt in the past, and graffiti scrawled on a nearby wall, reading 'ain't no black in the Union Jack'. (And I know London is no longer really part of England, but even so…)
4. Princelings from the so-called royal families of the UAE were still turning up in Pakistan to hunt (i.e. murder) rare houbara bustards. These birds, which are so rare that they are on the red list of threatened species, once flourished on the Arabian Peninsula. But because a load of ignorant Arabs considered their meat to be an aphrodisiac, they no longer do. And so Arabs with cash and connections take themselves off to Pakistan, where there is a remaining population of these birds to tidy up. One can only conclude that not only do UAE princes have undersized peckers (an established fact), but that their peckers don't even work. Maybe one day, with a bit of luck, they'll be on the red list as well.
5. Hopeless Harry, on his appointment as the 'Chief Impact Officer' for the mobile-based professional coaching, counselling and mentoring firm (?) 'BetterUp', issued a statement to explain what his goals would be in his new job. They would be 'to lift up critical dialogues around mental health, build supportive and compassionate communities, and foster an environment for honest and vulnerable conversations'. And couldn't we all do with more vulnerable conversations? (I can only wish Harry well with this one, but I do think that when next in the company of Medusa Markle in her Californian court, he shouldn't look too closely into her eyes for too long. She may be turning his brain to stone more quickly than he thinks. If he thinks.)

6. And lastly… a teacher at a grammar school in Batley – in which almost three-quarters of the pupils are from 'ethnic minority groups' – provoked protests by showing an 'offensive' cartoon of the Prophet Muhammad during a classroom debate on racism. The bloke probably succeeded in screwing up his career – for a 'blasphemous' act – in a country that has no blasphemy laws – yet.

So… you may begin to understand why my optimism had more or less shrunk away to nothing by mid-March, and why my pessimism had reasserted itself so strongly. With these reminders of our appalling treatment of the natural world, the gross behaviour of China, the despicable behaviour of people rather closer to home – and the tidal wave of witless wokery inundating much of the world – this result was inevitable. Just as it is inevitable that I will use this last chapter of my biography to take a peek into the future, where I will try to set out where I think 'my world' is going – before finally explaining why I think there is a place for this crystal-ball-gazing in an autobiography. And to whet your appetite for what is to come, I will reveal now that, within the swirl of mist inside my crystal ball, I will attempt to discern (a) what is in train for the human world, (b) what is already well underway in Britain and where this will lead, and (c) what awaits the natural world and ourselves as one of the many species it includes. So, first the human world…

OK. I have already regaled you with my observations concerning the spread of tyrannical regimes in this world – largely as a result of there being rather too many of us on the good ship Earth – and I've also provided you with a generous number of words of wisdom about the malevolence of Russia and the peril represented by that goliath of a country called China. However, to get to the core of what is in store for the human world, one needs only to focus on that last-mentioned country – the one that already has us in its grip…

Remember that China believes that it has been the most affronted nation on the planet, and that, after years of this effrontery (what happened to 'affrontery'?), it needs to take its rightful place in the world, that is to say, as the world's number-one, dominant nation. For which, of course, it needs lots of other nations to dominate…

Well, it's there already. And sorry to repeat myself here, but thanks to the West's negligence and its lax attitudes, it has been allowed to steal Western technology – by the bucketload – and then, by using this technology and, at the same time, systematically violating the principles of economic engagement, it has quickly become an economic behemoth upon which the world now depends. And an economic behemoth that is not averse to using its economic muscle. As many nations have already learnt to their cost, if you develop a close economic relationship with China, it will soon be used to bully you politically. Just ask Australia...

Nevertheless, China is not relying purely on its economic clout to dominate the world. It has a much more nuanced – and far-reaching – strategy than that, one that has been pursued for years and one that is just as systematic and ruthless in its nature as that being used to extinguish a separate Uighur culture within its borders. And it depends on networks – networks of people and institutions around the world that will promote its agenda and, at the same time, deflect any legitimate criticism of its actions or its ultimate intentions. It would take another book to list and describe every interconnected thread of this network, but please let me mention just a few.

To start with there are the 'enterprise model' universities of the West – institutions which have become addicted to funds, and which are therefore only too willing to take Chinese funds to support their research and Chinese student fees to maintain their academics' and administrators' otherwise unsupportable salaries. The fact that much of the consequent research findings will find their way back to the Chinese military and that many of the students under tuition will also be actively engaged in doing whatever is required of them by the motherland is of little consequence. And, incidentally, this latter student feature is really not very good news – for us here in the UK – as there are now 130,000 of these guys in residence at our own universities, all of them here at the whim of the Chinese government, and many of them wandering around and sniffing around our various dreaming spires. Indeed, it is little short of a scandal that this situation has been allowed to develop. And, as regards all that research funding, it is quite ironic – to say the least – that universities see no problem in accepting money from a state engaged in a massive programme of genocide, but lots of problems in even retaining on their campuses any statues of, or references to, their original conveniently dead benefactors, none of whom, I suspect, engaged in genocide, but just in the commercial practices prevailing in their day. Indeed, if I may go off at a tangent for just a second, I think it is very telling that the student Taliban at our universities direct all their fire at dead benefactors but none whatsoever at a very much alive despotic nation in the Far East. I doubt that the reason for this is a deliberate choice between the two, but merely the product of ignorance – in much the same way that the student body will howl about slavery in colonial times, but seems completely unconcerned that it is still happening now in places like Mauritania. Largely, I suspect, because 90% of those who have even heard of Mauritania – and its reluctance to forsake its traditions of slavery – could place it on a map. Or even in the right continent…

However, I am veering off the point, and to move on to another thread of the network, I need only mention Audi and Volkswagen, whose fortunes, like a few thousand other businesses, are now dependent on their access to the giant market of China, and whose executives have become masters in singing the praises of China whilst somehow remaining ignorant of some of its less than laudable practices. And I can think of no better example of this than when Herbert Diess, the chief executive of Volkswagen – which operates a plant in Xinjiang – claimed he was not aware of the detention camps in that region. One only had to look at his face as he was making this claim to know that he was lying through his teeth. I don't know why, when he was asked about these camps, he didn't just do a Basil Fawlty and collapse onto the floor in a not-very-convincing faint.

Anyway, to carry on, I can't fail to mention the West's financial industry, and especially the biggest serpents within this nest of serpents, who'd securitise and sell off the entire store of human happiness if they thought it could make them a quick buck. Principal amongst these pocket-stuffing operators is, of course, Goldman Sachs, a company that will do anything to generate business from China, including developing acute blindness whenever this is required – and employing any number of Chinese 'princelings'. These are the sons, daughters, nephews and nieces of top-ranking Chinese officials, who are taken onto its payroll to do nothing more than cement the company's vital relationship with China – and keep that part of the network in good order. And, to be fair, I should add that this hiring of princelings is not unique to Goldman Sachs. All the bastard banks do it.

And there's more. There are the elites: current or former members of that band of admirable folk who give up their lives to look after us, but who are not averse to looking after themselves when it suits them. And here I'm thinking of, for example, the well-connected members of the '48 Group Club', a London-based 'nonprofit organisation' dedicated to promoting trade between China and the United Kingdom, and including within its ranks such outstanding luminaries as Tony Blair, Alex Salmond, Jack Straw, Peter Mandelson, Ken Livingstone, Michael Heseltine and John Prescott! In reality, it is widely accepted that it is no more than the most powerful instrument of China's influence and information-gathering in the country. Now reaching into the highest echelons of Britain's political, business, academic and media elites, it never loses sight of its vital role of promoting a favourable view of China – and playing down anything that might not necessarily support this favourable view. That is why its chairman, Stephen Perry, commented positively on Beijing's response to Covid-19 back in February 2020, and stated that the Chinese government showed 'incredible sensitivity to the needs of the people'. Quite clearly, 48 Group Club is a very important part of China's huge global network of 'super-supine cheerleaders'.

So too, of course, is the Chinese diaspora around the world, all fifty to sixty million of them, any of whom might be persuaded or coerced to help his or her home country. And, of course, we mustn't forget all those various institutions dedicated to the cause of world dominance. And I don't mean just the large number of not-that-benign Confucius Institutes planted in hundreds of Western universities, or any number of Chinese-funded clubs, societies and think tanks around the planet, but also various UN agencies that have been harnessed to China's will and China's determined intentions. Indeed, there isn't a facet of life anywhere outside China that hasn't been infiltrated to some extent by those directing the 'great strategy' from within China – the strategy to cement its unassailable position at the top of the world's nations. Oh, and one last thing. You may be aware of something called China's Belt and Road initiative, a 'global infrastructure development strategy', adopted by the Chinese government to invest in the infrastructure of numerous countries, involving the building or rejuvenation of railways, roads, dams, airports, seaports and so much more. It has been sold by the Chinese as 'a bid to enhance regional connectivity and embrace a brighter future', but its real purpose is to forward Xi Jinping's cherished foreign policy objective of creating a Sinocentric international trade network – to underpin the wider network I've already discussed – as well as placing in Chinese hands a number of strategically sensitive facilities that they might have need of in the future. It's neocolonialism, Chinese style, and it seems to be unstoppable.

So, just to summarise briefly, China now has an economy that it can use to beat about the head any country it chooses. Through economic blackmail it can ensure decisions made by elected governments and their frightened bureaucrats are distorted in its favour, while at the same time its critics are silenced or ignored. But in addition, it has painstakingly developed the most comprehensive network of toadies, influence-peddlers, 'perception managers', propagandists, fellow travellers and information-gatherers, who, together with its own overseas citizens, have enabled it to erode resistance to its aims and advance its cause not from without but from within – from within the camps of all those countries that had the impudence to humiliate it for so long. And this is where I should draw a cartoon to illustrate what this relentless Chinese project means for the future of the West. But even though I might try, I know I am not up to providing the requisite cartoon with a requisite degree of professionalism. So, instead, I will try to draw the cartoon picture with words – and at the centre of this picture will be an old-fashioned wagon being pulled by a muscular beast and just approaching a high-walled compound...

On the back of the wagon, looking worn and distressed, is a tall man trying to keep at bay the snapping jaws of a big snarling dog, while all around him swarm a pack of rats, all trying to take small bites out of his legs. The man is the West, and that snarling dog, with Putin's dead eyes, is Russia, doing its best to bring him down – but with its broken, rotted teeth and its inept and rather feeble lunges, it will never do more than simply distract him. Which is what those rats are doing as well – rats with names such as 'Iran', 'North Korea', 'Terrorism', 'ISIS', 'Fundamental Islam' and 'Corruption'. And because he is so distracted by all these minnow creatures, he has not become aware that the wagon is being driven by a bloke called Xi

Jinping, and old Xi is goading forward that huge muscular beast whose own name is 'The Chinese Economy – a Gift from the West'. And the road ahead is being cleared of rocks and other obstructions by a host of Xi's compliant citizens, while four grease monkeys work below the wagon ensuring that its two axles are kept well-greased all the time, easing its progress towards that compound. Oh, and their names are 'Naïve Universities', 'Submissive Businesses', 'Money-grabbing Investment Banks' and 'Biddable Bastard Elites'. The compound is, of course, a huge internment camp, and above its large, oriental-looking gate is an elaborate banner, with, in big red letters, the words 'Chinese Hegemony', and in smaller letters below, the words 'Abandon hope all ye who enter here'. So, at least they've been honest with the signage. And the only thing wrong with this word-cartoon is that I've described the wagon as approaching the compound, whereas, in reality, it is already trundling through that gate, and that worn and distressed-looking guy, still distracted by the dog and the rats, will soon realise that he has something far worse to contend with than irritating animals. He has in front of him a future of complete Chinese control, and everything that means in terms of his freedoms and his very way of life.

This isn't sophistry. Just consider what has already happened. And let's start with Hollywood. Because a combination of Chinese 'official' censorship, coupled with the desire of American filmmakers to access the Chinese market, has, for years, led to all sorts of self-censorship, including the removal of any references to the 'Three Ts' – as in Tibet, Taiwan and Tiananmen Square – and any scenes depicting Chinese people in anything but a positive light. Then there is the overt bullying of both Taiwan and Hong Kong – accompanied by a rousing chorus of virtual silence from all those luminaries in the West. And if you want to experience total silence, then just listen to the barrage of criticism directed towards China for its proven illegal occupation and militarisation of islands in the South China Sea. One could hear a pin drop. And moving on quickly through China's success in normalising non-democratic regimes and its subversion of just about every rule of the World Trade Organization, let us for a moment consider Covid…

Had this originated in a black-pudding factory in Bury, and gone on to kill three, four or five million people around the world, as well as trashing the world's economy – but not that of Britain – can you imagine what the repercussions would be for our little country? We'd not only have overtaken North Korea in the pariah stakes, but we would also have been financially eviscerated as the rest of the world demanded compensation for their shredded economies. Not to mention some financial recognition for the impact of all those deaths. But what do we have when it is China that begat this pernicious plague, a plague that has devastated every nation on the planet – other than China? Answer: nothing. Not even an admission that it was responsible for this catastrophe, but instead just a report that its economy continues to grow while those of just about every other nation shrink like a willy in ice-cold water. One can only assume that its formidable network is doing a sterling job – in suppressing calls for restitution and muting any sort of criticism – and, at the same time, one can become even more concerned about what it will be able to get away with when it has achieved full dominance over the world.

For example, it might want to insist that its own ghastly surveillance and control system is implemented in all its vassal states – including this one – so finally bringing to fruition George Orwell's vision of the future. And, even worse than this, it will probably insist that its disregard for what were once the world's values is formally acknowledged and that it can therefore take whatever it wants from wherever it wants. And this wouldn't be bad news only for us, but it would be very bad news for the wider natural world. And to illustrate what I mean, please just consider what China has already done close to that magical archipelago called the Galápagos...

Three hundred Chinese vessels recently paid a visit to that part of the world, supposedly staying just outside the archipelago's own waters, but with many of them having disabled their public tracking devices – presumably for a reason. They then extracted tons of squid (a vital food source for Galápagos fur seals and endangered hammerhead sharks) along with other fish species important both to the local ecology and to the local fishing industry. Indeed, China is already acknowledged as the world's worst fishing nation, being regularly implicated in overfishing, targeting of endangered shark species, illegal 'intrusion of jurisdiction', false licensing and false catch documentation. So, just imagine how its programme of expunging every iconic and not-so-iconic animal on the planet will accelerate if it has absolute power and no challenge whatsoever to its egregious ways. We won't be looking at a continuing Holocene extinction event anymore, but instead at a Sinocene one – on fast-forward. And one accompanied by no compunction and no compassion.

So, it's just as well that we Brits will have something else to divert our attention from China's tidying up of the world's wildlife and its ordering of the affairs of the world's nations. And this I know because I am now looking in my crystal ball to establish what I listed as item (b) just a few pages back. That is to say 'what is already well underway in Britain and where this will lead'. And before I start, may I offer another word of warning – to all our more delicate readers. Because what I am about to write concerns a subject of which they will already have caught glimpses in this book, but which will now be presented in all its full-frontal horror. Oh, and I should just say that much of what I am going to discuss applies just as well to Western Europe as it does to Britain – albeit not all. And anyway, I'm sure you will be able to do the necessary multiplication to extend my British-centric observations to France, Germany, Italy, Spain and all those other nearby countries that are also being overwhelmed…

Ah, I may have given the game away there. So, I might as well come straight to the point, which is that Britain will soon not be Britain. Quite some time ago, our elite, in common with other European elites, found us indigenous plebs not quite up to scratch, and they embarked on replacing us with others. And these next generations were not to be sourced from our near neighbours, but from other continents. We would welcome not foreigners into our country but people with habits and beliefs that meant that they might better be described as aliens. After all, as far as I know, the folk of Brittany do not indulge in FGM, and even those hot-headed types from Andalusia draw the line at forced marriages and honour killings.

Yes, we had happily embarked on a process that would entail turning *our* home into a home for the world. Even though it was the only home we had, we would willingly turn it into a mini United Nations, and cast aside something that was the product of centuries of political, social and cultural evolution. Quite why this was allowed to happen, I do not know. But it was probably helped on its way by a good helping of misplaced colonial guilt, and our tradition of fair play that required us to give all those people whom we had colonised in the past the opportunity finally to colonise us. And to stay. This, despite immigration being the public's major concern for decades and, according to national surveys, being about as welcome as a home visit by Donald Trump.

Mind, one can't blame all those people for coming – and still wanting to come. They know very well that when they reach our shores – legitimately or otherwise – they will be very well looked after. They will even find that their cultural identity is more important than ours is, and whilst they will be free to enjoy the benefits of Britain, they will not be pressured in any way to become British. They can live parallel lives and essentially pretend they are still in their home countries – albeit with a lot more comfort and a lot more in the way of benefits.

That is why there are now millions of households in Britain where English is not spoken. Why any official form arrives with a Tower of Babel insert. Why English people are a minority in their own capital. Why a quarter of children under eighteen in Britain have at least one parent who was born abroad. And why those of us who have been here for some time quite often feel that we are homeless in our own country, or at best just a bunch of unwelcome lodgers.

Sometime in the 2060s, we native folk will be a minority in Britain. We will then have to accommodate thinking, practices, customs, traditions, habits beliefs, demands and even laws that will be truly alien – as any minority would. And bear in mind that some of these beliefs are entirely counter to our present insistence on the separation of the Church and the State. And I will go no further on that because I still value what remains of my life.

Instead, I will simply say that my Baby Boomer Britain has already become just a pleasant memory, but that even the very imperfect Britain that has replaced it will soon be shown to be merely a transient phenomenon. Because just over the horizon is a 'New Britain' – already revealing itself on our TV screens and in all forms of public debates and 'social adjustments' – and this will come to establish itself, before moving over to allow the establishment of a whole series of new New Britains, culminating in something that bears no relationship whatsoever to 'my' Britain. And it probably won't bear much relationship to what millennials currently regard as *their* Britain either. But, there again, it will have a nice mix of national cuisines that will make the rest of the world mightily envious. Including, no doubt, more than just a few that are Chinese...

Well, that's probably my cue to move on to the third and final item in my crystal ball, which is what is to happen to the natural world and to ourselves as a species. And worry not. This last insight I am about to provide will require far fewer words than I supplied on China, and possibly even fewer than in my previous account of the death of Britain. After all, there is only so much one can say about 'the end', particularly when one has already dealt with how we will get there...

Yes, you may recall that more than half a book ago I talked about the rapidly accelerating process of species extinction in this world combined with the equally rapid reduction in the populations of the remaining (non-human) species – all thanks to the efforts of man. Well, it's now time to revisit this issue, even if it means repeating more than a little of what I've already written. Not least because it is, without question, the biggest issue facing this planet at the moment. And note I said, the planet – not us. For once, it is necessary to take a less than human-centric view of what is happening to this world. And what is happening to this world is that we are impoverishing it at a speed that a fifteen-year-old Baby Boomer would have considered impossible. Because he or she would probably have had difficulty in coming to terms with quite how fast the world's population would balloon, and how rapacious this population would become.

It is a fact that cannot be repeated too many times: the world's population has tripled in the lifetime of us Baby Boomers. What started off as an overpopulated world is now bursting with far more specimens of *Homo sapiens* than it has ever hosted before, and far, far more than it can sustain – even if these humans were to kill off every other life form on the planet. And, unfortunately, that seems to be exactly what they are doing. Whether they're Chinese or one of the lesser races. Hence we have in progress the Holocene extinction event already referred to (and the prospect of the Sinocene that it will soon become) and we are well on track to establishing for ourselves the loneliest future imaginable, one where it will be just us living in some dreadful prosthetic world, with no other creatures as our companions, and even with little in the way of natural flora to lift our hearts. We will have proved that as well as being the most intelligent animal ever to have lived, we will also be the most stupid. The future, both for us and for all living creatures, has never looked bleaker…

However, do not be dismayed. There is possibly some good news of sorts. At least for all those other living creatures, if not for us. Because (as I have already reported in this book) it is becoming ever more likely that we are quite close to wiping ourselves out. So, at the distinct risk of repeating myself… this encouraging news comes not from the watchers of international friction, where despite there always being the possibility that things will spin out of control and, before you know it, you have a nuclear conflagration on your hands, this outcome might just as likely be avoided indefinitely. And nor does the news come from climate-change watchers, who report only a remarkable degree of resilience on our part to the impact of rising temperatures. No, it comes from the pathogen watchers: that band of microbiologists, epidemiologists and others who together have already concluded that we will meet our end through the agency of organisms much too small for us to see with the naked eye. For years they have been aware that all sorts of pathogens – with our help in the form of such things as the overuse of antibiotics – have been gaining the upper hand. But they have now realised that the strength of this invisible army has become almost as great as our hubris, and that it has already launched its final assault.

Well, still at the risk of repeating myself… Covid-19 might well be 'containable'. But even if it is, it will have merely acted as a dry run for the next devastating pandemic. Or maybe for the next one or the one after that. Never forget that viruses and all sorts of pathogens have been around for aeons, and it's not as though they're in any particular rush. They have all the time in the world to bring to an end our time in the world. And at some point, probably quite soon, they will do this. Indeed, the only meaningful debate one can have is whether they eliminate us entirely, or whether, through the agency of natural immunity, some of us are left as a breeding pool – in order to breed hosts for future generations of similar pathogens. But, in any event, I suspect we might hear a cheer from whatever residue of wildlife we haven't got around to dispatching. For them it will be Christmas every day – for countless millennia. After all, there will be either none of us around to persecute them, or just so few of us that they will be able to regard us as just irritants – and not the steamroller of death we've now become.

Right. Before I dress these pages with any more words of wisdom, I should probably point out that I *am* available for children's parties. If those little kiddies have had all they can take of miserable magicians, feeble face-painters and pathetic puppeteers, then maybe it's time for a stimulating dose of apocalyptic prognostication from one of Britain's most accomplished doomsayers. If nothing else, it will stop them getting overexcited...

Anyway, to return to my theme, I should possibly apologise for taking quite so much of your time in this final chapter to give you my views on the future. After all, I could just have said that Ming the Merciless is already taking over from that nice Uncle Sam; we Brits are in the process of losing our home; and the whole of mankind is heading for a fall. And the only cheering aspect of this otherwise appalling outlook is that, if they survive, the Chinese and the inheritors of Britain will find that they have only a truly threadbare world to further abuse or, if they don't survive, the natural world will be proven to be the final winner. However, I wrote all that detail because I wanted to underline something – in the thick lines of a marker pen. And this is that not only has my life been rewarding and enjoyable in so many ways, but it has also been perfectly timed!

Countless other people from past generations will have been able to claim that they had a wonderful childhood, a loving family environment, a great education, a challenging career, an ideal soulmate for a spouse – and the ability to travel, to enjoy some of the finer aspects of life and even to write. But how many, not of the Baby Boomer generation, would have been able – or, in the future, will be able – to record that they lived through peaceful times, through times where advances in technology provided them with more and more comforts and more and more opportunities – and times that fortunately preceded an age where it would all start to fall apart?

Now, I do accept that this process of decline has already started. On my travels around the world, I have seen too many ugly manifestations of humanity's disregard for its environment and too many once-pristine environments no longer pristine (and denuded of their wildlife) to think otherwise. But what I am talking about here is how that decline is now accelerating – rapidly – and, as a result, how all those millions of people who, unlike my Baby Boomer counterparts, still have a lot of life to live, can now only look forward to a world that is going downhill fast. I know I'm a pessimist, but can anybody seriously argue that the world's population can be controlled and that it won't go on to demand more and more from a world that has already been forced to give too much? And how about climate change? Will that be reversed? And then there's pollution and basic resource depletion. We might find more resources in the Arctic – and then fuck that up with our mines – and we might, sooner than you think, do the same in Antarctica. But where do we go after that? And don't say the Moon or Mars. Because the idea of keeping things afloat on Earth by pillaging other planets is about as harebrained as all those mega-rich idiots who see their legacy as the construction of futile giant fireworks that are only good for consuming even more of the world's scarce resources. Oh, and let's not forget those pathogens. Is Covid-19 going to be the last time mankind has to put life on hold while it tries to deal with a deadly microorganism? And will it even properly succeed with this one, let alone all those others waiting in the wings?

I don't feel smug – really. But I can well understand any reader of this book deciding that he or she has just read through the smuggest conclusion to an autobiography ever. Not only has this bastard had an incredibly charmed life, but he's even claiming that it's doubly charmed in the sense he will be ducking out of it before any apocalyptic ordure hits the fan. And he certainly won't be around to have to align himself with Chinese thinking or whatever new thinking comes to characterise life in the New Britain. However... what can I say? How can I possibly not speak the truth – in what will be the only autobiography I will ever write? And 'thank God' I hear you say to that...

Well, however smug or otherwise you may think I've been, the end is now really nigh. No, not that worldwide end, but just the end of this book. So, as I learnt to say as a conclusion to a number of my speeches (whenever I was forced against my will to deliver a speech), it only remains for me to thank you... for devoting a measurable slice of *your* life to reading about *my* life. If you've enjoyed it only a tenth as much as I enjoyed writing it, you may have thought that time well spent. And if you didn't, then 'sorry'. At least there won't be a sequel. In fact, the only thing that will follow these 400-plus pages is a series of appendices, which, as referred to before, contain some of my questionable poetry. And I don't think any of that is smug.

And now go off and write your own autobiography. You'll wonder why you've not got around to doing it before…

Appendices

I – Some limericks from *A Leap Year of Limericks*

There was a young woman who saw
Her own husband procuring a whore
Well, unlike his grief
The procurement was brief
And so was the punch to his jaw

There once was a man who relied
On a method much trusted and tried
When out on a date
He'd just ask for it straight
And if that didn't work, he just cried

There was a young man who suggested
That his wife should be much bigger breasted
This advice was ill-thought
And I have to report
The divorce, it will not be contested

There was a young actor from Derby
Who just knew that one day he'd a star be
But his dreams came to nought
When one night he was caught
With a full-size inflatable Barbie

There was a young tart called Marie
Who wanted more business, you see
So, her calling card said
'If you take me to bed
You can try one and get one for free'

There once was a chappie from Crewe
Who of todgers had no less than two
So, for years he looked out
For a girl kitted out
With a rare but compatible flue

There was a young chap from Long Lartin
Whose car was a blue Aston Martin
And an orgy for two
In his Aston so blue
Was what he so loved to take part in

There was a young girl from Kuwait
Who felled trees with the help of a mate
Six in a day
She could cope with OK
But she'd choke if she had to fell eight

There was a young man who was found
On a golf course laid out on the ground
He'd been hit on the head
By the woman he'd wed
When she found he'd been playing a round

There was a rich woman from Fleet
Who was not what you'd call just petite
Both her home there in Hants
And what lived in her pants
Were described as her large country seat

There was a young student from Herm
Who had only twenty-three sperm
He'd had a lot more
But that was before
The start of the Michaelmas term

Young Jack with the help of a friend
Would a brick from his penis suspend
His ambition, you see
Was not one brick but three
– and he did pull it off in the end

There was a young man from Moncrief
Whose todger was armed with sharp teeth
Well, strangely enough
It put women off
But it did help him once catch a thief

There was a young man who became
A girl with a quite different name
There were changes as well
To the way her clothes fell
– and her pants drawer was never the same

There once was a randy old goat
Who'd seduced this young girl on his boat
But when down on the deck
He got just a stiff neck
'Cos his Viagra got stuck in his throat

There was a young laddie from Crewe
Whose 'transactions' with ladies were few
In fact, they were none
And all he had done
Was once get a full-frontal view

An Aussie young lady would wonder
Why it was that her suitors all shunned her
Till a friend pointed out
That without any doubt
They'd all hoped that they'd see her down under

There was an old man who was irked
At the poor way his manhood now worked
But a pill did he find
– of a marvellous kind –
And up now his manhood has perked

There was a young woman called Gert
Whose boyfriend designed her best skirt
And I have heard it said
That before they were wed
He did have a hand in her shirt

I have quite often heard it opined
When a man on his own is confined
That the way he'll react
Is to seek out an act
That in due course will make him go blind

When Annie's libido was started
It was not for the weak or fainthearted
It would lovers so strain
That they'd end up in pain
Or as one of the dearly departed

There was a young man from Burundi
Who liked to have sex on a Sunday
With a manhood so strong
And inclined to stay long
It quite often stretched into Monday

There was a young man called Legrande
Who could pleasure himself on demand
But the pleasure, it ceased
When his member, he greased
And the whole thing got well out of hand

There was a young woman from Keele
Whose fine sense of touch was surreal
After only a week
At a men's club in Speke
She could tell all the members by feel

There was a young Tesco shelf-packer
Whose Christmas could not have been blacker
His girlfriend, my dear
Threw him out on his ear
And he then had to pull his own cracker

There was a young priest who would say
That the limerick had now had its day
So, who would have seen
That by humping the dean
He would help it to not go away

On holidays, Jim wore his shorts
When he swam or he played different sports
But their failure to hide
What was lurking inside
Got him banned from at least five resorts

Young Karen's degree was first class
And so too, I'm told, was her arse
But her arse was of use
(to her boyfriend, Big Bruce)
While her so-called degree was a farce

There was a young woman from Devon
Whose 'men in a day' count was seven
But that was before
On one cricket-team tour
When her record shot up to eleven

There was a young lady from Harborne
Who once snagged her blouse on a car horn
Well, that's what she said
To the guy whom she'd wed
To explain how she'd had her new bra torn

Young Steve who was born under Taurus
Once slept with a girl stegosaurus
When the steg then produced
Was when Steve then deduced
That the condom he'd worn had been porous

There was a young prince who liked beige
And encounters with boys underage
But his crimes came to light
On one dark moonless night
When his insert went in the wrong page

There was a young chap called Carruthers
Whose tackle was not like his brother's
In fact, as I know
If observed from below
It looked rather more like his mother's

There once was a woman from Mali
Who was painted by Salvador Dali
He showed her as blue
And with two eyes askew
And a third one in place of her charlie

There was a young lady from Hants
Who just yearned for a bit of romance
And if not true *amour*
Then at least rather more
Than 'Eh luv, what's this in yer pants?'

There was a young man who designed
A free-standing woman's behind
Quite what it was for
He wasn't too sure
But he did keep it very well shined

The girl of a paperback writer
Soon found that his work could delight her
He'd open real well
His action would gel
And his climax would always excite her

There was a young major called Bruce
Who once stuck his head in a noose
He wanted to die
And the true reason why
Was his privates were no bloody use

There was a young girl from Chicago
Whose boobs could be classed as bulk cargo
So huge were this pair
That when travelling by air
She'd have them sent on by Wells Fargo

There was a young girl from Australia
Who, with boys, was an absolute failure
Although she looked great
She could not get a date
'Cos the poor girl was named Jenny Talia

II – Some other ‘poetic attempts’, mostly from *Eggshell in Scrambled Eggs* and *The A–Z of Stuff*

Eggshell in Scrambled Eggs

The muesli was good
And the toast was just fine.
And as for the jam
It was simply divine.

But then came the egg
As in ‘scrambled on toast’.
And that’s when I knew
I had ‘gambled and loast’.

For there on the mush
Was a sliver of shell.
And the shell of an egg
I could do without well.

And no way, I knew
Would there be just one piece.
And like lives of a cat
There'd be eight more at least.

But losers learn slow
And I picked the piece off,
And then I commenced
My repast to re-scoff.

And wouldn't you know
The first load was just fine
And so number two,
And then three up to nine.

And then number ten
And it happened at last:
A ruddy great scrunch
And the good times were past.

With shell in my teeth
And with more on my tongue
My spirits sank low
And my ho lost its gung.

For what could be worse
Than a mouthful of bits
(If you don't count the droop
Or a bad case of squits)?

And covered in egg
And the remnants of toast,
So you can't spit it out,
Which you'd like to do most.

You just have to grin
And digest as you can
And then end your meal
As your meal first began.

That's with muesli and milk
And with toast and with jam
And with no other eggs
Save the 'eggs' in 'eggsam'.

Yes, 'eggsamine' your meal
And confirm that there's not
Another egg there
Be it cold, warm or hot.

Or coddled or poached
Or hard-boiled or just fried
Or worst of all scrambled
Where eggshell can hide…

Exercise Bikes

I pedal round and go nowhere
But stay just where I am
'Cos if I stay here long enough
I'll lose another gram.

But what a trial this nonsense is
And what a bloody chore.
And worse than this by quite a way
It's such a bloody bore.

And that's because there's nowt to do
Apart from feeling stressed
(And hoping that the stress won't lead
To cardiac arrest).

But stress is not the sort of thing
To keep me quite enthralled.
If only in some sleazy club
I'd had my bike installed.

'Cos then I could have pedalled round
While watching strippers tease
And that would chase the boredom off
And would my interest seize.

And then I could go on and on
Until I'd lost a stone
(Or till I'd found I had, at last
No more testosterone).

And then I'd be both slim and fit
With legs the size of logs.
And all because I'd parked my bike
Where girls take off their togs.

And if it worked that well for me
Then why not others too?
And what I mean is why not brand
My 'cycle while you view'?

I see it now, a new 'must have'
For strippers everywhere.
The 'ogle ride' – to shed those pounds
While they shed underwear.

I'd make a mint without a doubt
By renting out this brand.
The 'ogle ride' would make me rich
And known throughout the land.

So, rich and famous, slim and fit
And all from pedalling round
And all because that pedalling stuff
I was so off with browned.

And if you doubt I was so browned
And bored as bored can be,
Then bear in mind I wrote this ode
While pedalling rapidly.

Yes, all this junk is just my way
Of dealing with the drudge
Of sitting on a stupid bike
That will not ever budge.

So 'ogle' brands and stripper views
Are all just fantasy
And just like when I pedal round
Will go nowhere with me…

Packaged Butter Pats

A butter pat
Should be just that:
A blob of yellow stuff.
All on its own
And quite alone.
That's really quite enough.

But then they hide
The stuff inside
A silly plastic box,
To get in which
Without a hitch
Would test a wily fox.

And as for me
I helplessly
Just pull and tear the foil,
While hoping that
Who wrapped the pat
Would go his head and boil.

And when you're in
The smear's so thin
You need another one.
So once again
You suffer pain
To get it too undone.

Oh, what I'd give
A life to live
Where 'packs' they are eschewed
And foil is banned
And plastic's canned
And butter turns up nude…

Government Waste

A public servant bit on 'waste',
Chewed it round and liked its taste.
And that is why there's now a trend
For those in power to spend and spend.

And spend and spend without a thought
For what they'll get for what they bought
For what they bought the other day,
For just how much they've pissed away.

And as it's us who pay the bill,
Their lust for waste, we'll never kill.
It feeds, it breeds, it lives, it thrives,
It rules the roost and never dies.

And so we find they waste our cash
On projects daft and projects rash.
On training schemes that fail to train,
On three-lane roads with no third lane.

On IT schemes that cost the Earth,
On IT schemes of no real worth,
On IT schemes that get delayed.
And how about that foreign aid?

And how about consultants too,
And quangos old and quangos new,
And rafts of folk who get employed
To spoil the things we once enjoyed?

And HS2 – what is the word
For something seen as so absurd?
How can a pair of metal rails
Cost more than what we'd get for Wales?

And so to health and failing schools
Where standards lack and nonsense rules.
And jails and law and legal aid
And all those roads they've let degrade.

And then we have the welfare stuff.
To make quite sure we've all enough.
But here as well, there's waste in spades
As greed attacks and fraud invades.

And so it goes, a tale of woe
With waste so gross, it's hard to know
How those to whom we give our tax
Can act in ways that seem so lax.

Oh, how I wish they'd start anew
And act just like those slimmers do.
Yes, what I mean is 'please make haste
And shed some pounds from off your waste'.

'Cos if you don't, we'll all revolt
And you, yourselves, we'll soon assault.
And then you'll wish, I do declare,
That with our loot, you'd shown more care!

Trucks That Ruin Grass Verges

I love to live a country life
Away from towns and city strife.
But though I try, there’s still a scourge;
It’s called a roadside, nuisance verge.

It runs along my house outside,
A strip of grass but five feet wide.
And whilst not mine to sow or reap
I spend long hours, it trim to keep.

And this is bad enough, I know,
As through the year, the grass doth grow.
But worse than this by quite a way
Are trucks with loads that tend to stray.

You know the sort of thing I mean
A truck that says it’s ‘European’,
And underneath that truck there be
Some sixteen wheels as tall as me.

And eight of these have just one urge:
To gouge a trough along my verge.
A trough that sinks to one foot deep,
A trough that makes me want to weep.

For whilst it’s quick, this heinous crime,
For me to fix, it takes some time.
And why I do, I know not why,
’Cos soon another truck’s come by.

And then it’s there all o’er again,
A one-foot trough, this time by Ken,
The driver of the truck that strayed
To leave its mark of what it weighed.

I've lain awake on countless nights
To try to dream up scares and frights,
Which might just keep the trucks from off
That verge I want without a trough.

But hidden spikes and mines below
Cannot deter if not on show.
And if the scare is in full sight
Then it itself will cause a blight.

So, this is quite a con-un-drum
To cause a long extended 'um??'
For how the hell can one, I mean,
Devise what works but can't be seen?

Well, what I need's some circling sharks,
Which, on the surface, leave no marks.
But that they're there, just down below
Is quite enough to make you know...

That near that place, you should not be,
A danger żone within the sea.
And all the time, the sea remains
Unscarred by signs or posts or chains.

So, that's the end to which I strain:
To find a land-based shark to train.
And now my search has had a surge...
So, don't you scoff, I'm on the verge...!!

The Joy of the English Seaside

Down the M5 with them all packed aboard,
A family of five in their bright green Accord.
Their speed rather slowed as they got near the coast,
So, Mum filed her nails and Dad read the post.

It was well after ten when their goal was in reach,
And well after noon when their feet hit the beach.
For the parking (as always) was not near at hand,
And for more than a mile, they had walked to the sand.

Deckchairs were parked, and their bums parked on these,
And then it was time for the Branston and cheese.
But that's when it started, the worst of all things,
A wind of such strength, you could fly without wings.

First went the beach ball and then Sammy's hat
And then went the lilo they'd bought free of VAT.
But now it was free of the family as well,
And off down the coast, like a bat out of hell.

Dad used a swearword and Mum gave a scream
And Sammy just stood there as though in a dream.
But Sally and Tommy were more self-possessed
And wolfed down their sarnies and then got undressed.

The wind might be strong and the surf might be rough,
But of cars and of walks they had had quite enough.
And now all they sought was a play in the sea,
While Dad stayed behind and Mum made the tea.

So, off they both went and left Dad in the gale,
And Sammy still standing, his vest like a sail.
And Dad used more swearwords and Mum gave a curse,
And wouldn't you know it, the gale got much worse.

The wind was a nightmare, and that's no mistake,
And all Dad now wants is the beach to forsake.
But Sally and Tommy are still in the sea
And all he can do is have more of that tea.

What should have been fun on a fine, sunny day
Is now as much fun as a drunk Ronnie Kray.
And all 'cos the wind blew up and blew strong
And when it had come it then blew for so long.

It was still blowing hard when the hour came to four
When even the kids couldn't take any more.
So, stuff was packed up, and they made for the car
With Mum now complaining of sand in her bra.

But this was forgotten as soon as she spied
Their bright green Accord and its windless inside.
The relief was immense as they wedged themselves in
And Dad couldn't wait for their return to begin.

Nor could he wait to find out how he might
'Wind down' on a beach with the aid of a flight.
Yes, to English seashores he would not go again,
But instead try his luck on a seashore in Spain…

The Shark's Revenge (ideally on those who drink shark's fin soup)

The shark is a creature of beauty.
He's as sleek and as lean as a cat.
And in water, as lithe as a leopard,
And in menace, as mean as a rat.

We kill him for kicks and for pleasure.
We kill him to 'harvest' his fin.
Which is why, when we meet him while swimming,
He'll be wearing a great, leering grin.

At last he has found his oppressor
In a place where it can't do him harm.
And the only decision he's faced with
Is to bite through a leg or an arm.

It can't be a pleasant sensation,
A deep, tearing wound to incur.
And to realise that after that mouthful
You're not now the man that you were.

But really there's no need to worry,
'Cos that mouthful will not be his last.
In a minute he's back for another,
And from there on, it's downhill quite fast.

While you started with all your components,
And with everything working quite well,
You're now just a soup in the ocean,
With bits washing round in the swell.

So, when you next swim in the ocean,
Remember those sharks are there too.
And the soup of the day won't be shark's fin
But it might be a soup made of you.

The BBC

The BBC is big and strong
With wavelengths short and wavelengths long.
But even so, I have to say
I think the Beeb has lost its way.

To start with there are all its folk
Whose jobs are just a dreadful joke.
And worse than this, or so I'm told,
There's quite a few paid pots of gold.

And then there are its flagship shows,
The sort that simply curl our toes.
And what I mean is all that stuff
That's full of glitz and noise and fluff.

But worst of all's its state of mind
That means it might be very kind
To those who share its pinkish views
But not to those of other hues.

Yes, toe the line, and it's OK,
But if you don't, then go away.
It's what one sees on any night;
The 'you are wrong and we are right'.

In fact, I've often wondered why
The Beeb's not thought to give a try
To make the word 'diversity'
Apply to *thought* – so it might see...

That hiring staff of every tone
Is not the way to stop my moan.
No, what I want is *points of view*
To be diverse – and not taboo.

If that were so, I do declare
Soon Maitlis would be off the air.
And lo, we'd see the BBC
Be like the Beeb it used to be…

Banks

In days gone by, the greedy sort
Might rob a bank – and might get caught.
But now in banks they get a job
'Cos once-robbed banks themselves now rob.

Islamb

'Is lamb a good thing?'
Asked the queen of her king.
The king said, 'Of course,
But it does need mint sauce.'

London

London’s quite a funny place
With lots of things, except much space.
In fact, it’s ‘got it all’, and more.
At least for those who aren’t too poor.

And so it’s grown as more arrive
To taste its fruits or just survive.
And we all help, us country folk
This engine huge, its fires to stoke.

And in return it rules us all,
The thin, the fat, the short, the tall.
The trouble is, it doesn’t see
It’s not like you and not like me.

No, London’s not just funny now,
But foreign too, and so I vow
To see it cleaved from England fair
And shipped to where I do not care.

Yes, London is another state,
A place from which to separate.
Of this there is no room for doubt.
So, let’s get on and ship it out.

Far Too Many People

Foe eons long, the Earth remained
A place of charm where nature reigned.
And then came men – and women too,
Not hordes of them, but just a few.

So years went by, and all was fine
For deer and thrush and oak and pine.
Until the day, the human race
Commenced a surge – at quite a pace.

And with this surge it wasn't long
Before the few became a throng,
A throng of such a super size,
It won itself a super prize.

The prize, of course, was Earth itself
A world that still enjoyed good health.
But not for long, as man got round
To making off with all he found.

And burning up and chopping down
And turning green to muddy brown
And trapping here and killing there
And even screwing up the air.

So now the Earth is very ill
And hopes and prays and waits until
That stupid race, it starts to shrink
Or, better still, becomes extinct…

The United Kingdom – an Alternative Perspective

Long years passed before was built
The land of rose and leek and kilt.
But soon this land, it had acquired
An empire large and much admired.

But not content with lands abroad
It pushed itself until it soared
Above the rest, with mighty wealth
Amassed through work and not through stealth.

With engines steamed and looms engaged
It stoked the fires of minds uncaged.
And so it came to be supreme
And number one in self-esteem.

Enabling it to soar some more
In science, art and even law.
Nowhere was there upon this Earth
A place so blessed with so much worth.

And then came wars, not one but two
To test the red 'n' white and blue.
And though in both we nearly failed
In both we in the end prevailed.

With other nations we had gained
A future bright and unrestrained,
A world set up for peace and health,
Where empire'd morph to commonwealth.

And though at home we had our share
Of disappointment and despair
We still were able, ere too long
To build again a nation strong.

And so much so that to these shores
Arrived some folk, first in their scores.
And then in thousands still they came
The old, the young, the fit, the lame.

And now together we all live
A mix of men who hardly give
A passing thought for what has been
The greatest kingdom ever seen

Young People

The young are quite a funny lot.
They think they know what they know not.
And if you have a different view
Then yours is 'false' and theirs is 'true'.

It seems to me they should see sense
And not cause quite so much offence.
'So just grow up. And on the way
Indulge in sex three times a day'.

III – Some Covid odes – and one Covid carol

To Wuhan City Came a Bat

To Wuhan City came a bat
(in which an un-named virus sat)
This bat – and many others too
Was destined for a Chinese stew
Yes, in the land of Xi Jinping
They make their stews from anything
That's anything of any size
That swims or crawls or walks or flies
Sometimes they put the whole thing in
Sometimes it's just a hacked-off fin
And if it's scarce or very rare
Then frankly they just couldn't care
In fact, if rare they'll just pay more
For wing or head or spleen or paw
And this is why we'll soon be left
With forests, swamps and seas bereft
Bereft of all those special beasts
That ended up as special feasts
But let's just focus on that bat
The one in which the virus sat

'Cos when that bat to market came
The virus chose to get a name
And this it did without a plan
But just by trying 'plat de man'
For after all, while bats are fine
There aren't a lot on which to dine
In contrast men are everywhere
A world-sized meal of tempting fare
And so our Covid got its name
And China, lots of well-earned blame
'Cos if its folk had stuck to food
That once had clucked or once had mooed
– And hadn't flown around at night
With claws to grasp and teeth to bite
– Then viral problems would have stayed
Where all those bats, their roosts had made
And then, of course, the Chinese hid
The news that Wuhan had Covid
By doing this they guaranteed
That on us too the blight would feed
At first it fed on very few
And life went on as life will do
But then it found that those at sea
And those who lived in Lombardy
Would make a tasty starter for
A feast involving many more
The deaths they rose in Spain and France
Which meant we Brits had not a chance
We'd kept the Nazi hordes at bay
But with this chap there was no way
So, Reaper Grim, he scythed away
With more poor sods cut down each day
Until our Boris made a choice
Announced with scowl and sombre voice
'We're stuffed, my friends,' he sternly said

'I think we all should stay in bed'
And if not bed, then in our house
– With kids and cat and dog and spouse
And so we learnt to shop online
And how, at home, to drink and dine
– And then a new vocabulary
Of viral loads and PPE
And all the while we didn't earn
And all that grew was our concern
For how the hell we'd ever get
Beyond this plague and free of debt
And as for our economy
Well, think of butter gone to ghee
All melted down until it flows
And down the plughole quickly goes
In fact, the only source of joy
Was Mr Trump, the constant boy
The boy who thought that Covid's fake
(But chloroquine is what to take)
The world of gloom was often lit
By all his hair and all his shit
But let's get real and give a thought
To what this plague has with it brought
A weakened West that can't resist
The march by those who won't desist
Who won't desist in what they want
A world where they are out in front
A world where China's number one
And freedom's banned along with fun
(Just ask that guy called Mr Fong
Who once had both in 'free' Hong Kong)
So, what's to do to meet this threat
And not end up as China's pet?
Well, how about (though not enough)
A quarantine of Chinese stuff

To make quite sure it's Covid-free
For fifty months it's kept at sea
And meanwhile we would source elsewhere
And anywhere but 'over there'
And yes, of course, it would make sense
To think about some recompense
Some recompense for what we've lost
For all the dosh this plague has cost
So, lawyers all, come do your best
And take their shirt and then their vest
Three trillion quid would be OK
But four or five would make my day
And if they sought to trim the bill
Remember what first made us ill
Yes, bats in stews and bats in soups
And this is where this poem loops
'Cos what we need is habits changed
A view of wildlife rearranged
So, if they want to pay us less
(And make amends for our distress)
Then let them promise that from now
That what they eat is normal chow
That sharks and bats are left alone
That scoffing snakes becomes unknown
That bears are left with all their bile
That cooking cubs goes out of style
They might still rule the roost quite soon
(And even grab the bloody Moon)
But if their habits are revamped
And wildlife eating out is stamped
Then finally our world would be
A better place for beasts – and me

And for you. I've not forgot
It's just I've spied a pickup slot!

Good King Xi Jinping

(To be sung to the tune of 'Good King Wenceslas')

This old codger last went out…
Well, I can't remember
But I know the summer's gone
Now we're in December
Bloody hell, I've had enough
– Of lockdowns and of Zoom
Forty weeks without a pint
Gath'ring chronic gloo-oo-oom

If only China had not launched
That deadly Covid saga
I could be inside a pub
Downing pints of lager
Oh thank God there's wine online
And gin and brandy too
'Cos without those vital goods
It'd be just ho-ome brew

Never mind, we've Christmas soon
At last we can be merry
Turkey, spuds and Brussels sprouts
Nuts and port and sherry
But flippin' heck, I've just found out
We're in a second stew…
Santa's got Covid-19
And Rudolph's got the flu-u-u

How the hell can we sort out
Those vital Christmas presents?
'Specially now we're all so broke
As poor as rotten peasants
Rishi Sunak might have loot

To sort it for a few
But his buying gifts for all
Is more than he can do-oo-oo

Ah, I have it, I know how
We can get what is needed
After all, there is one place
That's thrived and so succeeded
Xi Jinping's the man we want!
– To put a false white beard on
And to ride a Christmas sleigh
All the way from Wu-u-han

This old codger would be pleased
To see his sleigh arriving
And to know that with his gifts
Our Christmas was surviving
And furthermore, we could tell Xi
That wealth or rank possessing
Ye who now will bless the poor
Shall yourself find ble-ess-sing

(With apologies to the original author of 'Good King Wenceslas')

Vacillating Over Various Vaccines?

A deadly virus did one day
Decide in Wuhan not to stay
Away from China it would go
To lands afar to thrive and grow

And soon it ruled the lives of all
The thin, the fat, the short, the tall
No longer would we meet or roam
But under lockdown, stay at home

And like a Justin Bieber song
This all went on for far too long
A life reduced to emailed clips
Bereft of pubs and foreign trips

But then one day the vaccines came
That rotten virus soon to tame
But which of these should we select?
And which of them should we reject?

Well, let us start with vaccine 'Pfizer'
Known by some as 'Increase-sizer'
Because, of course, this firm doth make
Those pills of blue that lovers take

Well, lovers of the man-type kind
Whose manhood might have now declined
So, these same men might well select
'The vaccine with a side effect'

For just imagine, if you will
The joy of now not getting ill
But then combined with quite a chance
Of some (supported) real romance

However, this may not appeal
To those whose kit is still ideal
Nor, of course, to those whose kit
Is more designed to just admit

Yes, women, girls and all young men
Might choose instead the Astra Zen
The vaccine made by Oxford dons
The one that won the vaccine bronze

... But only in its headline rate
Of making germs attenuate
And what is known to just a few
Is Astra Zen's real winning coup

Not how it's kept or its low price
But something else that gives it spice
Yes, Astra Zen – for Jill and Jack
– is 'Astra-aphrodisiac'!

Both men and women in its trials
Have all been seen with outsize smiles
The sort of smiles one knows are due
To carnal acts involving two

So just imagine, if you can
How many passions this would fan
How many folk a gut would bust
To wake again some dormant lust

If word gets out that this is what
This jab can do to make us hot
It won't be long before, no doubt
The Astra Zen is running out

It's just as well there's one more choice
A vaccine with a 'modern' voice
I mean, of course, Moderna's jab
A vaccine best described as 'fab'

For though it doesn't replicate
The 'blue-pill way to pollinate'
And lovers' potion it is not
(It doesn't even get them hot)

What it can do that others can't
Is in our minds a thought implant
The thought that we have still to see
What proved to be an absentee

I mean, of course, the year just passed
The one that wasn't quite a blast
The one that thanks to old Cathay
Was filled with just acute dismay

Yes, sex is fine and so are ways
To help out stuff that needs a raise
And help those folk who do require
A booster to their own desire

But what if we could start anew
That year that we have just been through?
If we could get what we have lost
Twelve months of life at so much cost

And that is what Moderna does
It gives us back that year because
It is a sort of time machine
And not just a Co-vid vaccine

So, go for this one if you can
And start again in last year's Jan
You've twelve months catching up to do
Those twelve months that the Chinese blew

Or, if you like, you can like me
Take Russia's 'Sputnik', which, you see
Is as a vaccine so intense
It even rids one of one's sense…

Yes, don't believe a word I've writ
Because, you see, I'm not too fit
That vodka jabbed into my arm
I think has done me quite some harm…

Covid Curtailments

A Chinese peasant, he did buy
A pair of bats, their meat to fry
And that is why your Auntie Flo
Last went to town twelve months ago

Why Flo and also Auntie Jean
Now do their shopping on a screen
Why, as with others in this land
Their trips to Primark are now banned

And then there's poor old Auntie Pat
With Archibold, her one-eyed cat
Together in their house they stay
– With one essential litter tray

For who could manage with the task
Of fixing on old Archie's mask?
You might as well ask Xi Jinping
To spread the flu throughout Beijing

So, Auntie Pat and Archibold
Are forced to live a life on hold
And as regards that trip to Beer
There is no way t'will be this year

And think of what that means for Lee
The Beery man whose B&B
Is now as empty and distressed
As Rishi Sunak's treasure chest

How he like many other folk
Is now fed up and stony broke
And all because that Chinese chap
Eschewed a simple cheese-filled bap

I only hope he's in disgrace
For what he chose to feed his face
Though given how his country's run
The chance of that is next to none

And meanwhile aunties in their 'caves'
Are forced to live like captive slaves
That's idle slaves who might get plump
Or addled-brained like Donald Trump

But worse than this I might propose
Is what it means for folk like Rose
– And Rose's boyfriend, Jason 'Jay'
Who lives from Rose, ten miles away

For Rose and Jay have courted long
With real true love and feelings strong
But now those feelings cannot be
Well, shared between them… physically

And let's not beat about the bush
'Cos two young folk who share a crush
Will often seek a path to bliss
That calls for more than just a kiss

Indeed, it often calls for stuff
Involving being in the buff
And then for two indulging in
What Auntie Pat might think a sin

But Auntie Pat has always been
A prude since she was just fourteen
She even looks the other way
When Archie does his bum display…

So, back to poor old Rose and Jay
And how two lovers miles away
Can straighten out what they do need
To see their carnal stuff proceed

I mean, this is of more concern
Than normal shopping to return
A trip to Primark's very nice
But cannot match some sexual spice

I deeply wish I could work out
How Rose and Jay might end their 'drought'
But like a Winnie, as in Pooh
I haven't really got a clue

With Amazon you now can get
A chocolate-flavoured clarinet
A life-size doll with bright green hair
And probably a wind-up Blair

But even Jeff, the Bezos guy
Cannot a coitus yet supply
At best he might in five years' time
– When Rose and Jay are past their Prime…

Which brings me to the point I need
For you to try to take some heed
For whilst I've writ this ode for fun
For lots of folk, of fun there's none

I mean, of course, those folk who yearn
For proper love to soon return
The 'Rose and Jays' throughout this land
Whose 'contact sport' has now been canned

I'm sure some do sort out how they
Can organise some 'mutual play'
But many others can't do this
– Or even snatch a measly kiss

What can one say to these poor guys
With whom we all so empathise?
Well, just one thing, and that, my friend
Is 'one day soon this curse will end'

And when it does both Jean and Flo
Will off to Primark promptly go
And no doubt prudish Auntie Pat
Will straightway let out the cat

And as for Rose and desperate Jay
What they will do I need not say
And not just once, of that I'm sure
But ten times what they've done before

And here's a thought to cheer us all
(Which, when we're free, you might recall)
It's just the fact that what we'll eat
Will not be bat but 'normal' meat

And that's because we will not be
In Xi Jinping's huge purgatory
I mean, of course, the land that did
Provided the world with vile Co-vid

And that's because we're English folk
– From Redditch, Bath and sunny Stoke
Yes, folk who dine on baps with cheese
– And folk who'll never be Chinese!!!

At Last...

At last, at last, I do declare
With jabs and tests we're nearly there
And soon we all can bid farewell
To Covid's far from magic spell

With lockdowns due to be unlocked
Our lives at last will be unblocked
And 'normal' won't be kept at bay
For one more week or one more day

Yes, all those things we haven't done
And all those treats we've had to shun
Will, after what's been quite a haul
Be there in spades for one and all

So straightaway one might decide
To try a pub – and go inside!
That's if, of course, there's one that's near
That still knows how to keep good beer

Or how about a trip to town
To find a shop that's not closed down
To find a shop that soon will not
Be just a vacant building plot...

Mmm, p'raps a trip to see a play
Might not cause quite so much dismay
Except, of course, I fear we must
Admit our local theatre's bust...

Perhaps instead what we should do
Is take ourselves off to the zoo
But bloomin' heck, I've just been told
The whole damn thing has just been sold

That really sucks, but never mind
There is a way we can unwind
I mean, of course, a stay-vacation
In our lovely pint-sized nation

And all we need's a place to stay
Where we can while away the day
A place where we can start to see
That finally we are now free

But oh my God, we are undone
Of cottage lets, there are just none
They've all been booked by other folk
– Or what they cost is just a joke

Which leaves us with one option more
– To seek somewhere a foreign shore
Yes, let us take ourselves abroad
To somewhere that we can afford

– Although, of course, I have to say
That anywhere beyond Calais
With Macron's help and Merkel's too
Is in a bloody awful stew

Without the jabs that we have had
To go there now would just be mad
And months will pass before we're sure
In Covid's grip they are no more

Which means, of course, for quite a while
We'll still be on this bless-ed isle
It's just as well then, for us all
That *relatives* await our call!

That's uncles, aunts and all the clan
All keen to see you when they can
And share with you their pure delight
At having got through Covid's blight

So, when you talk to Uncle Fred
– The one whose jokes you really dread –
He'll no doubt ask you straightway
To come and share a dreadful day

The sort of day that's made much worse
By Fred's wife, Jane, who can't converse
In fact, they're both such splendid bores
They both could bore through several floors

And that's the same with Mitch and Dawn
– Or Mr Dull and Mrs Yawn
Your siblings who for many years
Have made you wish for sound-proof ears

And as for Dawn's young daughter, Jan
A PhD awaits the man
Who can explain how with a screen
A girl becomes a dumb machine…

My God, why would you think it wise
To share your freedom with these guys?
When all along you have those *friends*
The guys on whom your 'id' depends

I mean, there's Joe, your long-time chum
The well-known 'friendly bearded bum'
– The one who's not responded to
A single email sent by you…

Yes, come to think, there are a few
Whose time as friends might now be through
I mean all those who've not done much
To check on you or keep in touch…

And then there's Carl and 'big-nose' Jack
Who told those lies behind your back
And not forgetting spendthrift Sid
Who still owes you one hundred quid…

And as for Jane and Jane's mate Jude
Their place as friends should be reviewed
It's quite OK to copulate
But not in view and at a fête…

Perhaps it's best to give some thought
To which friendships have come to nought
And which friendships should now be seen
As worthless as a French vaccine…

In fact, with pubs and bistros bust
And curbs put on our wanderlust
And feelings wearing rather thin
For certain friends and kith and kin…

One wonders whether we should stay
At home and from the world away
And with our books and pets and spouse
Delay emerging from our house

If nothing else we'd be secure
And of our health be super-sure
And more than that, we could prepare
For what next year we'll have to bear

I mean, of course, the latest beast
That's due from what we'll call 'the East'
Yes, not a simple Asian flu
But Covid number twenty-two!

Only kidding. Honest.

The Wig-bug

Eric liked football and hot, buttered toast
But making black puddings was what he liked most
In Wigan he worked with his helper, young Ron
And between them they made this rare *noir saucisson*

All was just dandy till one fateful day
When Ron started coughing before turning grey
He'd got something nasty, and that was for sure
And this was confirmed when he fell to the floor

Off with the medics he went pretty quick
And then it was Eric – who went and got sick
Not long thereafter it was Eric's wife Jane
(Along with her milkman. I need not explain.)

Something was spreading with dist-urbing speed
Yes, something that needed just humans to breed
And breed did it do, so in less than a week
The outlook for Wigan was no less than bleak

It wasn't just puddings that weren't leaving town
'Cos soon all those medics imposed a lockdown
Yes, people were told that they'd now have to stay
Within Wigan's boundaries with rules to obey

'Keep in your house and don't even think
Of going elsewhere for a quick, crafty drink
Now it's essential you do as you're told
Until we can see how events might unfold'

Well, unfold they did do, and before very long
A case of 'Wig-bug' had cropped up in Hong Kong!
And then there were more in Penang and Honshu
And even Jinping, he came down with the 'flu'

A black-pudding virus had left its hometown
And, as it spread out, it brought more people down
And lots of these people who weren't in their prime
Would not get back up for a very long time

Indeed, there were some who in all likelihood
Would never get up but remain down for good
Which meant – as I'm sure you yourself have worked out
A pandemic is what this odd ode's all about

Millions were dying in lands far and near
And *billions* were living in unbridled fear
For even the use of some harsh quarantines
Did little to help when there were no vaccines

However, the news wasn't totally crap
'Cos one place had followed a 'fruitful' road map
This first called for Wigan to be tightly sealed
And then for a vaccine to be soon revealed

Yes, Britain had stopped the disease in its tracks
And this meant its people could chill and relax
– and work to exploit what was happening elsewhere:
Economies plugged into intensive care

Ah yes, I've not mentioned (because I'm abashed)
It wasn't just lives that were totally trashed
So too were the fortunes of states big and small
(And even that one with the whopping Great Wall)

This was all very good – for ourselves in this land
Until we began… well, to more understand
That everyone else who was in such a mess
Didn't much care for our own huge success

Then things became worse when we would not agree
To let in a team to have a look-see
(In Wigan they wanted to find, if they could
The role played by Wigan's now world-famous pud)

Well, this just incensed a whole world full of folk
Who now, thanks to Wig-bug, were pretty-well broke
Even Ms Thunberg, the saint with the glare
Now trained her guns on 'those Brits over there'

A barrage of censure began to emerge
Us singled out as the source of the scourge
And then this great barrage, it only got higher
And soon we'd the status of 'full-blown pariah'

Why, people asked, would a country so fine
See 'pigs' blood and fat' as on something to dine?
Didn't they know that by eating odd fare
What might be let loose was a friggin' nightmare?

And they didn't mean Corbyn or dear Frankie Boyle
Or even a Maitlis draped only in voile
They meant a pandemic that gets out of control
And makes half the world spend some time on the dole

It also, of course, cost most countries so much
If taking out others they would have to go Dutch
And that's why our nation of still-solvent Brits
Was soon overwhelmed by a torrent of writs…

We tried to ignore them as much as we could
But frankly, that tactic was no bloody good
We were only a minnow compared to the rest
As was only too clear as then matters progressed

The writs called for trillions to make recompense
(Against which we clearly had no real defence)
But having been lax with our state credit card
To give them just *billions* would prove very hard

And so they took steps – to obtain their redress
Steps that would cause quite a lot of distress
'Cos what they embarked on – with no master plan
Was 'claim, seize and take it – wherever you can'

Gibraltar went first – to an indignant Spain
And then it was isles near the old Spanish Main
That's Anguilla, Bermuda and dear Monserrat
Scooped up and placed in old Uncle Sam's hat

Our overseas territories were soon down to none
And what would come next would be even less fun
'Cos into our land did our creditors come
– in order to take rather more than just some…

China took Bristol and Southend-on-Sea
(Not, in my mind, what you'd call a *Grand Prix*)
But France was more canny, and took all of Kent
And then charged the Kent folk exorbitant rent

Egypt demanded the lochs of Argyll
Their waters to take back to top up their Nile
And London was bagged by the Russians, of course
– with what they would claim was just minimal force

And when we were down to that island of Rum
And some of the grottier parts of old Brum
The vultures decided to take certain measures
That led to the loss of some national treasures

First went the wonderful Dame Judi Dench
And then t'was the turn of who else but Dawn French
Joanna Lumley was nicked by Bahrain
And shipped off to there with a case of champagne

Then they took Chelsea along with West Ham
The rights to the music of Coldplay and Wham!
The secrets of Stilton and Cheddar, of course
And even the patent on Worcestershire Sauce

So, I hope you now see how our poor choice of food
Inevitably meant that we ended up screwed
You simply can't choose to eat as you please
If this leads to a world that's consumed by disease

And you cannot expect, when three million have died
Your guilt for those deaths to successfully hide
And nor should you think that you'll not pay the cost
Of helping out nations for all they have lost

And if only… it wasn't this land of the Crown
That had let loose the Wig-bug to bring the world down
If only instead it had been a disease
Brewed in a place that's, say, full of Chinese…

'Cos I'm sure, unlike us, those folk, with the help of the Chinese Communist Party, would have accepted their culpability immediately, and recompensed us all handsomely. No question about it.

PS Black puddings are terribly maligned in this ode, for which I apologise unreservedly. I love them. And I don't actually know whether they are made in Wigan, but… well, Wigan/Wuhan. I'm sure you understand…

Afterword

One would think that after all those thousands of words and all those rhymes on the preceding pages, I would have nothing more to say. However, one of my few faults is that I always have more to say. I just can't help myself, and hence this brief afterword. It won't echo what I wrote in the last chapter of my biography – before the rhymes – which means that the end of the world as we know it will barely feature at all. Instead, there will just be a few further comments on what is the undeniable subject of the autobiography: namely me (in order to enable me to then make some more comments on my entire generation).

I will start by asking you to consider what opinion you have formed of me if you have actually managed to get through all those pages. Because I suspect that, if asked to choose the words that best describe me, you might pick some of the following: opinionated, arrogant, non-empathetic, hard-hearted, disrespectful, conceited, disdainful, flippant, misguided, delusional, self-satisfied, naïve, smug, irreverent, sacrilegious, bigoted, xenophobic, racist, fascist – and lucky. In my own opinion, some of these words would be apposite; some of them would be wrong – as wrong as the word 'bad'. Because whatever faults I may have, I do not think of myself as a bad person.

I do not believe that I have ever intentionally hurt anybody or any animal directly (other than numerous mosquitoes and numerous and various biting flies in the often-futile defence of my body). I have, of course, been responsible for a good deal of indirect harm – as has every human on the planet who has lived to my age. After all, one cannot exist as a human without damaging the natural world through one's needs and one's actions, no matter how careful one might seek to be. And if you're now thinking that jetting around the world for year after year is hardly the best way to be careful, I will reiterate the point made in the body of my autobiography that taking occasional flights – often to provide the much-needed financial support to a string of wild places that would not remain wild without that support – is not being unduly reckless. And in terms of its damaging the world, it pales into insignificance when one compares it to the chain reaction of harm unleashed by all those whose procreation habits saddle the world with multiple new humans, some of whom will go on to saddle it with a lot more. And, as was also made clear in my book, I am of the firm opinion that virtually all the world's problems stem from it having to host not just too many people but far, far too many people. The planet cannot cope with seven billion of us. It would, however, be able to cope quite comfortably with, say, just seven *million* of us…

OK. I seem to have drifted off my principal theme there – which is, you will remember, me. And to return to that theme, I want now to expand on that claim that, whatever else I am, I am not bad. Because you might possibly remember that somewhere in my autobiography I did refer to the fact that many younger people regard the whole of my generation as bad. And how could they not? After all, didn't all us Baby Boomers take what we wanted, ruin the world in the process, and then not leave anything for those who have only recently arrived at the party?

Well, you know what? I think that belief is tantamount to racism – one race of smooth-skinned young people condemning another race – of wrinkly, grey-haired people – just because they are wrinkly and grey-haired. And if any millennial disputes that view by maintaining that the condemnation is a result not of what us wrinklies look like but instead of what us wrinklies have done, then I maintain that what we actually did was no different to what those millennials would have done had they been born fifty years before. Forgive me for repeating myself, but, like me, the vast majority of Baby Boomers were not and are not bad. Indeed, in many ways, one could argue that they were exceptionally good – in terms of their manners, their decency, their sense of self-responsibility and their work ethic. And they were never, of course, digitally lobotomised through an addiction to screens. Which is not an insignificant plus point.

However, what I am really trying to say is that a whole generation should not be disparaged because of the timing of their birth and for their simply doing what every generation of humans has ever done: behave clumsily, thoughtlessly and shortsightedly, but without any malice. I repeat: most of them were and still are good people, and it is not their fault that they lived through what will probably prove to be a golden age. They might merit envy, but not blanket vilification.

Mmm… all that sounds a little bitter, doesn't it? And it may conveniently ignore the fact that there is a lot of shit coming down the road – as admitted in my book – and that this shit will have to be dealt with by all the young people in this world and not by us Baby Boomers, because we'll all soon be dying off. Nevertheless, it can get a bit much when one is showered with opprobrium not only for being white and English and proud of one's country and one's history, but also for being the age one is – about which one can do very little at all. Even digitally.

So, in conclusion, I, the Baby Boomer of this book, am not bad, and neither are 99.something per cent of all Baby Boomers. We are not that different to those who seek to criticise us – and who should bear in mind that, in fifty years' time, they themselves might well be attracting censure from a generation as yet unborn. And in no way deserve it.

So endeth the afterword and the lesson…

All my other books – so far

Brian's World Series

Brian on the Brahmaputra (with Sujan in the Sundarbans)
A Syria Situation
Sabah-taged
Cape Earth
Strip Pan Wrinkle (in Namibia and Botswana)
Crystal Balls and Moroccan Walls
Marmite, Bites and Noisy Nights (in Zambia)
The Country-cides of Namibia and Botswana
First Choose Your Congo
Absolutely Galápagos
Melanesia, Melancholia and Limericks
A Man a Plan a Canal Panama

The Renton Tenting Trilogy

Dumpiter
Ticklers
Lollipop

Light-bites

Eggshell in Scrambled Eggs
Crats
The A-Z of Stuff
A Leap Year of Limericks

Not so funny

Darkness
Survival

www.davidfletcherbooks.co.uk

This book is printed on paper from sustainable sources managed under the Forest Stewardship Council (FSC) scheme.

It has been printed in the UK to reduce transportation miles and their impact upon the environment.

For every new title that Matador publishes, we plant a tree to offset CO_2, partnering with the More Trees scheme.

MORE TREES
LET'S PLANT A BILLION TREES

For more about how Matador offsets its environmental impact, see www.troubador.co.uk/about/